A NARROW SEA

A NARROW SEA

The Irish–Scottish Connection
in 120 Episodes

JONATHAN BARDON

Gill Books

Gill Books
Hume Avenue
Park West
Dublin 12
www.gillbooks.ie

Gill Books is an imprint of M.H. Gill and Co.

978 07171 8059 2

Print origination by O'K Graphic Design, Dublin
Edited by Síne Quinn
Proofread by Ruairí Ó Brógáin
Indexed by Eileen O'Neill
Printed by TJ International, Cornwall

This book is typeset in 10.5/14 pt Minion.

The paper used in this book comes from the wood pulp of
managed forests. For every tree felled, at least one tree is
planted, thereby renewing natural resources.

A CIP catalogue record for this book is available from the
British Library.

5 4 3 2 1

To Carol

and in memory of
Zoë Lutton
laid to rest in Aberlady Parish Church Yard,
East Lothian, 26 June 2018

CONTENTS

PREFACE

A round 12,000 years ago the rising tides of the north Atlantic Ocean began to spill over and cascade into a vast and deep ravine, forming as they did so the Narrow Sea. Until then so much water was still locked up in ice sheets in the Northern Hemisphere that the sea level remained low – low enough to keep both Britain and Ireland not only connected to each other but also to the European mainland. A thousand-year 'cold snap', as scientists refer to this last manifestation of the Ice Ages, seems to have come to a rather sudden end. As temperatures and the oceans rose, Ireland became an island for the first time. Henceforth turbulent straits – once remembered as the Sea of Moyle and known today more prosaically as the North Channel – would keep these lands apart even though at its narrowest point only twenty kilometres separate Scotland's Mull of Kintyre from Torr Head in Antrim.

In the ancient epic tale, the four children of Lir, a ruler of the fairy folk, the Tuatha Dé Danann, were turned by a spell into swans at Lough Derravaragh by the king's intensely jealous second wife, Aoife. Nine hundred years would pass before they could once again assume human form. Their greatest torment by far was the time spent on the Sea of Moyle: here for three hundred years they were battered and separated by constant storms and their webbed feet were often frozen hard on to the rocks. The final three centuries spent sheltering behind the Erris peninsula in the far west proved to be benign by comparison. Certainly, the Narrow Sea is known for its surging tides and its treacherous waters, but it is quite wrong to see it as a barrier. A major theme of this book is that for nearly all of its history, when travel was easier and more rapid by water than by land, this channel was a conduit, a routeway, where peoples and cultures constantly blended.

In 2010 I was asked by BBC Radio Ulster to write 60 five-minute programmes to trace Ulster's connections with Scotland from the earliest times. These episodes were broadcast every weekday between Monday 3 January 2011 and Friday 25 March 2011. Each programme was to tell a story from the past about the Narrow Sea, joining subsequent programmes to describe and explain how those people inhabiting the lands on each side did so much to shape the history, not only of Ulster and Scotland, but of all of Ireland and Britain, and ultimately of many lands across the world. The aim of each broadcast was to be sufficiently self-contained and satisfying for those listeners who had not heard the previous broadcast. In the same way the reader should be able to open this volume at random to enjoy a fully understandable snippet of history. To create this book the number of episodes has been doubled and these, read in sequence, provide a narrative history of a part of north-western Europe which played a pivotal role in determining the fortunes of the continent and in time of other places elsewhere on the globe.

In a book of this scope, spanning almost all the time that humans have been in both Scotland and Ireland, the author is especially reliant on the published findings of specialists. I hope that these writers will consider acknowledgement of their work in the references and bibliography in part an expression of my gratitude. It has been a real privilege to be reminded of the vigorous good health of historical research on both sides of the Narrow Sea. The extraordinary increase in the quantity of publications has not resulted in any fall in quality. In the process many long-held assumptions have been convincingly challenged. For example, by the beginning of the new millennium scholars had reached a new consensus: Dalriada was *not* created by invaders and colonists crossing over from eastern Ulster to overwhelm Argyll during the fourth and fifth centuries AD. Instead, this kingdom long straddled the Narrow Sea, and its people, protected by rugged countryside on its south-eastern borders from both Roman conquest and interference by Strathclyde Britons, shared the Gaelic language then spoken over all of Ireland. Archaeologists have played a key role in persuading historians that this was the case.

By the beginning of the twenty-first century archaeologists had reached another more startling conclusion: only fourteen land mammals can be considered native to Ireland. A few had been able to survive the thousand-year cold snap between 11,000 and 10,000 BC. They included: the hare, stoat and woodmouse which subsequently evolved into distinct Irish species; otters, able to swim across; and brown bears, wild cats, lynx and wolves eventually driven to extinction by human hunters.

In Scotland Mesolithic Stone Age hunters had a wide choice of game, such as wild cattle, red and roe deer, wild boar, badgers and beavers. The first arrivals in Ireland discovered that these creatures, up to then forming the main part of their diet, were simply not there. Even the range of freshwater fish was limited to a handful of migratory species such as eels, salmon and sea trout, with landlocked trout, char and pollan transformed into freshwater fish as the ice retreated. Certainly, shellfish were gathered from the shore and hazelnuts, raspberries, blackberries, crab apples, waterlily seeds, fungi, edible bracken, goosegrass and vetch could be harvested in season from the woods. But human pioneers in Ireland found the fare on offer in Ireland was disappointingly limited. It would have required 250 eels to provide the same number of calories as a single wild boar, for example.

'Bring your own' is the arresting title given by the archaeologist J. P. Mallory to his explanation that, almost from the outset, the first hunter-gatherers to settle in Ireland felt they had no choice but to transport over animals from Britain to bring comfort and variety to their lives. By far the most important were wild boar – even if half their young were killed and eaten, enough remained to breed and multiply. Foxes, red squirrels and pine marten were probably brought over for their fur. Badgers came too (in the eighteenth century the Irish gentry relished 'badger flambé') and 'native' red deer do not seem to have been carried over by boat (probably as fawns in wicker baskets) until the beginning of the Bronze Age.

Produced and directed by Laura Spence, each programme in BBC Radio Ulster's *A Narrow Sea* was dramatised. The skill and versatility of the actors, particularly in their interpretation of annals, proclamations, letters and other documents from the past, were crucially important in persuading listeners to continue to tune in to subsequent episodes. *A Narrow Sea* was the most-downloaded podcast for Radio Ulster over the period with 127,452 requests over three months. This shows the huge appetite there is for both well-told history and Ulster-Scots material. The original 60 broadcasts, with their scripts, can be heard and viewed on the BBC Ulster-Scots website: http://www.bbc.co.uk/ulsterscotslibrary/a-narrow-sea

Laura Spence and Alister McReynolds were extremely generous with their time. I drew greedily on their vast store of knowledge in many conversations, which both followed up subsequently with helpful emails. Had I acted on most of their suggestions this book would be at least twice the length it is. As I write, my study is partly filled with piles of books and pamphlets lent to me by Laura from her great collection of works on so many aspects of Ulster Scots and American Scots-Irish history. I am grateful to those who agreed to apply their expertise by looking over some episodes, though I hasten to add that they bear no responsibility for the final product. They are: Jim Bennett, Chris Hudson, Will Lutton, Nico McGeagh, Alister McReynolds, William Roulston and Patrick Tweedale. My wife, Carol Tweedale, valiantly undertook the task of reading draft chapters to comment on how the text might be received by the non-specialist, and her advice urging further clarification was not only deeply appreciated but, I have no doubt, proved vital. Sincere thanks are due to the following for many kindnesses, particularly for giving me helpful comments, implanting fresh ideas and drawing my attention to useful sources: Brian Acheson, Norbert Bannon, Victor Blease, Jane Conroy, Gerald Dawe, Anne Devlin, Isabella Evangelisti,

Alison Finch, Tommy Graham, Richard Hawkins, David Hayton, Bronagh Hinds, Brian Lambkin, Ian Lutton, Kay Muhr, Nonie and Frank Murray, Rosemary McCreery, Babs McDade, Medb McGuckian, Máire Neary, Raymond O'Regan, the late Aodán Mac Póilin, Margaret O'Callaghan, Patrick Speight, Trevor Parkhill, Chris Parr, Errol Steele, John Waddell, Brian M. Walker, John Waugh and Paul Weir. I benefit enormously from the intellectual stimulation and friendship I receive from my association with that venerable organisation, the Belfast Natural History and Philosophical Society, especially from Angélique Day, Winifred Glover, Rosana Trainor and Brian M. Walker. Members of the Northern Ireland Tour Guides Association have been providing me with warm support and constant historical inspiration, in particular, Catherine Burns, Marty McAuley, Catherine McKimm, Min Shen, and Laura Spence.

A group of men of my own vintage who meet once a month in Belfast to discuss Ireland's past, the country's cultural heritage and the present condition of both the island and that of the United Kingdom, were amongst those who provided many valuable insights. They are: Maurice Blease, Victor Blease, Douglas Carson, Seán J. Connolly, David Coffey, Brian Garrett, Liam Kearney, John Knox, Eddie McCamley, Alister McReynolds, George Orr, Peter Spratt, Thompson Steele and Barry White. Zoë and Ralph Lutton went out of their way to familiarise me with all the sites of historical importance in Edinburgh: without those exploratory outings, for example, I would not have been convinced of the importance of Hugh Dubh O'Donnell's momentous pact with James IV made in the Renaissance splendour of the castle here in 1513.

The coastlines on both sides of the Narrow Sea are amongst the most hauntingly beautiful to be found in all of western Europe. On a calm and peaceful summer's day, it is not immediately apparent that these straits and the lands enfolding them were the scene of a succession of so many memorable happenings. Looking back over time they include: the setting off of the Allied armada just prior to the Normandy landings of 1944; evidence of the industrial and commercial power of both Belfast and Glasgow in the early twentieth century; the steamers carrying migrant workers from Donegal to labour as 'tattie hokers' on Scottish farms; the flight of fever-ridden victims to Glasgow during the Great Famine of the 1840s; the emigration of tens of thousands of Ulster Scots from Belfast and neighbouring ports during the eighteenth century to settle the thirteen colonies across the Atlantic; the criss-crossing of new liberal ideas from Ulster to Scotland and back again to help form the Enlightenment; the landing on 3 April 1642 at Carrickfergus of Major-General Robert Monro leading a great Scots army to crush Irish rebels and, incidentally, to set up the first Presbyterian congregation in Ulster; the flow of colonists from Portpatrick and Stranraer in the early seventeenth century to take part in the most ambitious scheme of colonisation in western Europe in modern times; the expedition led by Captain Francis Drake to slaughter MacDonnells taking refuge on Rathlin in 1575; the disembarkation of Scots, fresh from their victory at Bannockburn, at Larne in 1315, as Edward Bruce began his campaign to make good his claim to be King of Ireland; the ravages of Viking raiders who were to leave an indelible mark on every island and headland; the missionary expedition of Columcille in the sixth century which was to make Iona the most renowned Christian centre in north-western Europe; and the first crossings to Ulster made by Stone Age hunter-gatherers around 8,000 BC, about a thousand years after the first human settlements had been made on the eastern side of the Narrow Sea. The aim of this book is to bring such events to life.

I am grateful for the assistance of the staffs of the Public Record Office of Northern Ireland, the Linen Hall Library, the National Library, Belfast Central Library, the McClay Library in Queen's University, the Ulster Historical Foundation, the Jackie Clarke Collection in Ballina, the Ulster-Scots Agency, the Ulster-Scots Community Network, the Ultach Trust and BBC Northern Ireland. Throughout I enjoyed the staunch support and encouragement provided by Conor Nagle, Sheila Armstrong, Teresa Daly, Dilia Eckert and Avril Cannon. I am also exceedingly grateful to Síne Quinn who edited the text for this book with painstaking care and sensitivity, as well as impressing me yet again with her knowledge and insight.

Silent, O Moyle

Silent, O Moyle, be the roar of thy water
Break not, ye breezes, your chain of repose
While murmuring mournfully Lir's lonely daughter
Tells to the night-star her tale of woes

When shall the swan, her death-note singing
Sleep, with the wings her darkness furl'd
When shall Heav'n, its sweet bells ringing
Call my spirit from this stormy world.

Silent, O Moyle, to thy winter-wave weeping
Fate bids me languish long ages away
Yet still in the darkness doth Erin lie sleeping
Still doth the pure light its dawning delay

When will the day-star, mildly springing
Warm our Isle with peace and love?
When will Heav'n, its sweet bell ringing
Call my spirit to the fields above.

Thomas Moore

THE CLASSICAL WORLD LEARNS ABOUT SCOTLAND AND IRELAND

Three hundred and twenty five years before the birth of Christ, Pytheas, a navigator from the Greek colony of Massilia (now the city of Marseille in the south of France) set out on an epic voyage of exploration. He managed to slip past the Carthaginians guarding the Pillars of Hercules, through the Straits of Gibraltar, into the Atlantic Ocean. After making landfall at Cornwall, he set out northwards again. Pytheas, the first man from the Mediterranean to describe the Orkneys, then sailed on towards Iceland and Norway to witness the summer midnight sun, the Northern Lights and icebergs.

Though Pytheas's account of his explorations does not survive, clearly it circulated widely in his classical world. It gave Mediterranean traders for the first time the correct position of the 'Pritanic Isles', the British Isles. Himilco, the Carthaginan, had journeyed to the 'Tin Isles of Scilly' 150 years earlier and had warned of dense sea entanglements and threatening sea monsters just beyond Cornwall – by circumnavigating the British Isles Pytheas had proved him wrong.

And what of the peoples inhabiting these islands in the ocean on the far north-western edge of Europe? For a time Paleolithic peoples had been able to settle in the far south of Britain. Scotland and Ireland, however, remained among the last places on earth to be inhabited by human beings. Why? The explanation is the hostile climate: ice sheets, in some places a mile thick, ensured that for thousands of years Britain and Ireland were completely uninhabitable. Only after the last Ice Age was over, about 10,000 years ago, could human beings return to Britain and Ireland.

At Cramond on the Firth of Forth just outside Edinburgh archaeologists excavating an ancient habitation site found burned hazelnut shells in a fire pit. Radiocarbon analysis of the shells, dated at around 8,500 BC, established that this is the earliest habitation site in Scotland that we know of. In exactly the same way, analysis of charred hazelnut shells at Mount Sandel just outside

Coleraine confirmed a date of about 7,000 BC. Radiocarbon testing proved that this was not only the oldest human settlement known in Ulster but also, at the time of discovery, in all of Ireland.

Though separated by more than a thousand years, the Stone Age hunter-gatherers of Cramond and Mount Sandel appear to have had very similar lifestyles. Both communities erected large circular huts, each about six metres wide, made of saplings driven into the ground and bent over to form a domed roof by being lashed together, and then covered with bark, deer hide and grass turfs. Pieces of hard stone, chert at Cramond and flint at Mount Sandel, were roughed out into axe heads, arrowheads, knives, hide scrapers and other tools. They lived by harpooning fish, gathering nuts, seeds and berries in season and hunting wild pigs in the wild wood.

The Lebor Gabála Érenn (The Book of the Taking of Ireland), written in the eleventh century AD, claimed that the Gaelic Irish had been led by the sons of Míl directly to Ireland from Spain. A great many of our ancestors did indeed come from Spain but it is much more probable that, instead of attempting to brave Atlantic storms to cross the Bay of Biscay, they worked their way northwards along the west coast of France to cross the Channel over into Britain. From there they and their descendants travelled further north into Scotland. It seems very likely that the first bands of human beings to come to Ireland crossed the North Channel between Galloway and the Ards peninsula or between the Mull of Kintyre and the north Antrim coast, or made their way westwards from the Isle of Man. Indeed, it could be said that the forebears of those who eventually became Irish were – at least for a time – British. There was to be much coming and going across the North Channel, the legendary Straits of Moyle, for century after century, which would do much to shape the history of these islands.

Fresh arrivals brought the latest information from abroad. Knowledge of farming, first developed in the Middle East, arrived more or less at the same time in Ireland and Scotland about 6,000 years ago. Finds of exquisitely crafted brooches, torcs, swords and axes show that the skills of moulding and fashioning gold, copper and bronze were established some 2,000 years later. Around 500 years before the birth of Christ iron was being smelted, cast and forged throughout these islands. By then all the inhabitants of Britain and Ireland were speaking a Celtic language of one form or another.

During the last century before the birth of Christ, Julius Caesar led his legions into Gaul and one by one he conquered the Celtic-speaking tribes there. He then laid plans to invade what Pytheas had called the Pritanic Isles. Caesar called it Britannia and he intended to make it a province of the Roman Empire.

AGRICOLA, CALEDONIA AND HIBERNIA

During the spring of AD 43 the King of the Orkneys (an archipelago 16 km off the far north-east of Scotland) made the long and perilous journey by sea to Camulodunum, now the city of Colchester in Essex. This had been the capital of the British tribe, the Trinovantes; now it was a stronghold of the Roman Empire. Here the King – we do not know his name – along with ten other British kings bowed his head in homage before the Emperor Claudius. Julius Caesar had invaded Britain twice, first in 55 BC and again in 54 BC, but on both occasions he had been forced to withdraw. It was Claudius who had overseen the conquest and now he was here in person. He would make sure these kings would accept that Britannia was now a province of the Roman Empire.

That Empire stretched from Egypt and the sands of the Sahara in the south, from Persia and Mesopotamia in the east, and north to the Danube and the Rhine. That the King of the Orkneys had travelled so far south was a striking recognition that he regarded Claudius as ruler of almost all of the known world. Could the Roman Empire expand further to include all of these islands set in the Atlantic Ocean, here on the edge of the world? Could it encompass Scotland, the land the Romans called Caledonia, and that mysterious island to the west, known to the Romans as Hibernia?

One man developed a burning ambition to achieve this goal. Gnaeus Julius Agricola had first been posted as a military tribune to Britannia in AD 61. Here he served under Suetonius Paulinus, leading his cohorts forward during Boudicca's rebellion to crush the Iceni and Brigantes with unflinching ruthlessness. Rewarded by being given command of the 20th Valeria Victrix Legion, he directed the Irish Sea flotilla. Perhaps it was then he thought that Hibernia was an island worthy of conquest.

Recalled to take up a post in the province of Asia in AD 64, Agricola went on to become Tribune in Rome and after that Governor of Aquitania, a province of Gaul. Then, after 21 years' absence, Agricola was appointed Governor of Britannia in AD 78. At last he had been given the opportunity to achieve the

dream of his youth. First he descended on the Ordovices who had wiped out
Roman cavalry stationed in north Wales. He crushed these Britons mercilessly
and forced survivors desperately holding out on Mona's Isle, Anglesey, to make
abject submission to the power of Rome. Then in AD 79 Agricola led his legions
on to overwhelm what is now the north of England and the following year
he crossed the Uplands into Caledonia. Within two years he had established
Roman power as far north as the line across the country marked by the Clyde
in the west and the Forth in the east. Here, along the forty-mile strip of land
between these two rivers, Agricola had a chain of twenty forts built by AD 81.
The Britons living south of these forts – the Damnonii, the Novantae, the
Selgovae and the Votadini – came to accept Roman rule and their chiefs sent
their sons to learn Latin and be schooled in Roman ways.

Could Agricola advance further across the Highland Line to the wild northern
regions of Caledonia where mysterious barbarians who tattooed and painted
their skins held sway? And surely Hibernia, known for its lush pastures, would
be a fine addition to the Empire? In AD 82 Agricola turned west, to that tongue
of Scottish mainland closest to Ulster, now known as Galloway, to conquer the
British tribes there. It was then that he decided to invade Ireland. Agricola's son-
in-law, Tacitus, informs us that Agricola now planned an invasion of Ireland
with a king in exile:

> Agricola received in friendly fashion an Irish petty king who had been
> driven out in a civil war, and kept him for use when opportunity offered.
> I have often heard him say that Ireland could be conquered and held by
> one legion and a modest force of auxiliary troops; and that it would be
> advantageous in dealing with Britain too if Roman forces were on all sides.

Was this king Túathail Techtmar, founder of the Ulster Uí Néill dynasty,
106th King of Ireland and believed to be of mixed Irish and Scottish descent,
who had been forced to seek aid in Britain to recover his throne? We cannot
be certain. Agricola summoned the Irish Sea flotilla to the Solway Firth and
called all available cohorts to Galloway. But the invasion of Ulster never took
place. A legion of Germans stationed in Galloway mutinied, and there was
disturbing news that the barbarians in the Highlands were massing for an attack
southwards. Setting aside his plan to conquer Ireland, Agricola now gathered
legions from across the Empire to bring all of Caledonia under Roman rule.

'LOATHSOME HORDES OF SCOTS AND PICTS'

Eighty-four years after the birth of Christ, Gnaeus Julius Agricola, Governor of Britain, led the greatest Roman army ever to appear in Caledonia deep into the Highlands. Facing him at a place called Mons Graupius were 30,000 barbarians, known to the Romans as Picts because they painted and tattooed pictures or 'picts' on their bodies. There Agricola won a famous victory the Empire would not forget. According to his son-in-law Tacitus, the Picts lost 10,000 men:

> The next day … an awful silence reigned on every hand; the hills were deserted, houses smoking in the distance, and our scouts did not meet a soul.

But it was a hollow victory. The wild Highlands proved beyond the capacity of Rome to subjugate. The Picts were proving themselves far less barbarous than the Romans thought them to be. Occupying the most fertile land in Scotland, they could sustain long campaigns and use to great advantage their intimate knowledge of the glens and hills to harass the enemy with their fierce attacks. Indeed, soon the empire was becoming overstretched. Forty years after Mons Graupius the Romans pulled out of Caledonia altogether and built a wall from the Tyne in the east to the Solway in the west. Painted white with lime to make it visible at a great distance, and reinforced with watch-towers and forts, Hadrian's Wall took the work of three entire legions over six years before it was completed in AD 122. It was a defensive wall 80 Roman miles (17.5 kilometres) long and 20 feet wide in places (6 metres) and over 11 feet high (3.5 metres). With no equal in all of the rest of the Empire, it was the largest Roman artefact anywhere.

For the next two hundred years Hadrian's Wall served its purpose well. Then the Roman Empire, weakened by bitter internal disputes and its frontiers overrun by barbarians, began to fall apart. Legion after legion was withdrawn from Britain, many of them sent to defend the River Danube where Germanic tribes from the north and east were massing. One by one the Roman castellae were abandoned. At Inchtuthil, a Roman legion left behind almost one million unused nails, carefully hidden below the floor of a workshop. The Votadini, a British tribe long allied to the Romans, evacuated their great hill fort of Trapian Law in East Lothian on the Scottish borders so rapidly that they abandoned a treasure hoard of immense value. As the fourth century drew to an end, the writer Ammianus Marcellinus chronicled the desperate situation:

> At this time, with trumpets sounding for war as if through all the Roman world, the most savage tribes rose up and poured across the nearest frontiers. At one and the same time the Alamanni were plundering Gaul and Raetia; the Sarmatae and Quadri Pannonia; the Picts, Saxons, Scots and Attacotti harassed the Britons with continual calamities.

And who were these Scots mentioned by this Roman author? Scoti – meaning marauders or pirates – was the Latin name the Romans gave to the Gaelic-speaking people in Ireland. Many centuries would pass before the word Scot would mean an inhabitant of that part of Britain north of Hadrian's Wall or, indeed, before there would be a kingdom of Scotland. And now these Gaelic-speaking Irish, sailing east from Ulster, joined the Picts from the north in pillaging an empire becoming weaker by the year. Gildas, a Briton from Strathclyde who later settled in Wales, described the worsening situation:

> Britain was robbed of all her armed forces, her military supplies, her rulers, cruel as they were ... Britain remained for many years groaning in a state of shock, exposed for the first time to two foreign tribes of extreme cruelty, the Scots from the north-west, the Picts from the north....
> [As]the Romans returned home, the loathsome hordes of Scots and Picts eagerly emerged from their coracles that carried them across the gulf of the sea, like dark swarms of worms that emerge from the narrow crevices of their holes when the sun is high and the weather grows warm. In custom they differed slightly one from another, yet in their single desire for shedding blood they were of one accord, preferring to cover their villainous faces with hair, rather than their private parts and surrounding areas with clothes. Once they learned of the Romans' departure and their refusal to return, more confident than ever, they seized as settlers the whole northern part of the country as far as the wall.

Hadrian's Wall proved no defence and the Picts and Scots surged southwards:

> What more can I say? The townships and high wall are abandoned; once again the citizens are put to flight; once again they are pursued by the enemy; once again massacres yet more cruel hasten upon them.

On every frontier the Roman Empire was reeling under the attack of peoples from central and northern Europe seeking new corn lands and pastures. Legion after legion was withdrawn from the outposts to defend Rome. All to no avail: Alaric the Goth took Rome itself in AD 410. In the east the Roman Empire, with its capital of Byzantium, would survive for more than 800 years. But the western empire was no more. For the first time in over 800 years, its provinces were being carved into kingdoms by rampaging Germanic peoples, including Ostrogoths, Visigoths, Vandals, Burgundians, Lombards, Franks and – in eastern and southern Britain – Angles and Saxons.

Those English – described by Gildas, the sixth-century monk, as 'fierce Saxons, hated by God and men' – were soon to play their part in shaping the land we now know as Scotland.

EPISODE 4

DALRIADA

During the first century after the birth of Christ the Roman Empire was approaching the height of its power. Its legions overran Britain and advanced north as far as the Highland Line. But Ireland, known to the Romans as Hibernia (the Érainn, the Irish, called their country Ériu) was never to become part of that empire. Here a Celtic-speaking Iron Age society – very similar to that conquered by Julius Caesar in Gaul – survived undisturbed for many centuries.

Ireland was then a land of many kings. They enforced their rule from well-defended forts where high-born men served as a warrior caste riding on horseback, equipped with lances, throwing-spears and short iron swords held in richly decorated bronze scabbards, and defended with large round shields. No doubt several of these warrior kings had been driven westwards out of Gaul and Britain by the might of Rome. All Irish kingdoms had constantly shifting frontiers. Uladh, or Ulster, was then one of the island's largest. Its capital was at Emain Macha (Navan fort) in Armagh. At the kingdom's greatest extent its southern frontier ran from the Drowes River flowing into Donegal Bay in the west to the mouth of the River Boyne in the east. During the first centuries after the birth of Christ, however, Ulster was on the defensive. Claiming descent from the legendary Niall of the Nine Hostages (circa 370–450), members of the Uí Néill dynasty had emerged from their north Connacht homeland to thrust eastwards into Meath and northwards over the fords of Erne towards Inishowen. In wild country overlooking the marshland that separates the Inishowen peninsula from the rest of Donegal, the Uí Néill built the Grianán of Aileach. From this imposing circular hill fort, constructed massively of stone with inset stairways, wall passages and triple earthen bank defences, the power of the northern Uí Néill would in time extend over much of the rest of Ulster – but never including the lands along the western shores of the Narrow Sea.

About the middle of the fifth century Emain Macha fell to the northern Uí Néill. The over-kingdom of the Ulaidh gradually shrank to little more than the modern counties of Antrim and Down. Yet this shrinking provincial kingdom in the north-east of Ireland was intimately connected with the wider Gaelic world of Argyll and the inner isles of the Hebrides, west of Scotland. For a considerable time the lands on both sides of the Narrow Sea would be known as Dál Riata, better known in its anglicised form as Dalriada.

As the power of Rome began to decline the farmlands, towns and villas of Britannia proved tempting targets, not only for Picts from the north, but also for the Irish. Irish raids on Cornwall and Devon were so relentless that the population there abandoned their lands to make a new home in the Roman province of Armorica in the north-west of France, now called Brittany after them. Some of these Irish began to settle the lands they had been plundering in Wales, Devon and Cornwall. Indeed, Irish kingdoms were established for a time in parts of Wales. But did the Irish also conquer a kingdom for themselves in Scotland?

The seventh-century *Senchus Fer nAlban* ('History of the Men of Scotland') is possibly the oldest census record in western Europe. A register of all the households in Dál Riata, it enumerated the fighting men each one could muster for the king. Rewritten in the tenth century, it stated that the first Gaelic-speaking territory in northern Britain had been made by an Irish king, Fergus mac Eirc, who had crossed the Narrow Sea with his sons. He named the land he conquered Dál Riata in Argyll after the kingdom he ruled in Antrim. The Senchus also stated that the Gaelic language was first brought to Scotland by Fergus. We now know this is no more than a story, written possibly to back up the claim to territory in the north-east of Ireland made by one of the Argyll kings.

There is no doubt, however, that an identical language was spoken on both sides of the Narrow Sea. The place names of Argyll are almost entirely Gaelic, proof that this was the language of the indigenous inhabitants here. Rugged mountains, long narrow lochs and steep-sided forested glens had helped to prevent Argyll from being overrun by the Romans; and, after the departure of the legions, the nature of the landscape made regular overland contact difficult with the British along the Clyde and the Pictish heartlands far to the north and the east.

Movement then was much easier by water. Travel by sea from the Mull of Kintyre to the Glens of Antrim was no more difficult than making a sailing from there to Islay or Jura. The Narrow Sea was not a barrier, it was a channel of communication and trade. Here there was a shared culture; constant interaction amongst these maritime peoples over time led to the people of Argyll adopting the Gaelic language of their close neighbours, the Irish in Antrim.

Scholars today agree that the true origin of Gaelic spreading out to become the speech of so many Scots in ensuing centuries had nothing to do with an Irish invasion from the Glens of Antrim led by Fergus mac Eirc. Archaeologists point out that there is no evidence of significant colonisation from Ireland in Argyll. Precious ornaments found amongst other grave goods in Argyll are quite different from those discovered in Ireland. The warrior nobility of both Scotland and Ireland resided in massive circular stone forts (their presence indicated by the prefix 'dun', as in Dundonald in both countries) but most Irish families lived in circular enclosed homesteads known as ringforts. Around 45,000 remains of ringforts have been identified in Ireland. So far only two have been found in Scotland. Indeed, colonisation may have been in the opposite direction. Lake dwellings known as 'crannogs' seem to have been invented by the Picts. By the beginning of the Christian era they were being constructed all over Scotland, but not at all in England, Wales or Ireland – at that time. It was not until the sixth century that the first ones appeared in Ireland; they proved popular, and by the later Middle Ages at least 2,000 had been made here.

The most numerous people in eastern Ulster were the Cruthin or Cruithni. Who were they? Cruthin is the Gaelic version of Priteni, the word used to describe themselves. This was also the name given by Irish writers to the Picts on the other side of the North Channel. It does seem likely that either Picts (or were they Strathclyde Britons?) ensconced themselves in the present counties of Antrim and Down. Here they created a sub-kingdom, Dál nAraide, which held its own with considerable success for some centuries. They may have spoken a British language on arrival, but the Cruthin once they had settled in do not appear to have had a separate culture distinguishing them from the rest of the Irish – they spoke Gaelic like the rest of the inhabitants of Ireland and Argyll.

Dál Riata straddled the Narrow Sea for a hundred years and more. And throughout the seventh century this independent kingdom was ruled from Dunadd, the great capital of Argyll.

EPISODE 5

THE DOVE OF THE CHURCH

For more than a century the kingdom of Dál Riata flourished on both sides of the Narrow Sea: on one side of the kingdom the basalt cliffs of Antrim rising dramatically from the sea, bristling with hillforts, and the island of Rathlin; and on the other the Mull of Kintyre, the many islands of the Inner Hebrides and, adorned with mountains in season purple with heather, the peninsulas of Argyll thrusting into the sea. By the middle of the sixth century the Dál Riata kings had made Dunadd, in the heart of Argyll, their capital. Here at the southern end of Kilmartin Glen above Lochgilphead on a great rock rising 54 metres from the flat floor of the valley are the impressive remains of a mighty stronghold. Four massive circular embankments defended the fortress and its stone dwellings, storehouses and workshops.

At Dunadd crucibles for melting gold, silver and bronze, along with moulds for casting brooches, have been found in what clearly was a thriving royal capital. Here the kings of Dál Riata were inaugurated in the traditional manner. The Gaelic way was not to crown kings but, in a symbolic manner, to marry them to their kingdoms. At Dunadd the candidate for the throne proved himself worthy by placing his foot in a footprint carved on a smooth and level shelf just below the summit – successive waves of visitors have worn away the original footprint and it has now been replaced by a replica. On Ulster's north coast, built on a massive piece of basalt, broken away eons ago from the Antrim plateau, stand the remains of an ancient fort, Dunseverick. Today it looks rather modest and unprepossessing, but this was once the principal stronghold of the Kings of Dál Riata on the Irish side of the Narrow Sea.

The Gaelic rulers of Dál Riata steadily expanded their territory at the expense of their neighbours. Those neighbours were the Picts to the north and east; the Angles of the kingdom of Northumbria, then expanding northwards along the east coast to the Firth of Forth; and the Britons of Strathclyde, losing ground year after year to both the kingdoms of Northumbria and Dál Riata. The Strathclyde Britons were Christians but the Argyll Gaels, the Picts and the Angles had their own gods.

Christianity had been brought to the south of Ireland from Roman Britain and Gaul by traders and evangelists. Unquestionably, however, the main credit for bringing Christianity to most of Ireland, particularly the northern half of the island, must go to the man we now know as St Patrick. Not yet sixteen, he had been seized by Irish pirates from Bannaventum Taburniae, a Romanised town somewhere in western Britain, usually thought to be Wales. However, Patrick could have come from any part of the British-speaking lands not yet conquered by the Anglo-Saxons. It is quite possible, indeed, that he was a Strathclyde Briton. After six years he escaped back to Britain but, with the full support of his British Church, he returned to evangelise the Irish. By the time of Patrick's death, towards the end of the fifth century, Ireland possessed a flourishing Christian Church. It was not long before the new beliefs were being brought across the Narrow Sea to Argyll. The man who did most to launch that mission was an Uí Néill prince of Ulster, Colmcille or, in Latin, Columba, 'dove of the Church'.

Born at Gartan in Donegal, Colmcille studied to become a monk under Finnian at Moville in Co. Down and at Clonard on the Boyne, before returning to build his own monastery at Derry in 546. It seems that Colmcille was forced to flee across the North Channel after becoming embroiled in a dynastic dispute. Conall mac Comgaill, the Dál Riata king residing at his capital of Dunadd, welcomed this Uí Néill prince but also guaranteed his protection and granted him the island of Iona. Here on this Hebridean isle Colmcille built a monastery capable of housing 150 monks, scholars and novices, circa AD 563. Iona in time would become the most famous centre of Christian learning in the Celtic world, producing the finest illuminated manuscripts, including the Book of Durrow and the Book of Kells.

Colmcille's main achievement was the spreading of the Gospel to his fellow Gaelic speakers in Argyll. As he did so, Ninian was evangelising Galloway further south and turning Whithorn into a highly respected monastic settlement. Colmcille, however, pioneered the mission to the Picts. The Picts possessed some of the most fertile land in Scotland in Fife and East Lothian, in addition to the Highlands, Moray and the Northern Isles. Brude had succeeded in bringing all the petty Pictish kingdoms under his sway. This brought him into conflict with Dál Riata, expanding its frontiers at the time. It was therefore remarkably courageous of Colmcille to journey deep into Pictish territory through the Great Glen to meet King Brude by the River Ness.

There is no need to believe the miracles Colmcille is supposed to have performed there, and, while he does not seem to have made a convert of Brude, this king gave him permission to preach to his people. In the years that followed, clergy trained in Iona made sure that the Church was also flourishing in Pictland.

EPISODE 6

IONA

C olmcille, abbot and prince of the northern Uí Néill, was unquestionably the most energetic and influential churchman in the Celtic world during the sixth century. He established monasteries all over Ireland, most notably at Derry, Swords, Kells and Durrow, but his greatest foundation was at Iona in the Western Isles. Iona, a small but fertile island separated from the Isle of Mull by a narrow sound, is just 4.8 km from north to south and 2.4 km (3 by 1.5 miles) from east to west.

Iona became the power house from which the Gospel was brought to the many in Britain who had not heard it before. Pictish kings chose to be buried in Iona, including Kenneth Mac Alpin, the first King of Alba, and 'Rí Deircc', the Red King, MacBeth. They gave grants of land for new monasteries, most notably at Dunkeld which housed some of Colmcille's relics. Iona was also to lead the mission to convert the English of Northumbria. In 616, Aethelfrith, who had united Anglian kingdoms in Northumbria and extended his power northwards towards the Firth of Forth, was defeated and killed by his rival Edwin. Two of Aethelfrith's sons escaped. The eldest, Eanfrith, took refuge with the Picts and here in the royal court he was converted and baptised by clergy from Iona. The second son, Oswald, was taken in by the Dál Riata overking, Eochaid Buidhe, and he, too, became a Christian during a long stay on Iona. There he became devoted to the veneration of Colmcille.

In the year 634 Oswald returned and, after defeating his enemies, took for himself the crown of Northumbria his father had once worn. As soon as he could he sent a message to Iona to seek an evangelist. Travelling from the island by currach and by foot, Aidan, an Irish monk, deeply impressed Oswald by his piety and energy. Aidan received a gift of Lindisfarne and on this island a great monastic foundation thrived, modelled on Iona, becoming the dynamic centre of the mission to these pagan Anglians.

Colmcille and his successors made Iona the greatest centre of Christian learning in the north-west of Europe. A poem, almost certainly written by Colmcille, illustrates his devotion to scholarship:

> I send my little pen dripping unceasingly
> Over an assemblage of books of great beauty,
> To enrich the possessions of men of art –
> Whence my hand is weary with writing.

The earliest surviving Irish manuscript is a copy of the Psalms, known as the *Cathach* (the 'Battler') because it was later carried into battle as a talisman by the O'Donnells of Tír Chonaill. This was written in Iona and an ancient tradition, which may well be true, attributes the writing of the *Cathach* to Colmcille himself.

Until the arrival of Christianity all knowledge had to be committed to memory, particularly by the hereditary learned classes: in Gaelic society these members of the *aes dána* were the poets, the judges and law-keepers, and the seers. Now Scottish society (as Irish society had been) was transformed by the art of writing. Among the greatest achievements of this Celtic Church are the magnificent illuminated Gospels and other sacred texts. Most of these were written and decorated in monasteries founded by Colmcille and his successors.

The high point of manuscript illumination was reached in the Book of Kells. Despite its name, this was the work of scribes on the island of Iona and was later taken for safety to Kells in Meath after the Vikings had begun their attacks. This copy of the Gospels combines strong sweeping compositions with astonishingly detailed, almost microscopic, ornament. The most admired page combines the sacred chi-rho monogram (the first letters of the word Christ, Χριστός in Greek) with images of Christ, the Resurrection and the Eucharist; and the stately rounded script is punctuated with scenes such as cats pursuing mice, an otter seizing a fish, and a greyhound hunting. It has a good claim to be the most beautiful book executed during the first millennium. The finest English illuminated edition of the Gospels is the Book of Lindisfarne, a magnificent example of the blending of Celtic and Anglo-Saxon art.

Formidable resources were required to sustain this culture. It took the hides of no fewer than 185 calves to make the vellum for the Book of Kells. Colouring material included expensive orpiment from the Mediterranean for yellow colours and lapis lazuli from Afghanistan for the colour blue. The high cross seems to have been invented on Iona, with biblical scenes carved in the stone to aid the instruction of the illiterate. Iona was no backwater; along with Dunadd and Whithorn it had become a revered centre of the civilised world.

The literate clergy of the Celtic Church provided kings with a valued mandarin class. Adomnán, an abbot of Iona who had come from the monastery he founded in Raphoe in Donegal, was a skilled diplomat. At the end of the seventh century he negotiated the release of prisoners seized in a Northumbrian raid on Ireland. Adomnán's greatest achievement was his establishment of the 'Law of the Innocents' (Cáin Adomnáin) in 697. This was a kind of seventh-century Geneva Convention for the protection of women, children and clergy. Eventually this early declaration of human rights, providing stern punishments both on earth and in heaven for those who inflicted violence and slander on non-combatants, was guaranteed by no fewer than 50 kings in Ireland and Scotland.

One clause stated:

> Women may not be killed by a man in any way, neither by slaughter or by any other death, not by poison, nor in water, nor fire, nor by any beast, nor in a pit, nor by dogs, but shall die in their own lawful bed.

It even covered industrial accidents such as those resulting from exploding kilns. The law was renewed in 727 by means of a circuit of the relics of Adomnán.

Of course, the 'Law of the Innocents' did not end wars and, at the end of the eighth century, a new people appeared on the scene who were completely unaware of it – the Vikings.

VIKINGS

In *The Ecclesiastical History of the English People*, written in 731, the Venerable Bede stated that there were four peoples in Britain speaking five languages, including Latin, the language of the Church. All four peoples were to be found in what today is Scotland. The four languages were Gaelic, Old English,

P-Celtic and a Pict language – now lost completely. The Anglo-Saxons spoke Bede's language, Old English. Since the Kings of Northumbria had overrun much of the country as far north as Edinburgh, a form of this language – the ancestor of Lowland Scots – was being spoken over the Southern Uplands and the east coast up to the Firth of Forth. The Britons of Strathclyde and Dumbarton spoke a P-Celtic language (a subdivision of the Celtic language, also known as Gallo-Brittonic), almost identical to that spoken by the British in Cumbria and Wales, the ancestor of modern Welsh. By far the largest area in northern Britain, including the Highlands, the Outer Hebrides and the Northern Isles, was occupied by the Picts. Their language failed to survive but it seems also to have been a P-Celtic language. It survives only in elements of some place names such as Pitlochry – pett meaning a 'portion of an estate'. The fourth language was Gaelic, the speech brought by colonists from Ulster to Dál Riata. This was a distinctly Irish form of the Celtic language, known as Q-Celtic. It was spoken in every part of Ireland and now, across the North Channel, it was spreading widely out from Argyll. Many words in Gaelic begin with a Q or K sound. For example, Kin or Ken, meaning a headland or boundary, appears in place names all over Ireland and also over much of Scotland, including Kinlochleven, Kintyre and Kinross. Many words in the language spoken by the Britons began with a P. The equivalent of the Gaelic element Kin or Ken in British was Pen – it is found in place names such as Pentland, Pennersaughs and Pencaitland in Lothian and Penarth and Penrith in Cumbria. Then at the end of the eighth century a fifth people began to make their mark.

In 793 the Anglo-Saxon Chronicle recorded:

> On 8 June the ravages of the heathen men miserably destroyed God's church on Lindisfarne with plunder and slaughter.

The Viking raids had begun. Two years later both Iona and Rathlin were attacked. Then Bangor and Downpatrick were plundered. As a monk wrote some years later:

> Everywhere Christ's peoples are the victims of massacre, burning and plunder. The Vikings overrun all that lies before them and no one can withstand them.

An Irish monk wrote in the margin of his manuscript:

Fierce and wild is the wind tonight,
It tosses the tresses of the sea to white;
On such a night I take my ease;
Fierce Northmen only course the quiet seas.

The Northmen who bore down on Scotland and Ireland were for the most part Viking warriors from Norway. Undefended churches and monasteries suffered most in the early attacks, the raiders being attracted to them not only by precious liturgical vessels but also by their rich stores of corn. These raiders were formidably armed with fearsome battle-axes and long slashing swords edged with superbly welded hard steel and their bodies were protected by helmets fitted with protective nose pieces and flexible coats of mail. Their longships were not only designed to cope with the hazards of the ocean but also, with their shallow draught, capable of navigating rivers far upstream.

The lands ruled by the Picts suffered most. The Outer Hebrides were overwhelmed and the Picts living in the Shetlands and the Orkneys seem to have been almost completely wiped out. The Vikings came first to plunder but soon they were settling permanently in these islands possessing a milder climate than in their own homelands. In southern Ireland they built the island's first towns, some to grow later into cities, including Dublin, Limerick and Waterford. But in spite of penetrating deep into the heart of the province and, for a time, maintaining fleets of longships on Lough Neagh and Lough Erne, in Ulster they never managed more than a few toeholds, such as Strangford, Carlingford, Ballyholme and Larne. It seems that in Ulster the Vikings met such formidable resistance that they decided to settle elsewhere. For the year 811 the Annals of Ulster have this terse entry: 'A slaughter of the heathens by the Ulaid'. This must have been a significant achievement, because the same victory was recorded in the court of Charlemagne. The same annals record that in 866 Áed Finnliath, King of the northern Uí Néill, actually defeated the Vikings on their own element, the sea, on Lough Foyle.

If your surname is McKittrick, McIvor, MacDowell, McSorley, Sweeney, McLeod, MacDonnell, or MacDougall – all of them common in Ulster today – you certainly have Viking blood flowing in your veins. But people with these names were not to appear in Ulster until long after the era of the Vikings was over.

CINÁED MAC AILPÍN, THE KINGDOM OF ALBA AND THE STONE OF SCONE

Scotland was a land of at least eight kingdoms when the Vikings began their attacks during the 790s. With its long, indented coastline and many islands, Dál Riata in Argyll was fatally vulnerable to seaborne assault. On Iona all manuscript-writing and illumination ceased in the famous *scriptorium*: after the monastery had sustained no fewer than six devastating attacks by 824, the community's survivors left altogether, carrying what treasures they could to Kells in Meath. Meanwhile no Argyll Gael was likely to lay claim to the Irish part of Dál Riata: Vikings now coursed the Narrow Sea.

The Western Isles fell under Viking rule, the Isle of Man being the centre of power for quite some time. The English kings of Northumbria had extended their frontier northwards to the Lothians and over towards Galloway. But the ferocity of repeated attacks by Danish Vikings forced these Anglian rulers to abandon Scottish territory altogether. Nonetheless their language and institutions had taken root north of the Borders.

In a curious way, the Vikings helped the spread of the Gaelic language over most of Scotland at this time. Those who had brought the Gospel and veneration for Colmcille from Iona to the lands of the Picts were revered. Atholl, meaning 'New Ireland', was named long before there was any kind of Gaelic political control in that part of Perthshire. Now many high-born refugees from the ravaged lands of Dál Riata made their way eastwards to the kingdoms of the Picts, particularly that of Fortriu with its rich farmlands, extending from Dunblane to Perth and over to Forfar. Other members of the Gaelic elite set out for Moray in the north east. Meanwhile Pictish nobles, those who had not been evicted by incoming Gaels, were adopting the Gaelic language spoken all over Ireland but in Scotland, until recently, only in Argyll and the Hebrides. Now, in its heartland of Moray and Fortriu, the language of the Picts was about to die.

Protracted bloodletting and destruction convulsed Scotland again and again in these years. Nevertheless, this violence helped to clear the way for the creation of the kingdom of Scotland. Fortriu – unlike Dál Riata, the Hebrides, the Northern Isles and Northumbria – had not yet endured serious attack. That changed dramatically with a great Viking invasion in the year 839. Even though the King of Dál Riata came to aid the King of Fortriu, the Viking 'gentiles' slaughtered their men and killed both kings at an unnamed battle-site in Moray. The era of the Picts was coming to a close.

Emerging from this mayhem, after the Vikings had departed with their loot, was a mysterious warlord, Cináed mac Ailpín. Who was he? He claimed to be a descendant of a famous king of Dál Riata from the ruling kindred of Cenél nGabráin. This was probably an invention. Actually, he may well have been a Pict who, by now, had become a speaker of Gaelic. When Cináed died peacefully in his bed in 858 he ruled a territory that stretched from the North Sea across to the Atlantic. This kingdom he called 'Alba', a Gaelic name previously given to the entire island of Britain.

That frontier was to be extended further by another devastating invasion. In 870 a great Viking fleet set out from the tidal waters of the River Liffey commanded by the King of Dublin, Olaf the White, along with Ivar the Boneless and Ragnar Hairy Britches. Sailing up the Clyde, this Viking horde ravaged the British kingdom of Alt Clut and besieged Dumbarton Rock until after four months it fell. At the conclusion of this orgy of killing, the Viking raiders returned to Dublin with 200 longships filled with British slaves. Only a rump of a once-great British kingdom survived upstream on the Clyde at Govan, soon to be absorbed into the expanding kingdom of Alba.

The ruler who really secured the survival of Alba and its dynasty was Cináed's grandson, Constantine II, who came to the throne in 900. In 937 he marched a great northern coalition into Northumbria to confront the English King Athelstan. But Athelstan triumphed at Brunanburgh – 'no ravens went hungry' the author of *Egil's Saga* correctly reported, for this was the bloodiest battle of the century. Constantine survived this disaster, however, to weld together under his rule the shattered remains of the kingdoms south of the Forth and the Clyde.

Back in 843 Cináed mac Ailpín, making a spurious claim to be descended from ancient Irish royal stock, had himself inaugurated as king in a traditional Gaelic ceremony. This was at Scone on the eastern bank of the Tay at its lowest fording point. Here on Moot Hill, an artificial flat-topped mound, he was seated on a rectangular block of sandstone, the Stone of Destiny. Constantine had himself inaugurated in the same way. Rulers of Alba would be crowned on this stone for centuries to come.

THE EASTERN COASTLANDS OF THE NARROW SEA: NORMAN INFILTRATION

For centuries it had been Northmen who had posed the main threat to Scotland's independence. Then 1066 changed everything. At Hastings William, Duke of Normandy, made good his claim to be King of England. These Normans, descendants of Vikings settled in northern France, made certain their conquest would be permanent. In just a few short years of slaughter and destruction, an alien French-speaking caste swept away the Anglo-Saxon élite.

Malcolm Canmore, King of Alba since 1057, viewed William's invasion as an opportunity to make good his claims to Northumbria. In 1070 Malcolm took his army south only to be forced into a humiliating retreat. The Conqueror's retaliation was to invade Scotland in 1072 and when he reached Abernethy on the banks of the Tay, Malcolm 'made peace ... and gave hostages and was his man'. What did 'his man' mean? To Malcolm it was an empty phrase but to William, and those who came after him, this was proof that the King of Alba, ruler of the Scots, had acknowledged the King of England as his liege lord.

Malcolm refused to give up: in the last ill-advised expedition, in November 1093, he and his son Edward were killed at Alnwick. It was fortunate for the Scots that the Conqueror's successors were so distracted by internecine disputes that they were left alone. The Normans did not conquer Scotland by military force. But it could be said that, subtly, they were to take control by infiltration and invitation.

A profound cultural shift, which would begin the process of pushing the Gaelic character of the kingdom to the periphery, began at court. Here the principal instigator was an Anglo-Saxon princess, Margaret. After the Battle of Hastings this young, lovely, learned and pious lady fled to Scotland and there won the heart of King Malcolm. He made her his Queen in 1072.

Margaret now lived in a court where only Gaelic was spoken and, though her husband was bilingual, she depended heavily on the English advisers who had come north to join her. She brought Benedictine monks from the mother house of Canterbury to Dunfermline and launched a complete overhaul of the church in Scotland, bringing it into line with established practice approved by Rome.

In his own way Malcolm had assisted this cultural shift. The heart of his kingdom (which would not be called Alba for very much longer) was north of the Forth. The King moved the centre of gravity steadily southwards, strengthening his hold on the anglophone Lothian.

In the chaotic struggle for power following Malcolm's death, the Scottish kingdom appeared to be becoming a client state of England. For example, Malcolm's son Edgar got the throne in 1097 'in fealty' to King William II. Stability returned only with the accession of Malcolm and Margaret's youngest son, David, in 1124. His sister Edith had married King Henry I of England, and David had been brought up in his court, speaking French and learning Norman ways. In 1114 David, by marrying Matilda, widow of Earl Simon de Senlis, had inherited vast estates in Huntingdon and Northampton. Now this client of the English Crown, the Earl of Huntingdon, was also King of Scots.

David's mother Margaret had stamped an English character onto the Scottish court. Now David promoted Norman culture and procedures into a kingdom he was to rule for almost thirty years. Trusted Normans – a great many of them rather obscure undertenants and landless knights from Huntingdon – were invited into Scotland and given land to be held under feudal tenure. Among them were ancestors of future monarchs, the Bruces and the Stewarts.

This great influx did not, it seems, provoke as much resistance from native Scots as might be expected. Improving climate, allowing marginal land to be brought into production, helped to make it easier to accommodate the newcomers. And, above all, during his long reign, David not only extended the frontiers of his realm but also brought a new prosperity to Scotland. He created 16 royal burghs, including Edinburgh, Roxburgh, Dunfermline, Stirling, Berwick, Perth and Aberdeen.

David had control of silver mines at Alston near Carlisle and these provided the bullion with which he began to mint Scotland's first coins. Deeply pious, like his mother (who was to be canonised in 1249), the King of Scots used a great deal of his silver to found new monasteries. The decline of the Celtic church was signalled by new ecclesiastical arrangements, especially the division of most of the kingdom into parishes, each with a kirk built of stone and sustained by the levying of 'teinds' or tithes. By 1200 there were no fewer than 1,100 parishes in Scotland.

By that year, the Normans were in Down and Antrim, forging their way up the western coastlands of the Narrow Sea. They had come here to Ulster not by invitation nor by infiltration, but by armed conquest.

EPISODE 10

THE WESTERN COASTLANDS OF THE NARROW SEA: NORMAN CONQUEST

As in Scotland, the Normans had come to Ireland by invitation, but there the comparison ends. 'Strongbow', Richard FitzGilbert de Clare, the Earl of Pembroke and Strigoil, had come at the request of Dermot MacMurrough, King of Leinster, who had been driven out of the country by the High King, Rory O'Connor. From the moment their first contingent landed at Bannow Bay in Wexford in May 1169, the Normans had to fight their way – the Viking strongholds of Wexford and Waterford offered formidable resistance, but to no avail. Amidst the carnage of Waterford city, Strongbow was wed to Dermot's daughter, Aoife, thus securing his inheritance of the Kingdom of Leinster. Finally, in September 1171, the invaders overwhelmed a great host brought to the outskirts of Dublin by the High King. The Irish had no immediate answer to volleys of arrows fired by Welsh longbowmen, bolts shot by Flemish crossbowmen and the assault of securely mounted mailed knights. Dermot died in 1171 and, as agreed beforehand, Strongbow now possessed the lands of Leinster.

Henry II, the most powerful monarch in western Europe, ruler of England, Brittany, Anjou, Aquitaine, and much of Wales, viewed Strongbow's victories with some alarm. His subjects' victories presented him with a spectre – an independent Norman state which could threaten his empire from the west. Henry prepared a great expedition and on 18 October 1171 400 ships entered Waterford haven. The King's progress from there to Dublin was one of the finest triumphs of his long reign. Making camp outside the city walls, Henry held court and received the submission in his new title as Lord of Ireland. Rory was allowed to retain his now rather empty title of High King. Henry left Ireland the following spring.

The King gave the fertile kingdom of Meath to Hugh de Lacy, provided he could conquer it, but in 1175 he made an agreement at Windsor that further Norman conquest should be forbidden provided the High King would keep

Irish rulers at peace. This treaty proved impossible to enforce and no attempt was made to prevent John de Courcy as he set out to carve out a new patrimony for himself.

In February 1177 John de Courcy, a knight from Cumbria, sallied out from Dublin with 22 mailed horsemen and some 300 foot soldiers. The expedition marched through Meath heading north to the plain of Muirhevna, where it was joined by Irish allies. Then de Courcy led his men beyond the furthest limits of Norman territory over the Moyry Pass. Turning east, the invaders reached Lecale in fewer than four days. In front of Down, the capital of the kingdom of Dál Fiatach, the attack was prepared. 'John's followers were few in number', the chronicler Gerald of Wales recorded, 'but good, brave men, the pick of the army'.

So unexpected was this Norman incursion that the local ruler, Rory MacDonleavy, fled with all his people. To seize a kingdom by surprise was one achievement but to hold it with a small force was quite another. MacDonleavy invoked his authority as over-king of the Ulaidh and returned a week after his flight with a great host. Defensive earthworks, hastily thrown up by de Courcy's men, were too incomplete to be effective and so it was in the open – on the ground which slopes up from the River Quoile south to Downpatrick – that a battle was fought, as Gerald relates:

> So a fierce battle commenced. To begin with they showered down a hail of arrows and spears at long range. Then they came to close quarters, lance encountered lance, sword met sword, and many were killed on either side … After an intense and for a long time indecisive struggle between these unevenly matched forces, John's courage at last won him the victory, and a great number of the enemy were killed along the sea shore where they had taken refuge … For because the surface of the shore was soft and yielding, the weight of their bodies caused men to sink deep into it, and blood pouring from their wounds remained on the surface of the slippery ground and easily came up to the knees and legs of their pursuers.

An even greater Ulster coalition – including the Cenél Eóghain king, Máel Sechlainn McLochlainn, the Archbishop of Armagh and other leading prelates carrying holy relics – joined King Rory for a final attempt to oust the Normans in a great assault in June. Once again de Courcy triumphed.

The MacDonleavys were to fight again but their kingdom was lost. In a characteristic campaign of daring, the Normans had won a toe-hold in Ulster, and in their rapid overrunning of the coastlands on the western side of the Narrow Sea thereafter, they effected a radical alteration in the province's balance of power.

EPISODE 11

DE COURCY AND DE LACY

T he striking feature of John de Courcy's conquest is that all parts of it had easy access to the Narrow Sea. The sea was the essential Norman lifeline, made more secure when in 1180 de Courcy married Affreca, daughter of Gottred, King of the Isle of Man, who brought with her a formidable fleet as her dowry. This was a coastal lordship which ventured no further inland than the nearest shores of Lough Neagh at Antrim. The Normans first secured their conquests by throwing up mottes, most of them concentrated in east Down and south Antrim. It was here that de Courcy built the two mightiest fortresses in his domain: Carrickfergus Castle and Dundrum Castle.

Carrickfergus Castle was erected on a tongue of rock jutting out into Belfast Lough. Behind a surrounding wall, now the inner curtain, masons erected a massive rectangular keep with walls nearly 3 metres (9 feet) thick. Black basalt from close by, together with some red sandstone from Newtownabbey and cream Cultra limestone shipped across the lough, were used to build this tower four storeys high, rising over 27 metres (90 feet) above the rock. It was and remained the largest keep constructed anywhere in Ireland. On another defensible rock adjacent to the sea, Dundrum Castle stood sentinel over the land approaches to Lecale. The names of de Courcy's principal barons appear in witness to his charters. They include Richard FitzRobert, William Savage, William Hacket, William Saracen, Richard de Dundonald, Walter de Logan and Henry de Coupland (who gave his family name to the Copeland Islands).

Like David, King of Scots, de Courcy was exceptionally generous to the church, starting out by giving it his first conquest, Down, which he renamed Downpatrick. He founded the Cistercian Abbey of Inch, the first building in Gothic style raised in Ireland. Other gifts to the church included the Benedictine Black Abbey in the Ards, Augustinian houses at Muckamore and Downpatrick, and White Abbey near Carrickfergus. Affreca founded Grey Abbey in the Ards.

For a quarter of a century John de Courcy ruled his Ulster lands with as much independence as a warlord. Then shortly after John became King of England in 1199, de Courcy's luck ran out. John, a capricious monarch who trusted no one, relished retaining control by setting baron against baron. He particularly resented the unseemly independence shown by de Courcy. John liked to raise up men of modest standing to challenge those he considered over-mighty. Hugh de Lacy fitted the bill perfectly: younger brother of Walter, the Lord of Meath, he had inherited little and yearned for more. After fighting well alongside the king in northern France in 1199, Hugh advanced north in 1201 with royal blessing and quickly routed and ousted de Courcy.

The king summoned de Lacy to Winchester Cathedral on 29 May 1205. The king tied a sword around de Lacy's waist to symbolise his investiture as the Earl of Ulster – the first Irish earl. But King John being King John, de Lacy found his place in the sun did not last. It seems that the king almost immediately regretted having made de Lacy an earl. Finding that John did not need him any more, and well aware of growing baronial discontent in the king's Angevin dominions, de Lacy risked all by becoming an open rebel against the Crown. He championed his kinsman William de Braose, Lord of Limerick (and much else besides), who had broken with the king.

De Lacy miscalculated. Landing at Waterford on 20 June 1210, John brought over the largest army yet to be seen in Ireland. Brother Walter, most Irish barons and even Cathal Crobhderg, King of Connacht (the youngest son of High King Rory O'Connor), joined the English king in Dublin. Marching north alongside John was none other than John de Courcy; he, no doubt, advised the king not to risk ambush in the Moyry Pass but instead to build a bridge of boats across Carlingford Lough to take his army northwards. Using imposing siege engines, John took Dundrum and Carrickfergus Castles. De Lacy had already fled as the royal forces closed in on Carrickfergus, but his wife Lescelina was left behind in the castle (in the words of the Scotichronicon) 'because her husband detested her'.

De Lacy crossed the Narrow Sea and found refuge in St Andrews where, fortunately, he had made a pious donation some years before. Then he and de Braose made it to France. Matilda de Braose and her son William did not: King John had them starved to death in prison. De Braose died soon after but de Lacy now embarked on a new career. The landless Earl of Ulster joined the crusade against the Cathar heretics in Languedoc and the Midi. As a reward for his military prowess, he was given substantial estates there.

All had changed by 1221. The Cathars drove out the crusaders, leaving de Lacy bereft of land once more. But the Earl was not finished yet: he was on his way back to Ulster.

EPISODE 12

THE EARLDOM OF ULSTER

Hugh de Lacy, Earl of Ulster, had been driven out of Ireland by King John in 1210. He took refuge in France, and soon was in the thick of the crusade there against the Cathar heretics. Eventually the Cathars triumphed, however, and the Earl slipped back into Ireland in 1223, throwing the northern half of the country into turmoil for several years. Joined by Aedh O'Neill, King of Cenél nEoghain, de Lacy, after much blood-letting, gained the upper hand. The beleaguered King Henry III, John's son, beset by myriad problems, felt he had no choice but to restore the earl to favour in 1227. Never slow to take up arms against anyone who stood in his way, de Lacy devoted the rest of his life to strengthening his earldom and extending its frontiers.

The earl added the outer ward and the unique circular twin-towered gatehouse to Carrickfergus Castle; and it was he who built Dundrum Castle's massive drum. He raised another formidable bastion at Greencastle to guard the narrows of Carlingford Lough – and perhaps to prevent another royal bridge of boats. During de Lacy's exile in France, King John rewarded Normans, settled in south-west Scotland, who had come to his aid in Ulster. These barons were invited to cross the Narrow Sea to take up lands in the earldom. Duncan of Carrick was granted the Antrim Glens from Larne to Glenarm. His nephews – Alan, Lord of Galloway, and Thomas, Earl of Atholl – received coastlands from the Glens along the north coast as far west as Lough Foyle.

De Lacy made sure that all newcomers acknowledged him as their liege lord, and he may have forced some of these barons to return to Scotland. The northern coastland called Twescard, from the Irish *tuaisceart* meaning 'north', was centred on Coleraine and the lower Bush valley. The Earl of Atholl had built a castle at Coleraine, but it had been destroyed by O'Neill and had to be rebuilt. Twescard had become one of the most prosperous parts of the earldom by the time de Lacy died peacefully in his bed in 1242.

It seems to have been a condition of de Lacy's restoration that the Earldom of Ulster would revert to the Crown on his death. In 1264 Walter de Burgo, Lord of Connacht, was granted the earldom by Edward I. A major reason was that the free-spending Edward, 'Hammer of the Scots', was deeply in debt to this great lord. As one of the most powerful magnates in the land, the new Earl

of Ulster could be relied on to keep the Irish of the north from threatening
outlying manors of the Lordship of Ireland. Certainly Walter worked hard
to establish good relations with Aedh O'Neill. This King of Tír Eoghain was
betrothed to Aleanor, the Earl's cousin; he 'promised to bind himself under pain
of excommunication' to treat her honourably.

Next in social importance after the Earl were the four great baronial families:
the Savages, Bissets, de Logans and de Mandevilles. The Savages had manors,
mainly in Twescard. The Bissets originally of Norman origin had settled in
the Antrim Glens. The de Logans were from the Six Mile Water valley. The
de Mandevilles had manors in north Antrim, Donegore, Comber, Killyleagh,
Groomsport and Castleward. These vassals held great manors from the earl,
valued in knight's fees, that is, land for which rent was sufficient to maintain
the service of a knight. In the Six Mile Water valley, for example, there were
four knights fees, each about two square miles: Twywys (Ballynure); Lyn
(Ballylinny); Robertiston (Ballyrobert); and Waltirton (Ballywalter). Much of
the rent in the earldom was paid in corn. Some tenants paid peppercorn rent
only – literally in the case of the tenants of Frenestoun (now Ballyfrenis), who
paid a pound of pepper each year. John de Mandeville in Greencastle paid
'one soar sparrowhawk' at the feast of John the Baptist, 24 June; Nicholas
Galgyl of Greyabbey gave a pair of silver spurs for one farm and an otterskin
for another; and a tenant of Glenarm paid two pairs of white gloves for 102
acres there.

Towns grew up in the shadow of mottes and stone castles. The largest
was Carrickfergus, and Coulrath (Coleraine) vied with Downpatrick as the
town second in importance. Others included Le Roo (Limavady), Blathewyc
(Newtownards), Dunmalys (Larne), Portkamen (Bushmills), Portros
(Portrush), Grenecastell (Greencastle), Doundannald (Dundonald), Coul
(Carnmoney) and Le Ford (Belfast). Le Ford would have been no more than a
small village.

When Walter de Burgo died in 1271, his son Richard was only 12 years old. In
1280, when not quite of age, Richard was allowed to inherit his lands and castles.
Known popularly as the 'Red Earl', Richard de Burgo ruled with a firm hand and
pushed the frontiers of his great lordship still deeper into Gaelic Ulster. But he
was to live long enough to see his earldom all but destroyed by a Scots army
brought across the Narrow Sea by Edward and Robert Bruce.

NORMANS MAKING THEIR HOME IN SCOTLAND AND IRELAND

Trusted Normans – a great many of them rather obscure undertenants and landless knights from Huntingdon – were invited into Scotland and given land to be held under feudal tenure. The first and most lavish grant was to Robert de Brus, whose family had come from the village of Brix near Cherbourg. The estate Brus (later Bruce) acquired was Annandale, a great sweep of territory of 200,000 acres at the head of the Solway Firth.

Walter Fitzalan, the third son of a steward of the lords of Dol in Brittany, arrived in 1136 to serve as steward to three twelfth-century kings of Scots. He founded the family of Stewart which by 1200 had acquired a lordship extending across much of Ayrshire, Renfrew, Cowal and Bute. The de Balliol family, originally from Picardy, was given lands in the west of Scotland. David I, King of Scots, appointed William Comyn as his Chancellor and in the next century his family became the most powerful one in Scotland. Other Normans and Flemish coming in at David's invitation bore such surnames as fitz John, Umphraville, Oliphant, de Morville, Giffard, Mowbray and Riddel. Many had surnames which today would be regarded now without hesitation as uniquely Scots, including Carson, Douglas, Ramsay, Ogilvie, Fraser, Montgomery, Sinclair, Pollock, Gordon and Lindsay. David was determined to incorporate Moray in the north-east into his kingdom. Here the King's principal agent was a Flemish family called Freskin, which later changed its surname to de Moravia and, eventually, Murray.

During the seventeenth century great numbers bearing these surnames would be crossing the Narrow Sea to make a new home in Ulster … just as, during the nineteenth century great numbers with native Irish surnames would be travelling in the opposite direction to make a fresh start in Scotland.

The Normans, and those they brought over with them across the Irish Sea, never conquered all of Ireland. But by the end of the thirteenth century they had seized control of almost all of the fertile lands of Leinster, Munster and Connacht. The most successful in winning estates were the descendants of foreigners who came to help Dermot MacMurrough recover his kingdom of Leinster. They were as much Welsh as they were Norman and Flemish. At the core was a tightly knit family group, all descended from a remarkable Welsh princess, Nesta, daughter of King Rhys ap Tewdwr, who had children by Stephen, Constable of Cardigan; William fitz Gerald, Lord of Carew; King Henry I of England; and Gerald of Windsor, to whom she was married – and she had children by at least one other man. Even if Gerald was not actually their father or grandfather, most were happy to be named fitz Gerald and be described as 'Geraldines'.

Amongst those with Nesta's blood in their veins who spearheaded the invasion of Ireland in 1169 were Raymond 'le Gros' fitz Gerald, son of the Lord of Carew; Robert fitz Stephen, son of the Constable of Cardigan; Maurice fitz Gerald, son of Gerald of Windsor, and Meiler fitz Henry, grandson of Henry I. Their deeds were memorably recorded by Giraldus Cambrensis, 'Gerald of Wales', archdeacon of Brecon and tutor to the future King John. His father was William fitz Odo de Barri and Angharad, daughter of Gerald of Windsor and Nesta. Several of Gerald's relatives took part in the invasion of Ireland and their descendants were the founders of the Barry family in Co. Cork.

The greatest of the Geraldines became the Earls of Kildare and the Earls of Desmond. Henry II gave Meath to Hugh de Lacy and William de Burgo (or de Burgh) received lands in south Tipperary from King John before going on to conquer much of Connacht. The de Burgos in Connacht later went native and their descendants are the Burkes or Bourkes. The Dillons are descended from Sir Henry de Leon who served as John's secretary and got lands in Longford, Westmeath and Kilkenny. The Prendergasts, of Flemish origin, won substantial lands for themselves in Co. Wexford. The first members of the Fleming family were granted Slane in Co. Meath. Other surnames of Norman origin in Ireland dating from the Medieval period include Butler, Cusack, Cruise, Nagle, Power and Roche – how many Roches today know that their ancestors' surname was de la Rochefort? Fitzpatrick is not Norman but is the Gaelic *Mac Giolla Phádraig* normanised. Two names from this time of Welsh origin are Taaffe (ancestors of the Earls of Carlingford) and Griffith.

The Normans made less of an impression on Ulster than on the other three provinces. FitzGeralds, who founded Sligo town, tried to conquer Fermanagh only to be routed by the fords of Erne at Belleek. Only the coastlands of Antrim and Down, and later the north coast as far west as Inishowen, were successfully colonised. None of the conquerors – John de Courcy, Hugh de Lacy or Richard de Burgo – left a noticeable number of descendants carrying their surname in the north. But some of the barons who fought alongside them did: they include Savages, de Logans, de Audleys and Jordans. The Jordans got land in Jordanstown near Carrickfergus and in Ardglass, where their tower house still stands. The Savages, driven out of the Six Mile Water valley in Antrim by the Clandeboye O'Neills, took refuge in the southern half of the Ards peninsula where they held out for several centuries. Savage, from *sauvage*, 'a countryman', is the commonest surname of Norman origin in Ulster.

Scottish Normans, granted land in the earldom of Ulster by King John, returned home for the most part after Hugh de Lacy's warmongering return from southern France. The Bissetts, ensconced in the Glens of Antrim, proved an exception. The marriage of Margery Bissett to John Mór MacDonnell in 1399 was to change the course of Ulster's history. Making life difficult for genealogists, most Bissetts thereafter adopted the Irish patronymic *Mac Eoin*, anglicised as MacKeown.

EPISODE 14

THE RED EARL AND THE 'HAMMER OF THE SCOTS'

When Richard de Burgo inherited his lands and estates in 1280, he could consider himself one of the most powerful barons in all of western Europe. Now the 3rd Earl of Ulster, he was also Lord of Connacht and in possession of great estates besides in Leinster and Munster. After putting an end to a deadly quarrel between Henry de Mandeville and William FitzWarin in Twescard, de Burgo extended his lands westwards along the coast to Lough Foyle. In time he would take over Inishowen, raising there the great castle of Northburgh at Greencastle. De Burgo made sure he was fluent in Irish. Much of his success was due to his ability to win over the support and respect of Gaelic lords.

Known widely as the 'Red Earl', this man who possessed almost half the land of Ireland gave fealty to Edward I, Lord of Ireland and King of England. This meant that de Burgo was obliged to provide military service whenever called upon by the king, his liege lord. It was this feudal duty which was to draw him inexorably into the affairs of Scotland.

Ruthless and violent, even by the standards of his day, Edward I of England was at war unceasingly throughout his 35-year reign. In crushing Prince Llewelyn he left much of north Wales devastated. He did not stint treasure and men's lives to uphold his authority in Gascony. But the all-consuming ambition of this monarch was the subjugation of the realm of the King of Scots. When the Canmore dynasty, founded by David I, ran out, the Scottish parliament had actually invited Edward to choose their next king. Edward picked John Balliol, a man of Norman blood who had no hesitation in giving his fealty to the King of England. However, Edward destroyed what should have been a mutually beneficial relationship. His high-handed seizure of goods by purveyors and his burdensome exactions were bad enough, but when he called on the Scots to provide him with an army in Gascony they were driven into armed revolt in 1295. Leading Scots nobles and churchmen felt that they had no choice but to make a secret pact with King Philip IV of France – this was the beginning of what became known later as the 'auld alliance'.

In response, Edward led a great army of some 30,000 men northwards in the spring of 1296. When he took Berwick, then Scotland's most prosperous burgh, he refused the pleas of his clergy to show mercy. In an orgy of destruction and slaughter, as a chronicler relates, 'for two days streams of blood flowed from the bodies of the slain, for in his tyrannous rage he ordered 7,500 souls of both sexes to be massacred … mills could be turned round by the flow of their blood'. Even more lives were lost when the Scots army was shattered at Dunbar.

Edward depended on men, war material and food supplies from Ireland to secure his victory. There it was not so much the resistance of the native Irish but disputes amongst the Norman lords that on occasion threatened the security of his Lordship of Ireland. Indeed, in 1294 Richard de Burgo had been seized and held in the castle of Lea by John FitzThomas of Offaly – his pugnacious rival in the Midlands. FitzThomas had to be dragged to England before he would agree to release the Red Earl. The King desperately needed de Burgo to lead an army to support his expedition in Scotland. Edward was to write later that 'he relies on him more than any other man in the land for many reasons'.

On 1 January 1296 28 barons, led by the Red Earl, were summoned to muster with the royal army. The fleet setting sail across the Narrow Sea carried 3,157 men, 300 of them mailed horsemen and – taken out of Ireland for the first time – a troop of 261 'hobelars', native Irish skirmishers on light horses, later to prove their deadly worth in France. Hugh Bisset, from the Antrim Glens, had four ships, each manned by a crew of 40: these were 'to harass the king's Scotch enemies by sea'. During that summer the treasurer paid out £4,000 to royal purveyors to ship supplies to Carlisle.

Two years later, in 1298, the king ordered the following from Ireland: 8,000 quarters of wheat, 10,000 quarters of oats, 2,000 quarters of crushed malt, 1,000 tuns of wine, 500 carcasses of beef, 1,000 fat pigs and 20,000 dried fish.

These were provisions to sustain the Earl of Ulster as he returned to Scotland to assist Edward in his campaign against William Wallace. Wallace, an obscure knight from Elderslie, had revived the war against the King of England at a time when nobles in despair were giving up the struggle. Attracting the devoted support of thousands of ordinary Scots, Wallace overwhelmed the English at Stirling Bridge. Astonished at his success, the highest in the land rallied to Wallace, ennobled him and made him the Guardian of Scotland.

But Edward was not to be called the 'Hammer of the Scots' for nothing. The King marched on Scotland for the sixth time and, to be sure of success, once more he summoned the Red Earl to join him.

EPISODE 15

ROBERT THE BRUCE TAKES REFUGE ON RATHLIN

On 27 March 1306 Robert the Bruce had himself crowned King of Scots at Scone. The only mark of royalty was a circlet of gold since Edward I of England had taken away the crown and the Stone of Destiny. To be crowned was one thing, to make good his claim was another: on 19 June King Robert and his army were routed at Methven near Perth. Most of the noblemen who had attended the coronation three months earlier were hunted down and put to death.

Now on the run, Bruce took refuge with Angus MacDonald, Lord of Islay and Kintyre. Then, after only three days here in the stronghold of Dunaverty, Bruce heard that English troops were approaching in force. He decided to withdraw to safety with his 200 followers over the sea to the island of Rathlin. Meanwhile King Edward had appointed Sir Simon de Montacute to command a flotilla 'for service against the rebels lurking in Scotland, and in the Isles between Scotland and Ireland'. Sir Hugh Bissett, the Lord of the Glens, was ordered to assemble 'as many well-manned vessels as he can procure, to come to the Isles and the Scottish coast, and join Sir John de Menteith in putting down Robert de Bruce and his accomplices there, and in cutting off their retreat'.

Rathlin was a part of Bissett's lordship and the only reason Bruce could go there was that, unknown to the English king, Sir Hugh had joined him. Bissett had form: he had given his support in the past to William Wallace. Bruce's first place of refuge was a cave on the island – the story that King Robert was inspired there by the determination of a web-building spider owes its origin to Sir Walter Scott's writing 500 years later.

With Bruce were his brothers Edward, Thomas and Alexander; James 'The Black Douglas'; Robert Boyd; and, a former Guardian of Scotland, James Stewart. Arriving in September they spent that winter of 1306–7 recruiting support in Ireland. In February 1307 Bruce sent an advance party back to Scotland; but shortly after landing near Stranraer it was overwhelmed. Thomas and Alexander Bruce, along with two 'Irish kinglets', were captured and executed. On hearing this, King Robert without delay left Rathlin to land on the Ayrshire coast. It was only then that his fortunes began to change. A Scots victory at Louden Hill notwithstanding, seven more hard-campaigning years were to pass before the great triumph of Bannockburn.

The most detailed account of King Robert's campaigning is to be found in *The Brus*, a long poem occupying 20 volumes, written by John Barbour in 1377. To provide a flavour of the original, below are lines describing the three days spent at 'Donavardyne' (Dunaverty) before sailing to 'Rauchryne' (Rathlin):

> And in Donavardyne dayis thre
> For owtyne mair, then duellyt he.
> Syne gert he he his mengye mak them yar,
> Towart Rauchryne, be se to far.
> That is ane ile in the se,
> And may weill in myd watter be
> Betwix Kyntyr and Irland,
> Quhar als gret stremys ar rynnand,
> And als perilous, and mair,
> Till our saile tham in schipfair,
> As in the race off Bretangye,
> Or starit of Marrock in to Spayne.

Barbour tells us the journey was particularly 'perilous' in this Narrow Sea (which he compares to the Straits of Gibraltar between Morocco and Spain) because a storm blew up. In translation, he describes the voyage:

…had one been there he must have seen a great commotion of ships. For at times some would be right on the summit of the waves, and some would slide from the heights to the deeps, as if they would plunge to hell, then rise suddenly on a wave while the other ships at hand sank swiftly to the depths. Much skill was needed to save the tackle in such a press of ships, and among such waves; for, ever and anon, the waves bereft them of the sight of land when they were close to it, and when the ships were sailing nearer, the sea would rise so that the waves, weltering high, hid them from sight. Nevertheless they arrived at Rathlin, each one safely, and each blithe to have escaped the hideous waves.

The local people were terrified as they disembarked and fled to the fort now known as 'Bruce's castle'. Eventually they were reassured and came to an agreement that 'while he chose to remain there, they would send victuals for three hundred men'. Barbour continues:

The covenant was thus made, and on the morrow all Rathlin, man and page, knelt and did homage to the King, and therewith swore him fealty and good service. And right well they kept the covenant, for while he dwelt in the island they found provision for his company, and served him very humbly …

EPISODE 16

THE ROAD TO BANNOCKBURN AND LARNE

As his long reign was coming to an end, Edward I, King of England, Lord of Gascony, Prince of Wales and Lord of Ireland, was determined to keep Scotland as an integral part of his far-flung dominions. Now he faced the unflinching opposition of William Wallace leading Scots driven by his exactions and high-handed decrees to take up arms against him. Humiliated by Wallace's initial battle triumphs, Edward concluded that, to prevail, he had to have the assistance of his liege subjects in his Lordship of Ireland.

In 1303 Richard de Burgo received a letter from the king commanding him once more to lead a great expedition from Ireland to Scotland. A fleet of 173 ships, carrying 53 barons and over 3,400 men-at-arms, hobelars and foot soldiers, set sail for Scotland. These Irish mustered with King Edward's main army and together they saw to it that the Scots were utterly overwhelmed.

Captured by agents of Edward I in Scotland, William Wallace was dragged in bonds to London. He had lost everything. In Westminster Hall on 23 August 1305 this knight from Elderslie, once Guardian of Scotland, found himself condemned as a traitor to face a grisly death. Pulled over rough cobbles at the heels of a horse to Smithfield, he was first hanged and – while still alive – cut down, then emasculated, eviscerated, his bowels burned before him, beheaded and his corpse cut into quarters. Edward could be certain that Scotland was his and, as proof to his subjects, he had in his capital the crown of the King of Scots, the coronation Stone of Scone and that country's holiest relic: the Black Rood of St Margaret.

Yet it was only a year later that King Edward got news of a fresh insurrection against his rule in Scotland. This time it was led by a lord who had once campaigned by his side: Robert the Bruce, Earl of Carrick. Bruce had himself crowned at Scone as King of Scots on 25 March 1306, but only a handful of noblemen turned up for the ceremony. Again and again King Robert faced defeat. Forced to become a fugitive, King Robert sent Elizabeth, his wife and queen, to the north in the hope that she could find refuge in Norway; but she was captured at Tain and kept prisoner in Holderness. King Robert fled to the Isles and, almost certainly for a time, took refuge in Ulster on Rathlin Island.

When he returned to the Scottish mainland King Robert sustained yet more reverses. Edward I died in 1307 but his son and successor, Edward II, continued the war. In 1314 Edward in person led a great army into Scotland. King Robert preferred to avoid set-piece battles. But when the English advanced to relieve Stirling Castle, Edward Bruce, Robert's surviving brother, persuaded the King of Scots on this occasion to make a stand.

This battle ground King Robert chose with care. The schiltrons, hedgehog formations of well-trained men wielding spears, had the protection of trees behind and the boggy 'carse' in front. Camouflaged ditches flanked the firmer ground leading to the castle. On 23 June King Edward advanced with a force that outnumbered the Scots two to one. Seeing Bruce wearing his crown, one of Edward's young knights, Sir Henry de Bohun, charged at him only to have his head cleft in two by the King of Scots wielding his battle axe as the knight bore down on him. Unnerved, King Edward held back as night fell. Then at first light that midsummer dawn the disciplined spearmen broke into a trot and bore down on the English with devastating effect. Mounted English horsemen, driven back, either pitched into the hidden ditches or dislocated the ranks of their own archers. King Edward was fortunate to escape the carnage.

So many barons and knights were captured that, almost at a stroke, Scotland acquired great riches from the ransoms subsequently paid. Edward had no choice but to release hostages and captives – amongst them was Elizabeth, King Robert's Queen. Elizabeth had endured no fewer than eight years in captivity. She was none other than the daughter of Richard de Burgo, the 'Red Earl' of Ulster. Where now would the Earl's loyalty lie – with his son-in-law, the King of Scots, or with his liege lord, King Edward of England? This severe test was just a year ahead.

For King Robert had turned his attention to Ireland. He planned to strike at the heart of the English colony there which had long sustained armies fighting against him in Scotland. On 26 May 1315 a great fleet crossed the Narrow Sea. King Robert's brother Edward led the invading army. Edward had no less a mission than the complete conquest of Ireland. The Scots disembarked at Larne. According to Irish annals, Edward brought with him 'the men of three hundred ships, and his warlike slaughtering army caused the whole of Ireland to tremble, both Gael and Gall'.

EPISODE 17

'WASTING AND RAVAGING': EDWARD BRUCE IN IRELAND

In May 1315 Edward Bruce, brother of Robert, the King of Scots who had routed the English at Bannockburn the year before, invaded Ireland – the most formidable army to cross the Narrow Sea for as long as anyone could remember. First, Edward sought to bring ruin to the lands of the colonists in Ireland who for so long had sent fighting men on campaign in Scotland on behalf of the English Crown. His ultimate goal, however, was to conquer this island from end to end and have himself crowned as King of Ireland. Ever since he had taken refuge on Rathlin, Robert Bruce had taken care to establish his credentials as Gaelic monarch, since he was a descendant of the Kings of Alba. He secured the alliance of the most powerful Gaelic ruler in Ulster, Donal O'Neill, King of Tír Eoghain. Now King Donal made a great hosting across his kingdom, ready to serve King Robert's brother, Edward.

Transported by the notorious pirate Thomas Dun – 'a scummer of the se', according to the poet John Barbour – Edward Bruce 'came to Ireland', the Annals of Connacht record, 'landing on the coast of north Ulster' in May 1315. 'He began by harrying the choicest parts of Ulster, burning Rathmore in Moylinny'.

After disembarking at Larne, Edward plundered the manors of Six Mile Water, routed the local lord Sir Thomas de Mandeville, swept aside the MacCartans, and made rendezvous with his ally, Donal O'Neill, King of Tír Eoghain. Together they advanced south, forcing their way through the Moyry Pass, and razed Dundalk. It was in that colonists' town that Edward Bruce proclaimed himself High King of Ireland. The burning of the church of Ardee, filled with men, women and children taking sanctuary, was an early sign of the ruthless and destructive character of this war.

So unexpected was this Scots incursion that Edmund Butler, governing the Lordship of Ireland on behalf of Edward II (the same King of England defeated at Bannockburn), was in Munster, far to the south. At the same time, Richard de Burgo, the 'Red' Earl of Ulster, over in the west was not much closer: he was there attending to his extensive possessions in Galway and Mayo. Both lords hastened northwards to engage Edward Bruce. The Annals record that de Burgo brought together a great army from all sides to Roscommon,

> marching thence to Athlone and obliquely through Meath and Mag Breg, having with him Felim O'Connor, king of Connacht, their numbers being about twenty battalions; and this time the Galls spared not saint or shrine, however sacred, nor churchmen or laymen or sanctuary, but went wasting and ravaging across Ireland from the Shannon in the south to Coleraine and Inishowen in the north.

The royal governor decided to stay south of the Moyry Pass to defend the Norman manors of Leinster. Advised by O'Neill, Edward Bruce pulled back across Ulster to ravage the Earl's settlements at Inishowen and the Roe valley. De Burgo meanwhile came north and advanced down the right bank of the lower Bann, only to find that the Scots

> threw down the bridge of Coleraine to hinder the Earl; and he followed them up and encamped opposite Edward and the Ulstermen on the river at Coleraine and between them they left neither wood nor lea nor corn nor crop nor stead nor barn, but fired and burnt them all.

De Burgo's difficulties intensified when the King of Connacht decided to change sides and throw in his lot with this brother of the King of Scots, making submission to Edward as his High King.

At Coleraine a wide river estuary separated the two sides, as Barbour relates:

> The Bane, that is ane arme of the se
> That with hors may nocht passit be,
> Was betuix thame and Ullister.

... but not for long ... the Bann was crossed with Dunn's fleet and the Scots drew close to de Burgo, who prepared an ambush for them:

> The Erll and all that with him war,
> Ruschit on thame with wapyns bar.

This failed: the Earl was forced back to make a last stand by the Kellswater at Connor in Antrim. There on 10 September 1315 the Scots spearmen completely overwhelmed de Burgo's feudal host. De Burgo was imprisoned in Dublin for a time (perhaps he was suspected since his daughter was married to King Robert). Then, according to the annals the Earl 'was a wanderer up and down Ireland all this year, with nor power or lordship'.

After the Battle of Connor as many survivors of the Earl's broken army as could make it to Carrickfergus took refuge there in the castle on the north shores of Belfast Lough. In October 1315 the Dublin government's victuallers were ordered to supply 30 crannocks of wheat to the defenders, but ships carrying the grain were scattered by a storm and the supplies were diverted to Whitehaven and Skinburness. Those within the castle would have to survive on what lay within the storehouses. Lacking heavy siege engines, the Scots settled down to starve the garrison into submission, while the main body of their army prepared to conquer the rest of Ireland.

At first Edward Bruce swept all before him. Reinforced by fresh troops brought over by the Earl of Moray in November 1315, the Scots advanced south. There in the Midlands they routed armies commanded by the royal governor. The Scots fought a winter campaign knowing that their spearmen were at an advantage at a time of the year when horses were hampered by soft ground and shortage of grass. A terrible famine was sweeping Europe, however, and unable to live off the country despite their victories, the Scots were forced by hunger back into Ulster.

There would be much death and destruction to come.

EPISODE 18

'IN THIS BRUCE'S TIME ... FALSEHOOD AND FAMINE AND HOMICIDE FILLED THE COUNTRY'

For Henry of Thrapston, keeper of Carrickfergus Castle, the position was becoming desperate. Ever since the autumn of 1315 the Scots, brought to Ulster by Edward Bruce, had this great fortress under siege. Now, after more than five months, the men in his garrison were reduced to chewing hides. It was not until Easter 1316 that an attempt was made to bring relief; Sir Thomas de Mandeville put together a force in Drogheda and sailed to Belfast Lough. A fierce skirmish followed in the streets of Carrickfergus when the Scots were roused, but it was in vain that a desperate sally was made by the castle garrison; the Scots defeated the defenders and those who had tried to help them, and in the fighting Sir Thomas was slain.

A further relief expedition was diverted by Richard de Burgo, the 'Red' Earl of Ulster – the grain was given to the Scots as ransom for his cousin, Sir William de Burgo, captured the previous September. It was only a matter of time before Carrickfergus surrendered. During a parley the garrison seized 30 Scots and held them prisoner in the dungeons. According to the Laud Annals, eight of these men were later killed and eaten by the defenders. The annals explain that this 'pitiable circumstance' came about because 'no one came up with supplies'. Finally, after a year's siege, in September 1316 Carrickfergus capitulated.

Edward Bruce's hold on Ulster was now complete. The Earldom of Ulster's other strong bastions, Northburgh in Inishowen and Greencastle opposite Carlingford, also had fallen to the Scots. On 1 May 1316 near Dundalk Edward had himself formally crowned King of Ireland. But beyond the bounds of Ulster, he still had to make good his title. At Christmas, Robert Bruce, King of Scots, joined his brother, landing at Carrickfergus with an imposing force.

Early in February 1317 the two brothers broke out of Ulster to rout the 'Red' Earl in Meath. As the Scots approached Dublin, capital of the Lordship of Ireland, the Earl (who had taken refuge in the city) was imprisoned by the Mayor. The Mayor was not being unreasonable in questioning his loyalty: had not the Earl seized corn intended for the garrison in Carrickfergus? Had he not married his daughter Elizabeth to Robert Bruce, making her his Queen?

Desperate measures by the citizens saved Dublin from falling to the Scots. All the dwellings beyond the city walls were torched. The Bruce brothers lacked siege engines and pulled back from the capital to burn and plunder as far south as Limerick. Of their Irish allies, only Donal O'Neill, King of Tír Eoghain, continued to fight for them. Felim O'Connor, who had changed sides to ally himself with the Scots, withdrew from the campaign altogether and returned to his kingdom of Connacht. The Bruces were fast failing in their great enterprise and pulled back to Ulster in May 1317.

King Robert returned to Scotland on 22 May, leaving his brother Edward to face Roger de Mortimer, who arrived from England with an imposing army. He decided that the Earl of Ulster was loyal and had him released. Why did Mortimer and Edward Bruce not battle it out that summer? The answer is that, as famine continued to rage, neither opponent could muster the provisions needed to go on campaign. However, some good news arrived at Dublin Castle in July 1317: John of Athy, appointed Admiral of Edward II's fleet, defeated and killed at sea Thomas Dun the pirate lord in the pay of the Scots. Edward Bruce no longer possessed secure supply lines with Scotland.

The winter of 1317–18 was even harsher than the one before. Dearth was as severe as anyone could remember. 'Great famine this year throughout Ireland', the Annals of Connacht recorded, and the Laud Annals assert that Bruce's men 'were so destroyed with hunger that they raised the bodies of the dead from the cemeteries ... and the women devoured their own children from hunger'. The annalist believed this to be a punishment for eating meat during Lent, 'for they were reduced to eating one another, so that out of 10,000 there remained only about 300 who escaped the vengeance of God'.

Despite the previous famine and the harsh winter, the harvest of 1318 was a good one. In a final attempt, Bruce invaded south once more through the Moyry Pass only to meet an English army under the command of John de Bermingham at the hill of Faughart. In the words of the Annals of Connacht:

> Edward Bruce, he who was the common ruin of the Galls and Gaels of Ireland, was by the Galls of Ireland killed at Dundalk by dint of fierce fighting. MacRuaidri, king of the Hebrides, and MacDomnaill, king of Argyle, and their Scots were killed with him; and never was there a better deed done for the Irish than this, since the beginning of the world and the

banishing of the Formorians from Ireland. For in this Bruce's time for three years and a half, falsehood and famine and homicide filled the country, and undoubtedly men ate each other in Ireland.

HEBRIDEAN WARRIORS: *GALLÓGLAIGH* SEEK THEIR FORTUNES ACROSS THE NARROW SEA

Robert and Edward Bruce had failed in their mission to conquer Ireland but they certainly had left the English king's Irish Lordship seriously weakened. The exchequer in Dublin, the capital of the lordship, was frequently empty, and little help could be expected from the Crown, overstretched by numerous military commitments elsewhere. Descendants of Norman conquerors, particularly those most distant from Dublin, threw off their allegiance and became independent warlords adopting Irish customs and the Irish language, most notably descendants of the de Burgos in Galway and Mayo, known now as the MacWilliam Burkes. Native Gaelic lords began to build castles of mortared stone, many of them as formidable as any to be found in the English Pale. And, engaging the services of seasoned Hebridean warriors to stiffen the ranks of their own fighting men, they began to win back territories lost by their ancestors.

Vikings from the north – known in the Gaelic world as the Gall – had made the Hebrides their homeland and intermarried with the islanders, and their descendants came to be known as the Gall-Gael. They adopted Gaelic speech and abided by Gaelic laws and customs. Various attempts by the kings of Norway to assert their authority over this Scottish archipelago came to nothing and in 1266 King Magnus the Law-Mender felt he had no choice but to abandon his claim over the Western Isles. Meanwhile the King of Scots, Alexander III, determined that the Hebrides should be part of his dominions, began ferocious assaults on the Western Isles by laying waste homesteads on the Isle of Skye. In consequence Hebridean fighting men were deciding that Ireland might be a better place in which to seek their fortunes.

These men when they crossed the Narrow Sea to offer their martial services were known as *gallóglaigh*, 'young foreign warriors', shorthand for 'young warriors from Innse Gall', the Gaelic name for the Western Isles. In English these *gallóglaigh* were called 'galloglass'. The first major contingent arrived in 1259 when Aodh na nGall O'Connor, King of Connacht, married a daughter of Dougal MacRory, Lord of Garmoran in Argyll. She brought over as her dowry 'eight score' warriors.

After planting their harvests of oats in spring, gallowglass warriors would then gather their weapons and armour and sail in their galleys across the North Channel, there to offer their services to the highest bidder. When the summer season of fighting was over, these Hebrideans – those who had survived, that is – received their pay, mostly in the form of butter and hides, but also as live cattle firmly tied up for shipment; then they sailed back to the Isles in time to reap, thrash and winnow their harvests.

Galloglass sailed in galleys or smaller 'birlinns', clinker-built, open-hulled craft, with high sterns and prows. These direct descendants of Viking longships had their keels and frames constructed of oak, the overlapping planking of pine or oak, and masts of pine. Equipped with rectangular sails and propelled by between 72 and 24 oars, these were not only efficient troop carriers but capacious craft ideal for taking booty home. For protection in battle they wore quilted linen garments waterproofed with wax or pitch well rubbed in, and then given a covering of deer skin. Most had a metal helmet known as a 'bascinet' and a collar of mail over their padded coats. Some had a full coat of mail, an 'actoun' or 'habergeon' which had to be worn over a thick coat to prevent the rivets digging into the flesh. On their stone memorials galloglass liked to be portrayed with a sword; but for most this was too expensive a weapon. Their standard fighting kit was either a single-handed or double-handed axe, a firmly held spear and a short bow. Their style of combat was to fire their arrows first, then jettison their bows to charge, each protected with a round shield (either a buckler or the larger targe). One royal governor, Sir Anthony St Leger, observed that 'these sorte of men be those that doo not lightly abandon the field, but byde the brunte to the deathe'.

Some of these men began to make a new homeland for themselves in Ulster. Amongst Alexander III's fiercest opponents had been the MacSweeneys of Knapdale in Argyll. This King of Scots gave the Stewarts of Menteith authority to drive them out. Castle Sween fell and these MacSweeneys lost their lands.

The O'Donnell lords of Tír Chonaill needed reinforcements and invited them to settle. Three branches of the MacSweeneys of the Clann Suibhne established lordships here. All three were descended from Murchadh 'Mear' ('the Mad'), a lord of Knapdale: one branch drove the O'Breslins out of their peninsula to become MacSweeney Fanad; another became MacSweeney na Doe (*na dTuath* 'of the territories') who erected the near-impregnable Doe Castle, still standing today; and the third settled in the west of Tír Chonaill to become MacSweeney Banagh.

Other galloglass who settled in Ulster included the MacCabes, enegetic campaigners in the south of the province; the MacRorys; the Clann Síthigh, the MacSheehys; the MacDowells descended from Alexander Mac Dubhghaill (Dubhgall means 'a black-haired foreigner', i.e. a Danish Viking); and the MacDonnells, members of the Clann Somhairle, descendants of the legendary Viking lord of the Isles, Somerled. Some MacDonnells, in the service of the O'Neills of Tír Eoghain, got lands about Ballygawley but the most important branch settled in the Glens of Antrim, in time to play a pivotal role in shaping Ulster's future.

EPISODE 20

FROM THE ISLES TO THE GLYNNS: THE RISE OF CLAN DONALD

The Bissetts had crossed the English Channel with William the Conqueror and had been among those Normans who had subsequently slipped themselves, almost unobtrusively, into Scotland. But their descendants, John and Walter Bissett, were implicated in the murder of a member of the ruling Comyn family in Atholl in 1242. Narrowly escaping with their lives, they found refuge in the Glens of Antrim, to become founders of a great baronial family. There they made a new home for themselves and their people, obtaining lands from Richard de Burgo, the 'Red' Earl of Ulster. They thus acquired the seacht tuaithe, the 'seven territories', making up what for long was known as 'The Glynns'. A century later, in 1399, the heiress Margery Bissett, daughter of Eoin

Finn Bissett and Sadbh (herself daughter of the Lord of Tír Eoghain), married John Mór MacDonnell. That marriage was to be of momentous importance to those who dwelt on both sides of the Narrow Sea.

John Mór, son of John of Islay – grandson of Robert II, King of Scots – was a leading member of Clan Donald. Now, by marriage, John Mór had become Lord of the Glynns. Back in the twelfth century the Clan Donald had been founded by a Viking warlord, Somerled ('summer wanderer', in Gaelic Somhairle) who was acknowledged 'King of the Isles'. The Irish annals described him as *Rí Innse Gall*, 'King of the Islands of the Foreigners'. Somerled was also *Rí Airir Goídel*, 'King of Argyll'. His swashbuckling career ended when he was slain in battle in 1164. Somerled's descendants formed three kindreds: the Macdougalls, the MacRuairis and the MacDonalds. The Macdougalls were based in Lorn, Mull, and the Treshnish Isles; the MacRuairis, based in Garmoran; and the MacDonalds in Islay and Kintyre.

From the time that the Vikings overwhelmed them, the Isles formed a distinct entity held together by the sea. It took in all the islands from the Shetlands and Orkneys south along the Atlantic seaboard and through the Narrow Sea as far south as the Isle of Man. These were then territories owing allegiance to the King of Norway. Indeed, in 1097 Magnus Barelegs decided to prove that the peninsula of Kintyre was an island owing tribute to him as King of Norway: he stood at the tiller of his ship as it was dragged across the portage, the isthmus at Tarbert. Magnus was to meet a rather inglorious end in a minor skirmish with the warriors of Dál Fiatach close to Downpatrick in 1103.

The inhabitants of the Northern Isles spoke a dialect of Norse for many centuries. The remaining Isles were heavily colonised by the Vikings but the language spoken there by this blended population of Norse and Scots continued to be Gaelic. Norway's hold on the Isles weakened steadily and those local warlords who wielded real power there began to call themselves kings. Then in 1263 that Scandinavian hold was lost. Deliberately provoked by Alexander III, King of Scots, King Haakon Haakonson led a great fleet from Norway to descend on the Hebrides and the Firth of Clyde only to meet with ignominious defeat at Largs. In 1266 his successor, Magnus VI, decided to abandon Norway's claim to the Hebrides altogether. Norway did hold on to the Northern Isles for more than another century, nevertheless.

Norway's loss did not immediately become the Scottish kingdom's gain, however. It turned out than more than two hundred years were to pass before a King of Scots was able successfully to incorporate the Hebrides in his kingdom.

Angus Óg MacDonald (Aongus Óg MacDomnaill) supported Robert Bruce and this helped Clan Donald (Clann Domhnaill) to emerge victorious over their rivals, Clan Ruairi and Clan Dougal. Henceforth the head of Clan Donald described himself as 'Lord of the Isles' and this was tacitly accepted in Edinburgh. Angus's son John started out ruling Islay, Jura, Mull, Coll, Tiree, Morvern and Lochaber. Then in 1343 David II granted him Lewis and Harris; and through his marriage to Amy MacRuairi in 1346 he acquired Knoydart, Moidart, Uist, Barra, and Rhum. John cast Amy aside after four years and married Margaret, daughter of Robert the Steward, who became Robert II, and granted the Lord of the Isles Knapdale and Kintyre.

This extensive sea-girt dominion the Lord ruled with the close advice of the Council of the Isles – composed of the 'royal blood' of Clan Donald – meeting regularly at the centre of the lordship, the Isle of Loch Finlaggan on Islay. It did not seem particularly significant that, by the end of the fourteenth century, the Lordship of the Isles had also acquired a foothold in Ulster.

During ensuing decades the territorial reach of the Lordship of the Isles continued to expand. However, subsequent events would ensure that the lordship of 'The Glynns' would become a vital bolt-hole for the Clan Donald following catastrophic changes in its fortunes.

EPISODE 21

HOW DID DALRIADA, THE MOUNTH, GALLOWAY, TWESCARD, THE ROUTE AND THE GLYNNS GET SO CALLED?

Dál Riata means 'Riata's share' of the Gaelic kingdom which straddled the Narrow Sea from the time the Romans were abandoning Britain in the fourth and fifth centuries… but we do not know who Riata was. This became anglicised as Dalriada. In Argyll, three royal dynasties competed for the right to rule *Dál Riata*. The first to appear in the record was the *Cenél nGabráin*, 'Gabrán's kindred'. The Irish annals noted that Gabrán was defeated and killed in 559 by 'the son of Maelchon', Brude, the powerful overking of the Picts. *Cenél Gabráin*'s domains lay in Kintyre where Dunaverty was their principal stronghold. Gabrán's brother Comgall then became the main challenger. His descendants were *Cenél Comgaill*, 'Comgall's kindred', who ruled the Isle of Bute and the Cowal peninsula – they fought hard to annex some of the adjacent territory of Strathclyde held by the Britons of Alt Clut. North of *Cenél nGabráin* lands, *Cenél Loairn*, 'Lorn's kindred' held sway. Lorn seems to have been a fictional character, the brother of Fergus Mór mac Eirc, the equally fictional founder of Dalriada. In the ninth century the first King of Alba, Cináed mac Ailpín, declared that he was descended from *Cenél nGabráin* though it was more likely that he was a Pictish warlord seeking to reinforce his authority by claiming connection with a Gaelic royal bloodline.

For long the stronghold of the Picts was 'Fortriu', a kingdom north and south of 'The Mounth' – the name given to the eastern ridges of the Grampians, often referred to by local people as 'the hills', though this is by far the greatest mountain range in either Britain or Ireland. These wild, inhospitable uplands provided a valuable protective buffer against hostile assaults from Argyll. The lands from the Mounth to the North Sea are exceptionally fertile: these helped to sustain the Picts when threatened from not only by Dalriadan Gaels from the west but also by Anglian kings striking north from Northumbria through the Lothians.

Galloway, that part of the south-west of Scotland incorporating the historic counties of Wigtonshire and Kircudbrightshire, is a name derived from *i nGall Gaidhealaib*, 'amongst the Gall-Gael'. Perhaps no part of Scotland better illustrates how different people with different tongues left their mark as they blended. The people here were Britons, known to the Romans as the *Novantae*, speaking a P-Celtic language akin to Welsh. When the Romans left, these Britons created a kingdom known as Cumbria (not to be confused with that part of England further south with the same name). Then the English kingdom of Bernicia seized and settled these lands in the seventh century. Viking assaults from the eighth century onwards eventually drove out the English rulers and over the next two centuries Galloway was colonised and ruled by the Gall-Gael, a people of mixed Viking-Gaelic blood speaking Gaelic, probably from Ireland, possibly forced out of the Viking Kingdom of Dublin. Place names remind us of these different peoples. Examples include Guiltreehill, 'hill of the shining house' (British); Kelton, 'calf village' (English); Auchenairney, 'field of sloes' (Gaelic); and Southerness, 'south headland' (Norse). Scholars consider that Dumfries could well be a combination of British, English and Norse elements.

Early in the thirteenth century the north-east corner of Ulster (the Irish portion of *Dál Riata*) was conquered by Norman barons to become part of the Earldom of Ulster. The Normans called this fertile north coast region around Coleraine and Bushmills 'Twescard' from the Irish *tuaisceart*, meaning 'north'.

The English Crown lost control of this part of Ulster in the fourteenth century. The Norman de Mandevilles abandoned their manors here and the MacQuillans stepped into the vacuum created. Who were they? They seem to have been Strathclyde Britons in origin who went into service with Normans coming into Scotland in the twelfth century, duly adopting their language and culture. Some of those Normans were invited as colonisers over to the Earldom of Ulster in the early thirteenth century and that included MacQuillans – at that stage they spelled their name 'MacHoulyn'. They settled in County Down. Then, as the Earldom of Ulster disintegrated, the native MacCartans and Magennises drove them out. Most of the Anglo-Normans here, like the Whites of the Dufferin, fled to the safety of the Pale. The MacQuillans, instead, marched north and (pushing O'Cahans and others aside) conquered Twescard. By this time they were Irish-speakers and spelled their name 'Mac Uighilín'. To carve out a lordship for themselves here they must have been formidable fighters – the name for a private army in those days was a 'rout', from the Norman French *route*. The Irish renamed Twescard *an Rúta*, which soon became The Route, the name it still bears today.

In 1399 John MacDonnell, son of the Lord of Islay, married Margery Bissett and got the Glens of Antrim as a dowry. Though there are nine glens, the Irish called them the *seacht tuaithe*, the 'seven territories'. Royal officials in Dublin Castle, alarmed at so many Hebrideans coming over to live in these glens, referred to them in warning letters sent to London as 'The Glynns', a name the area retained for a long time. The MacDonnell lords (who overwhelmed the MacQuillans and seized the Route in the sixteenth century) were known as the lords of 'The Glynns and the Route'.

The nine Glens of Antrim are from south to north: Glenarm, Glencloy, Glenariff, Glenballyeamon, Glenaan, Glencorp, Glendun, Glenshesk and Glentaisie. Some argue that there is a tenth glen, Glenravel (south west of Glenariff). The title given today to the highly-respected annual journal of the Glens of Antrim Historical Society is *The Glynns*.

'DAUNTING THE ISLES': THE ROAD TO HARLAW

In 1370 David II, King of Scots, granted Uilleam MacDonald, Lord of the Isles, the title of Earl of Ross, after the province in north Scotland. This was not only a reward for consistent loyalty to the Crown but also a recognition that Uilleam had penetrated deep into the mainland facing Skye over as far east as Inverness. The martial strength of the MacDonalds was often augmented by reinforcements from the north of Ireland. For many years past the Hebrides had provided galloglass mercenaries, *gallóglaigh*, to Irish chiefs. Now the Lord of the Isles was able to hire *gallóglaigh* settled in Ulster to cross back over the Narrow Sea to ensure triumph on Scottish battlefields.

By the early fifteenth century, however, it was becoming clear that Clan Donald was overreaching itself. The MacKenzies and other clans in Ross and Caithness fought ferociously to win back their independence. And the lords of the fertile eastern coastlands, speakers of Doric Scots, regarded Gaelic-speaking Hebrideans as uncouth barbarians; they were concluding that the power of the Earl of Ross would have to be checked. To add to MacDonald problems, it was proving increasingly difficult to sustain warm relations with the Scottish court. In Edinburgh there was no liking for the Gaelic system of succession to lordships – lords of the Isles succeeded not by primogeniture as in the Lowlands, but by being chosen by those of Clan Donald 'royal blood' meeting on the Council Isle of Loch Finlaggan. As in Gaelic Ireland, the man picked was considered the strongest, not necessarily the eldest son of the previous lord. In any case, Scottish monarchs were becoming eager to extend royal authority by force ever northwards and westwards by 'daunting the Isles'.

'Daunting the Isles' proved to be a long-drawn-out business. In part this was due to frequent revolts by nobles, debilitating struggles for power at court and periodic conflict with English kings. In 1385, for example, Richard II brought 14,000 men as far north as Edinburgh: it took a major campaign ending in victory for the Scots at Otterburn in 1388 to counter that threat from the south, at least for the time being.

In 1406 the ailing Robert III, King of Scots, sent his son and heir, James, to the French court for his own safety. But on the way James was captured by pirates and handed over to Henry IV, King of England. Well-treated though he usually was, James was a prisoner for the next 18 years. In his absence Robert the Steward, Earl of Fife and Duke of Albany, seized power and made himself regent, as the Governor of Scotland. Albany refused to recognise Donald MacDonald, who had succeeded Uilleam as the second Lord of the Isles, as the Earl of Ross. Instead he conferred the earldom on his own son, the Earl of Buchan.

The scene was set for a mighty power struggle. Donald MacDonald risked all by allying himself with Henry IV of England in 1408. Then to make good his claim to the earldom, he took time to gather a great force, including many gallóglaigh from Ulster. The host assembled at Ardtornish Castle on the Sound of Mull in 1411 and then invaded Ross. After a fierce battle, primarily with men of the Clan Mackay, MacDonald captured Dingwall Castle. Outside Inverness he summoned fighting men from Boyne and Enzie to join him. Then he swept through Moray, particularly the lands of Alexander Stewart, Earl of Mar. Eventually this Highland horde reached Bennachie, the last hill of the Grampian range before the coastal plain between Inverurie and Aberdeen.

The Earl of Mar, illegitimate son of Alexander Stewart, the 'Wolf of Badenoch', and grandson of Robert II, called on the gentry of Buchan, Angus and Mearns to join his standard to defend Aberdeen and to drive back Donald, Lord of the Isles. The two sides confronted each other at Harlaw on 24 July 1411. The outcome was the bloodiest battle ever fought between Scots. On Mar's side were Irvings, Straitons, Lovels and others generally loyal to the King and speaking Scots, many wearing armour and wielding maces, spears and battle axes. They regarded their Gaelic-speaking, kin-based opponents – equipped with two-handed broadswords, axes, scians and round targe shields – as savages. Though almost a thousand of his followers lay dead on the battlefield, Donald MacDonald, Lord of the Isles, had won a decisive victory. Mar lost fewer men but at least half his army had been killed. Amongst the many high-born who fell was Sir Walter Lesley, laird of Balquhain, slain with six of his sons. Aberdeen did not fall but MacDonald had not been 'daunted'. Indeed, for generations to come the Lordship of the Isles remained triumphantly independent. And the shock waves of Harlaw were to be felt across the Narrow Sea in Ulster.

DONAL BALLACH MACDONNELL, THE GLENSMAN WHO LED THE ISLANDERS TO VICTORY AT INVERLOCHY IN 1431

In 1424 James I, who had been held a prisoner in England for 18 years, was freed by the English on the payment of the huge ransom of 60,000 merks. Now aged thirty, he acted with extraordinary ruthlessness to wipe out all opposition, real or imagined. Murdoch Stewart, 2nd Duke of Albany, who had been acting as Governor of Scotland on his return, was summarily executed along with his sons. Then followed further acts of royal treachery.

In 1427 this monarch, close to being psychotic, summoned a parliament in his newly constructed 'fortalice' in Inverness. Once there, the assembled clan chiefs, around 50 in number, were seized. Some were executed on the spot. Other chiefs were incarcerated, including Alexander MacDonnell of Islay, who had recently succeeded his father Donald as Lord of the Isles and Earl of Ross. The King of Scots also arranged the elimination of John Mór MacDonnell (in Scots John Mor MacDonald, in Gaelic Eoin Mór MacDomhnaill), Lord of Kintyre, Islay and the Glynns. He had fought side-by-side with Donald, Alexander's father at Harlaw in 1411. King James invited John Mór to travel from the Glens for a parley in Argyll only to have a party of Campbells there put him to death.

United as never before by the King's cold-blooded treachery, the Hebridean clans rallied to confront the King of Scots. Since Alexander, Lord of the Isles, was a royal prisoner, they chose Donal Ballach MacDonnell (in Scotland, Donald Balloch MacDonald), John Mór's eighteen-year-old son and heir, to lead them. Donal gathered up his men in the Antrim Glens and sailed across the Narrow Sea to the Isles. Here Clann Domhnaill – the MacDonalds – entrusted him with overall command. It proved a good choice.

Donal called a muster at the island of Carna in Loch Sunart. The Earl of Mar, granted the lands and titles forfeited by Alexander, had been sent north with a large army and encamped in the shadow of Ben Nevis at Inverlochy. Donal decided not to delay: he led a picked force of 600 clansmen and entrusted his uncle, Alasdair Carrack, to command a party of some 200 archers.

Sailing through the Sound of Mull and into Loch Linnhe on board a flotilla of war galleys, Donal led the main assault while Alasdair Carrach, making his way unseen north of the camp, then rained down arrows from a height on Mar's confused host. The Islanders lost only 27 men in slaughtering over 600 of their opponents, including Alan Stewart, Earl of Caithness. After ravaging about Lochaber to punish Mackintoshes and Camerons who had joined the Earl, Donal Ballach returned to the Glens of Antrim with a great store of loot. James I could never subdue the Isles and reluctantly released Alexander from imprisonment, restoring his titles as Lord of the Isles and Earl of Ross. He even appointed him Justiciar of the Kingdom North of the Forth.

King James was obsessed with a determination to bring an end to Donal Ballach. His problem was that the Glynns were beyond his reach. He got his parliament to outlaw unauthorised contact between his kingdom and Ireland. James wrote to Irish lords urging them to have nothing to do with the Lord of the Glynns, appealing to the 'alde friendschip betuix the king of scotlande and his liege and gude alde frende of Erschry of Yrlande' because of 'the perell forsaid'. He was furious that a younger son of Murdoch, James the Fat, had escaped execution by being given a refuge in the Glens. At the same time Anglo-Norman lords wrote to Henry VI of England warning him of the 'grete multitude of Scotes ... out of Scotteland' who were posing a grave threat to the Lordship of Ireland.

Donal Ballach, head of Clann Eoin Mhór, had made himself the most famous man in the Isles. He had forged the Hebridean clans into a formidable independent power and did much to sustain it after Inverlochy by his unwavering loyalty to Alexander, who was ruling the Isles rather well. At the same time, in the years that followed, Donal Ballach turned the Glynns into an Irish lordship to be reckoned with. The Glens of Antrim had served as an invaluable bolt-hole for his kin and allied clans, and would do so again. Donal proceeded to turn his lordship into one powerful enough to alter the political shape of Ireland in the middle of the fifteenth century and beyond.

PIBROCH OF DONUIL DHU 'THE WAR-PIPE AND PENNON, ARE AT INVERLOCHY'

Pibroch of Donuil Dhu,
  Pibroch of Donuil,
Wake thy wild voice anew
  Summon Clan Conuil;
Come away, come away
  Hark to the summons;
Come in your war array,
  Gentles and commons.
Come from the deep glen, and
  From mountains so rocky,
The war-pipe and pennon
  Are at Inverlochy.
Come every hill plaid, and
  True heart that wears one;
Come every steel-blade, and
  Strong hand that bears one.
Leave untended the herd,
  The flock without shelter;
Leave the corpse uninterred,
  The bride at the altar;
Leave the deer, leave the steer,
  Leave nets and barges:
Come with your fighting gear,
  Broadswords and targes.
Come as the winds come, when
  Forests are rended;
Come as the waves come
  When birlinns are stranded:
Faster come, faster come,

Chief, vassal, page, and groom,
Tenant and master.
Fast they come, fast they come,
  See how they gather!
Wide waves the eagle-plume
  Blended with heather,
Cast your plaids, draw your blades,
  Forward each man set!
Pibroch of Donuil Dhu
  Knell for the onset.

Sir Walter Scott, *The Battle of Inverlochy*

Sir Walter Scott was inspired to write this poem by encountering a Gaelic song celebrating the victory won at Inverlochy by men of the Isles over the Earl of Mar in 1431. It had been passed down from generation to generation. It begins:

Piobaireachd Dhonuil Dhuidh, piobareachd Donhuil
Piobaireachd Dhonuil Dhuidh, piobearachd Donhuil
Piob agus bratach air faiche Inverlochi
The pipe summons of Donald the Black
The pipe summons of Donald the Black
The war-pipe and the pennon are on the gathering-place at Inverlochy

The *pibroch* is the gathering-call for the clan. Donuil Dhu is the piper. Clan Conuil is *Clann Domhnaill*, Clan Donald (often referred to as 'Clan Connell' in the nineteenth century), the MacDonalds of the Isles. Birlinns are the Islanders' clinker-built war galleys.

Alexander, Lord of the Isles and the Earl of Ross, had been imprisoned by James I, King of Scots. The man appointed to lead the assault on Mar's army was the 18-year-old Domhnall Ballach (anglicised as Donal Ballach MacDonnell in Ireland and Donald Balloch MacDonald in Scotland). He was 'The Tanister', deputising for the Lord of the Isles, and Lord of the Glynns, Islay and Kintyre. His father John Mór, who had acquired the Glens of Antrim by marrying Margery Bissett, had just been treacherously murdered in Argyll by the agents of James I.

It was from the Antrim Glens that Donal Ballach set out with his men to rendezvous with the rest of the clansmen on the island of Carna at Loch Sunart, there to agree on a plan of attack on Mar's camp at Inverlochy.

'DAUNTING THE ISLES': THE FALL OF CLAN DONALD

James I, King of Scots, had met a grisly end at the hands of some of his disaffected nobles. He was setting a pattern: his successors – James II, James III and James IV – were also to meet with violent deaths while still in their prime. All four kings were constantly distracted by the challenge of attempting to bring the Hebrides and Highlands to heel. This sprawling Gaelic-speaking territory was a world apart from the realm of the Scots-speaking lands of the Lowlands and the Borders. Alexander MacDonald, Lord of the Isles, had used all his diplomatic prowess to keep his archipelago dominion independent and to avoid provoking further attacks sanctioned by royal command. But his son John, who succeeded him in 1449, was to hasten the destruction of all that he had worked for.

John MacDonald made an alliance of mutual support with William, 8th Earl of Douglas, the most powerful magnate on the Borders. At a dinner in Stirling Castle in February 1452, King James II called on the earl to end this pact. The earl refused, whereupon the enraged king rose to his feet and plunged his knife deep into William's body. Others there also stabbed the earl and then threw his body out of the window. The earl's corpse was found below with 26 wounds and his head cleft with an axe.

Hearing of this, John, Lord of the Isles, quickly disengaged to protest his loyalty to the King of Scots who – not particularly worried that in fury he had stabbed to death one of his leading subjects – now waged a ferocious and vindictive war on the murdered earl's kin, seizing all their lands. At least that drew his attention for the time being away from the Isles. Then, on Sunday 3 August 1460, James II lost his life quite accidentally in another campaign: as he was launching the siege of Roxburgh Castle, the King was close to one of his own field guns when, on being fired, it burst its casing, killing him instantly. He was just thirty years old.

James III was but nine when he became King of Scots. MacDonald tried to take advantage of his minority by seeking to profit from the conflict between the Lancastrians and the Yorkists. In 1462 he joined a conspiracy with the Yorkist

Edward IV and the exiled 9th Earl of Douglas to divide Scotland between the three of them. By the time James III learned of the plot, which was not until 1475, the Lord of the Isles found himself in a helpless situation. King Edward of England had only sought a diversion and had no intention of advancing north. And Douglas had no followers left to speak of. John MacDonald hastened to court to make abject submission.

With his claymore held by the blade and wearing only a shirt and drawers, MacDonald knelt before the High Altar at Holyrood and handed his sword to King James. He was stripped of his titles of Earl of Ross and Lord of the Isles, and his best lands were made the property of the Crown. Outraged members of the Clan Donald, led by John's illegitimate son Angus Óg, could not take this humiliation. They drove John out of his home and plunged the Isles into civil war. The death knell of this Gaelic world was sounded when both sides fought a savage sea battle in the Sound of Mull in 1481. Angus Óg claimed victory in this 'Battle of Bloody Bay' but too many lives had been lost and around half of all war galleys in the Isles had been sunk or smashed to smithereens. The resuscitation of the Lordship did not prove possible. The incorporation of the Lordship of the Isles in the Kingdom was postponed to 1493, but this was little more than a formality. John MacDonald died in Dundee in 1503.

James III, in adulthood as brutal as his father had been, succeeded in alienating most of his nobles. When the high-born rebels got the help of the English, who besieged Edinburgh Castle for a time, all was over. In June 1488, the King was routed at Sauchieburn close to Stirling Castle, then chased from the battlefield and murdered.

The Stewart dynasty, however, was coming close to extending its rule over all the land of Scotland. James III had got the Northern Isles in lieu of a dowry when he married Margaret, daughter of King Christian I of Denmark. Nevertheless, incorporated into the Kingdom though it was, the former Lordship of the Isles proved extraordinarily turbulent for the next century and more.

Meanwhile, repeated reverses and unprofitable blood-letting had prompted more and more Islanders to cross the Narrow Sea to build a new life there. Here the MacDonalds – known as MacDonnells in Ireland – from their base in the Antrim Glens created the most powerful lordship in north-east Ulster.

EPISODE 26

'SURROUNDED BY IRISH AND SCOTS ... WITHOUT SUCCOUR OF THE ENGLISH FOR SIXTY MILES'

As the fifteenth century was coming to a close the Stewart dynasty was near to extending its rule over all the land of Scotland. James III had got the Northern Isles in lieu of a dowry when he married Margaret, daughter of Christian I of Denmark. More important, the independent power of the Lordship of the Isles had been broken by 1475. Though the Hebrides proved extraordinarily turbulent for the next century and more, they were becoming an integral part of the realm of the King of Scots. The only Islanders remaining beyond the reach of the Scottish Crown were the MacDonnells and their kin in the Antrim Glens.

In spite of these successes, James III – known for his brutality – succeeded in alienating most of his nobles. When these high-born rebels got the help of the English, who besieged Edinburgh Castle for a time, all was over. In June 1488 the King was routed at Sauchieburn close to Stirling Castle, then chased from the battlefield and murdered. At the tender age of fifteen, James IV, the King's son and heir, had become King of Scots. Along with an accomplice dressed as a priest, he had helped to knife to death his father, who had taken refuge in a barn, an act for which he was to do penance every day for the rest of his life. James IV was to become an able and fair-minded ruler, much loved by his people, a flamboyant Renaissance prince who united his subjects as not one of his predecessors had been able to do. The young king not only looked out for enemies in Ulster, he also sought allies there.

The collapse of the Lordship of the Isles and the protracted blood-letting which ensued there brought Islanders to Ulster in unprecedented numbers. Many had only the most tenuous kinship with the MacDonnells of the Glynns, but they were given protection and land. And, of course, they were valued as fighting men. Two centuries earlier Hebridean warriors, gallóglaigh, had bargained with Irish kings and chiefs for their martial services. Now in the sixteenth century a fresh flood of Scots mercenaries poured into Ulster. One of them, a Highlander who was also a priest, explained to Henry VIII that they were called Redshanks because 'wee of all people can tolerat, suffir, and away best with colde, for botthe somer and wynter (except when the froeste is most vehemante) goinge always bair-leggide and bair-footide ...'

Except in name, the Earldom of Ulster had all but disappeared. Emerging from their woody fastness of Glenconkeyne, the descendants of Áed Buidhe O'Neill – a former King of Tír Eoghain – crossed the lower Bann and carved out a new lordship for themselves from the shattered remnants of the earldom. Janico Savage, the earldom's seneschal, had written a desperate appeal to Edward IV in 1467 saying that unless help was sent the Irish 'in short tyme finally and utterly woll destroye your said Erldome'. He concluded:

> We mekely at the Reverence of almighty Jesu which by his profete Moises delyvered the children of Israel oute of the thraldom and bondage of Kyng pharoo besecheth in way of charite.

The 'charite' of £66 10s sent by the king was not enough. Janico was killed the following year, and in 1481 his son, Patrick Óg, was captured, blinded and castrated by Conn O'Neill. O'Neill's ally, Glaisne Magennis, drove the remaining settlers from Lecale. The Whites of Dufferin (the 'Black Third', on the western shores of Strangford Lough), abandoned their inheritance for the safety of the Pale, while the Savages, driven out of the Six Mile Water valley, hung on precariously to the tip of the Ards. The Magennises and MacCartans engulfed central and south Down, while the Clann Aodha Buidhe dominated a sweep of territory extending from Larne inland to Lough Neagh at Edenduffcarrick (now Shane's castle, near Randalstown) and taking in the castle of Belfast and north Down, including much of the Ards. This territory the English called Clandeboye after the ruling family that had conquered it.

Carrickfergus was left isolated, described in 1468 as 'a garrison of war ... surrounded by Irish and Scots, without succour of the English for sixty miles'. Then in 1485 Henry Tudor at Bosworth Field brought the wasting Wars of the Roses to an end. Henceforth English monarchs could begin the process of restoring the authority of the Crown across the Irish Sea. Many years would pass, however, before this would threaten the independence of Ulster warlords. There the balance of power had simply shifted from one Gaelic lordship to another. Vicious succession disputes amongst the O'Neills tore apart the hegemony of Tír Eoghain in a few short years. Now it was Tír Chonaill which prevailed. James IV, King of Scots, found it well worth his while seeking the friendship of the O'Donnells there who were turning this lordship into the most powerful one in all of Ireland.

EPISODE 27

LORDS OF TÍR CHONAILL, ALLIES OF THE KING OF SCOTS

Hugh Dubh O'Donnell succeeded his father Aodh Ruadh in 1505 as Lord of Tír Chonaill – without question the greatest Gaelic lordship in the country. Meaning 'Land of Conall', Tír Chonaill was approximately the same shape and size as the present county of Donegal except that it then incorporated all of the west bank of the Foyle, including the monastic site of Derry. O'Donnell power, however, thrust far beyond those borders, deep into other parts of Ulster and into the province of Connacht. The Maguire island stronghold of Enniskillen was taken in 1508 and in 1514 the O'Neills of Tír Eoghain confirmed that Inishowen, Fermanagh and Cinél Móen (the fertile tract between the Foyle and Letterkenny) were part of the Tír Chonaill lordship. The O'Donnells also exercised direct control over O'Cahan's country (now the northern part of Co. Londonderry) and the Route in north Antrim. Hugh Dubh, in addition, ensured that he was overlord of Iochtair Connacht – almost all of the northern half of the province, including the port of Sligo. At the height of his power Hugh Dubh had either direct or indirect control extending into nine counties.

In addition to numerous fortified tower houses and crannogs, this Tír Chonaill lordship was defended by a chain of castles stretching from Derry to Bundrowes, the strongest being Lifford, Castlefinn, Donegal, Belleek and Ballyshannon. The O'Donnells maintained an impressive fleet which rivalled that of the piratical O'Malleys who dominated the Connacht coastline from Achill almost to the ramparts of Galway city. Indeed, the O'Malleys made an ill-advised assault on Killybegs in 1513 only to be comprehensively routed by Brian MacSweeney who was known thereafter as Brian an Cobhlaigh, 'Brian of the Fleet'. A permanent O'Donnell flotilla also patrolled the entire Erne waterway from the falls of Assaroe at Ballyshannon upstream by river and loughs as far east as Cavan. The Tír Chonaill lords took care to sustain the loyalty of their sub-chieftains. The leading ones were O'Doherty, O'Gallagher, O'Boyle and the MacSweeney chieftains. O'Doherty was lord of all Inishowen, who put the best-mounted warriors into the field. The O'Gallagher chief, *marascal sluaigh* 'marshal of the hosts', was in command of O'Donnell's household troops. Sub-chieftain O'Boyle was lord of Boylagh. Fanad, Doe and Banagh were the three MacSweeney galloglass chieftains. A council of lords and chiefs met regularly to ensure internal political stability, the key to Tír Chonaill's prosperity and power.

This lordship's population was concentrated on the fertile lowlands which boasted of great herds of cattle and flocks of sheep, and broad stretches of unenclosed ground for the cultivation of oats. Captain Charles Plessington, an English naval officer, observed that the southern part of the lordship was 'very fertile and full of corn and cattle, especially around Killybegs, Donegal and Ballyshannon'. The sparsely inhabited highlands and rugged western coasts were only used for grazing stock during the summer and as a source of timber, peat and game – according to Philip O'Sullivan Beare, the Tír Chonaill woods sheltered 'most dense herds of fat deer'. Tribute to the overlord, in addition to military service, was paid largely in cattle, a levy referred to as 'The kingly beefing of O'Donnell'. O'Doherty paid 'sixty bullocks', MacSweeney Fanad 'eighteen bullocks … three times a year' and the other two MacSweeney lords and the termon (sanctuary) land of Derry each had 18 bullocks demanded of them. The O'Friel family, in charge of church lands at Kilmacrennan, kept bees and their tribute to O'Donnell was in the form of methers of mead.

And without the substantial regular income generated by the great salmon and herring fisheries – particularly from Bristol merchants and Spanish netsmen – the lords of Tír Chonaill could not have imposed their will over such an extensive part of the island. Each year the Bristol Company sent vessels into the Erne estuary. There they stayed for two months to buy and salt down some of the thousands of salmon returning from the seas around Greenland and the Faroes preparing to leap the falls of Assaroe to reach their spawning grounds upstream. The O'Donnells also had control over the equally prolific salmon fisheries in the Foyle and Moy estuaries. Vast shoals of herring attracted fishing fleets from Drogheda, Scotland, Brittany and Spain to exploit what the Irish called the *garbhushe*. The Spanish got permission to land on Arranmore and the Rosses to process the herring they netted. Henry VIII was informed that the ruler of Tír Chonaill was known to overseas traders as 'the best lord of fish in Ireland and he exchangeth fish always with foreign merchants for wine by which in other countries he is called the king of fish'.

In addition to Bristol, merchants travelled from the ports of Saint-Malo and Morlaix in Brittany, and from Glasgow, Ayr and Wigtown in Scotland.

Signing formal documents, the Bretons and the French exchanged wine, salt, gunpowder and firearms for fish, tallow and hides.

The Scots played a major role in introducing guns to Tír Chonaill. The first mention of firearms in any of the Irish annals is in 1487 when an O'Donnell killed an O'Rourke with his musket as Bréifne was being subdued by Aodh Ruadh. Aodh and his son Hugh Dubh were amongst the first in Ireland regularly to employ cannon and other artillery, largely made possible by the warm relations they maintained with the Scottish Crown.

Shortly before his death in 1507 Aodh Ruadh wrote to King James IV from Tír Chonaill: he had heard that the King of Scots intended to set off on a pilgrimage to the Holy Land and he begged him not to do so on account of the dangers involved. James wrote back to assure Aodh that he had no intention of leaving Scotland unless he was certain that his realm would be safe in his absence. Hugh Dubh kept up the correspondence begun by his father, an indication that he, too, valued close relations with the King of Scots.

That friendship led to a military pact, sealed in Edinburgh in 1513.

EPISODE 28

1513: JAMES IV AND HUGH DUBH O'DONNELL MAKE A PACT

Much as his nobles admired him for his martial prowess, James IV knew that protracted warfare with England did nothing for the prosperity of his subjects. As for Henry VII, he preferred extravagant display and ambitious building programmes to costly campaigning. In 1502 a 'Treaty of Perpetual Peace' was solemnly signed at the new Tudor palace of Richmond. Both kings agreed that 'there be a good, real and sincere, true, sound, and firm peace, friendship, league and confederation, to last all time coming'. The treaty was sealed by the marriage of Henry's daughter, Margaret, to the King of Scots.

For the remaining years of Henry VII's reign, the peace held firm. And it could be said that no King of Scots was more successful than James IV at winning over the loyalty of his subjects.

At 11 p.m. on Saturday 21 April 1509, Henry VII expired. His eldest son, Arthur, had died in 1502. So it was his second son who, at the age of seventeen, now became Henry VIII. The new king obtained special papal dispensation to marry Arthur's widow, Catherine of Aragon. It was not long before Henry VIII was abandoning his father's determination to maintain the peace. He aspired to emulate Henry V in conducting a glorious campaign in France. This was an immediate threat to the 'Perpetual Peace'.

As long as he could, James IV resisted the clamour of his nobles to fight, but when Henry prepared to set out across the English Channel, he felt he had no choice but to revive the 'auld alliance' with France. Scotland was now at war with England. The moment had arrived when King James needed all the support he could get – and that must include Hugh Dubh O'Donnell, Lord of Tír Chonaill. The King of Scots was not to be disappointed.

Hugh Dubh had worked hard to sustain his friendship with James IV. In 1507 he sent over his ambassador, Aeneas Mc Donyall, accompanied by two servants, to deliver letters to the King. They came back with replies from James a month later. The following year Hugh shipped over to the king a present of Irish hawks for the hunt, peregrines almost certainly.

In 1510 the Lord of Tír Chonnaill, not expecting international war, decided to travel abroad. He arrived in Rome just as the Sistine Chapel was close to completion. He had an audience with Pope Julius II and on his way home called in on Henry VIII of England. Hugh spent no fewer than 32 weeks in Henry's court and, while he was there, was knighted by the king.

Back in Donegal Castle in 1511, Hugh Dubh O'Donnell rather suddenly had to decide whose side he was on. The Treaty of Perpetual Peace was falling apart. In 1512 Henry VIII declared war on Louis XII of France. Knight of the English realm though he was, Hugh chose to back France's ally, the King of Scots. The Lord of Tír Chonaill crossed the Narrow Sea himself accompanied by a bodyguard and a retinue which included his harper. Entertained liberally, Hugh Dubh was in Scotland for three weeks.

On 25 June 1513 fanfares of trumpets announced the arrival of 'Prince' O'Donnell at Edinburgh Castle. Here, in a magnificent ceremony, he was welcomed in the castle's Great Hall, completed just a few years before. Donegal Castle was surely the finest and most elegant modern palace in Ulster, but it could not compare with this hall, a structure fit for a Renaissance monarch with its coped crenellated parapet with half-cannon spouts, its mullioned and transomed windows with stained leaded glass, and cast-iron downpipes with hoppers and fixings decorated with fleurs-de-lys, roses and thistles. The hall's interior was no less impressive, its most arresting feature being the huge hammerbeam roof, its great beams resting on stone corbels engraved with heads and symbols, from which hung decorative gothic copper pendant lamps. Here the highest in the land of Scotland had gathered in all their finery to greet this powerful Irish lord.

The list of those who witnessed this Irish alliance is by far the longest for any agreement made in James IV's reign. It included the Earls of Angus, Argyll, Lennox, Arran, Eglinton, and Glencairn; the Archbishop of St Andrews, the Archbishop of Glasgow, the Bishop of Galloway, along with two abbots, an archdeacon and a dean; Lords Seton, Lindsay of Byres, and Sinclair; Patrick Paniter, the King's Secretary; and Robert Colville of Ochiltree, Director of Chancery.

James had this hall built to celebrate his marriage to Margaret Tudor, Henry VII's daughter. That union was made to seal the Perpetual Peace and that was why carvings of the thistle and the Tudor rose were side by side. Now the King of Scots and Henry VIII were at war. The Lord of Tír Chonnail had a crucial role: to prevent Henry's allies in Ulster from reaching Scotland and to attack the English in Carrickfergus, James promising to provide artillery, ammunition and quarriers 'for undirmynding of wallis'.

EPISODE 29

1513: A SCOTS NAVAL ASSAULT ON CARRICKFERGUS

Early in the year 1511 vessels sailing up and down the busy Firth of Forth seaway could see that they were dwarfed by a mighty ship rising up from the new royal docks of Newhaven. Named after the archangel who protected crusaders, the *Michael* was almost immediately known to all as the *Great Michael*. When she was launched the *Great Michael* was the largest and best-equipped ship afloat in Europe, possibly in the world.

This great flagship, manned by 300 sailors and capable of carrying a thousand troops, was armed with 12 cannons on each side, in addition to 3 large basilisks and numerous smaller pieces such as serpents, falcons and 'double-dogs'. The *Great Michael* was designed not only to fire heavy shot but also to withstand it – its walls were reckoned to be ten feet thick. The *Margaret*, launched a few years before, was not much smaller and altogether James IV had an impressive navy of 38 vessels. These warships were mobile gun platforms and, back in 1504, Admiral Andrew Wood with such vessels had been able to smash up shoreline forts manned by rebels in the Isles. Then in 1513 the King of Scots would put his navy to sea for a very different purpose: to take part in a European war.

James IV was the first king to bring all of Scotland under his sway. This King of Scots could put an army in the field larger than any of his predecessors could have mustered. And to demonstrate that his kingdom was an independent power to be reckoned with, James now had made Scotland a significant naval power.

King Henry VIII declared war on France and prepared an invasion force in June 1513. King James could no longer resist the clamour of his nobles to mobilise in support of King Louis XII. That same month Hugh Dubh O'Donnell, Lord of Tír Chonaill, had crossed the Narrow Sea to sign a solemn pact of alliance in Edinburgh Castle. As the most powerful Gaelic lord in Ireland, Hugh would engage the forces of the English Crown there, and, at the same time prevent the MacDonnells of the Glynns and their Hebridean kindred from making trouble while the King of Scots was campaigning in the south.

Decisions had to be made at speed in Edinburgh. The highest in the land, churchmen included, were summoned to muster their fighting men. From Edinburgh they would advance south to the Borders. But how would the navy be best used? Louis XII wanted Scots vessels in the English Channel, there to disrupt Henry VIII's invasion force and supply lines. Henry knew this and had his ships waiting in the Downs ready to engage the Scots when they appeared. James, aware that (in spite of possessing the *Great Michael* and the *Margaret*) Henry's navy was larger than his own, decided that his navy, commanded by James Hamilton, 1st Earl of Arran, should take a completely different route. His fleet would need to steer north past the Orkneys and reach the English Channel by sailing along the Hebrides and down through the Irish Sea to rendezvous with the French fleet.

This was a fateful decision. Without loss, the Scots vessels did successfully negotiate the Pentland Firth to sail round Cape Wrath, down past the Isle of Skye into the North Channel. The problem for King James was that time was running out: the English expeditionary force was now crossing to France largely unimpeded. To make matters worse, Arran decided on a diversion – he would attack Carrickfergus. As the English Crown's strongest post in Ulster, this was a legitimate target – but had the assault been authorised by James or was it in revenge for a previous attack made on the Isle of Arran from Ulster? Robert Lindsay, the chronicler of Pitscottie, had no doubt that Arran was disobeying orders: the Admiral 'keipit no derectioun of the king his minister bott passit to the wast sie wpoun the cost of Ireland and their landit and brunt Carag-forgus witht wther willages'.

In its only action in Scottish service, the *Great Michael* bombarded Carrickfergus Castle; it was not taken, however, but Arran's men sent ashore, as the chronicler recorded, burned the town and neighbouring villages and slaughtered many of their inhabitants.

More time was lost when storms blew up and Arran took his fleet to Ayr for repairs. Here the Scots 'repossit and playit' for 40 days. By the time the Scots navy had reached the coast of Normandy it was mid-September. Henry VIII was safely on French soil with his supplies and he was winning battles. Storms blew up and the *Great Michael* was moored, impotent, in Brest. When sent out to sea in October, embarrassingly, the great warship ran aground off Picardy and was fortunate not to be wrecked.

By this time the Battle of Flodden had been fought and King James IV was dead.

EPISODE 30

1513: THE BATTLE OF FLODDEN

During the late summer of 1513 Henry VIII was in France winning famous victories. Thomas Howard, Earl of Surrey, had had the temerity to speak out against this expensive and risk-laden adventure; as punishment he had been refused permission to join the young English King across the Channel. Instead Surrey was entrusted with patroling the north. The seventy-year-old earl set out for Northumberland determined to restore his family to favour. There he quickly learned that England was in peril. The responsibility for halting a Scots invasion of unprecedented size now rested solely on his shoulders.

James IV, in alliance with Louis XII of France, had advanced south in command of at least 34,000 men, by far the largest army ever to invade England. Having taken or destroyed all the castles defending the Borders north of Newcastle upon Tyne, known as the English East March, by 1 September, James crossed the River Tweed to occupy Flodden Hill, there to make a stand against the English. The Scots spent days making this position as impregnable as possible.

At Newcastle upon Tyne, Surrey found that the task before him was formidable. He had nothing like James's artillery firepower and the King of Scots commanded 8,000 more than he had. Then disaster struck: English bandits attacked his supply wagons and robbed them of all they carried.

What was Surrey to do? He could pull back and wait to be resupplied but that could shatter morale, bring dishonour on his captains and ensure ignominy for the Howards. He decided on the only alternative: to seek battle with the Scots without delay. This veteran of many campaigns now confused his enemy by an elaborate feint. He marched north, bypassing Flodden Hill.

At first light on 9 September the Scots discovered that Surrey had reappeared and now was making for the nearby Branxton Hill. By securing this hill, the English could attack Flodden Hill from the north without facing heavy guns.

What was the King of Scots to do? James made the fateful decision to try to get to Branxton Hill before the English. Moving away from Flodden Hill, where the defences had been so well prepared and the artillery pieces so meticulously placed and sighted, was full of risk. Tempestuous rain fell ceaselessly. James did get to Branxton Hill before the English and this, apparently, gave the Scots a position of dominance.

For the first time on British soil a battle began with a duel between field guns. But here on Branxton Hill the Scots had no time to build platforms for their heavy pieces. Hastily placed, Scottish ordnance fired wide of their targets, either over the heads of the English or into the mud. Lacking platforms, the heavy guns recoiled back several feet, making reloading a slow business.

English guns, smaller and lighter, and mounted on wheels, could more easily be pulled back into position after recoil and the shot, just two inches in diameter, was capable of killing or maiming four or five men in line. Seeing his soldiers being felled by this deadly fire, King James gave the command to advance downhill. This was to put into effect the tactic which had proved so effective in battles in northern Italy: at a steady disciplined pace, foot soldiers, each holding a pike 18 feet long, bore down on their foes.

But Branxton Hill's sloping ground was soft and waterlogged. Now thousands of Scots were churning up the sodden ground into mud and sinking up to their knees – none more so than nobles, each suited in about 50 pounds' weight of armour. Since it became well-nigh impossible for the Scots to make effective use of their pikes, Surrey's men armed with shorter eight-foot bills (hooked weapons similar to billhooks used in farming) began relentlessly to slaughter their opponents in the quagmire.

Flodden was the first major battle in England or Scotland to feature an exchange of artillery fire. It was also the last battle in which the longbow had a significant part to play. As the fighting was drawing to a close, English longbowmen (until now able to do little because their bowstrings had slackened in the wet) fired at almost point-blank range with terrible effect. One of those wounded was James IV: an arrow struck him in the jaw, disabling him long enough for bill men to hack him to death.

Earls Argyll, Bothwell, Caithness, Cassillis, Crawford, Lennox, Montrose and Rothes lay dead. Other high-born who met their end included Alexander Stewart, Archbishop of St Andrews; George Hepburn, Bishop of the Isles; William Bunch, Abbot of Kilwinning; Lawrence Oliphant, Abbot of Inchaffaray; and Lords Avandale, Borthwick, Elphinstone, Erskine, Hay, Herries, Innermeath, Ross, Semphill, Seton and Sinclair.

Around 10,000 Scots lost their lives at Flodden. The English suffered about 4,000 dead and not a single lord was killed. Notwithstanding the terrible loss it had sustained, Scotland managed to retain its independence. The stability James IV had created survived him.

Meanwhile, on the other side of the Narrow Sea, the erosion of the independence of Gaelic Ireland was already well under way.

EPISODE 31

'THE REEK OF MAISTER PATRIK HAMMYLTOUN': THE SCOTTISH REFORMATION BEGINS

In the driving rain on 29 February 1528, Patrick Hamilton, Abbot of Fearn and great grandson of a King of Scots, James II, was tied to a stake in front of St Salvator's College in St Andrews. Earlier that day a council of bishops and clergy, led by Cardinal David Beaton, Archbishop of St Andrews, had found him guilty of all 13 charges of heresy brought against him. During his studies in Paris and Leuven, Hamilton had been won over to the reformed faith as set out by Martin Luther; and from the time he had returned to Linlithgow in 1527 great numbers had come to hear him preach.

As the fire was lit at noon Hamilton declared to the watching crowd:

As to my confession I will not deny it for awe of your fire, for my confession and belief is in Jesus Christ … I will rather be content that my body burn in this fire for confession of my faith in Christ than my soul should burn in the fire of hell for denying the same.

It was already dark when he uttered his last words: 'Lord Jesus, receive my spirit' – the poorly seasoned wood around the stake burned so slowly that it took him six hours to die. The Protestant Reformation in Scotland had its first martyr. One witness warned the Cardinal that 'the reek of Maister Patrik Hammyltoun has infected as many as it blew upon'.

Seeking answers in a time of uncertainty and political turmoil, the literate in Scotland had been turning increasingly to the Scriptures. It was in the Bible, they were certain, that the truth was to be found. The number of those who could read was rising: it helped that James IV had made it law that sons of landowners must be properly educated. Some of John Wyclif's fourteenth-century English Bible was translated into Scots by Murdoch Nisbet and, after 1526, William Tyndale's New Testament was smuggled in.

John Gau returned from Malmö in Sweden with a Lutheran treatise entitled *The Richt Vay to the Kingdom of Heuine* by Christian Pederson that he had translated into Scots. George Wishart brought back a more radical doctrine from Switzerland. He was a disciple of John Calvin who preached an uncompromising faith: the fate of mankind was predestined; only God's elect would be saved; and the Bible could not err. Wishart translated Calvin's doctrine with the title *The Confession of the Fayth of Sweserlands*. Calvinism rather than Lutheranism was to be the variety of Protestantism which would prevail in Scotland.

Those who could not read, the great majority, imbibed the reformed faith not only by listening to preachers but also by learning vernacular songs, paraphrases, versified Psalms and metrical versions of the Catechism usually set to popular tunes. One song began with the words, 'The Paip, that pagan, full of pride …' and went on to castigate all ranks of churchmen. After every verse, this was this curious chorus: 'Hay trix, trim go trix, under the greenwood tree'

This was subsequently published in a volume entitled: *The Gude and Godlie Ballatis*.

A few senior clergy were attempting to draw attention to the sorry condition of the Church in Scotland but, ultimately, to no avail. Parish churches and their clergy were starved of funds because tithes – known as 'teinds' – were mostly appropriated by higher clergy to be lavished on cathedrals and abbeys, and on good living for themselves. Indeed, the Church had too great a share in the national wealth: its revenue was at least £300,000 a year at a time when the Crown's patrimony brought in only around £17,500. Monasteries had long ceased to serve any worthwhile function. Monks at Inchcolm in Fife kept women in their monastery. Patrick Hepburn, Bishop of Moray, had nine illegitimate children. Marion Ogilvie, Cardinal Beaton's mistress, gave birth to eight children the Cardinal had fathered. Several other women also had children by Beaton.

In February 1546 Beaton had George Wishart arrested: this charismatic preacher had alarmed the hierarchy by his compelling sermons. At St Andrews Wishart was sentenced to die at the stake; there his clothes were packed with gunpowder to ensure that this martyr, unlike David Hamilton, burned well.

Then three months later the Cardinal was dragged by 16 Protestant zealots from his bed and from the arms of one of his lovers in his castle at St Andrews, and then stabbed to death. His corpse was crammed into a barrel with his severed genitals stuffed into his mouth. The struggle for the hearts and minds of Scots had begun violently. Victory for the reformers was achieved with such speed that there were to be fewer Catholic and Protestant martyrs in Scotland than in almost any other country in Europe.

EPISODE 32

SUCCESS FOR THE PROTESTANT REFORMERS IN SCOTLAND

In the early hours of the morning of 29 May 1546, Cardinal David Beaton was murdered and mutilated in St Andrews Castle by Protestant zealots. Those men who had carried out the assassination were lairds, an indication that the progress of the Reformation in Scotland was being hastened by the support of most of the country's nobles. Decisions made in Paris and London also did much to determine the outcome. France stood for the old religion while Henry VIII of England, as he was severing his ties with the Papacy, had defied the Pope to divorce Catharine of Aragon; he had married Anne Boleyn but then had her executed; and by now he had wed Jane Seymour. The King was increasingly surrounded by courtiers who were enthusiastic Protestants. Indeed, it seems likely that King Henry had given his backing to those who had slain Cardinal Beaton.

James V had died in December 1542. Just three weeks later his daughter Mary was born in Linlithgow Palace. Since James had no legitimate male heir, Mary was now Queen of Scots. She was in constant peril from the moment she was born partly because, as the granddaughter of Margaret Tudor (Henry VII's daughter and James IV's Queen), she had a direct claim on the throne of England. Henry VIII wanted his son Edward raised as a Protestant, betrothed to his cousin the infant Queen of Scots. When he failed to get his way, he sent battalions north with orders to kill, burn and spoil. Mary's mother, Mary of Guise, seized the reins of government in Edinburgh. She revived the 'auld alliance' between Scotland and France and, in response, the French shipped over advisers, troops and munitions. Those who had assassinated Cardinal Beaton had been holding out in the Castle of St Andrews; in July 1547 they were forced by gunners from the French fleet to surrender. One of those captured here and taken to France as a galley slave was John Knox – at one time he had carried a two-handed sword as a bodyguard for his teacher, George Wishart, the reformer subsequently burned at the stake at the behest of Cardinal Beaton in February 1546. On 29 July 1547 the five-year-old Mary sailed from Dumbarton to France. The Queen of Scots was now betrothed to the Dauphin, the heir to the French throne. They were to marry in 1558.

Scotland was close to becoming a client state of France. The great majority of Scots nobles loathed this dependence on a Catholic power and, in consequence, hostility to Mary of Guise – the Queen regent who was acting as temporary head of state until her daughter came of age – mounted. She persuaded Parliament to pass an Act in 1552 that formally condemned printers of 'Ballattis, sangis, blasphematiounis, rymes' both in 'Latine' and 'Inglis'; but the reformed faith continued to gain ground across the Lowlands. A network of congregations using the English prayer book sprang up in the principal burghs; their ministers were mainly priests who had become reformers. In 1557 and again in 1558 the annual Catholic procession on St Giles's Day in Edinburgh was attacked.

Released from his term as a galley slave at the request of Henry VIII's son and successor, Edward VI, Knox divided his time between England, Geneva and Scotland. While abroad, he wrote *The First Blast of the Trumpet against the Monstrous Regiment of Women* – a vituperative tract aimed at Mary of Guise and the Catholic Queen Mary of England, who had succeeded her brother Edward in 1553. In the spring of 1559 Protestants gathered in Perth as Mary of Guise planned the trial of four leading preachers and their resolve was strengthened when Knox disembarked to join them. His fiery denunciations of idolatry encouraged mobs to wreck religious houses in the city.

Victory for Protestantism came with remarkable speed. France and England made peace, both agreeing to leave Scotland alone. When the French left, Mary of Guise was helpless. To make matters worse for her, she lost the support of the French court. Mary Queen of Scots was for a brief time Queen of France, but her husband François died of an ear infection in December 1560. Catherine de Medici, the queen mother, had no time for the young widow. Mary had no choice but to return to Scotland.

Mary arrived to find that the Protestant nobility were in full control – despite her mother Mary of Guise's best efforts. Back in December 1557 five 'Lords of the Congregation' had made a 'band' or covenant to quit the Roman Church and make Scotland Protestant. Very quickly they got the backing of their peers. They ordered friars to clear out by 'flitting Friday' 12 May 1559. Parliament, better attended than anyone could remember, met in Edinburgh in 1560. There the members solemnly abolished the authority of the Pope, forbade the celebration of the Mass and adopted 25 'Articles of Confession of Faith'.

The Church of Scotland had become the established church, the 'kirk'. The Protestant Reformation had triumphed in the Lowlands and in the ensuing decades of the sixteenth century it would be accepted willingly by the great majority of Gaelic-speaking Highlanders and Islanders. In stark contrast, Protestant doctrines were to be vehemently rejected by the Gaelic-speaking people of Ulster on the other side of the Narrow Sea.

EPISODE 33

'SUCH MIRROURS OF HOLINESS AND AUSTERITIE': THE REFORMATION RESISTED IN GAELIC ULSTER

Bishop Chiericati, papal nuncio to the court of Henry VIII, was in Downpatrick in 1515. 'In this place I could not walk in the street', he reported, 'because everyone ran to kiss my dress, understanding that I was nuncio from the Pope, so that I was almost compelled by force to stay in the house, so strong was their importunity, which arose from strong religious feeling'. But in the same year, a correspondent signing himself 'Pandor', assured the King that Irish souls fell to

> Hell in showers, for ther is no archebysshop, ne bysshop, abbot, ne pryor, parson, ne vycar, ne any any other person of the Churche, highe or lowe, greate or small, Englyshe or Iryshe, that useth to preache the worde of Godde, saveing the poor fryers beggars.

'Pandor' was right to refer to the work of the 'poor fryers beggars' and, had he been able to visit Gaelic Ulster, he would have seen that the mendicant orders of friars, notably the very strict and pious Third Order of Franciscans Regular, had made the Church more popular there than perhaps it had ever been before. These men, instead of cutting themselves off from the world, embedded themselves in the community and won the admiration of ordinary people by adhering rigidly to their vows, in particular to the vow of poverty, and by reaching out to them by their emotional preaching and pastoral work. They preferred humble dwellings and lived, not by tithes or compulsory dues, but by the offerings of the people, usually given in kind. The English scholar Edmund Campion, later executed as a Jesuit traitor, thought the religion of the Gaelic natives, the 'uplandish Irish', to be composed of 'idle miracles and revelations vaine and childish'. But he did admit that lay people influenced by the friars were 'such mirrours of holiness and austeritie, that other nations retain but a shewe or shadow of devotion in comparison of them'.

The nobility of Ulster vied with each other to give lavish patronage to mendicant orders. Aodh Ruadh O'Donnell, then the most powerful Gaelic lord in all of Ireland, brought Franciscan Observantines into Tír Chonaill in 1474. Over the next 14 years he had a splendid friary built for them in Donegal. The distinct 'Irish Gothic' style of Donegal friary was imitated across Ulster. Máire, wife of Ruaidhri MacSweeney, Lord of Fanad, erected a friary at Rathmullan for the Carmelites in 1516. In other parts of Tír Chonaill friaries sprang up at: Magherabeg, Ballysaggert, Killybegs, Balleeghan, Kilmacrenan and Ballymacsweeney. The Clandeboye O'Neills founded friaries at Massereene, Larne and Lambeg. Rory MacQuillan, Lord of the Route, built Bonamargy around 1500. The MacDonnells then took Bonamargy over after ousting the MacQuillans from the Route and made it the most important centre of devotion in the north-east. Altogether 90 friaries were founded in Ireland between 1400 and 1508, 68 of them in the ecclesiastical provinces of Armagh and Tuam. A striking feature of Gaelic Ulster at this time was that many who became friars were drawn from ruling families and the traditional learned classes.

When Aodh Ruadh O'Donnell died in 1505, his wife Fionnghuala spent the next 22 years in the habit of St Francis before she was buried alongside him in Donegal friary. Tuathal Balbh, chieftain of the O'Gallaghers, was so moved by the preaching of Franciscans that he would only take prisoners in battle rather than break the commandment: 'Thou shalt not kill'.

The Church in Gaelic Ulster was in many respects deeply conservative. Reforms brought to Ireland in the twelfth and thirteenth centuries had barely touched the far north-west. Back in 1397 John Colton, the Archbishop of Armagh, an Englishman who lived in Drogheda, at great personal risk visited the far north. In Derry he had confirmed Hugh MacGillebride as abbot on condition that he 'dismiss and expel from your dwelling, cohabitation and care that Catherine daughter of O'Doherty whom it is said you have lately taken into concubinage'. Though he was warmly welcomed and prevailed upon to celebrate Mass in the open air for 'the thousands of people who had gathered out of respect for the said father', Colton failed to make MacGillebride comply with his order. In this remote part of the western Christian world celibacy was impossible to enforce and the children of clergy bore surnames such as MacEntaggart (son of the priest), MacAnespie (son of the bishop), Mac an Abbot, McVicar and McParson.

Thanks to donations of land over the previous centuries, the Church in Gaelic Ulster was well supported and across the province families – such as the MacGraths of Pettigoe in Fermanagh – acted as conscientious hereditary guardians of Church land. Local lords did succeed in taking over some of these lands but their rapacity could not be compared with their counterparts in Scotland. In short, the inhabitants of this part of Ireland, where the authority of the English Crown barely existed, saw no reason for root and branch reformation of the Church. And when the champions of the Reformation did appear, they were seen to be alien despoilers and conquerors.

EPISODE 34

'A HERESY AND A NEW ERROR': THE REFORMATION'S FAILURE IN ULSTER

The Annals of the Four Masters – the popular name for *Annála Ríoghachta Éireann* ('Annals of the Kingdom of Ireland') was compiled in Donegal Abbey's sister house of Drowes between 1632 and 1636. The author was a Franciscan friar, Michael O'Clery, assisted by three collaborators: Farfassa O'Mulconry, Peregrine O'Duigenan, and Peregrine O'Clery. Relating the island's history from Noah's Flood onwards, this is one of the great works of Gaelic literature. At its core it is a heartfelt lament for the destruction wrought by the English Crown on the Church. This is how the reader is told of Henry VIII's break with the Papacy:

> A heresy and a new error sprang up in England, through pride, vainglory, avarice and lust, and through many strange sciences, so that the men of England went into opposition to the pope and to Rome. And they styled the king Chief Head of the Church of God in his own kingdom … they destroyed the orders, namely the monks, canons, nuns and the four poor orders … They broke down the monasteries, and sold their roofs and bells … They afterwards burned the images, shrines and relics, of the saints … and they also burned the Bachall Íosa, the staff of Jesus, which was in Dublin, performing miracles from the time of St Patrick …

The dissolution of the monasteries, and the destruction associated with it, caused great distress to the inhabitants of the Pale and other parts of Leinster and Munster where royal authority had long been respected. Over most of Ulster, however, Henry VIII's laws made little impact for the time being. The Church there continued as before with the significant exception of Newry. Fleeing from his native Staffordshire where he had been accused of murder, Nicholas Bagenal served as military adviser to Conn Bacach O'Neill, Lord of Tír Eoghain. Bagenal persuaded O'Neill to make his peace with Henry, travel to

Greenwich and there be dubbed the first Earl of Tyrone. As a reward, Bagenal was knighted in 1547 and made Marshal of the King's Army in Ireland. In 1550 he was given the town of Newry and its extensive abbey lands. In Newry and to some extent in Carrickfergus, the reformed faith was gaining a toehold but hardly more than that.

Elizabeth I came to the English throne in 1558, a year before the triumph of the Protestant reformers in Edinburgh. From the outset she found it extremely difficult to get her subjects in Ireland to adopt the reformed faith. This was because it was associated with the influx of 'New English', dispossessing alike the Gaelic Irish and the 'Old English' (descendants of Norman conquerors and those they had brought over with them across the Irish Sea) of land and positions of responsibility. To people in Gaelic Ulster in particular, the reformed religion was seen as an alien attack on their identity and way of life.

Only towards the end of her reign did the Queen decide not to stint her treasure to ensure the conquest of Ireland from end to end. Hugh O'Neill, Earl of Tyrone, had united all the Gaelic lords of the north in a great rebellion against the Crown. This wasting war began in 1594. It took nine years of ruthless blood-letting and destruction before O'Neill could be made to submit. The great cost of Elizabeth's campaigning left almost nothing over to fund a proselytising mission. In any case, to the northern Irish the commanders championing Protestantism – most notably Sir Arthur Chichester, the governor of Carrickfergus – were brutal and intolerant conquerors. Significantly, the customary Irish words for a Protestant were *Albanach* or *Sasanach* – 'Scotsman' or 'Englishman'.

Even before the rebellion had got under way the opportunity to win the Irish over to Protestantism had been lost. John Kearny, on behalf of the royal government in Dublin Castle, produced a printed Protestant catechism and a Gaelic alphabet book in 1571 but not many copies were circulated. Only after 1600 was a considerable amount of Protestant literature printed in Gaelic. The contrast, not only with Gaelic Scotland but also with Wales, is striking. The Bible translated into Welsh appeared in 1588. In Wales the Tudor government treated Welsh identity with respect. In Ireland, however, the Crown and the New English saw the Gaelic bardic class as an impediment to their plans for the island. Trinity College, founded in 1594, even in its most productive years, was sending out fewer than five graduate clergy a year – and none of them were obliged to be fluent Gaelic speakers. And at that time, outside of Carrickfergus and Newry, very few understood English speech in Ulster. Little effort was made by the Crown to win over members of the hereditary learned orders and so very few men were available to preach the Protestant religion to the Gaelic Irish.

Across the Narrow Sea the King of Scots, James VI, the son of Mary Queen of Scots and great-grandson of Henry VII, patiently set about winning over the hereditary learned classes in the extensive Gaelic parts of his kingdom to the new reformed doctrines.

EPISODE 35

MARY QUEEN OF SCOTS AND HER SON JAMES VI

T he Scottish Parliament, meeting in Edinburgh in 1560, decisively removed the authority of the Catholic Church. In the weeks ensuing a committee drafted the *First Book of Discipline*, in effect the foundation document of the Presbyterian Church. Superintendents exercised authority formerly held by bishops and presided over Kirk courts. Laymen were given power and authority in religious matters and each parish appointed a Kirk Session to assist the minister. Preachers, speaking in Scots, had a central role in ensuring that the people came to know and understand the Scriptures. The seven sacraments of the Catholic Church were reduced to two: Baptism and Communion. Traditional religious festivals were banned, including Christmas Day.

Devout Catholic though she was, Mary Queen of Scots could do nothing to turn back the clock. At first this tall, beautiful and vivacious young queen seemed to manage a difficult situation with charm and diplomacy. Now a widow after her first husband François died, Mary undermined her position by two further marriages, both of them disastrous, first to Henry Stewart, Lord Darnley, her first cousin. Protestants were infuriated by the Catholic marriage on 29 July 1565 and, in any case Darnley proved a worthless playboy. He did father a son, who would become James VI. Darnley was murdered in mysterious circumstances on 9 February 1567.

Next Mary was forced to marry James Hepburn, 4th Earl of Bothwell, who may well have been responsible for Darnley's murder. This marriage provoked a rebellion and at Carberry Hill in June 1567, Bothwell fled the battlefield for Norway. Mary was seized and forced to abdicate on 24 July. Her 13-month old son was proclaimed King James VI. Mary's Protestant half-brother, James

Stewart, the Earl of Moray became Regent. He was the illegitimate son of James V and Margaret Douglas.

In 1568 Mary made the fatal decision to seek refuge from Queen Elizabeth in England. She moved to Tutbury, closely guarded for the next 16 years by the 6th Earl of Shrewsbury. Had she not continued to intrigue with Catholic plotters against Elizabeth, she might have avoided execution at Fotheringhay at the age of 44 on 8 February 1587.

By fleeing to England, Mary left Catholic nobles in Scotland in a severely weakened position. As a result, Protestantism continued to sweep across Scotland. Her flight brought about a profound shift in the relations between England and Scotland. Mutual support for the Reformation in effect put the two states into a permanent alliance. Mary's son, James VI, crowned King of Scots at the age of 18 months, did his best to uphold this alliance – after all, the failure of Queen Elizabeth to marry ensured that he was next in line to the English throne.

During his minority James endured an exceptionally harsh upbringing for a monarch, deprived of love, frequently whipped by his tutor, periodically locked up by his guardians and terrified by attempted assassinations and violent aristocratic feuds. His stern tutor, George Buchanan, nevertheless, ensured that James grew up to speak good English and to be accomplished in Latin, French and Italian, as well as being thoroughly imbued with Protestant doctrine. Considering that his mother Mary had her head chopped off, that his father, Henry Lord Darnley, had been blown up at Kirk o' Field, and that, as a five-year-old, he had seen the blood-stained body of his dying granduncle, James Stewart, Earl of Moray, being carried past him at Stirling Castle, James proved a level-headed monarch, ruling Scotland rather well.

Above all, James played his part in helping to promote religious harmony across his kingdom. By the standards of the day he could be described as an ecumenically minded Protestant. The king demanded loyalty first and, unlike Elizabeth, he did not set about persecuting nobles who remained Catholic – provided they remained loyal. He did not interfere when his wife, Anne of Denmark, decided in the 1590s to convert from Lutheranism to become a Catholic. And despite protests from the Kirk, for nearly 30 years James gave a key position in his government to Alexander Seton, Earl of Dunfermline, a Catholic educated by the Jesuits.

And it was largely due to James that there was no coercion used in the mission to convert Highlanders and Islanders to the reformed doctrines he so cherished.

JAMES VI AND THE MISSION TO THE *GAIDHEALTACHT*

No more than 25 Protestants and 2 Catholics suffered martyrdom in Scotland, most of them while Cardinal David Beaton was still alive. In Tudor England the number of martyrs of both faiths exceeded 500. This is striking proof that James VI, King of Scots, set his face against religious persecution in his realm.

James was helped by the fact that the arrangements made in 1560 establishing the new Protestant Kirk worked well, partly because the old Church office holders were allowed to draw two-thirds of their former revenues. There were tensions; moderates accepted the institution of superintendents or bishops while more doctrinaire Presbyterians, led by the scholar Andrew Melville after his return from Geneva in 1574, wanted no bishops and insisted that the Kirk be independent of Crown interference. As he reached maturity James proceeded with caution: he strove to maintain the authority of bishops and the Crown but at the same time he did not stand in the way of the growth of a nationwide structure of presbyteries – which gave the General Assembly of the Kirk a status similar to that of the Scottish Parliament.

The Reformation was triumphing everywhere Scots was spoken, but what about the *Gaidhealtacht*, the other half of Scotland? In the middle of the sixteenth century the most powerful Gaelic lord was Archibald Campbell, the 4th Earl of Argyll. He had played a pivotal role in the national revolution of 1559–60. Now he set himself the task of taking the reformed doctrines into the Gaelic-speaking world. The Earl, as was customary, travelled through his lands from castle to castle. Now, along with feasting and celebrations, he included Protestant services and preaching, and his wide network of relatives and clients was persuaded to do the same. His son, the 5th Earl, also called Archibald, carried on the work of extending the Reformation northwards and westwards.

As in Ireland, Gaelic lords had by their side hereditary orders of poets, jurists, annalists, physicians and other learned men. Their traditions were transmitted orally and these men were now enlisted to proclaim the Protestant message. Argyll found the perfect agent to forward his proselytising plan: John Carswell. Carswell was a notary appointed Superintendent and Bishop of the Isles, and given lands and castles to sustain his mission. In 1567 Carswell published a translation of *the Book of Common Order*, 'Knox's Liturgy' (*Foirm na n-Urrnuidheadh*), along with Calvin's small catechism. This was the very first book printed in Gaelic and, since it was in a literary form common to both countries, it could be understood across the Narrow Sea also.

The spread of the reformed faith in the Highlands and Islands depended not on print but on the spoken word. Indeed, there was no complete Bible translated into Gaelic until 1801. Members of the old learned families now served the Kirk and translated spontaneously from the English Bible into whatever local Gaelic dialect they encountered. They also used Carswell's catechism and perfected a compelling preaching style, much envied in the next century by the Franciscans. Operating from Ulster, the Franciscans attempted a counter offensive but only achieved permanent success in the remote islands of Barra and Uist.

Scotland during the reign of King James VI was remarkably peaceful by the standards of the time. At the same time, south of the Borders, England governed by Elizabeth was enjoying increased stability and fast-growing prosperity. On the other side of the Irish Sea, however, the island of Ireland during her rule was repeatedly convulsed by violence, nowhere more so than in Ulster.

EPISODE 37

THE MACDONNELLS AND THE 'CANKRED DANGEROUS REBEL', SHANE O'NEILL

Early in the sixteenth century, the O'Donnell lordship of Tír Chonaill was not only the strongest in the north but also by far the most powerful Gaelic lordship in all of Ireland. Then, rather suddenly, the O'Donnell tide went out and the O'Neill tide came in. The extension of English royal power in Connacht was partly responsible: Tír Chonaill lost access to the rich tribute it had for long exacted from that western province. The collapse of the O'Donnell hegemony, however, was due mostly to wasting and vicious succession disputes between male members of the ruling family. For example, Calvagh O'Donnell became lord only by tying up and imprisoning his own father until he died.

In May 1561 Calvagh himself was tied up and imprisoned after being routed by Shane O'Neill, lord of Tír Eoghain. For over two years Calvagh was kept in bonds, his neck in a collar chained to fetters on his ankles so that he could neither sit nor stand. Later he told how Shane's irons had been 'so sore that the very blood did run down on every side of mine irons, insomuch that I did wish after death a thousand times'. Meanwhile of her own accord Calvagh's wife, Catherine, widow of the 4th Earl of Argyll, became Shane's mistress.

O'Neill would stop at nothing to achieve his goal of ruling all of Ulster. James MacDonnell, Lord of Dunyveg and the Glynns, observed Shane's triumphant campaigning with growing alarm. MacDonnell's lordship, straddling both sides of the Narrow Sea, was a formidable one. But he had a unique problem: James was a subject of Mary Queen of Scots and, at the same time, as possessor of extensive lands in the Antrim Glens and the Route, was also (in theory at least) a subject of Queen Elizabeth. What was he to do? Shane's next unexpected move did offer a slim prospect that the MacDonnells might be left undisturbed.

On 4 January 1562 O'Neill was in Greenwich. In desperation Queen Elizabeth had invited him over to see if she could tame him. In the presence of ambassadors and all the court, Shane threw himself to the floor before the Queen. Then, rising to his knees, he made a passionate speech in Irish, punctuated by howls which caused great astonishment. 'For lack of education and civility I have offended ...' he began, the words of his speech being translated into English by the Earl of Kildare.

As soon as he was back in Ulster, however, Shane began breaking all the assurances he had given that he would keep the peace. Elizabeth plaintively asked how such a 'cankred dangerous rebel' might be 'utterly extirped'. After laying waste the Maguire lordship of Fermanagh, O'Neill prepared to crush the only part of Gaelic Ulster not yet in his power: the MacDonnell lordship.

As Shane bore down on the Glens in 1565, the MacDonells set their beacons ablaze on Fair Head and the high ground behind Torr Head to summon help from across the Narrow Sea. The men of Kintyre seized their weapons and manned their galleys, but it was already too late. Sorley Boy MacDonnell, who had been leading the defence of the Glens, fell back to join his brother James. Together they made a desperate last stand by the slopes of Knocklayd. Shane captured James and, refusing appeals from both Queen Elizabeth and Mary Queen of Scots to accept a ransom, he allowed him to die of his wounds. Sorley Boy, also made prisoner, Shane kept alive. Dunseverick fell, Ballycastle was taken, and – after Shane threatened to starve Sorley Boy to death – Dunluce capitulated.

Elizabeth launched an amphibious operation against O'Neill the following year but this came to an embarrassing conclusion when the English gunpowder store at Derry accidentally blew up. In the end it was Shane's neighbours in Ulster who brought about his downfall. In 1567 the indefatigable O'Neill lord of Tír Eoghain decided on another punitive attack on Tír Chonaill. But as the O'Neills crossed the River Swilly at Farsetmore they met a furious onslaught of O'Donnells and MacSweeneys, as the annals record:

> They proceeded to strike, mangle, slaughter, and cut down one another for a long time, so that men were soon laid low, heroes wounded, youths slain, and robust heroes mangled in the slaughter.

Shane's warriors retreated into the advancing tide, there to be drowned or cut down. O'Neill himself fled eastward to take refuge with the MacDonnells in the Glens. It was an extraordinary decision. Did he think he could trade Sorley Boy for help from these Island Scots? In an apparent mood of reconciliation, the MacDonnells prepared a feast at Glenshesk. Then they 'fell to quaffing' – as one report put it – and a quarrel broke out. O'Neill was hacked to death. Shane's head was sent 'pickled in a pipkin' to Sir Henry Sidney, Elizabeth's Lord Deputy of Ireland, who placed it on a spike over Dublin Castle's arch-gate.

Freed from captivity, Sorley Boy became Lord of the Glynns and the Route. All his very considerable diplomatic and military prowess would be needed to enable this lordship to avoid annihilation.

EPISODE 38

'THEY BE OCCUPIED STILL IN KILLING': A MASSACRE ON RATHLIN

Sorley Boy MacDonnell, lord of the Glynns and the Route, was certainly one of the most astute politicians in the Gaelic world. In the Isles he made peace with his people's traditional enemies, the Campbells. He arranged the marriage of his brother's widow, Lady Agnes (herself a Campbell), to the strongest ruler in Ulster, Turlough Luineach O'Neill, Shane's successor as lord of Tír Eoghain. Finola, Lady Agnes's daughter, was married in turn to Hugh O'Donnell, lord of Tír Chonaill. Finola – known as Inghean Dubh, the 'dark daughter' – was to prove herself a woman to be reckoned with. These arrangements formed the basis of a powerful defensive coalition of O'Neills, O'Donnells and Island Scots.

Sorley Boy also took care to maintain good relations with James VI, King of Scots since his mother Mary's forced abdication in 1567. This required exceptional diplomatic skill since, in the King's opinion, these Gaelic-speaking Islanders were 'alluterly barbares, without any sort or shew of ciuilitie … voyd of ony knowledge of God or his Religioun'. The gravest threat came from England: Elizabeth resisted all of Sorley Boy's blandishments. Instead the Queen approved an ambitious plan put forward by Walter Devereux, Earl of Essex, to make an English colony of eastern Ulster. Grateful for Essex's service in foiling an escape attempt by Mary Queen of Scots, she gave him title to most of Co. Antrim and money to cover half the cost of the thousand soldiers he had raised.

From the moment he set out from Liverpool in August 1573, Essex encountered one frustrating reverse after another. He wrote in complaint to Elizabeth that his gentlemen colonists had 'forsaken me, feigning excuses to repair home where I hear they give forth speeches in dislike of the enterprise'. In frustration he hanged some Devon men for attempted desertion. Essex recklessly invaded Tír Eoghain, burning corn and slaughtering a band of Turlough Luineach's followers taking refuge on a river island at Banbridge. Then in October 1574 Essex and his men were invited to a feast in Belfast Castle by the Clandeboye lord, Sir Brian MacPhelim O'Neill, who had no wish to provoke the English intruders. There, the annals record,

> as they were agreeably drinking and making merry, Brian, his brother, and his wife, were seized upon by the earl, and all his people put unsparingly to the sword … Brian was afterwards sent to Dublin, together with his wife and brother, where they were cut in quarters. Such was the end of their feast.

This treacherous cruelty did nothing to advance Essex's cause.

The following summer the Earl determined to smash the power of the MacDonnells. A fleet was fitted out in Carrickfergus harbour, including three frigates under the command of Francis Drake, already famous for seizing a Spanish treasure convoy. Captain John Norris (after whom Mountnorris is named) took command of the soldiers crowding on board the vessels bound for Rathlin. Rathlin was then an island of great strategic importance: it was a staging post across the Narrow Sea to the Isles. The island was a valued refuge when Kintyre on the Scottish mainland and the Antrim Glens on the Irish mainland were being attacked.

On the morning of 22 July 1575 the assault fleet reached Arkill Bay on the east side of the island. Essex reported that Norris's men, 'did with valiant minds leap to land, and charged them so hotly, as they drave them to retire with speed, chasing them to a castle where they had of very great strength'. The castle, with many women and children inside, was pounded by ships' guns for four days. But without a well, and with its wooden ramparts destroyed by red-hot cannon balls, it could hold out no longer.

At dawn on 26 July the garrison surrendered on condition that their lives were spared; but it was reported:

> The soldiers, being moved and much stirred with the loss of their fellows that were slain, and desirous of revenge, made request, or rather pressed, to have the killing of them, which they did all … There were slain that came out of the castle of all sorts 200 … They be occupied still in killing, and have slain that they have found hidden in caves and in the cliffs of the sea to the number of 300 or 400 more.

Essex passed on to the queen information he had received that Sorley Boy 'stood upon the mainland of the Glynnes and saw the taking of the island, and was like to run mad for sorrow (as the spy saith), turning and tormenting himself and saying that he had then lost all that ever he had'. Elizabeth did not condemn this blood-letting. Instead she promoted Norris and gave Drake a special audience at court.

But Essex was running out of men and money. He pulled back in despair to Dublin, where in September 1576, rather suddenly, he died of dysentery at the age of thirty-six.

For Sorley Boy this was only a temporary respite. For the sake of her realm's security, Elizabeth still hoped she could establish an English 'plantation' in eastern Ulster – and, of course, the creation of such a colony could be achieved only by driving the MacDonnells back across the Narrow Sea.

EPISODE 39

'THIS SCOTTISH WOMAN WILL MAKE A NEW SCOTLAND OF ULSTER': SIR JOHN PERROT'S 'RASH, UNADVISED JOURNEYS'

Turlough Luineach O'Neill, lord of Tír Eoghain, had married a member of the Campbell clan, a wealthy widow, Lady Agnes. As a dowry she brought over the Narrow Sea an impressive force of mercenary Redshanks. London could normally depend on the O'Donnells and the O'Neills to be preoccupied by warring with each other, cancelling out the danger they posed to the Crown. Now they were allies, the bond sealed by the marriage of Finola, Lady Agnes's daughter, to Hugh O'Donnell, lord of Tír Chonaill. To make matters worse, all of them were on excellent terms with Sorley Boy MacDonnell, Lord of the Glynns and the Route, the chief who had done most to forge this formidable defensive network.

'Here is a great bruit of 2000 Scots landed in Clandeboye', Sir Nicholas Malby wrote anxiously in a report he sent to Queen Elizabeth in the autumn of 1580. He was certain Turlough Luineach O'Neill's 'marriage with the Scot is cause of all of this'. This seasoned commander warned that

> if her Majesty does not provide against her devices, this Scottish woman will make a new Scotland of Ulster. She hath already planted a good foundation; for she in Tyrone, and her daughter in Tyrconnell, do carry all the sway in the North.

Malby fretted that the Ulster lords, along with Island Scots, would band together with European Catholic powers. Indeed, just as he was writing, Elizabeth's commanders were campaigning against rebels in Munster supported, alarmingly, by an expeditionary force sent by Pope Gregrory XIII to Kerry.

In 1584 Sir John Perrot took up his post as Lord Deputy of Ireland. He had once dismissed Ulster 'as a fit receptacle for all the savage beasts of the land'. Now Perrot, thought to be the natural son of Henry VIII, decided that it was worth his while to lead a campaign north. He had been informed, incorrectly, that a great force of Scots was about to invade the province.

As Perrot's army, the largest to be seen in Ulster for many a year, advanced down both banks of the lower Bann, most of the Scots retreated in their galleys to the Isles. With just 40 men Sorley Boy's youngest son, Randal Arannach, held out in Dunluce castle. Perched on a high, sea-tunnelled rock near Portballintrae, with a strong gatehouse and bristling with turrets, Dunluce seemed impregnable. But pounded for two days in September by the Lord Deputy's cannon, including a culverin considered the largest in the realm, the garrison capitulated.

Appalled by the expense of this and further expeditions into Ulster Elizabeth sent this stinging reproof in her own hand:

> Let us have no more such rash, unadvised journeys without good ground as your last journey in the North. We marvel that you hanged not such saucy an advertiser as that he made so great a company was coming ... take heed ere you use us so again.

Actually, a great 'company' was on its way. Sorley Boy held a meeting of Island chiefs on Bute and there won support for the recovery of his Antrim lands. As Rathlin was being recovered, troops encamped at Red Bay, commanded by Sir Henry Bagenal, were taken by surprise and overwhelmed. On the night of 1 January 1585 Sir William Stanley's men at Bonamargy Abbey came under attack. Stanley reported to Bagenal:

> About 11 of the clok the same nyght, came certayne troupes of Skottes on foote, and about VI horsemen with them, who had upon their staves wads lighted, wherewith they sodaynly sett the roufe of the churche, being thatched, on fyer. They gave us a brave canvasado, and entered our camp ... I had twelve choys men hurte, and myself with arowes, in the raynes of my bak, as I called forwarde my men; in the arme, and in the flanke, and through the thigh; of which wounds I am verie sore.

Perrot refused an offer of parley and so the Scots fought on. On Hallowe'en night 1585 80 Scots landed at Dunluce and, unseen, scaled the cliffs and ramparts with the aid of ropes twisted from withies. Peter Carey, the constable, fought to the last of his men; then he was hanged from the walls with a withy rope. 'I do not weigh the loss,' Perrot remarked when the news was brought to him, 'but can hardly endure the discredit.' It was some consolation to him that his men succeeded in slaying Sorley Boy's older son, Alasdair, who had taken refuge in a grave. A Captain Price opened the coffin and found 'a quick corse therein, and in memory of Dunluce we cried quittance with him, and sent his head to be set on Dublin Castle'.

In that year of 1585 England and Spain went to war. Men could not be spared for inconclusive campaigning against the MacDonnells. Sorley Boy came to Dublin the following year. Shown Alasdair's head on a spike he said, 'My son hath many heads'. Sorley prostrated himself before a portrait of Elizabeth, a small price to pay for recognition of his family's right to the Glens and the Route.

EPISODE 40

GAELIC ULSTER DEFIANT

In the late summer of 1588, raked by English cannon fire and scattered by fireships, the ships of the Spanish Armada could do no other than take flight up the North Sea, around the Shetlands and westwards deep into the Atlantic. In the mountainous seas many stricken Armada vessels foundered on Ireland's rugged coastline. Unable to return to Spain, some castaways tried to find refuge in neutral Scotland.

In the pitch blackness, close to midnight at the end of October, in a rising gale the *Girona* struck Lacada Point, a long basalt reef near Dunluce, and split apart. All but a handful of the 1,300 nobles, soldiers and sailors crowded on board this galleass perished as a strong tide swept them out from the shore. Provisioned by the MacSweeneys, these Armada castaways had sailed out of Donegal Bay northwards around Bloody Foreland in a desperate attempt to reach Scotland. Amongst those drowned that night was Don Alonso Martínez de Leiva de Rioja, Knight of Santiago, Commander of Alcuescar, the general-in-chief of the Armada's land forces entrusted by Philip II of Spain with the conquest of England. The *Girona* was the last of no fewer than 24 galleons and other Armada warships which that fateful autumn had been wrecked with terrible loss of life along Ireland's poorly charted shores.

For those in London deciding future policy for Ireland the Armada was a wake-up call. At one stage in September there were at least 3,000 Spaniards on Irish soil when the most Lord Deputy Sir William Fitzwilliam could muster was 1,000 armed men. The truth is that these castaways were too weakened by their privations to pose any serious threat, but Elizabeth and her counsellors did not know that. England had been spared a terrible fate, but an awful spectre remained: the queen's Protestant realm could once more be put in peril, threatened from the west, if a hostile Catholic power could make common cause with Ireland's many disaffected Gaelic lords. Elizabeth resolved not to stint her treasure until every corner of the island was made secure for the Crown.

More than any other province, Ulster was out of reach. Despite numerous punitive expeditions, only Carrickfergus and Newry remained firmly in royal control. To transform the north the queen put her faith in Hugh O'Neill. He seemed to owe all he had to the English. It had been an English king who had given an earldom to his grandfather Conn Bacach. After the murder first of his father, Matthew, and then of his brother Brian at the behest of Shane O'Neill, it had been Elizabeth who had affirmed Hugh as Baron of Dungannon in 1568. Carefully nurtured by the Crown and given a good English education in the Pale, Hugh had been proclaimed the Earl of Tyrone in 1585. It seemed that the English had been right to give Hugh their support – he had campaigned with the Earl of Essex, had given no aid to the Spaniards cast ashore in 1588, and often lent military aid to the lord deputy of the day. Yet O'Neill was to become the most dangerous and astute of Elizabeth's opponents not only in Ulster but in all Ireland.

Hugh O'Neill's burning ambition was to win unquestioned domination of all of Ulster. For a long time English help was essential in assisting him towards that objective. Patience and diplomacy were equally important. It took skill to settle in Dungannon while Turlough Luineach O'Neill, acknowledged by his people as 'the O'Neill' of Tír Eoghain, remained alive and while Shane O'Neill's sons were at large. It took vision to assuage the age-old enmity between the O'Neills and O'Donnells.

In 1591 Hugh O'Neill arranged the rescue of Red Hugh O'Donnell from Dublin Castle. Captured at the age of sixteen in 1587 and held hostage thereafter, Red Hugh (after having his frost-bitten toes amputated in Ballyshannon) was proclaimed Lord of Tír Chonaill at Donegal Castle. His mother Finola, the Inghean Dubh, the 'dark daughter' of Lady Agnes, Turlough Luineach's wife, had persuaded her aged husband, also called Hugh, to step aside in favour of their son.

Meanwhile Elizabeth's commanders and sheriffs were enforcing the royal writ across the country. When Fermanagh came under threat in 1593, its lord, Hugh Maguire, felt he had no choice but to rebel. But his castle at Enniskillen fell to the English. It was at this moment that Hugh O'Neill – to the astonishment of Dublin Castle – deserted the Lord Deputy's army, changed sides and put himself forward to lead the defence of Gaelic Ulster. In 1594 by the Arney river he scattered the queen's forces and organised the recovery of Maguire's castle.

One by one the Gaelic lordships of all Ulster – some by persuasion and others by force – fell in behind O'Neill, O'Donnell and Maguire. Hugh O'Neill raised a great host, calling up recruits each spring and giving these men training, discipline and modern firearms. Gallowglass warriors gave up the traditional battleaxe for the caliver and the arquebus – loaded with bullets cast from lead intended for the roof of Dungannon Castle and with powder imported from Scotland.

On the Earl of Tyrone's behalf the Clandeboye O'Neills took Belfast Castle and disembowelled all the English garrison there. Their neighbours, the MacDonnells of the Glens, tried to remain neutral. As this epic conflict got under way, that proved impossible.

EPISODE 41

'WE SPARE NONE OF WHAT QUALITY OR SEX SOEVER'

James MacDonnell, who had succeeded his father Sorley Boy as Lord of the Glynns and the Route, was at great pains to maintain good relations with both the King of Scots and the Queen of England. In 1597 he travelled to Edinburgh to pledge his loyalty to James VI, and was rewarded there with a knighthood. The author of the *Chronicle of the Scottish Kings* approvingly described MacDonnell as 'ane man of Scottis bluid, albeit his landis lye in Ireland. He was ane bra man of person and behaviour, but he had not the Scots tongue, nor nae language but Erse'. Sorley Boy had made his peace with Elizabeth and now his son was striving to uphold it. But could he avoid being drawn into the great coalition of Ulster lords led by Hugh O'Neill, Earl of Tyrone, at war with the English Crown?

Pugnacious action by the governor of Carrickfergus, Sir John Chichester, made it impossible for Sir James MacDonnell to stand aside. Chichester demanded that he hand over guns retrieved from the *Girona,* the Armada galleass sunk off the north coast in 1588. When he was refused, Chichester besieged Dunluce where the MacDonnells, he reported, 'have planted three peeces of ordnaunce, demi-cannon, and culvering, which were had out of one of the Spanish ships coming upon that coast after our fight with them'. After failing to take the castle, the governor then seized a large herd of MacDonnell cattle. Sir James led his men down to Carrickfergus to negotiate their return. 'What say you?' Chichester called to his officers during the parley. 'Shall we charge them?' In the rash attack that followed Chichester was shot through the head and 180 of his men were killed.

And so MacDonnell found himself at war with the Queen, after all. Indeed, without exception, every Gaelic lordship in Ulster had joined Hugh O'Neill's rebellion. When in July 1598 the Queen's Marshal, Sir Henry Bagenal, led a great army north, Sir James MacDonnell sent his younger brother, Randal, with a substantial contingent from the Antrim Glens to join O'Neill's Gaelic host being drawn up to confront the Marshal. As the over-confident Bagenal thrust across country beyond Armagh, his army was assailed by musket and caliver shot fired from behind dense woodland cover. Pack horses and cannon dragged by bullocks impeded regiments marching behind, while the van advanced to near annihilation. Bagenal rode back to help extricate a heavy gun stuck in the bed of a stream (the yellow ford which gave the battle its name), but when he raised his visor he was shot in the face and fell dying.

The Battle of the Yellow Ford was the most disastrous defeat the English ever suffered at the hands of the Irish. Within weeks one Gaelic lord after another in the other three provinces of Ireland joined the rebellion. English rule, not only in the extremities but over the whole island, was in peril. In 1599 Elizabeth sent over Robert Devereux, 2nd Earl of Essex, with the greatest English army yet seen in Ireland. But Essex achieved little and, to the queen's disgust, he made a truce with Tyrone before deserting his post to return to London.

In January 1600 Elizabeth appointed Charles Blount, Lord Mountjoy, as her Lord Deputy. He immediately proved himself a commander of great ability. Mountjoy prepared to break O'Neill's rebellion by an unceasing war of attrition; he preferred to fight in winter when it was more difficult for the Irish to hide in the leafless woods, their stores of grain and butter could be burned, and their cattle could be more easily stampeded and cut down. He would starve insurgent Ulster into submission.

Advancing from the south, Mountjoy forced O'Neill to abandon his elaborate defences in the Moyry Pass. Sir Henry Docwra sailed into Lough Foyle to establish a secure base at Derry; from there he engaged Red Hugh O'Donnell in Tír Chonaill. Sir Arthur Chichester, appointed governor of Carrickfergus after the MacDonnells had killed his brother John, crossed Lough Neagh to create havoc on the western shores. In May 1601 Chichester reported to Mountjoy:

We have killed, burnt, and spoiled all along the lough within four miles of Dungannon ... in which journeys we have killed above one hundred people of all sorts, besides such as were burnt, how many I know not. We spare none of what quality or sex soever ...

Mountjoy urged Docwra to 'burn all the dwellings, and destroy the corn on the ground, which might be done by encamping upon, and cutting it down with swords'. According to his secretary, the Lord Deputy himself 'destroyed the rebels corn about Armagh (whereof he found great abundance) and would destroy the rest, this course causing famine, being the only sure way to reduce or root out the rebels'.

The only hope now for those in arms against Elizabeth was that the Spanish would send the help they had promised. In September 1601 Hugh O'Neill got word that, at last, the Spanish had made landfall at Kinsale in Munster.

EPISODE 42

RANDAL MACDONNELL, THE GREAT SURVIVOR IN A TIME OF DEFEAT, DESTRUCTION AND CONQUEST

On Easter Monday 1601 Sir James MacDonnell fell dead, poisoned it is thought by an agent in the pay of the English. Without contest, Randal Arannach – so called because he had been fostered on the Scottish Isle of Arran – was chosen by his people to take his brother's place as Lord of the Glynns and the Route. After all, Randal had led MacDonnell fighting men to many memorable victories as they fought alongside Hugh O'Neill, Earl of Tyrone, in his great rebellion against the English Crown. By this year, however, Queen Elizabeth's armies, under the command of Lord Deputy Mountjoy, were penetrating deep into the Ulster countryside, wreaking havoc. The only hope now for the Gaelic lords of the north was the arrival of substantial foreign help.

In the autumn of 1601, a Spanish expeditionary force, led by Don Juan del Águila, made landfall in Munster and seized the walled town of Kinsale. Without delay, Mountjoy turned his army round to go south to besiege the Spaniards. O'Neill felt he had no choice but to respond to Águila's frantic appeals to join him. Randal, along with all the leading lords of Ulster, responded to the Earl of Tyrone's summons. That December, he led his men from the Antrim Glens to traverse the length of Ireland.

Overlooking the English encampment outside Kinsale with his great Gaelic host, O'Neill gave in to entreaties to make an immediate attack. The battle begun at dawn that Christmas Eve was a disaster. The element of surprise, crucial for success, was lost almost immediately. English sentries heard the Irish make preparation and saw their arquebus slow matches glowing in the dark. In the half light, and advancing forward over unfamiliar ground, many Ulstermen lost their way. Seizing the initiative, Mountjoy's armoured heavy cavalry swept down, inflicting a terrible slaughter. In a couple of hours it was all over, and Águila's sally from the walls to make assault on the English entrenchments came too late.

Kinsale was Ireland's Culloden: all of O'Neill's previous triumphs were wiped out at a stroke, and though the war continued for more than another year, the complete conquest of Ireland by the English was only a matter of time.

Sir Arthur Chichester had taken advantage of Randal's absence in Munster to lead out of Carrickfergus a punitive force with the aim of devastating the Glens and the Route. He advanced

almost as far as Dunluce, where I spared neither house, corne, nor creature; and I brought from thence as much prey as we could well dryve, being greatlye hindered by the extreame snowe fallen in the tyme of my being abroade.

At Kinsale almost the entire contingent of MacDonnell's several hundred infantrymen armed with firearms, together with archers and horsemen, was slaughtered. Fortunate to escape the battlefield himself, Randal returned to find himself almost impotent. Back in Ulster the English resumed their campaigns of slaughter and destruction. 'We do now continually hunt all their woods', Mountjoy reported, 'spoil their corn, burn their houses, and kill so many churls, as it grieveth me to think that it is necessary to do this'. His secretary described how Mountjoy spent five days at Tullahogue where the O'Neills of old custom were created, and there he spoiled the corn of all the country, and Tyrone's own corn, and brake down the chair wherein the O'Neills were wont to be created, being of stone, planted in the open field.

O'Neill on his return from Kinsale could manage no more than rearguard action in the Fermanagh woods.

In the autumn of 1602 Randal, seeing that further resistance to the Crown forces was futile, made his submission. He joined the final bloody stages of the campaign against O'Neill, with 500 foot and 40 horse supplied at his own expense. In gratitude, Chichester introduced Randal to Mountjoy at Tullahogue and there, at the foot of that ancient inaugural hill site, the Lord Deputy knighted him. O'Neill decided himself to surrender and, given a safe-conduct, made his way to meet Mountjoy at Mellifont in Louth.

On the night of 27 March 1603 Lord Deputy Mountjoy got news that Elizabeth had died. He kept the information to himself when O'Neill made his submission three days later. The King of Scots, James VI, was now also James I of England. In addition, he was King of Ireland, an island conquered by the Crown from end to end for the first time in its history.

Perhaps no one in Ireland benefited more immediately by the accession of King James than Sir Randal Arannach MacDonnell. One reason was that a few years before Randal had given vital assistance to James when Angus MacDonald of Dunyveg had risen in rebellion. James, eager to protect Randal 'from the violence of his bade kynesmen', confirmed him on 28 May in his possession of a vast territory (333,907 acres by modern measurement) stretching from Rathlin and the Route down the Antrim Glens to Larne.

Sir Randal Arannach MacDonnell had proved himself a great survivor.

EPISODE 43

THE ESCAPE OF CONN O'NEILL

During the final years of Elizabeth's reign Conn Mac Néill O'Neill was Lord of Upper Clandeboye, a territory encompassing north Down and the Ards peninsula. He had fought with the Earl of Tyrone against the Crown but after the rout of Kinsale he had submitted to the governor of Carrickfergus, Sir Arthur Chichester. Conn, however, failed to keep out of trouble and his antics were to lead directly to the most successful Scottish colonisation carried out anywhere in Ireland.

During a feast lasting several days in his tower house of Castlereagh, the wine, not surprisingly, ran out. Conn sent his men to Belfast nearby to get more. As the Montgomery family papers inform us:

> The said servants being sent with runletts to bring wine from Belfast aforesaid, unto the said Con, their master … then in a grand debauch at Castlereagh, with his brothers, his friends, and followers; they returning (without wine) to him battered and bled, complained that the soldiers had taken the wine, with the casks, from them by force … on this report of the said servants, Con was vehemently moved to anger; reproached them bitterly; and in a rage, swore by his father, and by all his noble ancestors' souls, that not one of them should ever serve him … if they went not back forthwith and revenge the affront done to him and themselves, by those few Boddagh Sasonagh soldiers (as he termed them).

Conn's men – 'as yet more than half drunk' – returned to Belfast and killed a soldier. Accused of levying war against the Queen, Conn was cast into a dungeon in Carrickfergus.

It was not long before news of Conn's fate travelled to Scotland across the North Channel to Ayr. Here Hugh Montgomery, 6th Laird of Braidstane who had commanded Scottish troops fighting for the Protestant cause in France, and 'forseeing that Ireland must be the stage to act upon', realised that he could profit from O'Neill's plight.

Both Hugh Montgomery and his brother, the Reverend George Montgomery, were close confidants of King James VI of Scotland. In effect they served the King as spies in England, employing a footman 'with letters of intelligencies and of business and advice, and in requittal he received more and fresher informations (touching the English Court and the Queen)'. Their moment came when Elizabeth died in the spring of 1603 and James VI of Scotland became James I of England:

> The said Laird in the said first year of the King's reign pitched upon the following way (which he thought most fair and feazable) to get an estate of lands with free consent of the forfeiting owner of them.

An elaborate plan was laid to spring Conn O'Neill from jail. Thomas
Montgomery, a relative of the Laird, was sent over to Carrickfergus in a small
boat to woo the Town Marshal's daughter, Annas Dobbin. This Thomas did
with striking success:

> This took umbrages of suspicion away, and so by contrivance with his
> espoused, an opportunity one night, was given to the said Thomas and his
> barque's crew to take on board the said Con, as it were by force, he making
> no noise for fear of being stabbed.

According to another account, Conn's wife Éilis assisted by smuggling
in rope in two big cheeses, 'the meat being neatly taken out, and filled with
cords, well packed in, and the holes handsomely made up again'. Annas Dobbin
opened the cell and Conn lowered himself down the rope to the waiting boat
to be taken across to Largs and freedom. At Braidstane Castle the deal was
finalised. In return for half his lands, the Laird would obtain for Conn a royal
pardon. Conn and Hugh then travelled to Westminster, there to meet George
Montgomery who for some months had been serving as chaplain to the King.
James received Conn graciously, knighted Hugh Montgomery and ordered that
the arrangement should be confirmed by letters patent.

It was at this point that two other Scots at court intervened. They were Sir
James Fullerton and James Hamilton, like Montgomery, natives of Ayrshire.
Both had lived for many years in Dublin, teaching there and acting as informers
for King James. Fullerton, now a gentleman of the bedchamber, approached the
King, saying that 'the lands granted to Sir Hugh and Con were vast territories,
too large for two men of their degree'. He reminded King James that he had
granted land in the Ards peninsula in 1604 to a London merchant, Thomas
Ireland, in return for £1,678 6s 8d, and that Hamilton had bought this patent.

King James quickly revised the grant, dividing Upper Clandeboye equally
between Conn O'Neill, Sir Hugh Montgomery and James Hamilton. The
crucial condition of the patents issued to Montgomery and Hamilton was that
they 'should promise to inhabit the said territory and lands with English or
Scotchmen'.

EPISODE 44

'PARISHES MORE WASTED THAN AMERICA'

During the final stages of the conquest of Ulster Queen Elizabeth's commanders had devastated the countryside by systematically destroying crops, burning stores of butter and corn, and slaughtering cattle. Sir Arthur Chichester, in command at Carrickfergus, concluded that it was not enough merely to attack the Irish for 'a million swords will not do them so much harm as one winter's famine'. The inevitable result was famine, a man-made horror that may have reduced the native population of Ulster by as much as one third. Lord Deputy Mountjoy observed 'there is growing so extreme a famine amongst them that there will be no possibility for them to subsist'. Fynes Moryson, Lord Deputy Mountjoy's secretary, reported incidents of cannibalism

> and a most horrible spectacle of three children (whereof the eldest was not above ten years old) all eating and gnawing with their teeth the entrails of their mother, upon whose flesh they had fed 20 days past ... roasting it continually by a slow fire.

That was in Down, one of the most devastated counties. And so it was that the great estates in that county granted by King James to his Scottish courtiers, Sir Hugh Montgomery and James Hamilton, had ample room for newcomers, if only because the population had been so drastically reduced by war and starvation.

The King's grant to Hamilton specifically stated that 'the said territories' were 'depopulated and wasted'. The former Lordship of Upper Clandeboye and the Great Ards was divided in April 1605 into three equal parts. Conn O'Neill, the former lord, was left with lands surrounding Castlereagh and its vicinity. The grants to Montgomery and Hamilton were so arranged that 'the sea coasts might be possessed by Scottish men, who would be traders as proper for his Majestie's future advantage'. Montgomery's estates were centred on Newtownards and Donaghadee, and Hamilton's lands included an estate on the western shore of Strangford Lough but were predominantly in north Down about Bangor and Holywood.

Meanwhile, several retired army commanders were also dedicating themselves to 'plantation', to colonisation. These 'servitors' may well have been outraged on hearing of the lenient terms agreed in 1603 with the defeated Hugh O'Neill; but they did not go empty-handed. In September 1603 Sir Henry Docwra had been granted the territory he had made his military base since 1600. It included the building of a dissolved chapel of nuns, the stone tower on what is still called the Bogside, 'with the whole island of Derry and all other buildings, gardens etc. in the said Iland'. Sir Arthur Chichester, appointed Lord Deputy in Mountjoy's place in 1604, urged 'that the city of Derry be cherished and countenanced in her infancy' since the 'erection of it hath cost so much money and lost so many men'. He himself, given Belfast and fertile stretches of south Antrim, was eagerly enticing officers who had served under him to settle here. Sir Thomas Phillips was establishing contacts with Scottish merchants to help him turn the confiscated abbey lands of Coleraine assigned to him into a thriving market. The colonising efforts of these English soldiers were dwarfed, however, by those of two Scottish lairds in County Down.

Montgomery and Hamilton had received their grants on the strict condition that they settle English and Scottish Protestants on their estates – indeed, this was the first time in Irish history that Scots colonists were given equal status with English ones. Both men set about meeting this obligation with considerable determination. During the winter of 1605–6 Sir Hugh returned to Braidstane with the purpose of inducing his neighbours to join him. He found many willing to do so. Initially, they included his wife Elizabeth's brother, John Shaw of Greenock; Patrick Montgomery of Blackhouse, married to Shaw's sister, Christian; Colonel David Boyd; Patrick Shaw, Laird of Kelsonephew; Thomas Nevin, brother to the Laird of Monkredding and Cunningham; Patrick Moore of Deugh, Kirkcudbrightshire; Sir William Edmonston, 7th Laird of Duntreath, from Sterlingshire; and John Neill of Mains-Neill near Braidstane. The surnames of Scots who in 1617 took out letters of denization – that is permission to live in Ireland – include Catherwood, Wyly, Boyle, Harper, Barkley, Hunter, Thompson, Crawford, Adair, Wilson, Cathcart, Maxwell, Fraser, Aiken, Harvey, Semple, Anderson, Martin and Speir. The majority settled on Sir Hugh's estates. Among those colonising the Hamilton estates were families with such names as Maxwell, Rose, Barclay, More and Baylie.

The Montgomery family papers describe the conditions the Scots encountered when first coming over:

We shall wonder how this plantation advanced itself (especially in and about the towns of Donaghadee and Newtown), considering that in the

spring time … those parishes were now more wasted than America (when
Spaniards landed there) … for in all those three parishes aforesaid, 30 cabins
could not be found, nor any stone walls, but ruined roofless churches, and a
few vaults at Gray Abbey, and a stump of an old castle in Newtown, in each
of which some gentlemen sheltered themselves at their first coming over.

It was not long, however, before these Scots were busy erecting houses and
ploughing. This was the beginning of the most successful British colonising
venture in Ireland in the seventeenth century.

EPISODE 45

'EVERY BODY WAS INNOCENTLY BUSY': COLONISING DOWN

It is to the Montgomery Manuscripts, the papers of the family of Sir
Hugh Montgomery, Laird of Braidstane, that we must turn for the most
detailed information on the Scottish plantation in County Down in the
early seventeenth century. 'After a short necessary stay for recruits of money'
and visits to prospective colonists in Edinburgh and Braidstane, Sir Hugh,
accompanied by Conn O'Neill, made their way to Ulster during the spring of
1606. Montgomery made Newtownards – then simply called Newtown – his
main residence. No time was wasted:

> Sir Hugh in the said spring brought with him divers artificers, as smiths,
> masons, carpenters, etc. … They soon made cottages and booths for
> themselves, because sods and saplins of ashes, alders, and birch trees (above
> 30 years old) with rushes for thatch, and bushes for wattle, were at hand.
> And also they made a shelter of the said stump of the castle for Sir Hugh,
> whose residence was mostlie there, as in the centre of being supplied with
> necessaries from Belfast (but six miles thence) who therefore came and set
> up a market in Newton, for profit for both the towns. As likewise in the fair
> summer season (twice, sometimes thrice every week) they were supplied
> from Scotland, as Donaghadee was oftener, because but three hours sail
> from Portpatrick, where they bespoke provisions and necessaries to lade in,

to be brought over by their own or that town's boats whenever wind and weather served them, for there was a constant flux of passengers coming daily over.

I have heard honest old men say that in June, July and August, 1607, people came from Stranraer, four miles and left their horses at the port, hired horses at Donaghadee, came with their wares and provisions to Newton, and sold them, dined there, staid two or three hours, and returned to their houses the same day by bed-time, their land journey but 20 miles. Such was their encouragement from a ready market, and their kind desires to see and supply their friends and kindred, which commerce took quite away evil report of woodkerns, which enviers of planters' industry had raised and brought upon our plantations.

At Newtownards Sir Hugh set about building himself a residence fitting his status:

Some of the priory walls were roofed and fitted for Sir Hugh and his family to dwell in; but the rest of these walls, and other large additions of a gate-house and office-houses ... with coins and window frames, and chimney-pieces, and funnels of freestone, all covered: and the floors beamed with main oak timber, and clad with boards; the roof with oak plank from his Lordship's own woods, and slated with slates out of Scotland; and the floors laid with fir deals out of Norway, the windows were fitly glazed and the edifice thoroly furnished within. This was the work of some time and years, but the same was finished by that excellent Lady (and fit helper mostly in Sir Hugh's absence) because he was by business much and often kept from home, after the year 1608 expired.

It was not long before the plantation in Down was flourishing:

Now every body minded their trades, and the plough, building, and setting fruit trees, etc., in orchards and gardens, and by ditching in their grounds. The old women spun, and the young girls plyed their nimble fingers at knitting – and every body was innocently busy. Now the Golden peaceable age renewed, no strife, contention, querulous lawyers, or Scottish or Irish feuds, between clans and families, and sirnames, disturbing the tranquillity of those times; and the towns and temples were erected, with other great works (even in troublesome times).

The author paints a picture that is far too flattering – for example, he failed to mention the eruption of an unseemly and expensive dispute over property between Sir Hugh Montgomery and James Hamilton. It cannot be disputed, however, that the Scottish colonisation of much of County Down was a solid achievement and that it would continue to develop and spread out from its core in the years to come.

Meanwhile, the man left with just a third portion of the former Lordship of Upper Clandeboye, Conn O'Neill, was struggling. For a start, his close relatives could argue that the two-thirds of his lordship alienated to Montgomery and Hamilton were not, by customary Gaelic law, his to give away. Certainly, the author of the *Montgomery Manuscripts* (1603–1706) was at pains to point out that 'Con's title was bad ... This being the pickle wherein Con was soused, and his best claim but an unquiet possession'. Conn O'Neill had swiftly to familiarise himself with English law and English practice in managing his estates. An early indication of his inability to cope in a new regime was his sale in August 1606 in Slut Neale (roughly between Ballylesson and Drumbo) of the valuable woods of four townlands to Montgomery.

EPISODE 46

PLANTING THE ISLES WITH 'ANSWERABLE IN-LANDS SUBIECTS'

Before ever turning his attention to Ulster, indeed before the 1603 Union of Crowns, King James prided himself on being a dedicated promoter of plantation. Always acutely short of money, this King of Scots convinced himself that there was great untapped wealth in the Highlands and Islands, parts of the realm – to his dismay – which at best contributed pitiful sums to the royal coffers. These lands, as he wrote himself, were 'maist commodious ... alsuelill be the fertillitie of the ground as be riche fischeingis be sey'. However, the backwardness of the indigenous people here had made the region 'altogidder unprofitable baithe to thame selffis and to all uthiris'.

King James had this vision of transforming these benighted, rebellious, Catholic, Gaelic-speaking Highlanders and Islanders into law-abiding, loyal, English-speaking, God-fearing Protestants ... who, of course, would willingly pay their dues to enrich the Crown.

He had been drafting proposals to colonise these parts of his realm with loyal Lowlanders since the 1580s. Finally, the King had been spurred into action when Angus MacDonald, chief of Dunyveg, decided that he should join Hugh O'Neill, the Earl of Tyrone, and Red Hugh O'Donnell, in their rebellion against Queen Elizabeth. James had good reason: he could not afford to affront the Virgin Queen as he was her designated successor.

Not known for bravery on the battlefield, James repeatedly shied away from personally leading military expeditions but in 1596 he made an exception. As he advanced towards Islay, he explained why he was on the march:

> Angus accumpanyed with a nowmer of rebellious and disobedient subjectis, inhabitantis of the Ilis, ar myndit, as the Kingis Majestie informit, to transporte thameselffis ouer to Irland, and to joyne with the Erll of Tyrrown, O'Doneill, and uthiris of the rebellious people of that land.

James MacDonnell, Lord of the Glynns and the Route, anxious to retain the friendship of the King of Scots, especially as to Elizabeth he was a deadly enemy, decided to support King James against Angus, kinsman though he was. Not long before, this MacDonnell lordship had straddled the Narrow Sea; now it was in the process of splitting into two, with Angus as chief on one side and James chief on the other. In 1597 this Lord of the Glynns, along with his brother Randal Arannach, set sail to engage Angus MacDonald. Along with King James's troops, the warriors from the Antrim Glens triumphed. The grateful King of Scots promptly knighted James MacDonnell.

The terms meted out to Angus MacDonald were harsh. He was 'as soon as convenient' to 'remove himself, his family and dependers ... out of the bounds of Kintyre and the isle of Giga' and 'keep good order in Yla, Colonsay, and Jura' to make way for 'lieges to whom his Majesty has granted title to any part thereof'. In short, King James wanted Angus to evict his entire clan from Kintyre and accept new Crown tenants on his other lands. Angus understandably refused. The fierce resistance he and his people put up resulted in Lowlanders given estates here in the Isles giving up and returning home.

King James got his parliament to pass an act in 1597 demanding that all chiefs in the Highlands and Islands, on the pain of forfeiture, produce their charters proving entitlement to their lands. This led to an orgy of charter forging and widespread fabrication of genealogies. The MacLeod chief of the Isle of Lewis could not or would not present his title deeds. His lands were confiscated. Making arrangements for 'inplanting' civilised Lowlanders, the King laid out his scheme for creating 'colonies among them of answerable In-lands subiects, that within short time may reforme and civilize the best inclined among them; rooting out or transporting the barbarous or stubborne sorte, and planting ciuilitie in their roomes.'

Ludovic, Earl of Lennox, agreed to lead the 'Fife Adventurers', a group of 12 men granted land on Lewis. Accompanied by around 500 settlers in the late autumn of 1599, they made landfall at Stornoway only to meet fierce opposition immediately from the MacLeods. If any opposition was shown, the King gave the Adventurers full permission to employ 'slauchter, mutilation, fyre-raising, or utheris inconvenieties'. The would-be colonists made themselves a fortified enclave at South Beach near Stornoway but they had to endure relentless attacks and the harshness of a Hebridean winter. Those colonists not dead of starvation or already murdered fled Lewis in 1601.

King James refused to give up. A second attempt was made to plant Lewis in 1604. It also failed. In the end it was another Gaelic chief, Archibald Campbell, the Earl of Argyll, who crushed the MacLeods and their allies, the MacGregors – indeed, the name of MacGregor was proclaimed as 'altogidder abolisheed'. The Earl of Argyll allowed MacKenzie clansmen to take over Lewis. In other words, James's schemes of colonisation in the Isles failed completely.

Just on the other side of the Narrow Sea they were to succeed. After his brother Sir James MacDonnell had been poisoned in 1601, Randal Arannach became Lord of the Glynns. To the King's great satisfaction, Randal was to create an enduring plantation in County Antrim, Randal's colonists being Presbyterian Lowlanders, many of them refugees from the failed plantations in Islay, Kintyre and Lewis.

EPISODE 47

COLONISING COUNTY ANTRIM

Sir Randal Arannach MacDonnell, Lord of the Glynns and the Route, Catholic and Gaelic-speaking though he was, made vigorous attempts to encourage Protestant Lowland Scots to settle on his estates. This was primarily to forge good relations with King James – after all he had fought with Hugh O'Neill, Earl of Tyrone, and Red Hugh O'Donnell, Lord of Tír Chonaill, against the Crown. Sir Randal had another reason. Much of Ulster was in a ruinous condition as a result of the scorched earth policy so ruthlessly and successfully pursued by English army commanders, and the MacDonnell lands were no exception. One patent stated in 1604 that 'the whole region of the county Antrim' was 'wasted by rebellion'.

Sir Randal was desperately short of ready cash and, in short, his estates sorely needed more inhabitants capable of bringing the land into full production and, crucially, capable also of paying rent. There is little doubt that the early success of Sir Hugh Montgomery and James Hamilton, lairds from Ayrshire, in settling Lowland Scots in County Down encouraged MacDonnell to seek new tenants on the other side of the North Channel. A supply was immediately available: Lowlanders planted on Kintyre at King James's behest by the Earl of Argyll had been forced to take flight after ferocious attacks in 1607 by Angus MacDonald of Dunyveg, former lord of the territory and, incidentally, Sir Randal's cousin. They gratefully signed leases to become tenants on MacDonnell lands and brought their own cattle with them.

Other Lowland Scots followed those driven out of Kintyre, particularly would-be colonists forced by the MacLeods to flee the Isle of Lewis. At the same time, more Gaelic-speaking Islanders joined their Hebridean relatives in the Glens. Between 1609 and 1626 Sir Randal allotted lands, ranging between 150 and 300 acres each to 25 Lowland Scots on long leases, many of them for 101 years and one for 301 years. These men, in turn, sublet farms to their relatives, neighbours and Scottish tenants. John Shaw of Greenock leased a large estate at Ballygalley – the castle he built there in 1625 is still in use as part of a hotel. Protestant Lowlanders were particularly attracted to the fertile lands of the Route, in particular the Boyds from Ayrshire and Largyan in Bute, the Hunters of Hunterston in Ayrshire, the Crawfords, some from Kilbirnie in Argyll, and Stevensons from the Lothians and Ayrshire.

Sir Randal made a futile attempt to recover lost lands in Kintyre and the Isles in 1607 but he lost out to the Earl of Argyll, the powerful head of the Campbell clan. Argyll obtained a ruling from the Scottish Lords of the Council to eject the inhabitants of Kintyre and a great many took refuge in the Glens of Antrim. Muster rolls and later surveys indicate where these Hebridean Scots settled. Leading families included the McAuleys in Glenarm and Carnlough and about Cushendall; the McCormicks in Glenshesk, Glenmakeeran and Carnlough; the Magills in Glenarm and Carnlough; the McKays in Glencloy, Glenarm and Glendun; the McNeills in Glenmakeeran, Cushendun and Carnlough; the

McAllisters in Glenaan and Glenariff; and a Highland branch of the Stewarts, originally of Norman origin, favoured Ballintoy.

Other Lowland Scots proved themselves vigorous colonisers in other parts of County Antrim. William Edmonston of Duntreath, Stirlingshire, originally crossed to Ireland with Sir Hugh Montgomery. In 1609 he moved from Down to Antrim where he bought 2,870 acres at Broadisland in the barony of Belfast near Carrickfergus. Here he built two 'slated houses'. Clearly William Edmonston decided that his future lay in Ireland because he mortgaged his Duntreath estates in Scotland for 15 years. William Adair, who settled in the barony of Toome, came from Kinhilt in Wigtonshire. Like Edmonston, he was prepared to lose most of his lands in Scotland to make a success of his venture in Antrim. In 1620 Adair was forced to sell some of his Wigtonshire land to Sir Hugh Montgomery as he was put to the horn (that is, taken to court in Scotland) for debt. Ballymena owes its early development largely to Adair.

English army officers, veterans of the Elizabethan conquest of Ulster, acquired estates in the Lagan valley and on the north side of Belfast Lough. The largest proprietor was Sir Arthur Chichester, appointed Lord Deputy in 1605. Others included Chichester's kinsmen Faithful Fortescue and Henry Upton; Sir Moses Hill; Sir Fulke Conway and his agent Major George Rawdon in Killultagh; Captain Hugh Clotworthy at Massereene; and Captain Roger Langford at Muckamore. On several of these estates Scots made up at least half of the British tenants brought in.

Chichester ordered the firing of more than a million bricks to build a town at Belfast but the duties of his office, as King James's chief governor in Ireland, weighed heavily on his shoulders – never more so than when, in September 1607, he got news of the Flight of the Earls from Lough Swilly.

EPISODE 48

THE FLIGHT OF THE EARLS

In March 1603 Hugh O'Neill, Earl of Tyrone, submitted after nine years of rebellion against the English Crown. At Mellifont he accepted terms more generous than he had dared to hope for. Provided he renounced the title of 'The O'Neill' and handed the church lands of Ulster to the Crown, the Earl was allowed to retain his lordship over most of his traditional territory. Elizabeth had died just a few days before and Lord Deputy Mountjoy was uncertain what the new King James intended. In June O'Neill and the newly elected Lord of Tír Chonaill, Rory O'Donnell, travelled with Mountjoy to London. There they were well received by King James, and O'Donnell was created the Earl of Tyconnell. This royal pardon infuriated those English officers who had risked their lives campaigning in Ireland. One of them wrote angrily:

> I have lived to see that damnable rebel Tyrone brought to England, honoured and well liked ... How I did labour after that knave's destruction! I adventured perils by sea and land, was near starving, ate horse flesh in Munster, and all to quell that man, who now smileth in peace at those who did hazard their lives to destroy him.

Such men felt they should have been rewarded with lands confiscated from the former rebels.

Officials appointed by King James now set out to undermine the Earl of Tyrone and other Gaelic lords in Ulster. Their moment came when their principal spokesman, Sir Arthur Chichester, was appointed Lord Deputy of Ireland in 1605. Chichester was warmly supported by the Attorney-General, Sir John Davies, who was eager to impose English law on 'the Irishry in the province of Ulster ... the most rude and unreformed part of Ireland, and the seat and nest of the last great rebellion, that the next generation will in tongue and every way else become English.'

And so Chichester and Davies whittled away at O'Neill's authority, so that, the Lord Deputy reported, 'now the law of England, and the Ministers thereof, were shackles and handlocks unto him, and the garrisons planted in his country were as pricks in his side'. Meanwhile the Earl of Tyrconnell's position was becoming desperate. A royal commission ruled that MacSweeneys, O'Boyles and others need no longer pay rent to the Earl.

A Scot played a key role in making life intolerable for the earls. George Montgomery, brother of Sir Hugh Montgomery, the Laird of Braidstane who was busy colonising much of County Down, had been appointed Bishop of Derry, Raphoe and Clogher. The Bishop took over fertile lands in Donegal, which had been a vital source of income for Tyrconnell, leaving the Earl impoverished. Then Montgomery laid covetous eyes on swathes of the Earl of Tyrone's lands. Tyrone wrote to the King, complaining that:

The Lord Bishop of Derry, not contented with the great living Your Majesty has been pleased to bestow on him, seeketh to have a great part of my lands, whereunto none of his predecessors ever made claim.

Cúchonnacht Maguire, Lord of Fermanagh, had had enough humiliation at the hands of English officials. A royal commission had taken away half his ancestral lands and, finding the new regime unbearable, in great secrecy Maguire brought a ship from France to Lough Swilly on 25 August 1607. Rory O'Donnell had also had enough, but fearing that he would be beggared by the Crown, Tyrconnell did not hesitate to take his family aboard. Meanwhile Tyrone had become convinced that his life was in danger – indeed the Spanish ambassador in London believed so, observing: 'I know that they wish to kill him by poison or by any possible means'.

On Friday 4 September Maguire, O'Donnell and O'Neill raised anchor at Rathmullan and sailed away along with 90 followers. Fierce contrary winds forced them to change course for France. From there they travelled to Spanish Flanders. The Earls had hoped that the King of Spain, Philip III, would fit them out with an army to allow them to return and drive the English out of Ireland. But Philip, close to bankruptcy, had made his peace with King James; he would not even permit these Irish to go to Spain. Instead they were sent to Rome; there followed barren years of exile, a stream of letters to Philip and many untimely deaths from fever.

This was a momentous turning-point in the history of Ulster. An Irish Crown officer wrote to the King's secretary: 'The undutiful departure of the Earls of Tyrone, Tyrconnell, and Maguire offers a good occasion for a plantation'. Chichester agreed and penned this advice to King James:

If His Majesty will, during their absence, assume the countries into his possession, divide the lands amongst the inhabitants ... and will bestow the rest upon servitors and men of worth here, and withal bring in colonies of civil people of England and Scotland ... the country will ever after be happily settled.

King James found much to attract him in his Lord Deputy's proposal.

THE REBELLION OF SIR CAHIR O'DOHERTY

K ing James hesitated following the flight abroad of the Earls of Tyrone and Tyrconnell in September 1607. Could he really confiscate all those lands in Ulster simply because their owners had left the country? Attorney-General Sir John Davies assured him that he could. Lord Deputy Sir Arthur Chichester added that there was no time like the present for 'the whole realm, and especially the fugitive countries, are more utterly depopulated and poor than ever before for many hundred years'. And so the earls were condemned as outlaws and, in December 1607 the lands of the departed Gaelic lords were confiscated and put in the possession of the King.

The King now threw himself with enormous enthusiasm into this grand project, which he named the 'Plantation of Ulster'. It would give him a unique opportunity to reward at little cost the many who had claims on his purse. The conquest of Ireland had cost Queen Elizabeth at least two million pounds. King James was left with a huge debt; many merchants and suppliers might be delighted to be paid with landed estates. Certainly his 'servitors', that is, the army commanders and senior civil servants, looked forward to generous grants of land in Ulster. Above all, the successful plantation of much of Antrim and Down – which had begun at the start of his reign in 1603 – gave every indication that the colonisation of the rest of Ulster could be a triumphant success.

The outline plan was to colonise in six counties: Tyrone, Armagh, Fermanagh, Cavan, Tyrconnell and Coleraine. The last two counties would be slightly altered in size shortly afterwards and be renamed Donegal and Londonderry. In the spring of 1608, while the King and his courtiers began discussions on the colonising scheme, Chichester and Davies set out from Dublin to survey the lands abandoned by the earls and to garner all the evidence they could to give legal justification for their confiscation. On their way they got news of a fresh rebellion in the north. This was to bring profound changes to the scheme of plantation.

Perhaps no Gaelic nobleman in Ulster was more deserving of the gratitude of the Crown than Sir Cahir O'Doherty, Lord of Inishowen. As a fifteen-year-old, O'Doherty had joined the Crown forces at Derry in 1600 and he had been knighted on the battlefield for his bravery. He took particular care to abide by English law and was chairman of the grand jury that had judged the departed earls to be guilty of treason. However, he was treated with contempt again and again by the Governor of Derry, Sir George Paulet, and after the governor had punched him in the face during an argument in the spring of 1608, O'Doherty rose in rebellion. He seized the fort of Culmore on 18 April and the following night laid siege to Derry, took it and set it on fire. Susan Montgomery, wife of the Bishop of Derry, was taken prisoner and Doe Castle fell soon after.

O'Doherty was quickly joined by his neighbours the MacDavitts, the O'Gallahers and the MacSweeneys and by many O'Hanlons further south. It seems likely that they believed that the Earl of Tyrone was about to return with a Spanish army. Why had Derry fallen when its garrison actually outnumbered its attackers? To recover his reputation, Chichester had to act quickly. He ordered a general hosting and, outflanked by experienced veterans, O'Doherty was cornered at Kilmacrenan and killed by the Rock of Doon 'by a happy shot which smote him on the head'. With five Royal Navy vessels, Sir Henry Folliott, Governor of Ballyshannon, pursued the remnants who had taken refuge on the islands while Marshal Sir Richard Wingfield crossed the mountains to Glenveagh, where the O'Gallahers made a last but futile stand in their island castle.

The English were getting to know the province they had conquered from end to end, parts of which Chichester admitted had been only recently as inaccessible as 'the kingdom of China'. O'Doherty's head was taken to Dublin to be skewered on a pike at Newgate. Surviving rebels were rounded up and, rather than being hanged summarily as they could be by martial law, were sent on to be tried for treason. When duly convicted they could then be hanged, drawn and quartered in the usual grisly way.

The government had already returned to the task of planning the colonisation of the confiscated lands of the earls of Tyrone and Tyrconnell. The scheme being perfected in London would soon be far more grandiose than originally envisaged. All the lands of six entire counties would now be confiscated. The enterprise would surely be jeopardised, Davies wrote, 'if the number of civil persons who are to be planted do not exceed the number of natives, who will quickly overgrow them as weeds overgrow the good corn'.

INVITING SCOTS TO PLANT

Attorney-General Sir John Davies was in Ulster as Sir Cahir O'Doherty's rebellion was being crushed. From Coleraine he wrote to King James assuring him that he had six counties 'now in demesne and actual possession in this province; which is a greater extent of land than any prince in Europe has to dispose of'. This could not be denied. Soon after, Davies would make his way to London, there to lay out in detail his advice on how the six confiscated counties of Ulster should be colonised with loyal British subjects. Lord Deputy Sir Arthur Chichester stayed behind in Ireland, but he, too, had recommendations to make which he sent over with the title 'Certain Notes and Remembrances'.

Perhaps the most original proposal made by Chichester was that Scottish as well as English Protestants should be invited to be become colonisers in Ulster. The Lord Deputy's proposal immediately appealed to King James – the Plantation of Ulster now became the great project of his reign which would unite his loyal British subjects, north and south. Indeed, he decided to direct the plantation personally.

Soon after he had news of O'Doherty's rebellion, James ordered that the recruitment of Scottish soldiers for service on the European mainland should stop immediately as they were needed for the 'intended subduing of the Isles' and the 'suppressing of our rebels in Ireland'. Andrew Stewart, Lord Ochiltree, had been putting together an expedition to bring the Western Isles to order and to create there a 'civil society'. Now he was commanded to redirect this force to assist in the suppression of O'Doherty. Shortly afterwards Ochiltree was playing a leading role in persuading his fellow Scots to join him in the Plantation of Ulster.

Some Protestants in Ireland – most notably Matthew de Renzy, a German adventurer who had become a naturalised Englishman – expressed opposition to Scots involvement in colonisation on the island. In both London and Edinburgh it was ignored. To the King the planting of loyal Protestants in the Western Isles and in Ulster was all part of the same project. Earlier, James had sanctioned projects to 'reforme and ciuilize the best inclined' of the inhabitants of the Isles who were 'alluterly barbares' by 'planting colonies among them of answerable In-Lands subiects' and by 'rooting out or transporting the barbarous or stubborne sort, and planting ciuility in their roomes'. After the suppression of O'Doherty's rebellion, Ochiltree was provided with extraordinary powers and those in the Isles who failed to submit he had authority to 'hunt, follow, and pursue with fire and sword ... and to repel and hald them, their wyffis, and bairnis out of the country'. Andrew Knox, Bishop of the Isles, assisted this process energetically. Because he had been responsible for 'reducing of the ignorant and wicked people of our Isles to the acknowledging of God and obedience of the King's Majesty', Knox was to be translated to the diocese of Raphoe in 1610 in order to have the 'ignorant multitude reclaimed from their superstitious and popish opinions and reduced to the acknowledging of God and His true worship'.

Towards the end of 1608 Sir Alexander Hay, Secretary to the Scottish Privy council, gave enthusiastic backing for the active participation of his fellow countrymen in the Plantation of Ulster. His colleagues agreed and – even before the plan of plantation was finalised – the council issued a proclamation on 28 March 1609, to be published on 28 March 1609. It seems that much of the text was written by King James himself:

> Forsameikle as the Kingis Maiestie haueing resolued to reduce and setle vndre a perfyte obedience the north pairt of the Kingdome of Ireland ... his Maiestie, for this effect, hes tane a verie princelie and good course, alswell for establischeing of religioun, justice, and ciuilitie within the saidis boundis, as for planting of colonies thairin, and distributeing of the same boundis to lauchfull, ansuerable, and weill affected subjiectis, vpon certane easie, tolerable, and profitable conditionis, and although thair be no want of grite nomberis of the cuntrey people of England, who, with all glaidnes, wald imbrace the saidis conditionis, and transport thame selfiss, with their families, to Yreland, and plenische the saidis hail boundis sufficientlie with inhabitis, yit, his sacred Maiestie, out of his vnspeikable love and tender affectioun towards his Maiesties antient and native subiectis of this kingdome ... hes bene pleasit to mak chose of thame to be Partnairis with his saidis subiectis of England, in the distribution foirsaid ...

The response to this proclamation was so immediate that within a very short space of time the Scottish Privy Council was able to draw up a list of 77 leading citizens, with sureties, who advanced claims to a total of 141,000 acres in Ulster. Fearing there would not be enough land left for Englishmen, courtiers in London decided that was far too many.

MAKING ULSTER VISIBLE – A CIVILISING ENTERPRISE WHICH WOULD 'ESTABLISH THE TRUE RELIGION OF CHRIST AMONG MEN ALMOST LOST IN SUPERSTITION'

C olonists need maps. Only when the Elizabethan conquest was drawing to a close did recognisable maps of Ulster become available. Making them was a dangerous business. One cartographer, Francis Jobson, observed that Ulster was 'inhabited with a most savage and rebellious people from whose cruelty God only by his divine power delivered me being every hour in danger to lose my head'. The man who produced the best maps of the province, Thomas Bartlett, was, indeed, decapitated in Donegal in 1609: as Attorney-General Sir John Davies explained, 'when he came into Tyrconnell the inhabitants took off his head, because they would not have their country discovered'.

Davies was a member of the plantation planning committee in London. In January 1609 these courtiers published a comprehensive scheme describing how the land was to be divided up and outlining conditions to be observed by the grantees. Soon, however, it became obvious that, in order to make clear grants, a detailed survey would have to be made.

To measure the lands of six entire counties in Ulster before grants were made was quite impossible, at least in the time scale envisaged. Therefore, 'to avoid His Majesty's further charge', the government decided to carry out a survey by inquisition, that is, by talking to the locals. A commission, headed by Davies, was appointed to sit in Dungannon. The problem facing these commissioners was that the native Irish did not measure their lands in acres or by anything equivalent. The largest unit in a Gaelic lordship was a *baile biatach* (literally, a territory that provides food, *bia*), anglicised as a ballybetagh and usually converted by the English into subdivisions of counties known as baronies. Each ballybetagh was the landed territory of a corporate kin-group or sept, such as the O'Hagans, electing a sublord, the *uirí*. In some places ballybetaghs had been divided into quarters or *sessiaghs* (that is, sixths). The basic land unit in each ballybetagh, quarter and sessiagh was what the English were to describe as 'townlands', known as 'ballyboes' in much of Ulster, as 'tates' in County Fermanagh and parts of County Tyrone, and as 'polls', primarily in County Cavan.

The size of these townlands was based on the productivity of the soil: in fertile areas they would therefore be small by comparison with those in mountainous or less fertile ones. Imagine how perplexing it was then to the English – to say the least, the rationale behind this Gaelic system of marking out land units was very imperfectly understood by the commissioners. Rather too hastily they decided that a townland was made up of 60 acres of 'profitable' land and that a ballybetagh of 16 townlands was the equivalent of 1,000 acres (405 hectares). Much trouble was to arise from these assumptions.

A second survey was commissioned in the spring of 1609, headed this time by Sir Josias Bodley, inspector of fortifications in Ireland. The surveyors, Davies explained:

> were sent forth into each barony ... and in their perambulation took notes ... These surveyors, being returned to the camp, out of their notes drew up cards or maps wherein every ballibo is named and placed in his proper situation.

Bodley further explained:

> We thought it our readiest course that ... we should call unto us out of every barony, such persons as by their experience in the country could give us the name and quality of every ballibo, quarter, tate or other common measure in any of the precincts of the same; how they butted or mered interchangeably the one on the other. By which means and other necessary helps, we contrived those maps.

The assistance Bodley and his team received from local people – described by Davies as 'the ancient natives, especially such as had been rent gatherers and sergeants to the Irish lords' – was vital. He noted that many of the locals 'spoke good Latin and that readily'. They made it possible to name each townland and determine its boundaries. Not all the Irish were so cooperative: it was during this survey that Bartlett was beheaded.

Brought over to London, the maps were beautifully coloured in. King James spent hours eagerly poring over them. The project would be, the King observed, a civilising enterprise which would 'establish the true religion of Christ among men almost lost in superstition'. Lord Deputy Chichester declared that he would rather 'labour with his hands in the plantation of Ulster than dance or play in that of Virginia'. Then, in April 1610, the final scheme was published with the title 'Conditions to be observed by the British Undertakers of the escheated lands in Ulster', usually referred to as the 'Printed Book' and sometimes as the 'Articles of Plantation'. From all over Britain prospective colonists rushed forward to get a copy to read the terms and conditions for planting the 'escheated' – that is the confiscated – lands of Ulster.

EPISODE 52

THE PRINTED BOOK

The 'Printed Book', the title usually given to the volume issued in April 1610 detailing the terms and conditions for grantees in the Plantation of Ulster, formally launched what was to be the most ambitious scheme of colonisation in western Europe in modern times. The lands of six entire counties – Armagh, Fermanagh, Cavan, Donegal, Tyrone and what would shortly be named Londonderry – were to be colonised. Antrim and Down were already being planted and Ulster's ninth county, Monaghan, was excluded because arrangements made in the 1590s were thought to be satisfactory. The confiscated land in each county was divided into 'precincts', and each one subdivided into great, middle and small 'proportions', estates of 2,000, 1,500 and 1,000 acres (809, 607 and 405 hectares).

The largest group of colonists, known as 'Undertakers', had to clear their estates completely of native Irish inhabitants and undertake to plant 24 English or 'inland' Scots who had taken the Oath of Supremacy – that is, Protestants – from at least 10 families on every 1,000 acres, and pay a 'quit rent' to the King of £5 6s 8d per annum. Each undertaker had strictly specified building obligations: 'a stone house with a strong court or bawne about it', for example, on each great proportion. Undertakers were to 'draw their tenants to build houses for themselves and the families … near the principal house or bawne, as well as for their mutual defence and strength, as for the making of villages and townships' – in other words, isolated farmhouses would not be permitted.

Servitors, army commanders and other senior servants of the Crown were to get about 15 per cent of the lands, rather less than they expected. However, the most prominent servitor, Lord Deputy Sir Arthur Chichester, had already been granted almost the entire peninsula of Inishowen as a reward for crushing O'Doherty's rebellion in 1608. Servitors were not obliged to plant but, if they did, their quit rent was reduced from £10 13s 4d to £5 6s 8d per 1,000 acres.

Servitors and favoured Irish were to have their estates in the same precincts, so that ex-officers would be in a good position to keep a watchful eye on the natives. Those 'deserving Irish' granted proportions were to adopt English farming methods, to build houses in the English style, and to run their estates on the same lines as could be found in the English Pale around Dublin – in short, to give up the taking of 'Irish exactions' from those under them in return for 'rents certaine' and pay the Crown £10 13s 4d per 1,000 acres each year.

All ecclesiastical lands, amounting to around 20 per cent of the total acreage to be planted, were to be assigned to the state Church. In addition, 60 acres (24 hectares) of glebe land were to be set aside for every 1,000 acres (405 hectares) for the upkeep of a parish clergyman and his family. Land was apportioned for the upkeep of a 'free school' in each county. Substantial estates were earmarked to provide a secure income for Trinity College, Dublin. Deadlines were set for arriving, colonising, building and rent payment, and conditions were laid down for building towns, bringing in craftsmen, founding schools and erecting parish churches.

Payment of rent was not to begin until 29 September 1614. The period of compulsory residence was to begin on 29 September 1610 – an almost impossibly tight deadline insisted on by the King who wanted no delay.

Chichester had not been a member of the committee in London that had drawn up the scheme of plantation. When he read it, he was deeply perturbed. He doubted if the undertakers, granted over 40 per cent of the acreage, had the resources to carry out their obligations on such large estates. The most experienced servitors, including two Scots commanders, Patrick Crawford and William Stewart, got only 15 per cent of the land, not sufficient to carry out the defensive role expected of them. Above all, the 'deserving' Irish favoured with grants had not been left with enough land, one fifth of the confiscated acreage, and some had these estates only during their lifetimes. This, the Lord Deputy believed, would threaten the stability of the entire plantation.

The original plan of allocating estates to undertakers by lottery had been dropped in favour of giving them to 'consorts' of English and Scots in each precinct. This meant that those Irish fortunate enough to get grants were likely to get estates outside the areas where they lived. Since undertakers could not let any land to Irish tenants this meant that natives – from the Gaelic gentry down to the humblest labourers – would have to uproot themselves and squeeze into those precincts set aside for servitors and the 'deserving' Irish. However, this arrangement suited Scottish undertakers particularly; they were anxious to be allowed to group together with relatives, neighbours and acquaintances from their home localities.

EPISODE 53

'MAKE SPEED, GET THEE TO ULSTER'

B y the end of July 1609 65 Scots had applied to the Scottish Council to become undertakers in the Plantation of Ulster. They sought to colonise 120,000 acres in total. Since Scots and English were to be treated equally, it soon became clear in London that too many Scots had applied for too much land. King James then took charge himself, selecting personally who would be the grantees. Revised plantation articles, issued in August, assigned specific precincts or baronies either to Scots or English planters.

This revision was in part due to the fact that the King had persuaded the London Companies to become undertakers. They were to be assigned the entire county of Coleraine, augmented by the barony of Loughinsholin detached from county Tyrone, nine townlands from County Antrim in order to include Coleraine, and a slice of Tyrconnell to make Derry available to the Londoners. Tyrconnell was renamed County Donegal and the enlarged county given to the Londoners was now named Londonderry. In the remaining five counties of the plantation, the Scots were apportioned nine precincts, two each in Donegal, Cavan, Fermanagh and Tyrone, and one in County Armagh.

Each precinct was to have a chief undertaker and the King chose those for the nine Scottish ones with particular care. He had to be sure that the men he picked had the resources required, heeding Lord Deputy Sir Arthur Chichester's advice that men of 'rank and quality' should be picked. Some were the cream of Scotland's aristocracy and the first to be chosen were the King's cousins, Esmé

Stewart, Lord Aubigny, and his brother Ludovic Stewart, the Duke of Lennox. Lennox had served King James as ambassador to France and had been involved in the abortive attempt to plant the Isle of Lewis in 1598. Aubigny had helped to negotiate the Union of the Crowns of Scotland and England in 1603. James Hamilton, Earl of Abercorn, it was observed, was 'induced' by the King to become a chief undertaker 'for a countenance and strength to the rest'.

Once the chief undertakers had been appointed, the business of selecting the 50 ordinary ones could begin. Far more applied for estates than were available. Lord Balfour, one of the chief undertakers, commented that in making his selection he had to reject 'divers famous and ansuerable gentilmen'. Men of substantial property, with experience in estate management, were preferred. All merchants, including wealthy ones from Edinburgh and Glasgow, were rejected. Most of those selected were related to the chief undertakers; apart from the noblemen, 11 were knights; and, no doubt as a result of the King's intervention, 10 were servants of the Crown. The great majority came from the Lowlands and the south-west: no fewer than 11 from Ayrshire; 8 from Haddington; 6 from Wigton; and Renfrew, Lanark, Stirling, Dumbarton, Edinburgh and Linlithgow were well represented. The unruly Borders, and the Highlands and Isles, provided no undertakers – Chichester had warned that if Islanders or Highlanders were chosen the result would be 'more trouble and less profit' than if the Irish were left in possession.

Undertakers next embarked on the task of persuading relatives, friends, neighbours, farmers and craftsmen to become tenants on their new estates. Printing presses churned out pamphlets to encourage British Protestants to join the enterprise. An English undertaker, Thomas Blenerhasset, argued that 'goodly Ulster for want of people [is]unmanured, her pleasant fields and riche groundes, they remain … desolate':

> Depopulated Ulster … presents her-selfe (as it were) in a ragged sad sabled robe, ragged (indeed) there remayneth nothing but ruynes and desolation, with very little showe of any humanitie: of herself she aboundeth with many the best blessings of God … make speede, get thee to Ulster, serve God be sober …
>
> Art thou rich, possessed with much revenue? make speede without racking of rents or other offencive meanes; thou shalt doe God and thy Prince excellent service … use there thy talent, it will be quickly a million.

And make speed to get to Ulster the Scots did. Farming equipment and cattle had to be assembled and transport arranged. Patents entitling them to their estates had to be made out. All this made it well-nigh impossible to meet the deadline of getting to Ireland by 24 June 1610. Parties of Scots could be found making their way to the ports. One group, led by Lord Balfour of Burley and Bernard Lindsay, a groom of the bedchamber, reached Ayr early in August. There the burgesses of the town entertained them with 'sweetmeats, confeittis and sugar'. Meanwhile the Lord Deputy had travelled up from Dublin to meet the undertakers as they arrived. Burley joined him in his precinct of Knockninny in Fermanagh on 13 August 1610.

Chichester wrote that the Scots arrived 'with greater port and better accompanied and attended' than the English, 'but', he added, 'it may be with less money in their purses'.

'GREAT THINGS MOVE SLOWLY'

By the late summer of 1610, 44 of the 59 Scottish undertakers granted 'proportions' or estates in the Plantation of Ulster had arrived. Many were shocked to find that the countryside was still ravaged by the recent wars. Everywhere buildings were in ruin and there was scarcely one church with a roof intact. Both Alexander and John Achmutie, court servants from Edinburgh, after just a few days' visit, sold their proportions in Tullyhunco precinct in Cavan to the purveyor of the King's mines in Scotland, Sir James Craig. George Smailholm from Leith took one look at his estate in Fermanagh and went straight home, never to return. Lord Burley, with a neighbouring proportion by Lough Erne, nevertheless, was pleased with his.

The nine chief undertakers, in charge of each precinct, had the first choice of land and they picked estates with fertile soil and close to rivers and loughs for easy access. Though his proportion in the precinct of Strabane included much mountainous land, the Earl of Abercorn had fertile ground on the east bank of the Foyle easily reached from the sea. The King also lent him the services of 25 men from the army to help him get started. Scots from Wigtonshire, given estates in the precinct of Boylagh and Banagh in County Donegal, had to cope with thin acid soil blasted by storms – the chief undertaker there, Sir Robert McClelland, made sure he got an estate well protected from the Atlantic. However, their neighbours in the Scottish precinct of Raphoe had better land, convenient to safe anchorages in Lough Swilly and Lough Foyle.

Because they were arriving in the late summer and the autumn, the planters had to bring enough food with them to tide their tenants over the winter. The devastated lands of Ulster could not supply them and so cattle and grain had to be brought in at great cost from Scotland. This was a considerable burden on Scottish undertakers because they appear to have brought over more families than the English. Undertakers had to erect fortified castles (known as bawns) and their tenants had first to build homes for themselves. The land needed to be ploughed for next year's crop and, breaking the condition of their grants that they were to remove all the natives from their proportions, Scots were not slow to let the humbler Irish stay on and employ them surreptitiously as labourers to help them with building and farming.

Meanwhile King James, rather unreasonably, was fretting that his Plantation of Ulster was falling behind schedule. Lord Deputy Sir Arthur Chichester assured him in October that 'great things move slowly'. The King ordered all undertakers to be present in Ireland by 1 May 1611 on pain of forfeiture. It proved an empty threat. So, in the summer of 1611, Sir George Carew, a former Lord President of Munster, was sent over to head a commission of inquiry. In his rather perfunctory survey report he stated that 17 Scottish undertakers had yet to make an appearance. Appalled by this, the King commissioned another survey in 1613, this time supervised by Sir Josias Bodley, director-general of fortifications in Ireland and brother of the founder of the Bodleian Library in Oxford. Bodley did a thorough job. Work had not yet started on 16 Scottish proportions, it is true, but progress on 25 of them was encouraging. Still bitterly disappointed, the King made fresh threats but he shrank from outright confiscation and contented himself with imposing fines.

His Majesty was especially infuriated by the continued presence of the Irish on undertakers' proportions: he raged that the clearing of natives was 'the fundamental reason' for the plantation. In the previous century, when James was arranging the colonisation of some of the Hebrides by Lowlanders, he had demanded a very clear separation between planters and Islanders. Included in the 'Articlis to be contracted amongst the Societie of the Lewis', published in 1598, was a clause stating that no 'marriage or uther particular freindschip to be any of the societies, without the consent of the hail, with any Hyland man'. The plantation of Lewis had to be aborted because of attacks by 'bludie and wiket Hieland men'.

Actually, he should have been pleased at Bodley's findings. All over Ulster new fortifications were springing up, many of them in the Scots baronial style. Striking examples can be found in County Fermanagh, for example. They include: Tully Castle, Castle Balfour, Crom Castle, Monea Castle and Aghalane Castle. Around 2,200 British males had settled in the 6 counties of the plantation. What is more, unlike most of the English colonising Virginia at the same time, the British had brought their womenfolk with them. From Bodley's report it can be calculated that 490 families, totalling around 1,700 adults, had settled on the Scottish proportions alone. Yet another survey, headed by Captain Nicholas Pynnar in 1619, found that the number of British adults settled in the 6 counties had risen to 4,420. Pynnar did not distinguish between English and Scots but the British population on Scottish estates had more than doubled between 1613 and 1619.

And more colonists were still coming over from Scotland – so many, indeed, that the Scottish Secretary of State complained that the 'cuntrey people of the common sorte do flock over in so greit nowmeris that muche landis ar lastin [lying] waste for lacke of tennentis'.

EPISODE 55

BORDERERS: 'A FRACTIOUS AND NAUGHTY PEOPLE'

During the first days following the death of Queen Elizabeth in 1603 riders broke out from the Borders all along the frontier between Scotland and England, slaughtering, looting, burning, and driving deep into Cumbria and Northumbria in search of plunder. This would be remembered as the 'Ill Week'.

For centuries this wild border country, the 'Debatable Land', had been lawless and violent. Riding nimble unshod ponies, known as 'hobblers', wearing steel helmets and jacks – quilted coats of stout leather sewn with plates of metal or horn – and armed with lances, bills, cutting swords and heavy pistols known as 'dags' – these border reivers brought their reign of terror to a climax in the sixteenth century. Gavin Dunbar, Archbishop of Glasgow, excommunicated them in what must be the longest curse in history, running to over 1,500 words:

I curse thair heid and all the haris of thair heid; I curse thair face … thair mouth, thair eise, thair toung, thair teith, thair crag, thair schulderis, thair breast, thair hert, thair stomok, thair bak, thair armes, thair leggis, thair handis, thair feit, and everilk part of thair body, frae the top of thair heid to the soill of thair feit, befoir and behind, within and without …

I denounce, proclaimis, and declares all and sindry the committaris of the said saikles murthris, slauchteris … theiftis and spulezeis, oppinly apon day licht and under silence of nicht …

I condemn thaim perpetualie to the deip pit of hell, the remain with Lucifer and all thair bodeis to the gallowis, first to be hangit, syne [then] revin … with doggis, swine, and other wyld beasts …

It did no good. From Nithsdale, Annandale, Eskdale, Ewesdale, Liddesdale, Teviotdale and Tweeddale the reivers continued to feud with one another and inflict slaughter, destruction and misery on their more peaceful neighbours. But, in the spring of 1603, James VI of Scotland was now also James I of England. The Borders, which he referred to as the 'Middle Shires' of his kingdom, must be thoroughly pacified. A special force, known as the Armed Guard, set up in Dumfries, began the purging process by sending 32 Elliots, Armstrongs, Johnstons and Battys to the gallows and outlawing 140 more. 'Hard trot' pursuits were launched repeatedly from both sides of the Border. Mass hangings followed in Dumfries and Carlisle. The pacification would take seven bloody years.

The most recalcitrant reivers, the Grahams of Eskdale, Leven and Sark, paid a particularly heavy price. The Border Commission, set up by the King in 1605, with special instructions to deal with 'the malefactors of the name of Graham', confiscated the lands of 150 of them, relentlessly carrying out orders to hunt them down forthwith, burn their homes and expel their families. The King later gave special immunity to Sir William Cranston, head of the commission, for executing outlaws without trial.

Then, to the government's astonishment, Sir Ralph Sidley, a landowner in County Roscommon, offered to settle the Grahams on his estate. King James was delighted and compelled local property owners to subscribe to a fund to transport large numbers of them there. In September 1606, after a 'prosperous voyage' to Dublin, they made their way to the west of Ireland. Sidley pocketed most of the money raised. Soon the Grahams were complaining that they could not understand the language, that the land was waste and that 'we … cannot get a penny to buy meat and drink withal'. They scattered and drifted north to Ulster. As Lord Deputy Sir Arthur Chichester reported:

They are now dispersed, and when they shall be placed upon any land together, the next country will find them ill neighbours, for they are a fractious and naughty people.

But once the Plantation of Ulster got under way, undertakers were eager to entice as many British as they could to become their tenants in order to fulfil the conditions of their patents. Meanwhile more Borderers arrived in Ulster, fleeing from harsh justice and repression in their homeland. Fearful of arrest, many went as far west as they could to Donegal and Fermanagh to find landlords who would take them on as tenants. Though their family had served the Crown for generations in organising 'hard trot' pursuits of the reivers, Fermanagh undertakers Sir John and Alexander Home gladly settled them on their estates.

Few Borderers became members of the landed class, but they arrived in Ulster in great numbers to become diligent farmers. A perusal of Ulster's telephone directories would reveal how many Border surnames there are. The commonest are: Johnston (the leading surname in Fermanagh until the census of 2001); Maxwell; Beattie; Elliot; Armstrong; Scott; Kerr; Graham; Crozier; Irvine; Bell; Crichton; Douglas; Robson; Nixon; Young; Davison; Hall; Tait; Burns; Dixon; Trotter; Oliver; Rutherford; Little; Carruthers; Carlisle; Storey; Noble; Forster; Hall; Turnbull; Routledge; and Pringle – and those are only from the Scottish side of the Border.

EPISODE 56

'POISONED WITH POPERY': STRABANE A REFUGE FOR SCOTTISH CATHOLICS

For King James the Plantation of Ulster was nothing less than a civilising enterprise which would 'establish the true religion of Christ among men … almost lost in superstition'. In short, he intended that his grandiose scheme would bring the enlightenment of the Reformation to the most benighted province in his dominions. Yet some of his most determined planters were, in fact, Catholics. How can this be explained?

Before 1603, when Scotland was his only kingdom, James had refused to persecute nobles who remained Catholic. Now, in this Plantation of Ulster, he was anxious to persuade men of position and substance to give a lead. No matter if they adhered to the Catholic faith, provided they were loyal. Already the devout Catholic, Sir Randal MacDonnell, was proving an assiduous coloniser in Co. Antrim.

James Hamilton, created Earl of Abercorn in 1606, was 'induced' by the King to become a chief undertaker in the plantation 'for a countenance and strength to the rest'. He was granted the proportions of Dunnalong and Strabane in Co. Tyrone. Though not a Catholic, his father had been a devoted supporter of Mary Queen of Scots, and many of his relatives were Catholics.

The Earl saw to it that other members of his family received grants, including his brother Sir Claud Hamilton of Shawfield, who got the adjacent proportion of Killeny and the proportion of Eden in the Plumbridge area. From the outset Sir Claud encouraged Scottish Catholics to join him. Robert Algeo, Sir Claud's Catholic agent, established good relations with the native Irish, the O'Devins (now Devines) in particular. Flouting the strict conditions laid out in the Articles of Plantation, the agent leased out land to the natives, most notably to Patrick Groome O'Devin, who rented (by modern measurement) more than 3,000 acres. In November 1613 Patrick travelled to Scotland to deliver £23 10s to Sir Claud in person.

In October 1614 Sir Claud was 'now in Straban taking ordour for his buildingis' but he died before the month was out. As his children were still minors, they were placed under the guardianship of their uncle Sir George Hamilton of Greenlaw, who had acquired lands in Leckpatrick and Ardstraw. Sir George was a Catholic and made sure that William, Sir Claud's eldest son and heir, was brought up a Catholic. The 1st Earl of Abercorn died in 1618, to be succeeded by his eldest son, James. In 1634 the earl's fourth son, George, inherited the manor of Dunnalong. Under the guardianship of his uncle Sir George, he too became a Catholic.

The result was that over ensuing decades many Catholic Scots – no doubt finding that the Kirk was making it increasingly difficult for them to prosper in their homeland – found refuge in this part of Tyrone. Here the Plantation rules were being openly flouted: Catholic Scots were not permitted to hold land in undertakers' proportions. Would action be taken against them?

On 4 January 1630 Thomas Plunkett, 'a man lately reclaimed from Popery', made a deposition before George Downham, the Church of Ireland Bishop of Derry. He reported that there was 'a great meeting of priests last November' led by the Catholic Vicar-General, Tirlagh O'Kelly, who 'lives with Scottish papists at Strabane'. He was often entertained by Claude Hamilton, second son of the 1st Earl of Abercorn, who 'lodged him when the Bishop of Derry and the Provost of Strabane thought to arrest him'. Plunkett added that Sir George Hamilton 'is praised for having made many converts during his residence in Ireland, both at Strabane and at Killybegs'. In his covering letter Downham observed that:

> Sir George Hamilton, who is otherwise a courteous and civil gentleman, has tried to draw people to Popery.
>
> Claude Hamilton, Master of Abercorn, would be a hopeful young gentleman were he not poisoned with Popery, but maintains Papists so much that there will be a revolt in Strabane if any more of the Scotch Papists come there. The Archbishop of Glasgow has sent to me hoping that I will not harbour in my diocese Papists who have been expelled from Scotland.
>
> Sir William Hamilton, a good scholar, was a Papist, and perverted his wife, a daughter of Lord Ards, who had been a Protestant. He used the influence of Blackney, the Jesuit, who perverted Lady Hamilton's waiting maid.

Charles I did impose a heavy fine on Sir William in 1631 but refused to authorise other punitive measures. In any case, many Scottish Presbyterians were also attracted to these Hamilton lands. For example, one of them, Hugh Hamilton from Priestfield in Blantyre, paid rent of 'one hogshead of Gascoign wine, one pound of good pepper, four pounds of loaf sugar and a box of marmalade containing at least two pounds of the preserve'. The muster of settlers capable of bearing arms in the manor of Dunnalong alone came to 106. Here, at least, the Plantation of Ulster was flourishing.

EPISODE 57

SMOULDERING RESENTMENT

In the Plantation of Ulster the English had more capital but the Scots were the more determined colonists. The Scots courtier, Sir William Alexander, observed: 'Scotland by reason of her populousnesse being constrained to disburden her selfe (like the painfull Bees) did every yeere send forth swarmes.'

Indeed, the great migration of Scots to Ulster was well under way, drawn from every class of society. The Reverend Andrew Stewart of Donaghadee claimed that 'from Scotland came many, and from England not a few, yet all of them generally the scum of both nations, who, for debt or breaking and fleeing from justice, or seeking shelter, came thither.'

Though it is true that the Irish Council ordered the imprisonment of vagrant and criminal Scots 'pestring and disturbing the northern plantations of this kingdome', Stewart's assessment was excessively jaundiced. By the end of King James I's reign in 1625 there were no fewer than 8,000 Scots capable of bearing arms in Ulster. Many Scots were now also settling on estates held by English servitors and undertakers. The London Companies' proportions proved particularly attractive to them. In 1637 more than half the inhabitants of the walled city of Londonderry were Scots. Sir Robert McClelland leased 23,000 acres in the Haberdashers' proportion east of the River Roe and persuaded many Scots, particularly from his own county of Kirkcudbrightshire, to become his tenants there. By 1641 perhaps as many as 100,000 Scots and 20,000 English had settled in Ulster.

Yet all was not well. True, the planters generally brought over the specified number of British families, but the undertakers had not cleared the native Irish from their estates as they were required to do. The failure to attempt a measured survey of the confiscated lands had resulted in proportions vastly greater in acreage than that stated in the grants – in most cases seven times greater. The colonists could not possibly farm their lands without the Gaelic Irish; they were too useful as labourers and as tenants prepared to pay high rent to avoid eviction.

Hugh O'Neill, Earl of Tyrone, had died in Rome in 1616. All hope of help from overseas had gone. Nevertheless, with no security of tenure, their burdensome rents set by informal arrangements from year to year, and their status severely reduced, the natives still yearned for a return of the old order. What is more these Gaelic Irish were confronted by alien planters adhering to a variety of Protestantism far distant from their own Catholicism. The Puritan beliefs of the colonists were held not only by the Calvinist Presbyterians but also by the leading bishops of the Established Church, including the Scots: George Montgomery, John Todd, James Spottiswood, James Dundas and Andrew Knox. Franciscans increased their numbers threefold between 1623 and 1639, and instilled a new zeal amongst native Irish Catholics. The uncompromising spirit of the Counter-Reformation faced the inflexible determination of the Puritan settlers. Hostility, suspicion and uncertainty created a dangerously unstable atmosphere in the province.

All over Ulster, with the exception of a few parishes in Antrim and Down, the native Irish everywhere outnumbered the British newcomers. In the forests lurked the woodkerne, landless men and former soldiers of O'Neill, who threatened the settlements. Many were rounded up and shipped to Sweden to fight for King Gustav Adolph. The greater threat, however, was the smouldering resentment of the native Irish who worked and farmed with the colonists.

Those Irish who had been granted estates in the plantation, or otherwise had been able to hold on to their lands, had to adapt to a much-altered regime. Many proved unable to cope. They had to find ready cash to pay regular rents to the King's sheriffs; for marriage portions for female children; for the education of male heirs by attending university or the Inns of Court in London; and for fines, especially for failing to attend Protestant church services. This was a big change from depending on a largely subsistence economy in which livestock was a commonly accepted currency. The incoming British often ruthlessly exploited the frequent inability of Gaelic landowners to understand the newly-introduced legal system and to manage their estates in the English way. The result was that most of the native Irish had to borrow, mortgaging land for ready money. This land was usually lost because debts could not be repaid.

Conn O'Neill, Lord of Castlereagh, at one time the Lord of Upper Clandeboye, sold all his townlands, one by one. The Magennises in Iveagh, County Down, lost possession of half their estates by 1641 and much of the land remaining to them was hopelessly encumbered by debt. By that time many native Gaelic gentlemen in Ulster, including those who had got land grants as 'deserving Irish', were fast becoming desperate. In Tyrone Sir Phelim O'Neill had mortgaged his estates for more than £13,000. He would lead the rebellion in 1641.

EPISODE 58

THE *EAGLE WING* AND THE BLACK OATH

C harles I, coming to the throne in 1625, did not share his father's enthusiasm for the Ulster Plantation. The King sought only to increase his personal power and for this he needed money which did not have to be sanctioned by Parliament. In 1633 Thomas Wentworth was sent to Ireland as the King's trusted Lord Deputy to raise funds for the royal coffers. Imperious and indefatigable, Wentworth soon alienated every interest group in Ireland. A Commission for Defective Titles sent ripples of alarm through the landed classes, including the British planters in Ulster.

As during the previous reign, Catholics of property had to pay heavy fines for refusing to attend Protestant churches. But Charles was also determined to enforce High Church conformity on Protestants in Ireland, and Wentworth was his willing agent. This immediately led to severe tension in Ulster. The Reformation had been a striking success in the Lowlands of Scotland. The variety of Protestantism brought there by John Knox was a Calvinist doctrine, Presbyterianism, opposed to formal liturgy and the rule of bishops. The Scottish Parliament ratified the break with Rome in 1560 and the Presbyterian Church became the established Kirk of Scotland.

Most of the Scots colonising Ulster in the seventeenth century were Presbyterians. They had brought their ministers with them but as yet there was no Presbyterian church there. During the reign of James I those ministers were accepted and funded as clergy of the Church of Ireland. In any case, a high proportion of English planters held Puritan beliefs, similar to those held by Presbyterians. Now Wentworth, assisted by Henry Leslie, a Scot appointed Bishop of Down by King Charles in 1635, demanded acceptance of the Book of Common Prayer and the rule of bishops.

Leslie made his first visitation to Down in July 1635 to demand from his clergy subscription to the doctrines and liturgy of the Church of Ireland. Five ministers in the diocese refused, so they were summoned to meet him in church at Belfast on 10 August. There, in his sermon, Leslie vilified those ministers who had succumbed to Presbyterianism:

> Hee that will take upon him the office of a minister, not being called by the Church, is an intruder and a thief that cometh not in by the doore, but climbeth up another way ... They think by the puff of their preaching to blowe downe the goodly orders of our church, as the walls of Jericho were beaten downe with sheepes hornes. Good God! is this not the sinne of Uzziah, who intruded himself into the office of the priesthood? ... They have cryed downe the most wholesome orders of the Church as Popish superstitions ...

After a tense debate, the ministers were deprived of their office and financial support. Forced to leave Ireland, they decided to join other Presbyterians determined to go to New England to preserve their religious liberty. In the autumn of 1636, the *Eagle Wing*, a ship of 150 tons built at Groomsport, was ready to sail for the New World. Setting out from Belfast Lough with 140 passengers on 9 September, the *Eagle Wing* was driven across the North Channel to Loch Ryan by contrary winds. After repairing a leak, they sailed out into the Atlantic and got almost as far as the Newfoundland Banks. One passenger, John Livingston, the excommunicated minister of Killinchy, wrote an account of what happened next:

> But if ever the Lord spake by his winds and other dispensations, it was made evident to us, that it was not his will that we should go to New England. For we met with a mighty heavy rain out of the north-west, which did break our rudder, which we got mended … Seas came in over the round-house … and wet them all that were between the decks … We sprung a leak that gave us seven hundred strokes in two pumps in the half-hour glass. Yet we lay at hull a long time to beat out the storm, till … it was impossible to hold out any longer.

After prayer, they decided to return, reaching Belfast Lough on 3 November.

Meanwhile Scots were preparing to resist the King's demand for conformity. Tens of thousands signed the National Covenant, a pact between them and God to refuse the Book of Common Prayer and the rule of Bishops. Aware that many Presbyterians in Ulster had signed the Covenant, Wentworth drafted a command that all Scots over the age of sixteen must take an 'oath of abjuration of their abominable covenant'.

This 'Black Oath' had to be taken kneeling and if it was refused, Bishop Leslie had the power to fine, imprison and excommunicate. Members of one family were fined £13,000 and imprisoned at their own expense in Dublin. But the anger of the Presbyterians was as nothing compared with the mounting fury of the native Irish, ready in Ulster to rise in rebellion.

THE 1641 MASSACRES AND AFTER

On the night of Friday 22 October 1641, the native Irish of Ulster, led by Sir Phelim O'Neill, rose in furious rebellion. Charlemont, Mountjoy, Castlecaulfield, and Dungannon fell to the insurgents within hours of each other. Shortly after, most of the province had been overwhelmed. In the west only the island town of Enniskillen and the walled city of Derry held out. In the east the planters' successful defence of Lisburn, besieged by Sir Conn Magennis, gave the defenders of Belfast, south Antrim and north Down time to resist.

Rebel commanders at first attempted to distinguish between the English (regarded as the enemy) and the Scots settlers. Sir Phelim issued this instruction: 'I protest that no Scotsman should be touched'. In Cavan Philip O'Reilly ordered his men 'not to meddle with any of the Scottish nation, except they give cause'. Soon, however, the leaders lost control of their men and all the colonists – Scots as well as English – were in peril. Hungered by harvest failures, and listening to wild prophecies and rumours of a Puritan plot to massacre them, the Irish threw themselves with merciless ferocity on the settlers.

The most notorious atrocity was the piking and shooting of English colonists at Portadown. Elizabeth Price saw the prisoners driven 'off the bridge into the water and then and there instantly and most barbarously drowned the most of them'.

The most horrific bloodshed, however, took place in the Clogher valley in south Tyrone: here nearly 400 Scots who surrendered were put to the sword. One leader, Turlough O'Neill, admitted to 'that ill favored massaker neere Augher'. Just how many colonists were killed will never be known. Perhaps a 1,000 were slaughtered in County Armagh alone and modern estimates range between 10 and 25 per cent of the settler population. One Scot, travelling through Ulster in November, observed:

> The most woeful desolation that ever was in any country in the sudden is to be seen here. Such is the sudden fear and amazement that has seized all sorts of people that they are ready to run into the sea.

A flood of refugees soon reached Scotland. Over 500 landed on the Isle of Bute and there were similar reports from Ayr, Irvine, Portpatrick and Stranraer. On 1 February 1642 the Scottish Privy Council ordered a collection throughout the country for 'by famine they will miserablie perish if they are not tymouslie supplied'. Once news of the rebellion reached Scotland, many of those with estates in Ulster, or relatives or friends with estates there, began to gather bodies of volunteers to be sent to Ireland.

Tension between Scottish Covenanters and London caused agonising delays. Finally, on 3 April, after landing at Carrickfergus, Major-General Robert Monro, set out southwards with a Scots army in pursuit of the Irish. A hardened veteran of the Thirty Years' War in Germany, he simply slaughtered his captives, first at Kilwarlin Wood, then at Loughbrickland, and finally at Newry. Further north along the Lower Bann 30 or 40 Irish making for the river were, according to Adjutant-General Peter Leslie, 'cutt downe, with sume wyves and chyldrene for I promis such gallants gotis but small mercie if they come in your comone sogeris handis.'

In August 1642 the English Civil War broke out. Ireland played a full part in the violent convulsion which followed. The Ulster Irish made common cause with the Old English, descendants of Norman conquerors and those they had brought with them. They were Catholic but loyal to King Charles and set up headquarters at Kilkenny. In July 1642 Eoghan Roe O'Neill, a veteran Irish officer in the service of Spain, had disembarked at Doe Castle in Donegal. Assisted by Spanish silver and weapons, he patiently trained his army in modern fighting methods. In 1646 he was ready.

Receiving fresh Scottish reinforcements, Monro advanced from Antrim with 6,000 men and 6 field pieces drawn by oxen. With no guns but an equal number of men, O'Neill attacked the Scots at Benburb, pressing them back to the River Blackwater. Between one third and one half of the Scots were killed. It was the most severe defeat the British ever suffered in battle at the hands of the Irish.

Curiously little came of the victory at Benburb. Disputes between O'Neill and the Old English gave the Scots time to recover their position in Ulster. Meanwhile the Roundheads, led by Oliver Cromwell, were advancing to victory in England. Charles I was executed in 1649, Cromwell became Lord Protector, and in August landed at Dublin. Taking revenge for the massacres of 1641, Cromwell slaughtered the garrisons of Drogheda and Wexford. One by one, strongholds across the island fell to the forces of Parliament.

Meanwhile the Scots, horrified by the execution of the King, deserted the Parliamentarian cause. Now Scots settlers in Ulster had to face the might of Cromwell's Ironsides.

EPISODE 60

A NEW SUNSHINE OF LIBERTY?

D uring the violent convulsions of the 1640s, only military help from Scotland had saved the Plantation of Ulster from extinction. Now, in 1649, the Scots colony was threatened by the might of Cromwell. Led by Lord Montgomery of the Ards, Scots settlers in Ulster, following the example of their homeland, had declared for Charles II – Charles I's heir. While he campaigned in Munster, Cromwell sent Colonel Robert Venables northwards to deal with them. Early in December Venables cut the settlers' army to pieces near Lisburn, killing 1,000 men, many hacked down in a relentless cavalry pursuit. Colonel Tam Dalyell then surrendered Carrickfergus.

Belfast had not resisted Venables and yet, we are informed, '800 Scots were afterwards turned out of the town, whither they had brought their wives and children to plant themselves there.'

Would the Scots be turned out of their lands in Ulster? Cromwell's prescription for Ireland was extremely harsh: all those who could not prove 'constant good affection' to the Parliamentarian cause would be punished. Very few in Ireland could provide such proof. In 1653, the year when peace at last returned to Ireland, the government issued a proclamation ordering 260 Scots from Antrim and Down, including Lord Montgomery, to be transplanted to Tipperary. Catholic worship was proscribed. The punishment meted out to Catholics was terrible: hundreds were hanged, priests were hunted down, and, after being told to 'go to Hell or Connacht', landowners lost their estates, receiving much smaller ones west of the River Shannon. With much truth, the poet Seán O'Connell described Cromwell's conquest as 'the war that finished Ireland'.

In the end, however, Cromwell realised that he needed the support of Protestants, whatever their past allegiances had been. The Tipperary transplantation plan was dropped. Protestants who could not prove constant good affection were allowed to keep their estates, provided they paid fines. The Marquis of Antrim, Randal MacDonnell, as a Catholic, was Ulster's most high-profile loser. The government confiscated his estates amounting to some 300,000 acres. Other Catholic estates, such as those of rebel leaders, including Sir Phelim O'Neill and several members of the Magennis family in Iveagh, were also confiscated.

During the 1650s Scots who had fled across the North Channel during the rebellion steadily returned to Ulster to bring their lands back into full production. Though they had to keep a wary eye on Anabaptists in power in Dublin, Presbyterian ministers were allowed to return and get their incomes restored. Lady Clotworthy persuaded Colonel Venables to allow her minister, Mr Ferguson, to return to Antrim and, as the Reverend Patrick Adair recalled:

> After this, the rest of the brethren returned from Scotland with passes from the English government there ... For Cromwell did labour to ingratiate all sorts of persons and parties ... Upon this favourable reception by those in power for the time, the brethren thought it their duty of meeting together presbyterially, as they had formerly done ... They met at Templepatrick, Cairncastle, Comber, Bangor, &c., for a while, till at last they settled their meetings as before. This was in the year 1654, when this poor Church had a new sunshine of liberty.

Between 1653 and 1660 the number of Presbyterian ministers in Ulster grew from around half a dozen to 70. And what of Cromwell? In 1658 one of the most controversial figures of Irish history, died of natural causes in England and was buried in Westminster Abbey. The Royalists gained back power two years later. When Charles II was restored to his throne in 1660, the Ulster Scots rejoiced. Cromwell's body, which had been buried with great pomp in the tomb of kings at Westminster, was exhumed and gibbetted at Tyburn and buried there. Not wanting to go on his travels again – as he said himself – the King was in no position to upset Cromwell's land settlement. A few favourites were restored to their estates, the most prominent being the Marquis of Antrim. Soon, however, Presbyterians found that the Church of Ireland, returned to favour, renewed its insistence on conformity. In 1661 61 Presbyterian ministers were turned out of the churches of Ulster by the bishops. Ministers were not restored to their livings but in 1672 they were given a regular stipend, known as the *regium donum*, or 'royal gift'. Presbyterians, however, like Catholics, were excluded from public office (such as being members of town corporations) and this became official in the 1673 Test Act – the test being proof of the receipt of communion in a Church of Ireland church.

The Irish economy made a remarkable recovery during the long reign of Charles II. The British settler population steadily recovered its numbers. Once again the leading immigrants were Scots. By 1669 Scots made up an estimated 60 per cent of the British inhabitants of Ulster, and 20 per cent of the population as a whole. And with every crisis in Scotland, more took ship for Ireland. King Charles had the Solemn League and Covenant declared illegal in Scotland and the attempt to reimpose Anglican Church rule there led to an uprising of Covenanters. Crushed at Bothwell Brig in 1679, many surviving Covenanters fled to Ulster to swell the Scots population there.

When Charles II died in 1685, however, the Scots in Ulster faced a fresh crisis.

EPISODE 61

'SEVEN ILL YEARS'

On 7 December 1688 a force of 1,200 Catholic soldiers in the service of Alexander MacDonnell, Lord Antrim, advanced on the city of Londonderry. King James II, the first Catholic monarch in London for more than a century, had ordered his Lord Deputy in Ireland to clear Protestants out of the Irish army and the country's administration. The alarmed nobility of England had invited William, Prince of Orange, to be their King and in November he had landed in the south of England.

British settlers in Ulster did not hesitate to declare for King William. From all over central and western Ulster, Protestants crowded into Derry. Now Scots faced Scots across the Foyle. The great majority taking refuge there were Scots or descendants of Scots. Lord Antrim's men were 'Redshanks', Hebridean Scots and their descendants from the Glens. As Redshanks prepared to cross the river, 13 apprentice boys closed the gates against them. The siege of Derry had begun.

King James, forced out of England to France, arrived in Ireland with a French army in March 1689. Soon all of Ireland had fallen to him, save the island town of Enniskillen and the walled city of Derry. When on 18 April James advanced towards Derry's walls and offered terms, he was greeted with cries of 'No surrender!' For 105 days some 37,000 thousand Protestants held out. The shared experience of bombardment and privation eroded differences between Scots and English. On the Sabbath the only place of worship within the walls, St Columb's Cathedral, was occupied by both – members of the Church of Ireland in the morning and the Presbyterians afterwards. Relief came with the breaking of the French boom across the Foyle on 28 July.

The long resistance of Derry and Enniskillen gave King William time to send the Duke of Schomberg over to clear the Jacobites – the supporters of King James – from most of Ulster. Then on 14 June 1690 William of Orange stepped ashore at Carrickfergus. He had with him the largest army yet seen in Ireland, 36,000 men. This was a professional, multinational force of Dutch, Danes, French Huguenots, English and Scots. Ulster Protestants joined William mainly as skirmishers, the most formidable being the 'Inniskillingers', the majority of them descendants of Borderers from Fermanagh, described by the army chaplain George Story as being

> half-naked with sabre and pistols hanging from their belts ... like a Horde of Tartars.

Then followed King William's triumph at the Boyne on 1 July and the flight of King James back to France. But it took more than another year to bring Jacobite resistance to an end: the Williamites won their greatest victory at Aughrim in east Galway on 12 July 1691 and Limerick did not surrender until 3 October.

Once again Catholics lost many of their lands and the British colony in Ulster quickly recovered. Landowners in the north looked for fresh recruits from across the sea to bring their estates into full production. In the 1690s Scots were to the fore, almost certainly in greater numbers than during any previous decade of the seventeenth century.

In 1693 Hekla in Iceland erupted with terrible force, spewing huge quantities of volcanic dust into the stratosphere. At the same time, on the other side of the world, the volcanoes of Serua and Aboina erupted in the Dutch East Indies, adding to the atmospheric haze filtering out the sun. The outcome was what climatologists call the Little Ice Age. Ruined harvests resulted in a terrible famine in Scandinavia – Finland lost a third of its population. In Scotland the harvest failed in 1693 and in every following year to the end of the century. The Scots called these the 'seven ill years'. Some parts suffered more than during the Black Death in the fourteenth century. The starving tried to survive by eating nettles and grass and then, fever-ridden, poured into the towns, dying there in thousands. Andrew Fletcher of Saltoun reckoned that one in five died from hunger, and others reported that a third of the people starved to death. It seems likely that the seven ill years killed at least a tenth of Scotland's population as a whole. Patrick Walker, an itinerant pedlar, wrote: 'I have seen, when meal was all sold in the markets, women clapping their hands, and tearing the clothes off their heads, crying, 'How shall we go home and see our children die in hunger?'

A Lowlander in the Highlands reported:

Some die by the wayside, some drop down in the streets, the poor sucking babs are starving for want of milk, which the empty breasts of their mothers cannot furnish them, everyone may see death in the face of the poor that abound everywhere.

Ireland escaped the worst effects of this climatic downturn. Many survivors of the Scottish famine headed for the Narrow Sea to begin a new life in Ulster.

EPISODE 62

SCOTS 'ARE COMING OVER HERE DAILY'

The last decade of the seventeenth century and the first years of the early eighteenth saw a new surge of Presbyterian Scots coming into Ulster. Even before the Jacobites had been defeated, it was observed that 'vast numbers of them followed the Army as Victuallers ... and purchased most of the vast preys which were taken by the Army in the Campaign and drove incredible numbers of cattel into Ulster'. The Church of Ireland Bishop of Tuam, Edward Synge, estimated that 50,000 Scots families came to Ulster between 1689 and 1715. This was certainly an exaggeration; but the true figure was high, probably around 40,000 persons.

The Catholic Bishop of Clogher, Hugh MacMahon, wrote in 1714:

Although all Ireland is suffering, this province is worse off than the others, because of the fact that from the neighbouring country of Scotland, Calvinists are coming over here daily in large groups of families, occupying the towns and villages, seizing the farms in the richer parts of the country and expelling the natives.

There was some truth in this observation. It is quite wrong to conclude that in the Plantation of Ulster the native Irish were left only with the poor land. But by the end of the seventeenth century the colonists, English as well as Scots, were concentrating in the more fertile lands such as the Clogher, Lagan, Bush and Foyle river valleys. Earlier, estate owners short of tenants had been willing to let farms to the Catholic Irish. Now that prospective British tenants were more abundant, they preferred to lease the good land to their fellow believers. The Catholic Irish in many parts of the north were not expelled but they often had little choice but to rent farms on land previously described as 'waste' – bogland and hillsides that in the past had been used only for summer grazing.

Clergy of the Established Church, the Church of Ireland, were particularly alarmed by this flood of Scots immigrants. In several parts of Ulster Presbyterians formed overwhelming majorities – Jonathan Swift was unhappy at Kilroot not just because he was thwarted in love but also because he had almost no Anglicans living in his parish. Ulster Presbyterians threatened the privileges of the Established Church and made inroads on Anglican congregations too often neglected by worldly or absentee clergy. Presbyterianism was particularly well organised and disciplined. Congregations grouped into presbyteries which supervised their affairs through regular visitations. There were five presbyteries in 1689 and seven by 1691. From 1691 ministers and selected elders began to meet annually as the Synod of Ulster. Discipline was strict: ministers and elders could punish offences such as adultery, fornication, drunkenness, slander, failure to pay debts and Sabbath-breaking. Dr Edward Walkington, Church of Ireland Bishop of Down and Connor, indignantly complained that: 'They openly hold their sessions and provincial synods for regulating of all matters of ecclesiastical concern.'

William King, Archbishop of Dublin, insisted that Ulster Presbyterians were very different from other Protestants in Ireland: 'They are a people embodied under their lay elders, presbyteries and synods … and will be just so far the King's subjects as their lay elders and presbyteries will allow them.'

At this time, all the states of Europe were confessional states, each with only one official religion. Louis XIV went so far as to expel Protestants from France, the Huguenots, in 1685. Many, including those with surnames such as Morrow and Molyneux, were to find refuge in Ulster. The Islamic Turkish Empire, which then ruled the Balkans, put the rest of Europe to shame by its tolerant approach to Christian and Jewish minorities. In central and western Europe realms were either Catholic or Protestant. Indeed, in nearly all Protestant states only one variety of Protestantism was established. The Church of Scotland was Presbyterian. The Church of England was Anglican with the monarch as head of the church. And London insisted that the established church in Ireland must be Anglican. Here Catholics formed a large majority and they suffered greatly from their refusal to conform.

Beginning in 1695, the Irish Parliament enacted a series of statutes to deprive Catholics of many of the rights they had previously enjoyed. By 1728 Catholics could not vote, be members of Parliament, hold public office, buy land, lease farms for more than 31 years, be members of the legal profession, carry arms, run schools or send their children abroad to be educated, or own a horse worth more than £5. Archbishop King gave this blunt explanation: 'The Irish may justly blame themselves ... since it is apparent that the necessity was brought about by them, that either they or we must be ruined.'

King, however, was also determined that what for him were the arrogant pretensions of the Presbyterians must be curbed. In 1704 he made sure that appropriate clauses were included in the Act 'to prevent the further growth of Popery'.

EPISODE 63

HANS SLOANE

Hans Sloane has a claim to be one of the most famous Ulstermen who ever lived. He is remembered as a scientist, an author, physician to Queen Anne and a pioneer in introducing the fruit of the cacao, chocolate, to Europeans, though at this stage it was only as a drink. He also brought over quinine, a Peruvian bark prized by Native Americans as an effective treatment for malaria. Sloane is also regarded as one of those who launched the Enlightenment. Yet there were sides to his character which, by modern standards, were certainly unenlightened, in particular his view on the treatment of slaves.

His family had come from Ayrshire to work on the Hamilton estates in Co. Down. Hans, born in 1660, had regular access to a well-stocked library in Killyleagh Castle. Largely self-taught, he made his way to London at the age of 19 with the intention of becoming a physician. He studied at one of Europe's most venerable universities, Montpellier, specialising in medicine. On returning to London he gained admittance to the Royal College of Physicians.

In 1687 Sloane sailed to Jamaica as physician to the governor, the Duke of Albemarle. Here the prosperity of the island depended on the production of sugar, only made possible by the slave trade, over which the Royal Africa Company had a monopoly. Not only did Sloane describe, approvingly, ways in which recalcitrant slaves were tortured and put to death, but he also put forward his own suggestions for making sure that 'lusty negroes' worked even harder. These included applying lighted candles to hands and feet. There was no pity in his account of how slaves 'often' took their own lives by cutting their throats.

In the Caribbean Sloane gathered material for his two-volume work, *The Natural History of Jamaica* and, at the same time, accumulated an extraordinary collection of plants, animals, crystals, coins, fossils and anything else which struck him as being of interest. The items ranged from African banjos to whips fashioned out of manatee hide used by sugar planters to keep their slaves in order. Meanwhile Albemarle drank himself to death and so, after 15 months in the tropics, Sloane returned to England with hundreds of specimens, including a seven-foot yellow snake, an alligator fed on chickens and an iguana. The iguana fell overboard; the snake escaped and was shot; and the alligator expired almost within sight of Plymouth.

In London Sloane was doing very well for himself. His medical practice there flourished and amongst his patients was John Locke, the greatest political philosopher of the age, who sought treatment for his diabetes. No doubt this distinguished patient did much to influence Sloane's thinking. In 1695 Sloane married a Jamaican planter's widow, and the settlement specified that he receive one third of the profits from the plantation – in effect, he had become a slave owner. Queen Anne (who became extremely fond of his chocolate drinks) appointed him as her physician in 1712 and helped him set up his Physic Gardens to grow his medicines in Chelsea. Queen Anne had had 13 pregnancies – but not one child had survived – and her husband Prince George had died in 1708. During her last illness Sloane strove hard to keep the Queen alive long enough for her Protestant successor, Georg Ludwig, the Elector of Hanover, to make his way to the capital. There were at least 50 Stuarts with a better hereditary claim than the Elector, but being Catholic they were excluded by Act of Parliament.

The collection, Sloane explained, was intended to cast light on God's grand design and contribute to 'the confutation of atheism and its consequences.' He regarded Catholicism as dark, cruel and superstitious. For example, against stones taken from the Giant's Causeway, Sloane added an explanation that the native Irish were so gullible that they actually thought that giants had once walked their land. Sloane was prominent amongst those who questioned commonly held assumptions and promoted rational, evidence-based scientific enquiry. Nevertheless, he is not remembered now as a great scientist like Newton or Linnaeus. Though he carefully preserved and labelled his vast store of items, or displayed them behind glass, he left it to those who came after him to subject them to more rigorous analysis.

The Elector, crowned as George I, made sure that Sloane was knighted in 1716. Helped by his wealth, Sloane had created a huge stockpile. It contained 50,000 books, 3,500 manuscripts, 35,000 cameos, coins and precious stones, and over 25,000 natural history specimens, including 12,500 sealed boxes of dried seeds and fruits, and resins. The collection continued to expand as men he employed shipped back yet more curiosities. Elected President of the Royal Society, Sloane attracted growing numbers of distinguished visitors to view his carefully arranged hoard.

Sloane died in 1753. He left his eclectic collection to the nation. His books and manuscripts formed the nucleus of what is now the British Library. All the rest became the kernel of the British Museum, which opened in 1759. He made an important stipulation in his will: visitors were to be admitted free of charge.

EPISODE 64

JOHN TOLAND, THE CHAMPION OF FREETHINKERS

Those who regarded the Bible as sacred, as the revealed Word of God, were on the defensive in western Europe as the eighteenth century dawned. To their dismay 'deism' seemed to be gaining ground. Deists accepted that God, or the 'Supreme Being', had created the world but they believed neither in divine intervention nor in biblical revelation. Their philosophy, their 'natural religion', derived the existence and nature of God from reason and personal experience. Deists rejected prophecy, miracles and other supernatural happenings.

The first standard bearer of international importance for deism was, perhaps surprisingly, an Irishman, John Toland. Reputedly the son of a Catholic priest, he was raised in County Donegal's Inishowen peninsula as Seán Ó Tuathaláin, until the school he attended at Redcastle near Derry encouraged him to anglicise his name. At the age of 16 Toland exchanged his Catholic faith for that of the Church of Ireland and went to Glasgow University (even though this was a Presbyterian foundation) to study theology. Then he moved to Edinburgh where he obtained his master's degree at the age of 19. He abandoned Anglicanism for Presbyterianism. In preparation for ordination as a Presbyterian minister,

Toland continued his studies at Leiden in the Netherlands only to become a freethinker and to give up his training altogether.

In 1696 Toland published *Christianity Not Mysterious*. In it he argued that the divine revelation of the Bible contains no true mysteries; instead, all the dogmas of the faith can be understood and demonstrated by properly trained reason from natural principles. For this he was chased out of Oxford and a few years later driven out of Dublin in 1697. The very same year Thomas Aikenhead, a student in Edinburgh, was executed for declaring that Christ was an impostor and that his miracles were 'pranks'. The Grand Jury of Middlesex ordered the hangman to burn Toland's heretical volume after which he fled to Dublin. Some members of the Irish Parliament actually proposed that Toland be burned at the stake. Since he had fled the country by that stage, it was left to the Dublin grand jury to order that three copies of his tract be consigned publicly to the flames by the common hangman. The author, now in London, compared members of the Irish Parliament to 'Popish Inquisitors who performed an Execution on the Book, when they could not seize the Author, whom they had destined to the Flames'.

Toland thereafter lived a precarious existence in London, managing nevertheless to spend time across the English Channel travelling as far east as Prague. Cantankerous, difficult, quarrelsome and hard-drinking, he was described by one admirer in Oxford as 'a man of excellent parts, but as little share as may be of modesty or conscience'. William Molyneux, the renowned scientist and pamphleteer – who along with a fellow Dubliner, the city developer, Robert, Viscount Molesworth, did his best to defend Toland – informed the philosopher John Locke that he alienated almost everyone by 'his unseasonable way of discoursing, propagating, and maintaining' his views volubly in coffee houses.

Nevertheless, Toland's influence on the eighteenth-century European Enlightenment was powerful. *Christianity Not Mysterious* became the handbook of deism, sending shock waves reverberating down the decades. After it, Toland wrote more than a hundred more books, most of them dedicated to condemning 'priestcraft' and criticising ecclesiastical institutions. Along with a growing number of Enlightenment figures, Toland argued passionately that political institutions should guarantee freedom and that reason and tolerance were the twin pillars of the good society. Just as he denounced church hierarchy, so he opposed hierarchy in the state. Toland died in 1722 but his republicanism, in addition to his deism, long continued to influence the thinking of many. Amongst them were Maximilien Robespierre and other members of the Committee of Public Safety. In addition to unleashing the Reign of Terror, the Jacobin government's bloody suppression of all royalist and clerical opposition in France, these dedicated revolutionaries made worship of the Supreme Being the state religion of France in June 1794.

EPISODE 65

'JET-BLACK PRELATIC CALUMNY'

The 1704 Act to Prevent the Further Growth of Popery was by far the most comprehensive of a series of statutes depriving Catholics of their rights. After its passage, a senior judge observed:

The law does not suppose any such person to exist as an Irish Roman Catholic.

The 1704 Act also included penal legislation directed at Presbyterians. Across the island, Presbyterians, nearly all of Scots origin, now almost certainly outnumbered Protestants of the Established Church, the Church of Ireland. Presbyterian congregations nearly doubled in number between 1689 and 1716. Because they were concentrated in Ulster, the authorities in Dublin feared their power. In any case, since Anne had come to the throne in 1702, the High Tories were in office in London, determined to enforce conformity to the Anglican Church.

The 1704 'Popery Act' restored the sacramental test: it stated that any person holding public office must produce a certificate that he had received the sacrament of the Lord's Supper 'according to the usage of the Church of Ireland ... immediately after divine service and sermon'. Since Catholics were already disqualified by previous penal laws, this sacramental test was really directed at the Presbyterians, who now could no longer be members of municipal corporations or hold commissions in the Army or Militia.

Ulster Presbyterians were now in something of a quandary. They were outraged by the test but at the same time they heartily approved of the Popery Act. Nevertheless, from his cell in Newgate, Daniel Defoe, the author of *Robinson Crusoe*, launched a fierce attack on the test. In his pamphlet, *The Parallel; or Persecution of Protestants the Shortest Way to prevent the Growth of Popery in*

Ireland, Defoe declared that since the Williamite War Ulster Presbyterians:

> instead of being remembered to their honour have been ranked amongst
> the worst enemies of the Church, and chained to a Bill to prevent the
> further growth of Popery ... Will any man in the world tell us that to divide
> Protestants is a way to prevent the further growth of Popery, when this
> united force is little enough to keep it down? This is like sinking the ship to
> drown the rats, or cutting off the foot to cure the corns.

Sure in the knowledge that Presbyterians would always rally to the Protestant
cause in time of danger, the Church of Ireland continued to harass dissenters,
those Protestants who were not Anglicans. Dr William Tisdall, Vicar of Belfast,
shared the view of Dean Jonathan Swift that Presbyterians were more to be
feared than the Catholics themselves. Swift may have helped Tisdall to compose
a pamphlet attacking the Presbyterians, ironically titled 'A Sample of True-Blew
Presbyterian Loyalty in all Changes and Turns of Government'. The citizens
of Belfast, overwhelmingly Presbyterian, reacted by obstructing the vicar's
collection of 'house-money' to support his clergy. They also brought back their
Presbyterian minister, John McBride, who had been forced to flee to Scotland
in 1708 when Tisdall accused him of being a Jacobite. Tisdall was quite unable
to suppress pamphlets he condemned as scurrilous, including McBride's
denunciation of the vicar, entitled: 'A Sample of Jet-black Prelatic Calumny'.

On 10 December 1712 ten Presbyterian ministers and two Probationers
drawn from all over Ulster gathered at Belturbet in County Cavan to set up a
new congregation. Hearing of the meeting, the Dean of Kilmore, Dr Jeremiah
Marsh, called on the local Anglicans 'to stop these pernicious designs ... to
pervert the people'.

The ministers were arrested and a county Grand Jury was empanelled to
bring in the unanimous verdict that the Presbyterians were guilty of disturbing
the peace. A couple of months later Robert Wodrow, an agent of the Scottish
Presbyterians visiting Ulster congregations, reported: 'I find our brethren there
are in very ill circumstances. High church is rampant and flaming.'

But events in Scotland suddenly brought an end to this persecution.

On 16 January 1707 the peers and commoners of the Estates, the Scottish
Parliament, had voted in favour of a Union between Scotland and England.
This Union was deeply unpopular with large sections of the Scottish people.
When Queen Anne died without an heir in 1714, the 1701 Act of Settlement
came into force: the throne passed to the nearest Protestant heir, passing over
many Catholics with a closer hereditary claim. In this way, George, Elector

of Hanover, was invited to become King. Louis XIV immediately recognised the Catholic son of James II as King James III. In 1715, led by the Earl of Mar, Highlanders rose in furious revolt in support of James. Ten thousand Jacobites swept south but on 13 November they were halted at Sheriffmuir by troops under the command of the Duke of Argyll. It was all over when James, later known as the Old Pretender, disembarked at Peterhead from a French vessel on 22 December. He sailed away a few weeks later.

Ulster Presbyterians unhesitatingly stood by their Protestant King, George I. For their loyalty they were rewarded by an Act of Toleration in 1719. Catholics, branded as Jacobites, continued to be oppressed by the Penal Laws.

EPISODE 66

FLAXSEED

At the beginning of the seventeenth century Ulster was reckoned to be the poorest of Ireland's four provinces. By 1700 Ulster was unquestionably the richest. How can this be explained? First, in order to attract British tenants to their estates in Ulster, landlords (unlike those in Scotland) were obliged to let out farms on long leases usually lasting 31 years but sometimes as many as 50. Settlers were given time to drain, lime and ditch their land, bringing their farms into full production, without the fear of eviction. During most of the seventeenth century colonists depended on cattle, just like the native Irish, as the main source of farm income. Nevertheless, government officials noticed that Scots in Ulster were more diligent than the English there in ploughing up the sward to grow corn.

Scotland, like England, was a birth-place of what later was to be known as the Agricultural Revolution. New methods of rotating crops and fertilising them, to eliminate fallow ground, and better ploughs, which delved deeper into the mineral-rich subsoil, were gradually introduced to Ulster across the Narrow Sea. But by far the clearest explanation for Ulster's new prosperity was the growth of the linen industry.

Huguenots, French Protestants, have usually been given credit for bringing the linen industry to Ulster. Actually, from very early times the native Irish had grown their own flax and made their own linen. This type of linen was still being made for local sale in the eighteenth century; however, its width was too narrow for the export market. It was really the Scots, and families from the north of England settling in Ulster, who established the manufacture of linen suitable for sale abroad. In 1700 50 per cent of all Scotland's exports to England by value were made up of linen. Scots making a new home in Ulster in the seventeenth century brought their skills with them, and the majority of them set parts of their farms aside for the growing of flax. Some of the leading Ulster planters, such as the Clotworthys of south Antrim, encouraged their tenants to grow and spin flax to tide them over hard times. Not only could flax be easily sold for ready cash in the market but it could also be kept at home and processed, spun and woven into linen for sale to drapers. These merchants then took the linen webs to the Linen Hall in Dublin and from there exported them to London.

In 1699 Westminster passed a Woollen Act forbidding the export of Irish woollen goods in order to protect the interests of English producers. This drastic legislation, which killed off a thriving trade, caused an outrage that united Protestants and Catholics alike. London, however, did not want to ruin the Irish economy and, in compensation, acted to encourage linen exports. Restrictions on the importation of linen to the American Colonies directly from Ireland were removed in 1705.

During the early decades of the eighteenth century the domestic weaving of linen became the main economic activity of eastern Ulster: Antrim, Armagh, Down, Monaghan and the eastern parts of Londonderry, Tyrone and Cavan. Weavers could not allow their hands to become rough by heavy farm work – in case they would catch in the fine warp and weft – and so food had to be imported from other parts of Ireland to areas concentrating on producing linen cloth. Often they were satisfied with holdings just large enough for a cottage that could house a loom and spinning wheels, and with enough land to grow flax and enough grass for a cow to supply the family with fresh milk.

By the end of the 1720s linen, nearly all of it produced in Ulster, accounted for a quarter of the total value of exports from Ireland. The success of this industry in turn greatly stimulated the emigration of Ulster Scots to the American colonies. The emergence of a flourishing trade in flaxseed explains this development. Just as its blue flowers were fading, the flax was pulled, ripped up roots and all, so that no part of the stem was lost and the fibres in the stem were as long as possible. This had to be done before the plant went to seed. It was therefore more economical for a family of weavers to buy the seed from elsewhere. Early in the century seed was nearly all from the Baltic, shipped to Ulster by Dutch merchants. Then, in 1731, Westminster permitted the shipment of flaxseed directly to Ireland from the Colonies. In 1733 it stimulated the trade with a bounty or subsidy and America became the exclusive supplier of flaxseed to Ulster.

Ship owners landing seed at Derry, Belfast, Coleraine and Newry did not want to return across the Atlantic in half-empty vessels. The most lucrative cargo proved to be people anxious for a fresh start in the New World.

EPISODE 67

'LIKE A CONTAGIOUS DISTEMPER'

T hroughout the seventeenth century, and particularly during the 1690s, tens of thousands of Scots had crossed the Narrow Sea to Ulster. Then, during the first years of the eighteenth century, this migration stopped rather suddenly. After a string of bad harvests in Scotland, yields of corn were so good that there was a surplus for the burgeoning gin trade in London. At the same time, in Ulster the restless Scots and their descendants began to contemplate starting a new life across the Atlantic Ocean.

The British colonisation of North America had begun at around the same time as the Plantation of Ulster in the early seventeenth century. By the beginning of the eighteenth century – despite abrasive competition with the French and wars with native peoples – the American colonies were thriving. The first emigrants were drawn from the Laggan district in north-east Donegal, and it was clear that the exodus had begun in earnest by 1718. In that year 11 Presbyterian ministers and nearly 300 members of their congregations petitioned the Governor of New England, Samuel Shute, for a grant of land there. At least one ship brought 100 passengers from Londonderry to New York, and *The Boston News-Letter* reported the arrival of 11 ships from Belfast and Derry in the summer and autumn of 1719. Between 1717 and 1719 as many as 7,000 emigrants left Ulster for America.

The authorities in Dublin were alarmed at this draining away of a Protestant population that had been so painstakingly settled in Ulster during the seventeenth century. William King, Archbishop of Dublin and a commissioner for the Irish government, wrote in 1718: 'No papists stir ... The papists being already five or six to one, and being a breeding people, you may imagine in what condition were are like to be in.'

Ten years later Hugh Boulter, Archbishop of Armagh, deputising for the viceroy, informed the Duke of Newcastle:

> The humour has spread like a contagious distemper, and the people will hardly hear any body that tries to cure them of their madness. The worst is that it affects only Protestants, and reigns chiefly in the North, which is the seat of our linen manufacture.

Indeed, most Catholics had at this stage neither the resources nor the inclination to go to the American colonies which were, in any case, still overwhelmingly Protestant. Presbyterians were the great majority leaving Ulster and were known in America as the 'Scotch-Irish'. In 1729 an Address of Protestant Dissenting Ministers to the King argued that the sacramental test – excluding those who were not members of the Church of Ireland from public office – was found by Ulster Presbyterians to be 'so very grievous that they have in great numbers transported themselves to the American Plantations for the sake of that liberty and ease which they are denied in their native country.'

Almost certainly this was not the main cause, though Presbyterian ministers had a key part to play in organising the first sailings across the Atlantic. Ezekiel Stewart of Portstewart observed in 1729:

> The Presbiteirin ministers have taken their shear of pains to seduce their poor Ignorant heerers, by Bellowing from their pulpits against their Landlords and the Clargey, calling them Rackers of Rents and Scruers of Tythes ... There are two of these Preachers caryed this affair to such a length that they went themselves to New England and caryed numbers with them.

In these more settled conditions, when memories of wars in Ireland were fast fading, demand for land rose sharply. As leases expired, rents were jacked up – not so much by the great proprietors (such as the London Companies and the Earl of Abercorn) but by 'middlemen', those who rented large tracts from them. It was these middlemen, those who 'underset' (or sublet) these farms, who doubled and tripled rents over as few as 15 years. In addition, the early eighteenth century witnessed a series of bad harvests, the worst being in 1741.

During 1740, Arctic weather descended on Ireland and this was followed by a prolonged summer drought and then by floods in autumn. The only outcome could be famine – so severe that 1741 would be remembered as Bliain an Áir, 'year of the slaughter'. That year, out of a population of 2,400,000, between 310,000 and 480,000 died as a direct result of famine and fever.

Map of Dál Riata, anglicised as Dalriada, around 600 AD. It was long believed that this Gaelic kingdom was created by invaders and colonists led by Fergus Mór MacErc crossing over from eastern Ulster to overwhelm Argyll during the 4th and 5th centuries AD. It now seems that no dramatic conquest was involved. (*Ulster Historical Foundation*)

Dunadd, in Kilmartin Glen, Argyll, was long the capital of the Gaelic kingdom of Dál Riata which straddled the Narrow Sea. The kindreds of Cenél nGabráin, Cenél Loairne, Cenél nOengusa and Cenél Comgall vied with each other to rule the kingdom, but it was usually Cenél nGabráin which dominated from Dunadd. Dunseverick was Dál Riata's principal stronghold on the other side of the Narrow Sea. (*Kilmartin House Trust*)

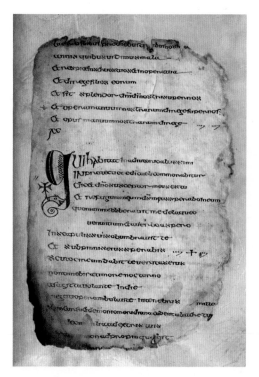

This copy of the Psalms was almost certainly written by St Columcille himself on Iona. It was known as the *Cathach* (the 'Battler') because it was later carried into battle as a talisman by the O'Donnells of Tír Chonaill. It is acknowledged as the oldest surviving manuscript in both Ireland and Scotland. (*Royal Irish Academy*)

Cross slab on Iniskeel, off Portnoo in Co. Donegal. As in the cross slabs at Fanad, a Pictish influence has been detected in the interlacing design. The monastery on this island was on an important pilgrim route which began in Mayo and continued through Tír Chonaill to Killadeas and Devenish in Fermanagh and on to Iona, Dunkeld, the Culdee foundation of Aberlady, and ending at Holy Isle, Lindisfarne. (*Rosemary McCreery*)

St Martin's Cross on Iona shows David with his musicians, along with other Biblical scenes and interlaced decoration. It seems that the Celtic High Cross was invented in Iona. Each was made in sections and, when put together, the arms of the cross were in danger of breaking under their own weight unless a ring was added to give support. (*Akela NDE/Wikimedia Commons*)

Chessmen from the Isle of Lewis. From the late 8th century the Vikings wreaked destruction on the Western Isles and forced the Church to abandon Iona. Not long after, however, they settled in large numbers in the Hebrides and adopted Gaelic speech and customs. Ulster also suffered devastating raids but, by contrast, the shortage of Viking place names there indicates little in the way of permanent settlement in the province by these northmen. (*Granger/Shutterstock*)

Elizabeth, daughter of the 'Red' Earl of Ulster, Richard de Burgo (or de Burgh), became Robert Bruce's second wife and queen. Here she is being captured by the English who kept her prisoner for eight years. Elizabeth's marriage to the King of Scots made her father, Earl Richard, rather suspect in the eyes of the English Crown. (*Alamy*)

Three branches of a prominent Hebridean galloglass family got land in Tír Chonaill: MacSweeney Fanad; MacSweeney na Doe (*na dTuath,* 'of the territories'); and MacSweeney Banagh in the west. In this section of a 1567 map of Ireland (where west is at the top), the MacSweeney na Doe warrior is wearing the characteristic galloglass decoration on his helmet. (*The National Archives (UK)*)

The Irish fighting men portrayed here by Albrecht Dürer are almost certainly *gallóglaigh*, galloglasses, mercenaries from the Western Isles who sold their services to Gaelic lords. Their method of fighting was to shoot their arrows first, then cast aside their bows to engage the enemy at close quarters with sword, battle axe or spear. (*Alamy*)

A model of the *Great Michael* built at Newhaven on the Firth of Forth for James IV, King of Scots, in 1511. The *Great Michael* was the largest and best-equipped ship afloat in Europe, possibly in the world, yet it achieved little. Sent by an indirect route around the Northern Isles and then south by the Hebrides to help Louis XII in 1513, all it did was bombard Carrickfergus ineffectively before reaching France too late in the season to be of any use in engaging Henry VIII's supply vessels. (*National Museums Scotland*)

The Great Hall, Edinburgh Castle. On 25 June 1513 fanfares of trumpets announced the arrival of the 'Prince' of Tír Chonaill, Hugh Dubh O'Donnell, to make a pact with James IV, King of Scots, now at war with Henry VIII. Six earls, three lairds, two archbishops and one bishop were amongst those who witnessed the document which sealed this alliance. (*Crown Copyright HES*)

On 29 February 1528 Patrick Hamilton, Abbot of Fearn and great grandson of a King of Scots, was found guilty of 13 charges of heresy. Burned at the stake over a damp fire in front of St Salvator's College in St Andrews, it took him six hours to die. He was Scotland's first Protestant martyr. (*Alamy*)

John Knox, forced for a time to serve as a galley slave for the French, returned from exile in 1559 as a champion of the Protestant cause in Scotland. He won fame for his fiery denunciations of idolatry and for his vituperative tract, the *First Blast of the Trumpet against the Monstrous Regiment of Women*. The reformers triumphed in 1560 and it was largely thanks to Knox that the variety of Protestantism adopted in Scotland was Calvinism rather than Lutheranism. (*National Galleries of Scotland/Getty Images*)

IOANNES CNOXVS.

This 16th century map of Portrush and Kintyre was made at a time when the English Crown was becoming increasingly anxious about the large numbers of Island Scots making a new home for themselves in Ireland's north-east. The MacDonnells had ensconced themselves in the 'Glynns' of Antrim, creating one of the most powerful lordships in Ulster. (*Public Record Office, London*)

Lordships in Ulster c. 1590. The English Crown then held little more than Carrickfergus, Newry and parts of Lecale. By 1603, however, the Crown had conquered the province from end to end. (from Mallory and McNeill, *The Archaeology of Ulster*)

James VI in 1595, 28 years after being proclaimed King of Scots at the age of 13 months. Considering that his mother Mary had her head chopped off, his father Lord Darnley had been blown up at Kirk o' Field and, aged five, he had seen the blood-stained body of his dying grandfather, the Earl of Moray, carried past him at Stirling, James proved a level-headed monarch, ruling Scotland rather well. (*Heritage Images/Getty Images*)

Francis Jobson's early 17th century map shows galleons and oared galleys carrying settlers and supplies across the Narrow Sea to Ulster. Jobson observed that Ulster was 'inhabited with a most savage and rebellious people from whose cruelty God only by his divine power delivered me being every hour in danger to lose my head'. As for his fellow cartographer in Tír Chonaill, Thomas Bartlett, 'the inhabitants took off his head, because they would not have their country discovered'. (*The Board of Trinity College Dublin*)

Part of John Speed's 1610 map, 'The Kingdome of Scotland'. Because James I regarded Island Scots as 'alluterly barbares', he specifically excluded them from the Plantation of Ulster. Nevertheless, many Hebridean Scots, such as the MacAuleys, MacAllisters and MacNeills, were settling into the nine Glens of Antrim with Sir Randal MacDonnell's approval. Lowland Scots were drawn in particular to north Down, north, mid and south-east Antrim, north-east Donegal and north-west Tyrone. Borderers were most numerous in Fermanagh. *(National Library of Scotland)*

Scots colonising Antrim and Down. Sir Arthur Chichester and Sir Randal MacDonnell brought in British colonists, most of them Scots (including John Shaw of Greenock at Ballygalley), to settle Upper Clandeboye in south Antrim. Sir Hugh Montgomery and Sir James Hamilton, bringing in Scots settlers to Lower Clandeboye and the 'Great Ardes' in County Down, could claim to be the most successful colonisers in Ireland in the 17th century. *(Ulster-Scots Agency)*

James I confiscated the entire counties of Armagh, Fermanagh, Tyrone, Donegal, Londonderry, and Cavan for his Plantation of Ulster in 1609. The counties were divided into 'Precincts' and assigned to Scottish and English 'Undertakers', 'Servitors' and 'deserving' natives. The arrangements made by Queen Elizabeth for Monaghan were allowed to stand and Antrim and Down were excluded because they were already being successfully planted by Sir Randal MacDonnell, Sir Hugh Montgomery and Sir James Hamilton. (From a map by T.W. Moody and R. J. Hunter in Moody, Martin and Byrne, *A New History of Ireland*, IX)

Francis Hutcheson is often regarded as 'the father of the Scottish Enlightenment'. A native of Co. Down, he became Professor of Moral Philosophy in Glasgow University in 1729. He believed that human beings are born free and equal with universal rights which apply everywhere regardless of status or origin. Only the people, or their representatives, should rule. His philosophy powerfully influenced those who led the drive for American independence. (*Alamy*)

Thomas Jefferson, with Benjamin Franklin on his right, presents the final draft of the American Declaration of Independence to John Hancock who presided over Congress. Hancock, the son of emigrants from Banbridge, is seated in the foreground. Standing behind him is Charles Thomson, born in Co. Londonderry and orphaned on the voyage to America. He was Secretary to Congress and was largely responsible for writing earlier drafts of the Declaration. (*Alamy*)

The Battle of Ballynahinch by Thomas Robinson. On 12–13 June 1798 the Crown forces, commanded by Major-General George Nugent, defeated the United Irish of Co. Down led by Henry Monro. In the foreground Captain Evatt is mortally wounded and, in the background, the insurgent pikemen are being cut down by cavalry on Ednavady Hill. Nearly all the defeated were Presbyterians and the rank-and-file of the Monaghan Militia, conscripted to fight for the Crown, were Catholics. (OPW *State Art Collection, Image courtesy of National Gallery of Ireland*)

Sarah Leech, born in 1807 in Taughboyne near Raphoe, lived in poverty all her short life. Her father died when she was three, leaving a widow with six children. Sarah attempted to make a living with her spinning wheel at a time when profits from hand-spun flax were being undercut by mill-produced yarn.

She composed poems in her native Ulster Scots; these were published by local benefactors in an attempt to ease her poverty but she died three years later at the age of 23.

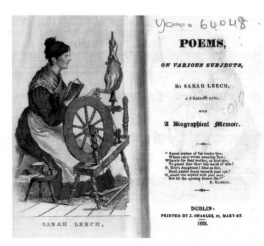

The first volume of Robert Burns' poetry to appear outside Scotland was published by James Magee in Belfast in 1787. Burns made a strong appeal to people in Ulster very conscious of their Scottish roots, people who shared his language, culture and religion. When the poet's eldest son of the same name came to visit his widowed daughter Elizabeth in Belfast in 1844, he was given a lavish official reception. (*Ulster-Scots Agency*)

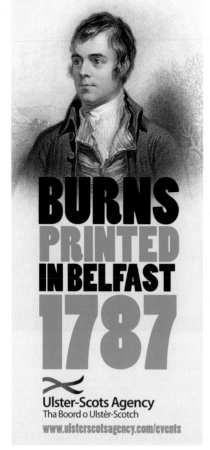

Andrew Jackson, the son of linen weavers from Boneybefore near Carrickfergus, was the first person of Ulster-Scots extraction to become a President of the United States – the Seventh, in 1829. Brought up in Waxhaw, South Carolina, he pursued a legal career in Nashville and was elected the first Congressman for Tennessee. Acquiring the nickname 'Old Hickory' as a renowned fighting frontiersman, Jackson treated Native Americans with ruthless cruelty – thousands of uprooted Cherokees died during their 800-mile mid-winter march, bitterly remembered as the 'Trail of Tears'. (*Alamy*)

WORDS NOT TO BE MET WITH IN OUR ORDINARY ENGLISH DICTIONARIES.

The following words, which are in everyday use in and around Belfast, are not to be met with in our ordinary English dictionaries. Generally speaking, they are in use among the low and vulgar only :—

Speel, to climb.
Wheen, a quantity; a number.
Sleekit, sly.
Cleek, a hook.
Bing, a heap.
Scringe, to creak.
Sevendible, thorough; sound.
Skelly, to squint.
Skelp, a slap; to slap.
Skelf, a small splinter.
Farl, a cake of bread.
Warsh, insipid; tasteless.
Thraw, to twist.
Sapple, to soak; to wet thoroughly.
Lappered, congealed; clotted.
Curnaptious, crabbed; captious.
Brash, a short or sudden illness.
Scam, to scorch.
Ramp, rank; rancid.
Dotther, to stagger.
Prod, to stab or thrust.
Slocken, to allay thirst; to quench fire.
Oxtther, the armpit.
Coggle, to shake; to rock.
Boke, to retch; to make an offer to vomit.

Fozy, spongy.
Thole, to endure or suffer pain or annoyance.
Hoke, to make holes; to burrow.
Thud, a knock or thump.
Smudge, to smirk.
Smush, refuse.
Dunt, a knock; a blow.
Dunsh, to knock against; to butt.
Scrunty, a niggard; niggardly.
Jundy, to jostle.
Scundther, to disgust.
Sheugh, a ditch.
Footy, mean; paltry.
Footther, to bungle; a bungler.
Stoor, dust.
Stoon, a pang; to ache.
Jubious, suspicious; mistrustful.
Jeuk, to elude by shifting; to dodge.
Floostther, to wheedle.
Stroop, a pipe or spout.
Dwine, to pine.
Clype, a large piece.
Cowp, to upset.

In 1860 David Patterson, teacher at the Industrial Institution for the Deaf and Blind, published *The Provincialisms of Belfast and Surrounding Districts Pointed Out and Corrected*. His purpose was to persuade his pupils to drop local speech and pronunciation and use standard English. The words he lists are, with the exception of 'sheugh' (from the Gaelic *síoc*), all of Lowland Scots origin. Close to half of these words then in use 'among the low and vulgar only' are still understood and spoken in Belfast today. (*Linen Hall Library*)

A hiring fair in Derry. To endure the hardships of becoming migrant workers in Scotland, thousands of boys and girls hired themselves out in preparation as farm servants for six-month terms – even as late as 1940 when this photograph was taken. Known as 'rabbles', these fairs in Ulster's north-west were held in May and November. Children often held a straw or peeled willow stick in their hands to indicate that they were for hire. (*Bigger & McDonald Collection. Courtesy of Libraries NI*)

Workmen leaving the Singer Manufacturing Company Works at Kilbowie c.1900. Isaac Singer, the German-American inventor of the sewing machine, decided to set up in Clydebank in the 1860s. Production in Glasgow began at Love Loan near John Street, moved to Bridgeton in 1869 and finally to Kilbowie. When it was completed in 1884, Kilbowie was almost certainly the biggest factory in Europe. (*Science & Society Picture Library/Getty Images*)

Shipwrights – known as 'Islandmen' – pour out of Harland and Wolff's shipyard on Queen's Island in Belfast at the end of a working day in 1911. The *Olympic* had been launched the year before as the largest ship in the world, leaving a vacancy in the high gantry in the background. Its even larger sister ship, the ill-fated *Titanic*, can be seen there, nearing completion. (*National Museum of Northern Ireland*)

On 9 October 1935 thirteen migrant workers, having spent months labouring in Scotland, had travelled back from Glasgow to Co. Donegal by boat and train. They arrived in Burtonport in the Rosses for the last stage of their journey over the sea to Árainn Mhór, Arranmore Island, and were joined by seven islanders who had come to meet them. In the darkness their ferry, an open sailing boat, struck rocks and overturned. It was fearfully long before anyone on land was aware that a disaster had occurred. Nineteen people drowned and there was only one survivor. (*National Library of Ireland*)

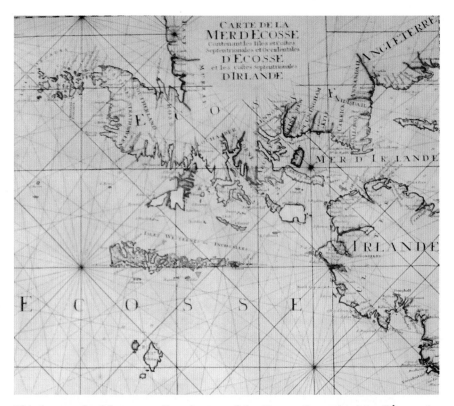

This is an early 18th-century French map of the Narrow Sea – the *Mer d'Écosse*, the 'Sea of Scotland', with adjacent coasts of Ireland. It is unique because (unlike other charts of the period) it gives a version of the name the Gaelic-speaking Hebrideans used themselves for the islands they inhabited. *Innse Gall*, 'Islands of the Foreigners', was in use from the 9th century onwards: the *Gall*, the foreigners, were descendants of Vikings from Norway who had settled these Western isles, intermarried with the locals and adopted their Gaelic language and customs. The map looks from west to east. (*The Jackie Clarke Collection, Ballina*)

Most of the victims were native Irish. A great many of the surviving British settlers in Ulster decided, as rents continued to rise, that it was time to move on to America. During the Plantation, many landlords allowed outgoing tenants to receive lump sums from incoming tenants to compensate for improvements made. This, which became known as the 'Ulster Custom', along with the sale of farm equipment, provided prospective emigrants with ready cash to pay their fares to the American colonies. As the eighteenth century wore on, the outflow from the north became a flood.

EPISODE 68

'IN AMERICA THEY MAY GET GOOD LAND'

So that the Bible could be privately consulted every day for guidance, the Presbyterian Church laid great emphasis on teaching its members to read. Incoming Scots did much, therefore, to make Ulster the most literate corner of Ireland. Presbyterians there could also read handbills advertising the opportunities awaiting them across the Atlantic. In 1729 the Justices of Assize for the North West Circuit of Ulster remarked on the lure of the New World for Protestants aggrieved at rent increases. They noted the success of agents sent around the province by ships' masters who 'assure them that in America they may get good land to them and their posterity for little or no rent, without either paying tithes or taxes, and amuse them with such accounts of those countries as they know will be most agreeable to them.'

British settlers in North America had found that flax grew readily there and raised crops every year, letting the plants mature well into the autumn. Then, in a process known as 'rippling', they drew the sheaves of flax through large fixed combs to detach the seeds. At this stage their flax was no longer good for making fine linen, but the seed commanded a ready price. Hogsheads of flaxseed were bought by travelling dealers, known as 'scowbankers', and taken down river to New York, Philadelphia, Boston and other ports.

In Ulster, flax was pulled in late summer, before the seed was set, in preparation for being retted, broken, scutched, hackled, spun, wound, woven, beetled and bleached into fine linen for sale at regular markets in Lurgan,

Armagh, Dungannon, Lisburn, Banbridge and elsewhere. But for a yearly supply of raw material, those making linen in their homes needed seed. This was supplied by the American colonies. In 1743 the Philadelphia merchant Samuel Powel wrote that 'the call for flaxseed to Ireland continues & increases ... It puts our people to sowing a great deal'. By 1751 Philadelphia alone was shipping out more than 69,000 bushels of seed a year, all of it destined for Ireland. In turn settlers in America were eager to buy Irish linen with the money they had raised in selling flaxseed. By 1760 Ulster was exporting 17 million yards of linen a year, most of it bound for the colonies.

Costly fine linen did not take up nearly as much room as seed on the return journey. Ship owners, therefore, competed with each other to fill the vacant space with passengers. The flaxseed trade and the emigrant trade were thus two sides of the same coin in this transatlantic commerce. Those who could, paid a fare of around £4 a person for the passage.

Since labour was scarce in America, merchants there put up money to pay for passengers who, in return, signed indentures before the mayor of the port of embarkation to work for no pay for around four years. The services of these 'indentured servants' were then sold, usually to farmers, for about £12 each, Pennsylvania currency. Other passengers, who ran out of money on the passage over, were known as 'redemptioners'. They also had to sign agreements and were allowed ashore to seek out friends and relations to find the cash owed. Redemptioners caused a good deal of trouble as frequent insertions in the press indicated:

> This is to desire Thomas Smiley, George Caldwell, Henry Robinson, and James Henderson, who came Passengers from Ireland with Capt. James Aspinall, in the Snow Frodsham, in the year 1735, that they would immediately pay the respective Sums for which they stand engaged, to James Mackey of Philadelphia, or they may expect to be arrested.

Most of the emigrants, setting out from Derry, Belfast, Larne, Newry, Coleraine and Portrush, disembarked at Delaware, Philadelphia, New York or Boston. Arthur Dobbs, from Castle Dobbs near Carrickfergus, had become Governor of North Carolina and he made energetic attempts to attract the Scotch-Irish to settle in his colony. In 1761 the South Carolina Assembly voted to pay £4 sterling for the passage of each poor Protestant brought to the colony. In the Low Country here in South Carolina, enslaved Africans were in a majority and plantation owners feared slave insurrections if Europeans were too few in number. Also, they felt, rightly, that the Scotch-Irish would be particularly skilled at colonising the 'backcountry', or hinterland. Charleston merchants, John Torrans and John Poag, engaged John Greg from Belfast to rustle up Ulster emigrants. Greg's ship *Falls of Belfast*, and the *Prince of Wales*, owned by Mussenden, Bateson and Company of Belfast, soon filled with passengers. They also hired the *Success*, a brigantine of 85 tons built in Philadelphia and part-owned by William Caldwell from Derry.

Soon these Scotch-Irish would be busy opening up the back country and coming into armed conflict with Native Americans, just as their forbears had done with the native Irish in the previous century.

EPISODE 69

THE DAWN OF THE SCOTTISH ENLIGHTENMENT

Shortly after 1700, when the seven 'ill years' of famine had ended, the great migration of Scots across to Ulster almost ceased. Nevertheless, the relationship between the north of Ireland and Scotland continued to be very close. Not only was trade brisk across the Narrow Sea but also new ideas flowed backwards and forwards. Both Scotland and Ulster were to play a pivotal role in what later became known as the Enlightenment – an intellectual movement crossing frontiers over much of western Europe and the British colonies in North America. In essence, the Enlightenment championed rational investigation, toleration, freedom of thought and religious liberty, and a belief in the essential goodness of human nature.

That Scotland emerged as a nursery for this profound revolution in thought is at first glance surprising – these were years of set-backs, uncertainty and turbulence. In March 1700 Scots settlers in Fort Andrew on the isthmus of Panama, enduring extreme privations after being besieged for a month by the Spanish, had no choice but to surrender. An imaginative plan to set up a colony which would draw trade from the Pacific overland to the Caribbean, the Darien scheme, had ended in catastrophic failure. Poor planning and provisioning, crop failures, an unwillingness to anticipate Spanish opposition, and – above all – devastating epidemics of disease, played their part. Some 2,000 Scots pioneers had died. Around a third of all money in circulation in Scotland, so enthusiastically invested in the scheme, had been lost. Nobles, merchants and many ordinary traders were ruined. Famine had already reaped a terrible harvest in the Highlands. Now the economy of the Lowlands was left prostrate.

Scotland's elite was therefore in poor shape to resist when London proposed a 'Treaty of Union' to create a single British state, the United Kingdom of Great Britain. A new British parliament would, actually, be no more than the one already existing at Westminster – apart from the addition of 45 MPs and 16 peers from Scotland. On 16 January 1707, as mobs rioted outside, Scotland's parliament, by 110 to 69, voted itself out of existence. It helped that the London government offered inducements including £20,000 in cash for 'expenses' and arrears of payment to office holders. The Scots did retain their legal system and, eventually, the Presbyterian Church was permitted to remain the established church, the Church of Scotland.

The last Stuart to reign, Queen Anne, died in 1714. By the Act of Settlement of 1701 Georg, Elector of Hanover, was now King George I. The throne passed, according to this Act, to the next Protestant heir, over the heads of many Catholics with a better hereditary claim. No fewer than 49 Stuarts had a better claim by blood to the throne, but they were ruled out by Westminster because they were not Protestants. In the autumn of 1715 John Erskine, 6th Earl of Mar, raised the flag of revolt on behalf of James Stuart, proclaimed in exile James III of England and James VII of Scotland. Mar proved a poor commander and, though some 10,000 rallied to him, the Duke of Argyll quickly blighted the dreams of these Jacobites at the battle of Sherriffmuir. When James, the 'Old Pretender', came ashore at Peterhead it was already too late.

Union would bring rich economic benefits, Daniel Defoe and others had argued. Only after two decades had passed were there definite signs that this prediction was proving correct after all. Scotland could now take part in direct trade across the North Atlantic. By 1727 50 vessels were making their way across the Atlantic every year from Glasgow to the tobacco landings on Chesapeake Bay. In 1741 they brought in 7 million pounds of tobacco; by 1751 they were unloading 21 million pounds; and in 1771 41 million pounds – a third of all Scottish imports, and close to two-thirds of the country's exports. The greatest profits were made in re-exporting to the Mediterranean and the Baltic. The population of Glasgow, 17,000 in 1740, rose to over 42,000 by 1780. The growth of Ayr, Greenock, Paisley, Aberdeen and Edinburgh, stimulated by colonial trade, was hardly less impressive.

After the Union Edinburgh ceased to be a national capital. The nobility moved south to reside in London, the source of power. Now a new middle class emerged to dominate Scottish society, an elite which included men of learning and letters determined to show the world that they, as men of intellect, could outstrip the English by creating works of international importance.

Ireland had only one university; England had but two; and Scotland had no fewer than four. At Glasgow, the largest, the tuition fee of £5 a year was one tenth that of Oxford or Cambridge and at least half the students came from middle class families. Glasgow University was acquiring an intellectual reputation of international importance. Presbyterians in Ulster, denied access to Trinity College in Dublin, formed a significant part of the student body there. In 1711 Francis Hutcheson became a student at that university. He was from Drumalig, half way between Belfast and Saintfield, and like other students from Ulster, he was entered into the roll as 'Scoto-Hibernicus'.

In time Hutcheson would achieve great fame and be known as 'the father of the Scottish Enlightenment'.

EPISODE 70

'THE PURSUIT OF HAPPINESS': FRANCIS HUTCHESON AND HIS LEGACY

In 1711 Francis Hutcheson crossed the Narrow Sea to become a student at Glasgow University. His grandfather Alexander was a Scot, a native of Ayrshire, who in 1657 had been appointed by Cromwell's Commonwealth government as the Puritan pastor of Saintfield in Co. Down. Evicted from the parish church on the restoration of Charles II in 1660, Hutcheson had managed nevertheless to return as minister to the Presbyterian congregation there. He had taken particular care in seeing that his grandson was given a sound education.

Francis graduated in 1716 as a 'New Light' Presbyterian who refused to believe that the world was the realm of the Devil. Returning to Ulster, he got a call to Magherally; but, perhaps realising that his opinions might be too advanced for this Co. Down congregation, he accepted an invitation to set up a Presbyterian academy in Dublin. Dublin was then the second largest city in King George I's Hanoverian dominions, about the same size as Milan and bigger than Madrid or Berlin. Here Hutcheson made his mark and got the opportunity to discuss the latest ideas with leading members of the city's intelligentsia. In Dublin he became powerfully influenced by the writings of Anthony Ashley Cooper, 3rd Earl of Shaftesbury, who had argued that benevolence was a natural human instinct. This was a view which became the basis of Hutcheson's ethical system. In 1725 Hutcheson published *An Inquiry into the Original of our Ideas of Beauty and Virtue; in two treatises, in which the principles of the late Earl of Shaftesbury are explained and defended*. Widely read, this work very soon made this Ulsterman one of the most admired intellects of his time.

Hutcheson set out to convince readers that every human being, each one stamped with the image of God's infinite goodness, is naturally inclined to be virtuous and kind to others. People can be vicious and cruel, of course, but that is not their true nature. Love is at the core of morality: 'There is no mortal', he wrote, 'without some love towards others, and desire in the happiness of some other persons as well as his own'. 'The happiest enjoyment of life', he was certain, 'consists in kind affections to our fellow creatures'. 'Action is best', he wrote in a phrase made famous by Jeremy Bentham a century later, 'which produces the greatest happiness for the greatest number'.

If anything, attacks on his writings in the columns of the *London Journal* by theological dogmatists – who wrongly accused him of being a freethinker – enhanced his reputation. In Dublin he was lionised, a frequent guest of the viceroy, Lord Carteret, and at least one bishop attempted, unsuccessfully, to persuade him to become a member of the Church of Ireland.

When the Chair of Moral Philosophy in Glasgow University fell vacant in 1729, Hutcheson was invited to fill it. His inaugural address, 'About the natural fellowship of mankind', was delivered in Latin, as were all lectures in the university. Thereafter Hutcheson broke with tradition by conducting his classes in English – indeed, he may have been the first professor in Europe to teach in the vernacular. His lectures and sermons were so earnest and compelling that colleagues and residents of Glasgow (women included) flocked to hear them. This indefatigable professor, as well as delivering a sermon every Sunday, gave additional lectures five days a week on morals, 'natural religion', jurisprudence and government. One of his students wrote later:

> He was a good-looking man, of engaging countenance. He delivered his lectures without notes, walking backwards and forwards in the area of his room. As his elocution was good, and his voice and manner pleasing, he raised the attention of his hearers at all times, and when the subject led him to explain and enforce the moral virtues, he displayed a fervent and persuasive eloquence which was irresistible.

The thrust of Hutcheson's teaching was, in his words, 'to change the face of theology in Scotland', to set aside inflexible Calvinist dogmas. Ministers of religion should aim to uplift and inspire congregations rather than preach fear and terror. One of his students recalled: 'If ever one had the art to create an esteem for Liberty and a contempt for tyranny and tyrants, he was the man!' Indeed, the most original and radical aspects of Hutcheson's thinking were on the rights of human beings. Human beings are born free and equal with universal rights which apply everywhere regardless of status or origin. Only the people, or their representatives, should rule. Hutcheson endorsed the right of resistance to bad government. He went further than his liberal contemporaries not only in championing the rights of wives, servants and children but also in teaching that slavery in any form, a totally unnatural state, was wrong. 'Nothing can change a rational creature into a piece of goods void of all rights', he concluded.

Hutcheson's influence on his generation was incalculable. In France the Encyclopédistes paid close attention to his thinking and some of his disciples carried his ideas across the Atlantic. Prominent amongst them was Rev. Francis Alison from Donegal, who had been Hutcheson's student at Glasgow University. A close friend and neighbour of Benjamin Franklin, Alison passed on these teachings, undoubtedly helping to shape the philosophy of this pivotal figure in the drive for American independence. And Hutcheson's philosophy was to be immortalised when Thomas Jefferson added 'the pursuit of happiness' to his list of inalienable rights in the American Declaration of Independence.

EPISODE 71

'IT IS TO SCOTLAND THAT WE LOOK FOR OUR IDEA OF CIVILISATION'

On 8 January 1697 Thomas Aikenhead was taken to the gallows on the road from Edinburgh to Leith and there he was hanged. This eighteen-year-old student had been condemned for blasphemy – according to his indictment he had said that 'the Holy Scriptures were stuffed with such madness, nonsense and contradictions', and reported that he had 'scoffed at the incarnation of Christ'. Appeals for mercy looked as if they might succeed but then the Church of Scotland's General Assembly, sitting at that time in Edinburgh, solemnly drafted a petition urging 'vigorous execution' to curb 'the abounding of impiety and profanity in this land'.

Aikenhead was the last person in Scotland to be executed for blasphemy. Bleak 'Old Light' dogmas were already being challenged by 'New Light' clergy and theologians, who argued that God – far from being vengeful – is a beneficent Creator who watches over the fate of his creatures. Certainly, Calvinist doctrines left little room for individual thought and liberty. At the same time, however, the Presbyterian Church from the outset had been a fierce opponent of public tyranny, giving approval to individuals to defy authority when it had become unyieldingly oppressive.

The origins of the Scottish Enlightenment can be traced back to an 'Act for Setting Schools', passed by the Scottish parliament in 1696, the very year that Aikenhead had been arrested. This established a school in every parish in Scotland not already possessing one. Each parish was to have a 'commodious house for a school' and a salaried teacher. The aim was to make certain that children, if possible girls as well as boys, must know how to read Holy Scripture for themselves. This was a momentous step: Scotland was rapidly on its way to becoming Europe's first literate society. It is reckoned that male literacy was about 75 per cent in 1750, by which time almost every town of any size had a lending library. Adam Smith, the political economist, reflected that the parish school system had taught 'almost the whole common people to read, and a very large proportion of them to write and account'.

At the same time Scotland's universities, Glasgow University in particular, were winning recognition as international centres of learning and liberal thought. At Glasgow Francis Hutcheson won prominence by taking on hardline conservatives of the Kirk and by inspiring his students with his vision of a compassionate God. Hutcheson, a native of County Down, had been appointed to the chair of Moral Philosophy at Glasgow University in 1729. The views he had expressed in *An Inquiry into the Original of our Ideas of Beauty and Virtue* and other publications were striking a chord with liberal thinkers not only in Britain and Ireland but also with the *philosophes* in France.

Hutcheson's addresses – delivered in a compelling speaking style in lecture rooms and churches packed with ardent listeners – were clarion calls for freedom; he memorably declared that it was the duty of governments to promote 'the greatest happiness for the greatest number'. Hutcheson believed passionately that the people, or their representatives, should rule. Neither inherited office nor even superior wisdom gave a right to govern.

Meanwhile, Henry Home, Lord Kames, endorsed Hutcheson's belief that morality is inborn but insisted that the rights and liberty of humans had to be protected by good law. This law lord inspired a brilliant coterie of thinkers and writers in Edinburgh, a city which was becoming this Enlightenment's centre of gravity.

It was a Catholic English poet, Alexander Pope, who declared: 'The proper Study of Mankind is Man'. A remarkable cohort of talented Scots went on to prove that dictum. In doing so they established themselves as leading founders of such social studies as economics, sociology, ethnography, psychology, anthropology and modern history. Adam Smith, author of *Inquiry into the Nature and Causes of the Wealth of Nations*, laid the foundations of classical free market economic theory. His friend, the philosopher and historian David Hume, argued convincingly that all human knowledge is founded solely on experience. William Robertson, the eminent historian who became Principal of the University of Edinburgh, emphasized the importance of material and environmental factors in determining the course of civilisation.

The Scottish Enlightenment produced great scientists, mathematicians, engineers and medical practitioners. They were all guided by the belief that science, and not tradition, should be the basis of the laws of the universe – any theory should be established by observation and the testing of hypotheses against the evidence. Amongst them was the physicist and chemist Joseph Black who discovered carbon dioxide and latent heat. 'Time is to nature endless and as nothing', the scientist James Hutton concluded; he was perhaps the first person to realise that natural forces had shaped the earth's surface over, not thousands, but millions of years.

'Scotland is the most accomplished nation in Europe', the English diarist Horace Walpole noted in 1758. François Voltaire, the greatest of the French *philosophes*, went further: 'It is to Scotland that we look for our idea of civilisation'.

EPISODE 72

'A GOOD WHEEN OF INGENS'

The journey of Ulster emigrants across the Atlantic in the eighteenth century was full of peril. In 1729, for example, 175 people died on board two vessels from Belfast during the crossing; and in 1741 the *Seaflower* sprang her mast en route for Philadelphia and 46 passengers died, 6 of their corpses being eaten in desperation by the survivors. In 1762 64 passengers died on the *Sally* during a passage of 14 weeks and 5 days between Belfast and Philadelphia. For many Ulster Presbyterians, however, these were risks worth taking. As David Lindsay explained to his Pennsylvanian cousins in 1758: 'The good Bargins of yar lands doe greatly encourage me to pluck up my spirits and make redie for the journey, for we are now oppressed with our lands at 8s an acre.'

An early pioneer was James McGregor, Presbyterian minister of Aghadowey, who in 1718 organised five ships to take a large part of his congregation, along with people from neighbouring congregations, from Derry to Boston in 1718. The New England Congregationalists tended to regard these immigrants from Ulster as uncouth, but Governor Samuel Shute set aside land north of the Merrimac River in New Hampshire for them. McGregor named the new settlement 'Londonderry' and from it other settlements developed with names including Antrim and Hillsborough.

Some Ulster immigrants stayed near the coast and prospered as merchants, particularly in Philadelphia. But the majority were restless, eager to seek out more land by moving into the backcountry. One commentator, William Burke, ascribed the settlement of the Southern backcountry to Irish migrants:

> who not succeeding so well in Pennsylvania, as the more frugal and industrious Germans, sell their lands in that province, and take up new ground in the remote counties in Virginia, Maryland, and North Carolina. These are chiefly presbyterians from the Northern part of Ireland, who in America are generally called Scotch Irish.

Passing through settled areas to the frontier, the Scotch-Irish settled on the Octarara Creek, between the present-day counties of Chester and Lancaster. From here pioneers pressed on in a north-westerly direction along the east bank of the Susquehanna River, founding the townships of Pequea, Donegal, Paxtang and Hanover. Crossing the river at Harris's Ferry, they came to the fertile Cumberland Valley. By the 1740s, the Cumberland Valley and the neighbouring York and Adams counties were densely settled. The Scotch-Irish pressed on westwards up the Juniata Valley, founding townships with names including 'Fermanagh', 'Derry', 'Tyrone' and 'Armagh' among the ridges of the Allegheny mountain range.

Others struck southward through the Great Valley, across the Potomac and into the Valley of Virginia. From this valley and the Carolina Piedmont, settlers moved into the mountain valleys of Appalachia, and from there they crossed the Appalachian range through the Cumberland Gap into Kentucky and Tennessee.

In 1720, James Logan, the Colonial Secretary of Pennsylvania who had been brought up in Lurgan, expressed his anxiety about the aggressive movements of Native American tribes on the borders of Quaker and German settlements: 'I thought it might be prudent to plant a Settlement of those who had so bravely defended Derry and Enniskillen as a frontier in case of any Disturbance.'

The westward advance of the Scotch-Irish was upsetting treaties made between the Pennsylvania government – committed to the Quaker ideal of non-violence – and Native Americans which set limits to white settlement. Known locally as the 'Dutch', Germans who were Amish, Mennonites and Dunkers, Protestant sects escaping religious persecution in their homelands, were also pacifists. This was not a view shared by pioneer Scotch-Irish in the backcountry.

The Scotch-Irish drove Native Americans out of the east side of the Susquehanna and as they crossed over to seize lands on the west side of the river, many fell victim to Delaware and Shawnee war parties. Nathaniel Grubb, a Quaker who represented Chester County in the Pennsylvania Assembly, thought these pioneers to be expendable. The *Pennsylvania Gazette* reported that Grubb 'being informed that sundry of the Back Inhabitants were cut off, and destroyed by our savage Enemies, replied, "that there were only some Scotch-Irish kill'd, who could well be spared".'

Ulster Presbyterians were already accustomed to being on the move and defending their land; woodkerne, tories and raparees at home had prepared them for frontier skirmishing with Ottawas, Shawnee and other Native Americans. The settlers' pugnacious attitude is tersely expressed in an urgent message sent by the backwoodsman James Magraw to his brother in Paxtang: 'Get some guns for us – there's a good wheen of ingens about here.'

Meanwhile the French were laying claim to a vast stretch of territory extending from the St Lawrence in the north to the Mississippi delta in the south. As Scotch-Irish pioneers began hunting and settling in the heart of this territory, the French – often at war with the British Empire – engaged Native Americans there to make war on them. Bloody conflicts ensued.

'THE PLEASANTNESS OF THIS SOLITARY WILDERNESS'

In 1755 British troops commanded by General Edward Braddock advanced into western Pennsylvania in an attempt to take Fort Duquesne from the French. On 8 July Braddock was killed and his men were slaughtered as they approached the fortification. Immediately afterwards, Native Americans allied to the French fell upon the Scotch-Irish settlements. In his leather-bound diary, James McCullough, an immigrant from Belfast, tersely recorded:

> Robert Clogston his son and Betty Ramsey her son was killed ... John Wood and his wife and mother in law and John Archer's wife was killed and 4 children take off ... Alexander Miller killed and 2 of his children taken.

Then, the following year, McCullough's two young sons were captured. The elder boy John was found at a Native American camp years later. He could no longer speak English and had to be tied up for the journey home.

John Armstrong, born in the parish of Brookeborough, County Fermanagh, on behalf of the Pennsylvanian government, took charge of operations in the Cumberland Valley. He built a chain of forts and raised a force of 300 men, nearly all of them Scotch-Irish. He advanced rapidly across uncharted mountains and fell upon the Native American encampment on the Allegheny River. Armstrong returned with dozens of scalps for which the Pennsylvanian government paid a handsome bounty – a government no longer pacifist as in days gone by when Quakers had a majority in the Assembly.

Conflict with Native Americans was certain to erupt again as Europeans relentlessly encroached on their lands. Pontiac, the Ottawa chief, formed a confederation of tribes, and in 1763 made a furious assault on the settlers and took several of their forts. Once again, Armstrong led the counter-attack. Some of his men, known as the Paxton Boys, were responsible for a notorious atrocity near Harrisburg. Here they massacred unarmed Native Americans under the protection of Quakers. One Scots-Irishman, William Henry, recorded that, across the dead bodies of a man and his wife

lay two children of about the age of three years, whose heads were split with
a tomahawk and scalps taken off ... a stout Indian ... his legs chopped off
with a tomahawk, his hands cut off ... the brains splashed for three or four
feet around ... men, women, and children spread about ... shot, scalped
and cut to pieces.

Government forces had to intervene to put an end to this Scotch-Irish revenge
killing. The war raged on and Pontiac besieged Detroit for five months. But the
Shawnees deserted him and the war ended in 1769 when Pontiac was murdered
by a fellow Native American. The Scotch-Irish enjoyed several years of peace to
resume their advance westward into the backcountry. One of these was David
McClure, a Congregationalist minister, who kept a diary as he journeyed into
the wilds of western Pennsylvania. 'I spread a bearskin for my bed ... kept awake
by the howling of wolves', he wrote, describing the attractions of this new land:

The soil is luxuriant ... white and black oak, Chestnutt, Black Walnut,
Hickory ... the sweetest red plums grow in great abundance ... [in] the
pleasantness of this solitary wilderness ... In the middle of the Creek a
small flock of wild geese were swimming, on the bank sat a large flock of
Turkies and wild pigeons covered one or two trees ... we had our choice
for supper.

Anxious to avoid repeated and expensive conflicts with Native Americans,
the government in London issued orders to halt further settlement of
the backcountry. These instructions were deeply resented by Scotch-Irish
frontiersmen – they were among the most vigorous in resisting attempts by
Westminster government to regulate the affairs of the American colonies on the
other side of the Atlantic.

Ulster Presbyterians continued to make their way to the colonies in great
numbers. An economic crisis at home, beginning in 1770, did much to ensure
that emigration from the north of Ireland reached a new peak. Some 40,000
tons of emigrant shipping left Ulster ports between 1771 and 1774, carrying
around 10,000 emigrants each year. In 1776 Benjamin Franklin reckoned that
the Scotch-Irish and their descendants formed one third of Pennsylvania's
350,000 inhabitants. This was the very year that the Secretary to the International
Congress, Charles Thomson, who had emigrated in his youth from Gorteade
near Maghera, put together the first draft of the Declaration of Independence.
The final version, written by Thomas Jefferson, was published on 4 July 1776.
By that year perhaps a quarter of a million Ulster people had emigrated to

America. Thomas Wright wrote from Bucks County to his fellow Quaker, Thomas Greer of Dungannon, in 1773. He advised him to allow his nephew to come to Pennsylvania: 'I believe with thy approbation I might venture to think that he or any young man may have ten chances to one to make a fortune here than in Ireland.'

Wright wrote again on 14 June 1774:

> The colonies at present is in a very dissatisfied position by reason of the impositions of Great Britain; Boston is entirely blocked up since the first of this month that no vessel is to pass or repass … some here is apprehensive the event will be attended with much bloodshed.

Indeed it was. The American Revolution was about to begin.

EPISODE 74

'OUR CAUSE WE LEAVE TO HEAVEN AND OUR RIFLES'

As the eighteenth century progressed, the ideas of the Enlightenment were carried from the Old World to the New. In particular, the clarion calls for liberty and an end to arbitrary rule, cogently expressed by Francis Hutcheson, Glasgow University's Professor of Moral Philosophy who hailed from County Down, were firmly planted in the American colonies by immigrants from Ulster. One of the most influential of these was Francis Alison, a Presbyterian minister from County Donegal, who set up an academy in New London, a Scotch-Irish settlement in Chester County, Pennsylvania. Amongst his students were men who went on to sign the American Declaration of Independence in 1776.

Since the end of its seven-year war with France and the conquest of Canada in 1763, George III's government in London had set about attempting to bring its American colonies under tighter control. Along the coast, merchants chafed against restrictive trade controls and diktats issued by ministers on the other side of the Atlantic. Inland and to the west, particularly in the backcountry of Pennsylvania, Virginia, Tennessee and the Carolinas, frontiersmen were outraged by orders refusing permission to seize or buy land occupied by Native Americans. For some, this encroachment on the territory of native peoples was a moral issue – the Irish writer Oliver Goldsmith declared that it was unjust to take over the lands of those who had 'been in possession from time immemorial'. Westminster's anxiety was that this westward expansion would provoke costly and bloody conflicts, distracting Britain from its wish to rein in French power.

The most numerous and determined Europeans in the backcountry were people of Ulster Presbyterian descent, known in America as the Scotch-Irish. In 1774, to punish Massachusetts for the Boston Tea Party the year before, Westminster enacted coercive legislation, which Americans quickly dubbed the 'Intolerable Acts'. At Hanover in Pennsylvania, the Scotch-Irish met to protest at this 'iniquitous and oppressive' legislation, adding that 'our cause we leave to Heaven and our rifles'. They were the first to threaten violent resistance. On the coast the reaction to the Intolerable Acts was the summoning of delegates from all 13 colonies to a Continental Congress. It met in Philadelphia in September and October 1774. Congress petitioned the King, but failing to get a response, the colonists began to mobilise. Their slogan became: 'no taxation without representation'.

The frontiersmen of Mecklenburg County in Pennsylvania, for the most part of Ulster Presbyterian descent, met early the following year and declared themselves independent of British rule. They were among the very first to do so. After British troops tried to seize supplies stored at the village of Concord in Massachusetts, colonial militia fought their first battle at Lexington in April 1775. The following month the militia, known as Minutemen because of the speed with which they could mobilise, seized Fort Ticonderoga. Though they held their ground, British troops sustained heavy casualties at Bunker Hill, overlooking Boston.

In June 1775 the Second Continental Congress elected George Washington to command its fighting force, named the Continental Army. The colonists in revolt now resolved on a complete break with Britain. The first drafts of the Declaration of Independence were compiled by Charles Thomson, born in County Londonderry and orphaned on the voyage to America when his father died within sight of the Delaware shore. Sold at the age of ten as an indentured servant, he became one of Francis Alison's pupils at New London. He acted as Secretary of Congress, a post he was to hold for 15 years.

Assisting Thomson in the drafting of the resolutions in the Declaration were two other Scotch-Irish lawyers, James Smith, like Thomson one of Alison's pupils, and Thomas McKean, whose family was from Ballymoney. Their words were then honed by Thomas Jefferson into the elegant and immortal prose of the final document which pulsates with the spirit of the Enlightenment. It was duly signed on 4 July 1776:

> We hold these truths to be self-evident, that all men are created equal, that they are endowed by their Creator with certain unalienable Rights, that amongst these are Life, Liberty and the pursuit of Happiness …

John Hancock, the son of emigrants from Banbridge, was the first to sign. Since George III was known to have poor eyesight, Hancock made sure his signature was large. He is reputed to have said: 'There, I guess King George will be able to read that'. In addition to Hancock, Smith and McKean, other signatories of Ulster descent included George Taylor, Edward Rutledge, Robert Paine, grandson of a Dungannon immigrant, Thomas Nelson from Strabane, and Matthew Thornton from Londonderry. The Declaration was first printed by an Ulster immigrant, John Dunlap of Strabane. The *Belfast News-Letter* was the first newspaper to publish the full text of the Declaration outside of America. It was by no means certain, however, that these colonists could achieve the independence they had declared.

EPISODE 75
———————

'AN IRISH-SCOTCH PRESBYTERIAN REBELLION'

Not all American colonists wished to make the break with Britain in 1776. Loyalists included some Scotch-Irish, especially farmers near the coast who sold their produce to the British forces and some, settled on the frontier of the Carolinas, who had little sympathy with the plantation-owners by the coast. Alexander Chesney, born at Dunclug near Ballymena, did not hesitate to join the Loyalist militia in South Carolina. Years later he served as a British Army officer suppressing the rebellion of fellow Presbyterians in the county of his birth in 1798.

The great majority of Ulster Scots descent, the Scotch-Irish, nevertheless, threw in their lot with the rebels. Indeed, several identified them as the most determined of the revolutionaries. Captain Johann Heinricks, a German mercenary serving with the British, declared: 'Call it not an American Rebellion, it is nothing more nor less than an Irish-Scotch Presbyterian Rebellion.'

George III characterised the Revolution as 'a Presbyterian war'. Horace Walpole, the writer and Westminster MP, said to his colleagues: 'There is no use crying about it. Cousin America has run off with a Presbyterian parson, and that is the end of it.'

In November 1776, Lord Dartmouth received a letter from his agent in New York, which concluded: 'Presbyterianism is really at the Bottom of this whole Conspiracy, has supplied it with Vigour and will never rest, till something is decided upon it.'

Presbyterian ministers were, indeed, in the forefront in urging Americans to back the rebellion. Several of them journeyed south from Pennsylvania to persuade the Scotch-Irish in the Carolinas to join George Washington's rebel army. A Loyalist clergyman, Charles Woodmason, sent this report:

> Itinerant Presbyterian preachers traverse this country Poisoning the minds of the People – Instilling Democratical and Commonwealth Principles into their minds ... Especially that they owe no Subjection to Great Britain – that they are a free People.

During the early stages of the conflict the Continental Army, raised by Congress and under the command of George Washington, suffered frequent defeats. In the autumn of 1777 the British put into effect their plan to cut New England off from the other colonies. Led by General John Burgoyne, a combined force of regular British troops, German mercenaries and Native American skirmishers, set out from Quebec Province towards New York. On 19 September, close to Saratoga, the British encountered deadly fire from a largely Scotch-Irish force of frontier militia men, under the command of an experienced veteran of the Indian Wars, Daniel Morgan. With their long-range Kentucky rifles these men succeeded in picking off virtually every officer in the advance company. After a lull in the fighting, battle was renewed with the main Continental Army on 7 October but, losing men from desertions and finding himself surrounded, Burgoyne surrendered on 17 October.

This disastrous defeat for the British at Saratoga was the turning-point of the war. France joined the Americans in 1778 and Spain the following year. Only in the southern colonies had the British made substantial progress. Here, in May 1780, Lord Cornwallis sent Colonel Banastre Tarleton inland to overwhelm the Scotch-Irish settlements in the North Carolina backcountry. Incensed by reports of the slaughter of those who had surrendered and of the burning of

Presbyterian churches (described by Tarleton as 'sedition shops'), the Scotch-Irish mobilised. By the banks of the Watauga River the Reverend Samuel Doak called on these 'over-mountain men', as they were called, to take up 'the sword of the Lord and of Gideon'. Using the cover of the trees, the buckskin-clad Scotch-Irish completely outgunned Tarleton's men at King's Mountain.

Early in 1781, the over-mountain men encountered Tarleton again at Cowpens in South Carolina. Under the command of Daniel Morgan, recently appointed Brigadier-General by Congress, the militia made a deadly attack at dawn. Such was the accuracy of their firing, in their first two volleys they ensured that 40 per cent of the British who fell were officers. Tarleton's army was virtually wiped out. Morgan, known affectionately by his men as the 'Old Waggoner', was awarded a gold medal by Congress. Though a Protestant, and regarded by those he led as Scotch-Irish, Morgan, an emigrant from Draperstown, was a rarity in North America at the time – he was born of native Irish Ulster stock.

Cornwallis withdrew from the Carolinas to Yorktown on the Virginia coast. A large French army had disembarked at Rhode Island, and during the summer of 1781 joined with George Washington's Continental Army north of New York City. At the same time the French West Indies fleet, commanded by the Comte de Grasse, sailed into Chesapeake Bay with 500,000 silver pesos to pay Washington's men. The Royal Navy, arriving to relieve Yorktown, was driven off. Cornwallis was trapped. After his defences had been stormed by the French and the Americans, Cornwallis had no choice but to capitulate on 19 October.

Effectively, the war was over.

EPISODE 76

CHARLES THOMSON: 'HE WHO SPEAKS THE TRUTH'

John Thomson, along with two brothers, crossed the Narrow Sea when Scotland was in the grip of famine in the 1690s, to lease a farm in the townland of Gorteade near Maghera. Then in 1739, attracted by the lure of cheap land across in America at a time when rents in Ulster were rising fast, Thomson, like many of his neighbours, decided to emigrate. His wife had died in childbirth that year and so he was the sole guardian of his three young sons as they set out across the Atlantic. The rigours of the voyage proved too much for him: almost within sight of Pennsylvania he died on board ship. As his property was stolen, possibly by the captain, his orphan boys were left with nothing when the ship docked at New Castle near the mouth of the Delaware River. All they could do was to 'indenture' themselves to work unpaid for several years in return for their keep.

The boys were separated from each other and one of them, Charles, aged only ten, was indentured to a blacksmith. Charles ran away from his employer and, since he risked imprisonment by doing this, he was extraordinarily fortunate to be taken in by a kindly woman. She saw to it that he was given an education, eventually in a school at Thunder Hill, run by Rev. Francis Alison, minister of the New London congregation in Chester County. Alison, who had come over from Donegal, had embraced the philosophy of Francis Hutcheson while a theology student at Glasgow University. Hutcheson's conviction that all people have universal rights, and are naturally inclined to be virtuous and compassionate, resonated with this widely respected Irish clergyman, regarded as the best Latin scholar in all of the 13 colonies. Since Charles was proving himself the most talented of his pupils, Alison introduced him to his friend Benjamin Franklin, the printer who became a renowned polymath, inventor, author, political theorist and diplomat, later remembered as 'the First American'. Much taken by Alison's pupil, Franklin invited him to stay with him in Philadelphia and to continue his studies there.

While teaching in a Quaker school Thomson sprang to the defence of Native Americans who had been tricked into handing over more than a million acres. Though he failed to get the land returned, he won the respect of these people who made him a member of their tribe and named him: 'He who speaks the truth'. Thomson expressed his indignation in a tract, *An Enquiry into the Causes of the Alienation of the Delaware and Shawanese Indians*.

When Thomson returned to Philadelphia the dispute between the colonists and the government of George III was coming to a head. There he became a member of the inner circle of those preparing the ground for the American Revolution. He was asked to become Secretary to the Continental Congress, a convention of delegates called together from the 13 colonies. Meeting first in Philadelphia in 1774, it became the governing body of the United States of America. Thomson held this position throughout the 15 years of the Congress's existence, always insisting on correct procedure and ensuring the accurate recording of debates and decisions.

Thomas Jefferson headed the committee of five that drew up the Declaration of Independence. Three Ulster men were integral in creating the Declaration: Dunlap, McKean and Thomson. These talented men were responsible for writing the draft, printing the declaration and designing the seal. It was Thomson, together with Thomas McKean (a businessman whose family had emigrated from Ballymoney), who put together the first draft of the Declaration – a draft in Thomson's elegant handwriting signed only by the two of them. This document, an act of treason, was then transformed by Jefferson into the immortal prose finally agreed. Adopted on 4 July 1776, the Declaration was taken by Thomson to be printed by John Dunlap. Dunlap had emigrated from Strabane in his youth.

The revolutionary government decided it needed a seal to authenticate official documents. Three committees failed in their attempt to find an acceptable design. Thomson's striking design was accepted. He had a bald eagle with outstretched wings clutching an olive branch, symbolising a preference for peace in its right talon, and a bundle of 13 Native American arrows, bound together to indicate the unity of 13 states. The eagle holds in its beak a scroll with the motto, *E pluribus unum*, 'Out of Many One'. Accepted as the Great Seal, it was used to ratify the Treaty of Paris on 14 January 1784, which ended the War of Independence and gave international recognition to the United States. Thomson's last official duty was to ride out to meet George Washington to tell him that he had just been elected first President of the United States.

The Declaration had proclaimed that 'all men are created equal'. This made no mention of women, slaves, and Native Americans, but at least they were not excluded by name. Thomson was almost alone among his revolutionary colleagues in being an abolitionist prepared to speak out publicly about the injustice of slavery. He described slavery as 'a sickness on this new country' – proof that he was a true product of the Enlightenment who never lost his passion for truth, fairness and liberty.

EPISODE 77

'WE SEEK FOR OUR RIGHTS'

After the humiliating capitulation at Yorktown in 1781, Britain – forced to fight across the globe and without any ally of consequence – had no choice but to sue for peace. Terms were finally agreed at Paris in 1783 and George III had to let his 13 colonies go. The Great Seal of the United States of America, still in use today, now had international recognition: it was designed by an immigrant from Maghera, Charles Thomson, Secretary of the Continental Congress. At a time when the War of Independence was not going well for him, George Washington had paid tribute to his supporters of Ulster descent: 'If defeated everywhere else, I will make my last stand for liberty among the Scotch-Irish of my native Virginia.'

However, an opponent called them 'the most God-provoking democrats this side of Hell'.

The War of Independence sent shock waves back across the Atlantic. The Americans had implemented radical ideas of the European Enlightenment – in particular the belief that all men are created equal with the inalienable right of liberty – in a manner which could not yet be matched in the Old World. Only later would Europeans be concerned that this transatlantic embrace of liberty included neither the tens of thousands of enslaved Africans nor the Native Americans being ruthlessly dispossessed in the backcountry. In the short term the virus of liberty carried from America challenged the rule and privileges of hereditary monarchs and aristocrats in Europe, and soon would lead to the convulsions of the French Revolution in 1789.

The impact of the American Revolution on Ireland was both immediate and profound. The sympathy of northern Protestants was with the colonists, for as the Presbyterian minister William Steel Dickson said in a sermon he gave in Belfast, 'There is scarcely a Protestant family of the middle classes amongst us who does not reckon kindred with the inhabitants of that extensive continent.'

Lord Harcourt informed London that Ulster Presbyterians were Americans 'in their hearts' and 'talking in all companies in such a way that if they are not rebels, it is hard to find a name for them'. In 1778, however, France joined the war on the side of the colonists and Ulster Protestants had no difficulty in recognising the traditional enemy. The American Revolutionary War was brought to the very shores of Ulster on 13 April 1778: Paul Jones, a Scot who had become an American privateer, sailed his ship *Ranger* into Belfast Lough and engaged *Drake*, a Royal Navy sloop stationed there. After an obstinate fight of 45 minutes off the Copeland Islands, Jones seized the vessel.

A Volunteer company formed in Belfast on St Patrick's Day now took on an urgent role. Recruitment was brisk. A French invasion of Ireland seemed imminent. The Government's position was fast becoming desperate. Since the treasury in Dublin was empty and the country had been stripped of regular troops to fight in America, the task of defending Ireland now depended on unpaid volunteers. The Volunteer movement rapidly spread from Belfast across the island. Since it was difficult for a Catholic to bear arms, this was very much a Protestant movement.

Very soon there were tens of thousands of armed Volunteers, completely outside government control. Now they were in a position to force the pace of political change. After all, Ireland's constitutional position closely resembled that of American colonies in revolt. Westminster alone controlled imperial and foreign affairs, and the viceroy and other members of the Irish executive were appointed, not by the parliament in Dublin, but by the government of the day in London. In any case, the Irish Parliament – utterly unrepresentative except of the leading Protestant landed interests – had its powers strictly limited: Bills passed in Dublin could be altered or suppressed in London; and Westminster could pass laws to be enforced in Ireland.

The government in Dublin was bankrupt and almost powerless. Lord North's Tory government in London, assailed by fierce criticism from the Opposition benches and reeling from news of catastrophic military defeats, had to make concessions. Hated trade restrictions on Ireland were removed. On 15 February 1782 the Volunteers flexed their muscles. Meeting in Dungannon's parish church, delegates representing 142 Volunteer companies passed resolutions which were, in effect, a clarion call for legislative independence. Their address to parliament mirrored the tone of the American Declaration of 1776: 'We seek for our Rights, and no more than our Rights; and, in so just a pursuit, we should doubt the Being of a Providence, if we doubted of success.'

Then, a few weeks later, North's government fell. The new Whig government granted all that was being asked for by the Volunteers and by the Patriots, their allies in the Irish Parliament. Henceforth the English Privy Council could not alter Irish Bills and Westminster could no longer legislate for Ireland.

For some Volunteers in Ulster this was not quite enough.

'A CORDIAL UNION'?

The eighteenth-century parliament in Dublin was even more unrepresentative of the people than the Westminster parliament. Protestant aristocrats and gentry decided who got elected. Catholics – three-quarters of the population – could not be MPs. Until 1793 Catholics were denied the vote. Presbyterians were very poorly represented in the Irish Parliament and it was from the north-east corner of the island, where they were most numerous, that the strongest demand was made for thorough-going change.

In the autumn of 1783 a Volunteer convention met in Dublin to demand parliamentary reform. Delegates from Belfast and Lisburn went further than most by insisting that Catholics be given the vote. But the time when the Volunteers could pressure the government was over. Peace had been made with the Americans and the French. The convention dissolved in confusion.

The euphoria surrounding the winning of legislative independence in 1782 soon evaporated. Power was monopolised by the Ascendancy – the privileged Church of Ireland gentry and their relatives. Then, in the summer of 1789, the Bastille was stormed in Paris. News of the outbreak of the French Revolution electrified the citizens of Belfast. Still only around one tenth the size of Dublin, Belfast nevertheless was growing fast. Since the owner of the town, the Earl of Donegall, spent most of his time on his estate in Staffordshire, life in Belfast was largely directed by a vibrant Presbyterian middle class. As streams were dammed, steam engines were installed and mills erected to spin by powered machinery the exotic tropical textile, cotton, Belfast became the nucleus of Ulster's industrial revolution. Here the Enlightenment had taken deep root. Well tutored in the egalitarian teachings of Francis Hutcheson, the middle-class elite of Belfast pressed hard for toleration and a genuine representation of all the people. Going further than Volunteers anywhere else in Ireland, Belfast Volunteers, along with those of Lisburn, called for the enfranchisement of Catholics. It was in Belfast that Catholics found their most ardent champions. In 1785 Protestant Volunteers had largely paid for the building of St Mary's, the town's first Catholic chapel, and had paraded to attend the first Mass there.

In every issue, the *Belfast News-Letter* reported events unfolding in France in meticulous detail. It described the revolution there as 'the greatest event in human annals' and exulted in the 'sublime' news that the French were 'bursting their chains, and throwing off in an instant, the degrading yoke of slavery'. On 14 July 1791 the Volunteers marched with bands, banners and cannon through the town to celebrate the second anniversary of the fall of the Bastille.

If the French could overturn arbitrary rule, could this not also be done in Ireland? This was a question being asked by idealistic young men in Belfast. In October they met in a tavern in Crown Entry and there founded the Belfast Society of United Irishmen. The Society's Declaration stated that 'We have no national government' and called for 'a cordial union among all the people of Ireland' and 'a complete and radical reform of the representation of the people in Ireland'. Their final resolution declared: 'That no reform is practicable, efficacious, or just, which shall not include Irishmen of every religious persuasion'.

All the founder members were Protestants. At first the Society was a pressure group and members passionately believed that they could win the day by argument, by the force of reason. The United Irishmen rapidly spread to towns close to Belfast, among Presbyterian farmers in Antrim and Down, then to Dublin and beyond. Events in France, however, were moving rapidly. Blood began to flow in the streets of Paris, war was declared on Austria in the spring of 1792 and in January 1793 Louis XVI was guillotined. In February 1793 Britain was at war with France. Those continuing to support the French could now be branded as traitors. Many original members of the United Irishmen withdrew. Others, led by Theobald Wolfe Tone, a Protestant lawyer in Dublin, now schemed to organise a revolution in Ireland, assisted by the French. The government cracked down on the radicals and imprisoned suspect conspirators.

Meanwhile, mid-Ulster was in turmoil. In this densely populated area the spinning and weaving of linen in the home was flourishing. Competition to rent land became fierce in the vicinity of market towns, bleach-greens and the water-powered wash-mills, dye-works and beetling mills. Here, where Protestants and Catholics lived in roughly equal numbers, the ideas of the Enlightenment had made little headway. Memories of seventeenth-century dispossession and massacre remained stubbornly alive. From the early 1780s sectarian warfare raged year after year, most intensely in County Armagh. Protestants called themselves 'Peep o' Day Boys' and Catholics named themselves 'Defenders'. Better armed, the Peep o' Day Boys at first swept all before them. The Earl of Gosford described them as: 'a low set of fellows ... who with Guns and Bayonets, and Other weapons Break Open the Houses of the Roman Catholics, and as I am informed treat many of them with Cruelty.'

For more than ten years this intercommunal violence convulsed the county and spread out to engulf almost all of mid-Ulster. It was brought to a climax in September 1795 when Defenders from south Armagh decided to counter-attack northwards.

EPISODE 79

'EVERY MAN WITH HIS DESTROYING WEAPON IN HIS HAND'

Since the early 1780s mid-Ulster was convulsed by a vicious sectarian war. For years on end appalling cruelties were perpetrated by both parties, the Catholic Defenders and the Protestant Peep o' Day Boys. In September 1795 the Defenders of south Armagh and Tyrone decided to invade north Armagh in search of arms. By the time they had reached a crossroads, known as The Diamond, the Peep o' Day Boys had mobilised and, as William Blacker witnessed, the Protestants opened fire:

> with cool and steady aim at the swarms of Defenders, who were in a manner cooped up in the valley and presented an excellent mark for their shots ... From the bodies found afterwards by the reapers in the cornfields, I am inclined to think that not less than thirty lost their lives.

The victorious Protestants then marched into Loughgall, and there, in the house of James Sloan, the Orange Order was founded. This was a defensive association of lodges: like the Defenders, it was oath-bound, used passwords and signs, was confined to one sect, and its membership was made up mainly of weaver-farmers. Blacker was one of the first members of the upper classes to join but he disapproved of the immediate outcome of the Battle of the Diamond. 'Unhappily', he wrote, 'a determination was expressed of driving from this quarter of the county the entire of its Roman Catholic population'.

In just two months some 7,000 Catholics were driven out of County Armagh. Far from shattering the Defender movement, the Protestants hastened recruitment over a wide area by scattering highly political Catholics to the south and the west.

Meanwhile, Wolfe Tone and radicals in the United Irishmen were plotting a revolution with the aid of the French. So far they had only managed to enlist young middle-class idealists in Belfast, Dublin and some other provincial towns, and Presbyterian farmers in Antrim and Down. Now tens of thousands of Catholic Defenders were clamouring to join the rebellion. Learning that the United Irishmen could put a substantial army in the field, the French revolutionary government despatched a great fleet to Ireland in the winter of 1796. The government was fortunate that fierce storms prevented the French from landing when they entered Bantry Bay in the far south-west.

Despite ruthless repression by the government, the rebellion went ahead without the aid of the French. It began in the counties surrounding Dublin in May 1798. Since most of their leaders were in prison, this was a Defender uprising of poor farmers and labourers. They sought to establish an Irish republic, but their motives were mixed, some merely wanting revenge against landlords and Protestant neighbours. They achieved their greatest victories in south-east Leinster where the insurgents took Enniscorthy by force and, without meeting resistance, seized the town of Wexford.

Not until 6 June was the standard of revolt raised in Ulster. That night United Irishmen in Larne drove the Fife Fencibles back to their barracks. Ulster Scots were fighting Scots. The following day, Henry Joy McCracken led men out of Belfast northwards while Presbyterian farmers took their pikes out of the thatch to join them in a coordinated attack on the town of Antrim. Their aims were clearer than those of the insurgents in Leinster – for them, above all, this was a fight for democracy. But, poorly armed and their movements betrayed by informers, they were routed in the narrow streets and scattered. The forces of the Crown soon snuffed out the rebellion in County Antrim, Ballymena being the last rebel stronghold to fall.

Presbyterian United Irishmen in County Down failed to persuade Defenders there to join them, but their turn-out was impressive. On 9 June they routed government troops at Saintfield and gathered afterwards at the Creevy Rocks south of the town. Here the Reverend Thomas Ledlie Birch preached to the insurgents. He took his text from Ezekiel: 'Cause them that have charge over the city to draw near, even every man with his destroying weapon in his hand.'

Here they elected the leader of the largest rebel contingent, Henry Munro, a merchant from Lisburn, as their commander. As Major-General George Nugent led his army out of Belfast, the insurgents withdrew to Ballynahinch. Driven back by cannon fire as light faded on 12 June, the United Irish were routed the following day. Munro was captured and executed by the Market House in Lisburn. Several Presbyterian ministers were also tried, convicted and hanged. After weeks in hiding, McCracken was arrested in Carrickfergus attempting to board a ship: he was hanged at the corner of High Street and Cornmarket in Belfast on 17 July.

Meanwhile the insurrection in Leinster was being crushed. Dense masses of pikemen on Vinegar Hill were slaughtered by a sustained onslaught of cannon fire and howitzer shells. Government retribution was terrible. The rebellion was not over, however: at the end of August 1798, the French made landing in the far west, at Killala Bay.

EPISODE 80

A YOUNG EYEWITNESS ON THE EVE OF BATTLE: BALLYNAHINCH, 12 JUNE 1798

On Saturday 9 June 1798 at Saintfield, Richard Frazer of Ravarna led a charge of United Irish pikemen, routing a force of York Fencibles and Newtownards Yeoman cavalry commanded by Colonel Chetwynd-Stapylton. Stirred by news of this victory, other County Down United Irishmen hurried to join the main rebel camp at Ballynahinch. Henry Monro, a linen merchant from Lisburn, took command. He was a direct descendant of Major-General Robert Monro who, sent over from Scotland with an army in 1642 to crush Irish rebels, had been comprehensively routed at Benburb in 1646.

On 11 June Major-General George Nugent, commander of the government forces, set out from Belfast to engage the United men. Columns of smoke rose into the still air as his troops set fire to farmhouses and haggards and burned Saintfield to the ground. Then Nugent halted to await the arrival of reinforcements from Downpatrick.

Next day, as the rebel army prepared to stand and fight, a 12-year-old boy, James Thomson, asked to join women carrying oatcakes, bacon, butter and boiled salt beef to the camp:

At my very particular and urgent request I was allowed to satisfy my curiosity, by accompanying them; as I was so young a boy, as to be secure against detention and danger ... When we arrived, there were on the ground a considerable number of females, chiefly servants, or daughters of wives of cottiers or small farmers. These were almost all employed in the same business as ourselves; though it is said two or three of them remained on the field during the battle ... Nothing could surpass the delicacy and kindness with which these female visitors were received and conducted through the camp ... two or three young men offered their services to conduct us through the field ...

The eye was presented with a mixed and motley multitude ...They wore no uniforms; yet they presented a tolerably decent appearance being dressed, no doubt, in their 'Sunday clothes' – The only thing in which they all concurred was the wearing of green: almost every individual having a knot of ribbons of that colour, sometimes mixed with yellow in his hat ...

Their leaders also in general wore green or yellow belts and some of them green coats; and many bore ornaments of various descriptions and of different degrees of taste and execution, the most of which had been presented as tributes of regard and affection and as incentives to heroic deeds, by females whose breasts beat as high in patriotic ardour as those of their husbands, their sweethearts and their brothers.

The most common of these decorations were the harp entwined with shamrock or bays, but without the crown; the British lion and unicorn in a falling attitude; the cap of liberty; and many other symbolic representations ...

In their arms there was as great a diversity as in their dress. By far the majority had pikes, which were truly formidable instruments in close fight ... These had generally wooden shafts seven or eight feet long with sharpened heads of steel of different forms and commonly ten or twelve inches in length. Some of these heads consisted simply of one longitudinal piece; but others had a piece crossing this and forming a sort of hooks, which were thought likely to be of use in dragging horsemen from their seats, or in cutting the bridles of their horses; others wore old swords, generally of the least efficient kind; and some had merely pitchforks. Those of the higher class were armed with guns. There were also seven or eight pieces of small cannon mounted on common cars which were not calculated to produce much effect ...

On a sudden an alarm was given ... In a moment all was bustle through the field; and a degree of trepidation and alarm pervaded the undisciplined mass. It is scarcely necessary to state that we instantly quitted the ground ...

After inconclusive fighting that evening, fighting resumed at first light. At around 7:00 am rebel ammunition ran out. Nugent's army overwhelmed the United Irish on Ednavady Hill. No quarter was give as the cavalry in relentless pursuit hacked down those in flight through lanes and byways. Betsy Gray of Gransha, who had stayed on the field of battle, was overtaken and killed with her brother George and her lover Willie Boal. Betsy was the first to die – she was shot through the eye by a yeoman, Thomas Nelson of Annahilt.

Two days later, Monro was captured and then condemned to death. At the gallows an officer present recalled: 'he settled his accounts as coolly as if he had been in his own office, a free man ... This done he said a short prayer ...'

Almost all the defeated were Presbyterians. With the exception of their officers, the men of the Monaghan Militia, who had won the day for the Crown, were Catholics.

James Thomson published his memoir in 1825 (see extract above); by then he was a teacher of mathematics at the Royal Belfast Academical Institution. He was father of the great scientist, Lord Kelvin.

EPISODE 81

'NEGOTIATING AND JOBBING': THE UNION

On 22 August 1798, commanded by General Jean Humbert, 1,099 French soldiers stepped ashore at Killala Bay in north County Mayo. Just five days later they routed a much larger government force at Castlebar. But without reinforcements and substantial local support, Humbert could not succeed. On 8 September, defeated at Ballinamuck in County Longford, he surrendered.

Britain had been at war with revolutionary France since 1793. The catalogue of defeats was a long one. William Pitt, the Prime Minister, as soon as he got news of the outbreak of rebellion, made up his mind to press forward with a Bill to unite the kingdoms of Great Britain and Ireland under one legislature at Westminster. For Pitt the last straw was the inability of the Ascendancy – the Protestant gentry and nobility of Ireland – to maintain law and order at a time when the Empire was in peril. Further embarrassing news of Humbert's dazzling military success with a tiny force at Castlebar only served to reinforce Pitt's fears – a more substantial French invasion, joined by thousands of disaffected Irish, was a prospect he just could not contemplate.

Back in 1782, Westminster had made an important concession: it had agreed that it could no longer make laws for Ireland. In short, there could be no Union unless the Irish parliament, as well as the Westminster parliament, gave its approval. This proposed Union would have to be like that between Scotland and England in 1707, that is, a treaty between both countries, ratified by both parliaments. Pitt's hope that his Bill for Ireland would get through more easily than the Scottish Union Bill was soon dashed. The Prime Minister was disturbed to read a note from an official in Dublin Castle. It warned that a Union Bill might well be lost in the Irish Parliament. It would be necessary, the official added, to have the Union 'written-up, spoken-up, intrigued-up, drunk-up, sung-up and bribed-up'.

So, indeed, it proved.

Feelings ran high in Dublin's College Green on 22 January 1799. This was the first opportunity the Irish Parliament had to express its opinion on the proposed Union. The debate lasted for 21 uninterrupted hours. Tempers flared. One government supporter reported to London:

> You would have thought you were in a Polish diet. Direct treason spoken, resistance to law declared, encouraged and recommended.

When it came to a division at dawn on 23 January, the government defeated the Opposition by just one vote. This was not enough to ensure the enactment of such a momentous measure. Lord Cornwallis, the viceroy, knew that exceptional effort would have to be put in to win a comfortable parliamentary majority in the final vote. The task of persuading MPs to change their minds fell to the Chief Secretary, Robert Stewart, Lord Castlereagh. Castlereagh, whose family had been Scots planters in Donegal and now possessed much of the Ards peninsula, was the first Irishman for many years to be appointed to such an exalted post. Some MPs would have to be flattered and cajoled; but others would seek more solid rewards such as promotion to the peerage, annual pensions from the state coffers or the appointment of relatives to senior positions – in short, they would have to be bribed. Cornwallis, who had to approve Castlereagh's behind-closed-door inducements, wrote in despair:

> My occupation is now of the most unpleasant nature, negotiating and jobbing with the most corrupt people under Heaven ... I despise and hate myself every hour for engaging in such dirty work.

The Irish Parliament was utterly unrepresentative of the Irish people, the voice only of the charmed Protestant elite of the country. Some attention would have to be given to public opinion, however. Across the island, most people were simply relieved that they had survived a rebellion that had claimed at least 30,000 lives. Cornwallis was surely right to observe: 'The mass of the people do not care one farthing about the Union'.

Catholics could not be MPs but they could vote in elections. Educated and propertied Catholics – with the notable exception of the lawyer Daniel O'Connell – tended to support the Union. They hoped it would be accompanied by Catholic Emancipation, that is, the right to be elected to Parliament. Protestants in Antrim and Down – many of whom had so recently been in arms against the Crown – also welcomed the Union. They were certain they would be more fairly governed by London than by a selfish clique in Dublin. Businessmen in Belfast were given the assurance that protective duties on the cotton they manufactured would remain in place.

Most rank-and-file Orangemen hated the Union Bill. They were certain it would be accompanied by legislation allowing Catholics to become MPs. Though the Grand Lodge of Ireland, with headquarters in Dublin, tried to be neutral on the issue, no fewer than 36 lodges from the counties of Armagh and Louth sent in petitions against the Union.

A full year passed before Cornwallis and Castlereagh had rustled up sufficient support to ensure the safe passage of the Union in the Irish Parliament.

EPISODE 82

MARY ANN MCCRACKEN: REVOLUTIONARY, RADICAL AND TIRELESS ACTIVIST

The Joys and McCrackens were typical of the Presbyterian merchant class that dominated Belfast's commercial and industrial life in the eighteenth century. Francis Joy had founded the town's first newspaper, the *Belfast News-Letter*, in 1737. His sons edited this news sheet, which almost certainly was the first to provide readers in Europe with the text of the American Declaration of Independence. Captain John McCracken lived next door to the Joys in High Street near Church Lane: shipowner, sailmaker and proprietor of a rope-walk just north of Chichester Quay, he had the distinction of importing the first bale of raw cotton into Belfast. In 1778 he joined with his brothers-in-law, Thomas McCabe and Robert Joy, and built the town's first cotton mill in Francis Street.

McCracken's forebears had been forced to flee from Ayrshire to Ulster during the suppression of Covenanters in the 1670s during Charles II's reign. The captain married Francis Joy's daughter, Ann, and they were to produce seven children. Mary Ann, their second youngest, was born in their High Street home in July 1770. She has a good claim to be Belfast's most famous woman.

The McCracken children were educated in a school embodying the spirit of the Enlightenment. David Manson advertised that in his school in Donegall Street children 'will be taught to read and understand the English tongue without the discipline of the rod'. 'Young ladies', it was recorded after his death, 'received the same extensive education as young gentlemen'.

Mary Ann and her brothers became active in the Society of United Irishmen, formed in Belfast in 1791. But when Britain declared war on revolutionary France in 1793, being a radical became a dangerous pursuit. Undeterred, Mary Ann and her brothers, Henry Joy and William, became drawn in to revolutionary conspiracy. Caught spreading sedition, Henry Joy McCracken was incarcerated for a time in Kilmainham Gaol in Dublin. He was only released because the authorities thought they had successfully crushed all revolutionary preparations in Ulster.

In 1798 the tectonic plates of the Age of Enlightenment and the Romantic Era were colliding with terrible seismic force. In Ireland the dreams of the bourgeois idealists became the reality of a furious rebellion characterised by sectarian slaughter, revenge killings and savage repression. Henry Joy McCracken led the 'Army of Ulster' to attack the town of Antrim on 7 June – only to see it routed and scattered. Mary Ann met her brother as he hid afterwards and gave him clothes, money, a forged pass and a promise of a passage on a foreign vessel. It was to no avail. Recognised and arrested in Carrickfergus, he was tried, convicted and condemned to be hanged. Mary Ann remembered:

> I took his arm, and we walked together to the place of execution ... clasping my arms around him, (I did not weep till then), I said I could bear anything but leaving him. Three times he kissed me, and entreated I would go; and looking round to recognize some friend to put me in charge of, he beckoned to a Mr. Boyd, and said, 'he will take charge of you ...'

The family's standing in the town ensured for McCracken a more dignified death that day, 17 July 1798, than for others executed as traitors at the time. The fly-blown heads of a Crumlin lawyer and two Ballynahinch insurgents already decorated a spike on the Market House.

For some years Mary Ann had been running a successful muslin business in Waring Street with her sister Margaret. This gave her the independent means to help pay for the unsuccessful defence of Thomas Russell in 1803, subsequently hanged in Downpatrick, convicted of attempting to join Robert Emmet's insurrection. Henceforth, like many other Ulster radicals, Mary Ann avoided direct involvement in politics. She did, however, play a prominent part in Belfast's cultural and public life. She acted as unofficial secretary to the great collector of traditional Irish music, Edward Bunting, was a founder member of the Belfast Harp Society and was elected President of the Committee of the Ladies' Industrial School for the Relief of Irish Destitution. She also looked after her late brother's natural child, Mary.

Robert Joy, Mary Ann's uncle, had been largely responsible for designing and raising the funds for the Poor House in Clifton Street, run by the Belfast Charitable Society. In 1827 a Ladies' Committee was formed and from the outset Mary Ann was the driving force. Her principal concern was the welfare of the children: usually around 100 of them and at one stage 242 in the house. The 1831 Annual Report observed that the children 'have been taught to spell and read two and three syllables – repeat and sing hymns – are instructed in the outlines of Arithmetic and Geography, and in the names and uses of Metals and Minerals'. Swings were provided; nuts and apples were given out at Hallowe'en; the children got a holiday for the Lammas Fair; and all were taken for swims during the summer.

As secretary Mary Ann deluged the governing body with detailed requests for improvements, particularly in sanitation and diet:

> The Ladies regret the slowness of the Gentlemen in attending to their suggestions respecting encouraging the old women to work by remuneration ... The Ladies have heard with infinite surprise and regret that the gentlemen are opposed to promoting industry in the House.

Again and again she showed that her committee refused to be thwarted:

> As the Gentlemen are so dilatory in deciding on the propriety of allowing the free course of industry in the House ... it is the duty of the Ladies to act

according to the best of their judgement in the interim, while the gentlemen are making up their minds on the subject ... The Ladies ... beg to remind the gentlemen that parsimony, and economy are widely different.

Throughout her adult life Mary Ann had campaigned against slavery. In protest against it, she refused to eat sugar. She led the Women's Abolition Committee in Belfast and would not give up when interest in the movement declined. In 1859 she wrote to the historian Dr Madden:

Belfast, once so celebrated for its love of liberty, is so sunk in the lore of filthy lucre that there are but 16 or 17 female anti-slavery advocates and not one man ... and none to distribute papers to American emigrants but an old woman within 17 days of 89.

She was referring to herself: at the age of 88 she was at the docks handing out anti-slavery leaflets to those boarding ships bound for the United States.

Mary Ann McCracken died at the age of 96 on 25 July 1866.

EPISODE 83

THE RHYMING WEAVERS

The Act of Union came into force on 1 January 1801. Henceforth, the Westminster Parliament would legislate for the United Kingdom of Great Britain and Ireland. It prompted little excitement in Ulster: the great majority were simply concerned whether or not they would have enough to fill their bellies.

For more than a century the manufacture of fine linen had been the mainstay of Ulster's prosperity. This was a rural activity: the flax was grown, pulled, retted, scutched and hackled on innumerable smallholdings; and the fibre was then spun in the home on treadle-operated spinning wheels by the women of the household and wound onto clock reels, ready for the weaver. Because weaving was heavy work, the weaver was usually the man of the house. His loom occupied the largest room in a long, low thatched cottage, well whitewashed against the weather. The floor had to be composed only of earth to maintain a cool, damp atmosphere to prevent the threads in the loom from drying and snapping. Linen cloth was usually woven into a 'web', a roll of cloth a yard wide and 25 yards in length. This was highly skilled, arduous and often lonely work.

At least the weaver's time was his own. He could prop a book against his loom and many became avid readers. Some composed verse. With them the poetry and songs of Robbie Burns became enormously popular. The Ordnance Survey memoir for the parish of Ballycarry in County Antrim observed disapprovingly: 'Their accent, idioms, and phraseology are strictly and disagreeably Scottish, partaking only of the broad and coarse accent and dialect of the southern counties of Scotland.'

The memoir for the neighbouring parish of Carnmoney commented: 'Their accent is peculiarly and among the old people disagreeably strong and broad. Their idioms and saws are strictly Scottish …'

The County Tyrone writer William Carleton referred to 'that intolerable Scot-Hibernic jargon which pierces the ear so unmercifully'.

Brought up in Ayrshire, Burns spoke and wrote a dialect of Scots almost identical to that spoken by descendants of Scottish immigrants in Ulster, most of whom had come from the south-west. He did much to convince Ulster Scots that they should be proud of their speech. Poets in Ulster treated Burns as one of themselves and several went to great lengths to visit him. Samuel Thomson of Carncranny, near Templepatrick, conducted a regular correspondence with him and, in one letter, Burns asked him for a pound of Dublin snuff. After the poet's death, Burns clubs sprang up all over eastern Ulster.

James Orr, born in Broad Island, became a weaver and won wide recognition as 'The Bard of Ballycarry'. He fought on the rebel side in the Battle of Antrim in 1798 and wrote a bitter, sardonic poem about it entitled 'Donegore Hill'. He commented scathingly on how quickly the insurgents fled the field of battle:

> The camp's brak up. Owre braces, an' bogs,
> The patriots seek their sections;
> Arms, ammunition, bread-bags, brogues,
> Lye skail'd in a' directions.

The revelation that Edward Newell, a local man, had informed on no fewer than 227 United Irishmen, prompted Orr to write 'Lines written under the portrait of Newell', the notorious informer:

Were these his looks? Indignant let me scan
Th' apostates' form, who sham'd the race of man.
Allied to friends and foes, but false to all,
He gain'd their confidence to work their fall ...
May dire Mischance arrest his odious frame,
Conscious Remorse his hopeless soul inflame,
Hunger accelerate the Death he fears ...

Newell was right to fear death: he was murdered in Templepatrick.

Orr wrote verse in praise of a beverage just beginning to be affordable by all:

WELCOME, my frien's, - ye're just in time,
The kettle's on, an' soon will chime;
An' gif', tho' us'd to strains sublime,
Ye'll listen me,
I'll clear my throat, an' rudely rhyme
In praise o' Tea.

But Ulster's domestic linen industry was fast running down. Hand-spun linen could not compete with cheaper mill-yarn, linen thread produced by power machinery. The Ballyclare weaver Thomas Beggs bemoans this loss of work in 'The Auld Wife's Address to her Spinning Wheel':

On the wintry night by the clear ingle side,
My wee bit lamp hung laigh in the lum;
An' I sung my sang, an' my wheel I plied,
An' Rorie was pleased wi' the hartsome hum
But now upon her I maun spin nae mair,
An' it mak's my heart baith sorry an' sair ...
Now men ha'e erected a new ingine,
An' left but little for us to earn.

David Herbison of Ballymena, who once walked to Belfast to buy a copy of Burns's poetry, wrote wistfully:

Oh had I the power the past to restore,
The reel wad still crack and the spinning wheel snore,
Mill-yarn wad sink doun as it never had been ...

Ulster's economy was being transformed.

EPISODE 84

SARAH LEECH, A FLAX-SPINNING POET IN DONEGAL

T he fertile Laggan district in north-east Donegal attracted Scots to settle during the Plantation more successfully than any other part of western Ulster. It retained its distinctive speech and this is reflected in surviving verse written in the eighteenth and early nineteenth centuries. These were years when the domestic linen industry provided a vital supplement to income earned by farming.

Sarah Leech, born in 1807, was the daughter of a linen weaver of Ballylennan, in the parish of Taughboyne, near Raphoe. She lived in poverty all her short life. Her father died when she was three years old, leaving a widow with six children. The problem at the time was that water and steam-powered mills in Manchester, Lanarkshire and Belfast were producing cheap cotton yarn at such a quantity and price that little could be earned by spinning flax into linen yarn by hand – and that was how Sarah and her family were attempting to make a living.

Sarah did get schooling until she was 12 years old. The poems she composed during long hours at the spinning wheel were published only because local benefactors thought a printed volume might earn her some money to ease her poverty. Years spent spinning in poor light in a damp cottage left her with failing eyesight and rapidly declining health. She died at the very young age of 23, only two years after the publication in 1828 of *Poems on Various Subjects*. This poem shows that she also helped with the reaping in season:

'On Killing a Mouse in Harvest'

Poor feckless thing, why did I kill thee?
The muse sic death could never will thee –
When some few grains o' oats wad fill thee –
The lib'ral lan'
Has often left an ear o't till thee
Wi' ripen'd han.

Ah! cursed sickle, ne'er again
Shall I thee use in reaping grain,
Nor e'er shall the ensanguin'd plain
Since by thee hapless mouse lies slain,
                    And I'm left pining.

It seems as fate had sae decreed,
That wanton lambs which safely feed,
Or range the plains and flow'ry mead
                    In sportive play,
Are doomed by epicures to bleed,
                    Some ither day.

Ye tears flow freely frae ilk e'e
How could I use sic cruelty
Upon a harmless mouse like thee,
                    As stop thy breath –
Thou mad'st a vain attempt to flee,
                    Impending death.

I wildly glower'd the scenes around,
O! how the thoughts my heart confound,
To think I should inflict the wound,
                    The mortal sore,
That laid thee sprawling on the ground,
                    In reeking gore.

Alas! Vain man can nought forsee,
Or such misfortunes he would flee –
Frail helpless creature, much like thee,
                    Beset with woes,
Still hoping better days to see,
                    He onward goes.

NEW LIGHT VERSUS OLD LIGHT

Committed Presbyterians always enjoy a lively discussion and there were many opportunities for debates on religion in Reading Societies which flourished in Ulster in the early nineteenth century. Differences of opinion, however, often led to disputes and partings. The Church of Scotland suffered from frequent ruptures and constant traffic across the Narrow Sea ensured that Presbyterianism in Ireland was often in a state of turmoil.

In Ulster as in Scotland, there were Covenanters and Seceders, themselves divided into Burghers and Anti-Burghers, in addition to mainstream adherents. All this was very confusing to those who were not Presbyterians, especially government officials responsible for administering the part-funding of ministers' salaries, known as the *regium donum* or royal grant. The main philosophical difference that emerged in Ulster was between 'New Light' and 'Old Light' Presbyterians. This schism originated with controversy over whether ministers should subscribe to the Westminster Confession of Faith. Drawn up by Presbyterian divines in 1643, this outlined the strict Calvinist doctrine as preached by John Knox.

During the eighteenth century, a growing number of Presbyterian ministers in Ulster – as in Scotland – objected to the orthodoxy of the Westminster Confession. At first, rather than expel these ministers, the Synod of Ulster placed them all in the Presbytery of Antrim. Known as 'New Light' Presbyterians, these men were profoundly influenced by the Scottish Enlightenment and tended to be liberal in politics and to uphold the right of private judgement in religion. The 'Old Light' Presbyterians condemned the New Light ministers, often unfairly, as being 'Arians', that is, those who denied the doctrine of the Trinity.

Meanwhile the Evangelical Revival was gaining strength in all the Protestant churches and was embraced eagerly by Old Light Presbyterians. Dr Henry Cooke, minister of Killyleagh congregation, was determined to uphold orthodoxy and launched his campaign at the Synod in Newry in 1822. He made a virulent attack on the Belfast Academical Institution, founded in 1810, declaring that the teaching staff there held heretical Arian beliefs. Cooke, originally Henry Macook of Maghera, had won notoriety by his powerful, emotional preaching and an attack on his colleagues for their lenient treatment of a minister who had confessed to 'ante-nuptial fornication'.

Dr Henry Montgomery, a professor at the Academical Institution, led a successful campaign to prevent the expulsion of New Light teachers; but in the larger struggle against orthodoxy he was the loser. At the synods held at Coleraine in 1825 and in Strabane in 1827 Montgomery failed to convince his fellow ministers that a range of beliefs could be tolerated within Presbyterianism. As a result, he and other New Light liberals felt that they had no choice but to withdraw and form their own rump synod in 1830. This eventually became the Non-Subscribing Presbyterian Church. The triumphant Cooke, meanwhile, won over the strictly orthodox Seceders and the great majority of Ulster Presbyterians united in 1840 to form the General Assembly of the Presbyterian Church in Ireland. Cooke was burned in effigy in Ballycarry and his inquisitorial visitations caused much resentment. But it was in vain that Montgomery looked back to the time when amidst 'a recognised variety of creeds there was a perfect unity of spirit, for every man, while rejoicing in his own liberty, respected the right of his brother'.

It would be quite wrong to conclude that all the Presbyterians of Ulster kept to the strict moral code laid down by their church. The enforcement of good living, keeping the Sabbath and avoiding frivolity and strong drink was a constant preoccupation of ministers and elders of congregations. The Ordnance Survey memoir for the overwhelmingly Presbyterian parish of Islandmagee, written in the 1820s, makes this clear:

> The inhabitants of all sexes and classes are perhaps a more immoral race than is to be found in any other rural district in Antrim. Their drunkenness and intemperance is everywhere proverbial ... What makes their immorality the more disgusting is the openness and want of shame with which it is exhibited. The women whenever from home ... drink raw spirits in such quantities as would astonish any but a native ... the number of sudden, violent and premature deaths among them, solely from the effects of intemperance, is appalling ... Some have fallen off carts or staggered into a hole on their way home. Others have been smothered, 2 have committed suicide, several have lost their reason, and many still remain as examples and warnings, in their paralysed bodies and shattered intellects, to those who are treading in their footsteps.

Meanwhile evangelicals had thrown themselves into the first major drive in more than a century to convert Irish Catholics to Protestantism. Over a period of ten years the Religious Tract and Book Society alone distributed 4,400,000 tracts. Though this was largely funded by wealthy English Anglicans, the

Presbyterian Church lent its support and sent out preachers. In rural Catholic Ireland this missionary campaign caused deep resentment and inevitably heightened sectarian tensions.

'MR. O'CONNELL, LOOK AT BELFAST, AND BE A REPEALER – IF YOU CAN'

The Catholic Church responded vigorously to the drive, by all the main Protestant sects, to convert Catholics to Protestantism. A new generation of Catholic bishops organised the previously overlooked confirmation of adults, and there was a fresh insistence on regular attendance at Mass, religious instruction and devout behaviour. The competition for souls heightened tensions and there was an alarming increase in sectarian clashes, especially in Ulster.

The Catholic Renewal was accompanied by growing Catholic political self-confidence. Educated Catholics had been bitterly disappointed that their expected emancipation did not immediately follow the Act of Union in 1801. The drive for Catholic Emancipation – that is, the right of Catholics to become MPs at Westminster – was brilliantly orchestrated by the Kerry lawyer Daniel O'Connell. Dr Henry Cooke, Ulster's leading Presbyterian divine, declared that he contemplated Catholic emancipation with 'horror, disapprobation and dismay'. But O'Connell's peaceful popular campaign eventually pressured the Duke of Wellington's government to yield. In 1829 Catholic emancipation became law.

O'Connell's next target was repeal of the Act of Union. To resist the Repeal movement, Cooke mobilised Presbyterians to join forces with Anglicans of the Established Church (often at odds with each other in the past). Sons of Presbyterians who had fought the Crown in 1798 were now alarmed at the growth of Catholic power and did not hesitate to support Cooke's political stand. O'Connell had to face massive hostile demonstrations when he travelled north in January 1841 and he was forced to leave Belfast protected by mounted police. In the other three provinces, great gatherings of repealers, known as 'monster meetings', failed to persuade Westminster to abandon the Union. Opposed to violence, O'Connell's movement began to run into the sand.

For the great majority in Ireland, the Union had failed to deliver prosperity. Following the end of the Napoleonic Wars in 1815, the price tenant farmers could get for their agricultural produce had fallen inexorably. And yet rents remained high because, as the population rose from 5,000,000 in 1801 to 8,250,000 by 1841, the demand for land was rising. Only in the north-east corner of Ireland did the industrial revolution take deep root. For a time Belfast became the centre of the island's cotton industry and then, from the late 1820s, the power-spinning of flax took off and tall mills began to dominate the town's skyline. The need for specialised machinery prompted the formation of a flourishing engineering industry. Belfast became the fastest-growing urban centre in the United Kingdom. At a 'Grand Conservative Demonstration' held to celebrate O'Connell's hasty departure in January 1841, Dr Cooke declared:

> Look at the town of Belfast. When I was myself a youth I remember it almost a village. But what a glorious sight does it now present – the masted grove within our harbour – (cheers) – our mighty warehouses teeming with the wealth of every climate – (cheers) – our giant manufactories lifting themselves on every side – (cheers) – our streets marching on … And all this we owe to the Union. (Loud cheers) … Mr. O'Connell … Look at Belfast, and be a Repealer – if you can. (most enthusiastic cheering, and loud shouts of approbation).

The population of Belfast leaped from 19,000 in 1801 to well over 70,000 in 1841. As tens of thousands poured in from the countryside, particularly from the densely populated counties of mid-Ulster, the composition of the town's population altered dramatically. The Belfast accent, once very similar to that of Ballymena, now changed to become an accent clearly originating primarily in County Armagh. Catholics, only a tiny minority at the start of the century, by the 1830s formed one third of Belfast's population.

But the great majority of the inhabitants of Ulster continued to live in the countryside. Here the domestic linen industry, which had flourished until the Battle of Waterloo, was in steep decline. Spinning wheels and handlooms in rural Ulster could not compete with steam-powered machines in Belfast, Lanarkshire, Lancashire and the West Riding of Yorkshire. The result was a drastic loss of income in rural Ulster. Paying high rents for farms that were the smallest on average in Ireland, tenant farmers, labourers and increasingly redundant weavers were ever more dependent on what the overworked soil could produce.

Then, in the summer of 1845, disaster struck. Crops of potatoes – the staple diet of the majority – were infected with a deadly fungus, *Phytophthora infestans*, and rotted in the ground. The Great Famine had begun. Only parts of Ulster had been afflicted in 1845. All of Ulster was ravaged in 1846. By 1847 there were no more tubers left to be planted. Their bodies weakened by hunger, people fell victim to disease. Thousands of fever-ridden, destitute victims poured into Belfast and other towns as the potato blight returned. Those who did not die in the streets and workhouses, now sought escape to America, to England ... and to Scotland.

'SWARMING WITH VAGRANTS FROM THE SISTER KINGDOM'

For centuries the human flow across the Narrow Sea had been overwhelmingly from Scotland to Ulster. Then rather suddenly, in the 1840s, the tide reversed dramatically. Ireland was in the grip of the Great Famine and destitution drove tens of thousands overseas. Most made for North America; those who could raise the passage money chose Australia; and a great many travelled over to England. But for people in Ulster desperate to leave, Scotland was the nearest land of escape.

Before the Famine, parts of Scotland had become used to seasonal migrants from Ulster, County Donegal in particular. They travelled to Glasgow, usually from Derry, and walked from there to seek out farmers looking for labour to cut, bind and thrash their corn, and for 'tattie hoking', lifting potatoes. The *Glasgow Herald* referred to them as 'those interesting and useful yearly visitants'. When the season was over, they returned with their wages sewn into the lining of their coats. Some stayed longer to work as navvies on the Union Canal, which began construction in 1818 to link the Forth with the Clyde.

Those who flooded over to Scotland during the Famine were not seasonal migrants but immigrants. Many arrived with the hope of earning enough to pay for passage to America. Those who were to make Scotland their permanent home tended to be the poorest of all. In June 1847 the *Glasgow Herald* ran a feature entitled, 'The Irish Invasion':

> The streets of Glasgow are at present literally swarming with vagrants from the sister kingdom, and the misery which many of these poor creatures endure can scarcely be less than what they have fled or been driven from at home. Many of them are absolutely without the means of procuring lodging of even the meanest description, and are obliged consequently to make their bed frequently with a stone for a pillow.

The *Edinburgh Medical Journal* described conditions at Glasgow Infirmary:

> Many poor, starved, destitute, and diseased creatures were brought and laid down before the door of the infirmary, their relatives, if they had any, not knowing what to do with them, and in numerous instances it was destitution and starvation more than fever which was their chief affliction. Numbers also were sent to hospital in such a weak state that ... of the deaths from all diseases, including fever, occurring in the infirmary during the last year 133 died within 36 hours after their admission.

In 1847 the Royal Infirmary of Glasgow was forced to erect a temporary wooden shed, containing 140 beds, on the green outside to accommodate the overflow of fever patients. Of a total of 9,290 treated in the Glasgow hospitals in that year, 5,316 were Irish.

In 1848 Asiatic cholera swept through the industrial towns of Scotland. The hard-pressed authorities were becoming desperate. In March 1849 the Glasgow city chamberlain urged that the strongest barriers should be erected against Irish immigrants: 'No time must now be lost to ward off from Liverpool and Glasgow, the scourge of wandering and famishing Irish'.

By 1849 the parochial authorities of Glasgow were sending paupers back to Ireland at the rate of a thousand a month. And yet people from Ulster continued to land in their thousands. Paddle steamers picking them up from Derry and Belfast erected cattle-pens on decks awash with animal mire. Calls of nature had to be relieved in public in the pens.

In 1853 the *Glasgow Herald* railed against

> the annual inundation of pauper Irish with which we are afflicted. They are landed by thousands, we may say, since the Irish famine, by tens of thousands, at the Broomielaw, just like sheep, at sixpence a head ... We

have thus to bear the expense of supporting the lives of perhaps the most improvident, intemperate and unreasonable beings that exist on the face of the earth, who infest us in shoals and beg our charity because the land of their birth either cannot or will not support them. Our hospitals are filled with them, our police are overwrought by them, our people are robbed and murdered by them.

The 1851 census listed the number of Irish immigrants in Scotland as 207,367 out of a total population of 2,888,742. Statistics were not gathered on the religion of the immigrants, but it is clear that the great majority were Catholics. But large numbers of Ulster Protestants also arrived and set up Orange lodges where they settled. Many native Scots eagerly applied to be sworn in to them.

Sectarian clashes, mirroring those in Ulster and now also in Liverpool, regularly erupted, most frequently in the sugar refineries at Greenock and the port of Glasgow. Places convulsed by sectarian rioting included the Dennie and Rankine shipyard at Dumbarton in 1855; Coatbridge in 1857; Shotts and Dykehead in 1865; and Partick in 1875. The ferocity of these encounters eased over time and Ulster immigrants and their descendants were in time to blend contentedly with the indigenous inhabitants and to contribute notably to a burgeoning Scottish economy.

Meanwhile many who had crossed the Narrow Sea from Ulster to Glasgow were taking ship for America and Canada.

EPISODE 88

'OLD HICKORY' AND THE 'TRAIL OF TEARS'

The 13 colonies of North America, while under British rule, were reluctant to accept Catholics as settlers. For a time they had to take in some native Irish given sentences of transportation until Botany Bay was chosen as a penal settlement in 1787. In any case, very few Catholics had the resources for willingly crossing the Atlantic. Nevertheless, some did make it: Ulster Irish surnames – such as Gallagher, Heaney, Devlin, Keenan and Mulholland – crop up in settlements regarded as overwhelmingly Scotch-Irish. Some became Protestants before setting out and many changed their surnames: a good number of McCains were originally O'Kanes from County Londonderry, for example. Legal barriers to Catholic immigration were cast down by the Declaration of Independence of 1776 which guaranteed religious freedom. It has been calculated that by 1790, out of a total white population of around 3,000,000, the Irish stock population of the infant United States was 447,000: two-thirds were 'Scotch-Irish', of Ulster Presbyterian origin, and the remaining third were mainly Catholic Irish, for the most part from the south of Ireland.

The Scotch-Irish continued to take the lead in pushing back the frontier. In the 1780s they had forged through the Cumberland Gap into Tennessee and Kentucky, and from the Carolinas to Georgia and Alabama. In 1794 the British abandoned fortresses barring migration from Pennsylvania north-west into Indiana and Wisconsin. The following year Spain opened the Mississippi to navigation and in 1802 the United States purchased the western half of the Mississippi basin from France.

The main losers were the Native Americans. Settled communities along the east coast objected to the expense and bloodletting involved in western expansion. The Scotch-Irish, however, had no qualms about battling along the frontier for new farmlands. Their leading champion was Andrew Jackson, the son of linen weavers from Boneybefore, one mile north of Carrickfergus, brought up in the Waxhaw settlement in South Carolina. He moved to Nashville to pursue a legal career and was elected the first Congressman for Tennessee. Acquiring the nickname 'Old Hickory' as a renowned fighting frontiersman, Jackson routed the Creek Indians of Alabama at the Horsehoe Bend of the Tallapoosa in March 1814. In January 1815, at the close of a brief and pointless war between the United States and Britain, Jackson won acclaim for his successful defence of New Orleans against the Irish general Sir Edward Pakenham.

After crushing the Seminole tribe in Florida in 1818, Jackson cowed the Cherokee, Chocktaw and Chicksaw tribes into ceding land in 1820, opening up much of the Mississippi basin to European settlers. Jackson's view was that native tribes should be forced to move across the Mississippi, and his moment came when he was elected the seventh President of the United States in 1829, and the first with Scotch-Irish roots. Seminoles tried to hold out in the Florida Everglades and the well-organised Cherokees, with an elected government, tried to seek redress in the courts. It was to no avail. The Cherokees were among five nations ruthlessly uprooted by US troops and forced to move west to unsettled territory in Oklahoma. Thousands died from cold, disease and starvation during their 800-mile mid-winter march, bitterly remembered as the 'Trail of Tears'.

Sam Houston, whose family had come from the Ballynure district in east Antrim, lived for a time with the Cherokees and learned their language. That did not stop him joining Jackson when he was campaigning against the Creek Indians. Like Jackson, he moved to Nashville, was appointed a district attorney and a major-general, and became a Governor of Tennessee. In 1833 the restless Houston moved to Texas where the presence of English-speaking pioneers was challenged by the Mexican dictator, Santa Ana. After all the able-bodied defenders of the Alamo, led by Davy Crockett, had been wiped out by the Mexicans, Houston led a force that shattered Santa Ana's army at San Jacinto in April 1836. Texas became a state of the Union and Houston was elected governor in 1861.

Houston converted to the Baptist faith towards the end of his life. Many Scotch-Irish did likewise. The Presbyterian Church insisted that its ministers receive a university education, and only a handful of its ministers were prepared to brave the perils of the frontier. In any case, families in the backwoods were captivated by a succession of revivals, led by Baptist pastors specialising in emotional preaching, and attracting huge numbers of penitents and converts.

Meanwhile, the Irish were flooding into the United States in unprecedented numbers. Between 1815 and 1855 well over 3,500,000 emigrants left Ireland, most of them destined for North America. In the early 1800s, Ulster continued to supply more emigrants than each of the other three provinces. But during the Great Famine of the 1840s, when at least a million fled Ireland's shores, it was the destitute from southern and western counties who crowded into 'coffin ships' for the perilous journey across the Atlantic.

EPISODE 89

DIVIDED LOYALTIES: THE SCOTCH-IRISH AND THE AMERICAN CIVIL WAR

As the debate on Ireland's political future intensified in the nineteenth century, the great majority of Ulster Presbyterians became passionate supporters of the Union with Britain. There were exceptions, however.

One of these was John Mitchel, a solicitor in Banbridge and the son of a Non-Subscribing Presbyterian minister near Dungiven. He called on Irishmen to rise up in revolt to secure independence. Convicted on the charge of treason-felony in 1848, Mitchel was sentenced to 14 years' transportation to the penal colony of Van Diemen's Land, now Tasmania. In 1853 he escaped and got a ship to New York. Here he found that the United States was drifting towards civil war. A brilliant journalist, Mitchel wrote passionately against the growing demand for the abolition of slavery and in favour of those states seeking to break from the Union.

South Carolina was the first to secede from the Union in 1860, followed in a short time by ten other Middle and Southern states. These 11 states formed the Confederacy in 1861. War broke out on 12 April 1861 when Southern forces opened fire on Fort Sumter, South Carolina. The Scotch-Irish, those of Ulster Presbyterian stock in America, were divided on the issue.

Geography usually dictated which side was taken. Ulster immigrants had been primarily responsible for opening up the back country of Pennsylvania in the eighteenth century. Now Pennsylvania was on the side of the Union. The great numbers of Irish Catholics who had emigrated to America, particularly during and after the Great Famine of the 1840s, had settled in the cities on the eastern seaboard – cities like New York and Boston that were firmly on the Union side. The Scotch-Irish were most numerous in states that joined the Confederacy, especially Virginia, the Carolinas, Georgia and Alabama. However, the backcountry of Virginia, with a large Scotch-Irish population, broke away to form the new state of West Virginia and declared for the North.

From the outset Scotch-Irish commanders were prominent on both sides. They included Major-General George B. McClellan who led the Union army in its first campaign. The Confederate forces opposing McClellan were commanded by Joseph E. Johnston and included Colonel Thomas J. Jackson and Lieutenant Colonel 'Jeb' Stuart, all three of them Scotch-Irish.

McClellan won the first round by defeating Johnston at Rich Mountain in July 1861, thus securing West Virginia for the Union. The next Union assault on Johnston's Confederates was led by another Scotch-Irishman, Major-General Irwin McDowell. His aim was to take the Confederate capital of Richmond. Facing superior numbers at Bull Run, Confederate troops began to fall back but Jackson's Virginian brigade stood firm. General Barnard Bee cried out:

'Look! There is Jackson standing like a stone wall! Rally behind the Virginians!'

Next moment the general fell mortally wounded, but Jackson turned the tide of battle – and became known as 'Stonewall' Jackson thereafter. The Union army broke and streamed back north towards Washington.

Outnumbering the Confederate forces three to one and in control of the lion's share of America's industrial output, President Abraham Lincoln's Union armies should have won at an early stage. But President Jefferson Davis, President of the Confederacy, had troops that were better organised and who were fighting in friendly territory. The Confederate commander-in-chief, General Robert E. Lee, was a brilliant tactician and his generals fought with flair. Stonewall Jackson, whose great-grandfather had emigrated from Coleraine, marched his men so fast that they were known as 'Jackson's foot-cavalry'. He famously enveloped a Union army during the Battle of Chancellorsville south of Washington in the spring of 1863. It was his last campaign: on 2 May he was accidentally shot dead by a Confederate picket. In contrast with the plainly dressed Jackson, 'Jeb' Stuart appeared on the battlefield wearing a hat cocked to the side with an ostrich plume and a yellow sash draped over his red-lined cape. This audacious cavalry commander won many dazzling engagements but he could not win the war.

In Ulysses S. Grant, President Lincoln found a general equal to the task. Grant, whose forebears came from Tyrone, turned the tide of the war when he outmanoeuvred the Confederates and took the imposing fort of Vicksburg in Mississippi. This gave the Union control of the entire river, splitting the Confederacy in two. Early in the summer of 1863 the Confederates thrust north almost as far as Baltimore only to be halted at Gettysburg. This hard-won Union victory left 43,000 men dead on the battlefield. The manpower of the South was now almost exhausted. By 1864 Union forces captured Atlanta and completed a march of destruction through Georgia to the sea. Lee surrendered to Grant on 9 April 1865.

More than twice as many Americans were killed in this conflict as during the Second World War. Two of Mitchel's sons were amongst those who lost their lives.

'A SECOND BELFAST OF THE WHOLE PROVINCE': CANADA

T he United States of America was always the preferred destination for emigrants from all parts of Ireland. Nevertheless, Canada was also a popular choice, particularly for northern Protestants. During the war between Britain and the USA in 1812 Irish Orangemen had been mobbed and murdered in the streets of Baltimore – incidents of this kind may have encouraged Ulster Protestants that they might get a warmer welcome in British North America. During Daniel O'Connell's campaign for repeal of the Union, a County Cavan farmer wrote to a relative who had gone to Canada: 'The polaticks have taken a queer turn. I think popery will rule with a rod of iron ere long; you had a fine escape out of it'.

Another observed that Canada was a place where Ulster Protestants could live safely under the 'fostering shade' of Britain's 'Incomparable Constitution which their forefathers defended with their blood in the days of William of Glorious memory'.

To attract European settlers, the Canadian government offered what the United States never did – free land. From 1819 it made grants of 50-acre plots in Upper Canada (now the province of Ontario). During the first 40 years of the nineteenth century twice as many people left Ulster for North America as had emigrated there during the whole of the previous century. A majority of these were Protestants, almost as many Church of Ireland members as Presbyterians. By the early 1840s Irish-born and their offspring in Ontario, around 134,000, formed over a quarter of the population of the province. Two-thirds of them were Protestants, largely from Ulster. Settlers had to learn to adapt to the extreme continental climate: long, freezing winters and great swarms of biting insects during the hot summers.

Then, as potato blight struck in the 1840s, unprecedented numbers of Irish people flooded across the Atlantic; 60 per cent made landfall in Canada because timber vessels returning from the United Kingdom offered the cheapest fares. Over 30 per cent of those bound for North America perished in these 'coffin ships' or shortly after landing. Most of those who survived the journey travelled south to find work in Boston or New York. Many were to stay, however, to farm and to find work on the waterways and railroads.

The arrival of great numbers of Catholics could unsettle community relations. The engineer Sir Richard Bonnycastle described the newcomers from Ireland as 'Orangemen who defy the pope and are loyal to the backbone and repealers, sure of immediate wealth who kick up a deuce of a row; for two shillings and sixpence is paid for a day's labour ... a hopeless week's fortune in Ireland.'

Here southern Irish Catholics, still speaking Irish, described Ulster Protestant settlers as 'Far Downs': *fear an Dúin* meaning 'man of Down'. Tensions were greatest in Toronto where some Protestants, known as 'blazers', tried to 'line off' or corral Catholics into their own districts. These attempts at segregation failed completely.

The Orange Order in Canada was largely established by southern Protestants. The first lodges were formed in Halifax in 1799 and in Montreal in 1800. John Rutledge, acquiring three lots of land in 1819, deeded a parcel of land for an Orange Hall. Ogle Gowan, the son of a County Wexford landlord, did most to build up the Order, particularly along the St Lawrence and the northern shores of Lake Ontario. By 1834 there were 154 lodges with 14,000 members. The first Twelfth parade was recorded as early as 1818 and by 1870 no fewer than 930 lodges operated in Ontario. Many who joined had no Irish connections whatsoever. In parts of rural Ulster population density had been as high as 400 per square mile. In the Ontario countryside it was only around 20 per square mile. Lodges in Canada therefore formed an important function of bringing people together for convivial occasions. LOL 215 in Leslieville, Ontario, spent almost all of its 1839 budget of £3 16s on refreshments, including a quart of spirit, four and a half gallons of whiskey and a great deal of brown sugar. In 1858 the Grand Master of Quebec was disturbed by reports that

> Some of the lodges spend the funds, which should be transmitted to this Grand Lodge, in drinking and carousing at their Lodge Meetings, which, if true, is deeply to be regretted, as it will justify the assertion of our enemies, who denounce us as drunken and blood thirsty.

Lodges also assisted immigrants from Ulster to find work. Some Toronto department stores and factory owners virtually guaranteed employment to loyal Protestants born in Ballymena. One Catholic Irishman complained that the Orange Order in Ontario was encouraging 'brethren' from Ulster 'to go there and make a second Belfast of the whole province'.

Membership of Canada's Orange Order fell away rapidly in the twentieth century but by then Canada had become an ever more popular destination for Ulster emigrants.

EPISODE 91

AN INDUSTRIAL HUB: BELFAST AND GLASGOW

T he American Civil War in the 1860s was the bloodiest conflict anywhere in the world in the nineteenth century. It sent shockwaves back across the Atlantic to Europe, having a profound effect on two cities on either side of the Narrow Sea, Belfast and Glasgow. When the Union commander-in-chief, General Ulysses Grant, sent Major-General William Sherman on his notorious march through Georgia in 1864, the cotton fields there were devastated. Meanwhile the Union fleet imposed an effective blockade on Confederate States, shutting off their exports. The price of cotton rose from 9d an ounce in 1861 to £1 4s in 1864. Deprived of raw material, the machinery of the United Kingdom's cotton mills fell silent. Glasgow, which was home to half of Scotland's 200 cotton mills, was particularly hard hit.

Long before, Belfast had given up its attempt to compete with Lancashire and Scotland in producing cotton. Instead it specialised in making linen by power machinery. Linen was then the nearest substitute for cotton and so Ulster faced the challenge of making up the shortfall. A boom followed in the Ulster linen industry quite without equal in the nineteenth century. By 1867 the province's mills and factories – most of them in Belfast – reached a remarkable capacity of 900,000 spindles and over 12,000 power looms. Belfast had become the greatest centre of linen production in the world and would remain so for many years to come. In 1895 the president of the Belfast Chamber of Commerce, H. O. Lanyon, made this estimation:

> I find the length of yarn produced in the year amounts to about 644,000,000 miles, making a thread which would encircle the world 25,000 times. If it could be used for a telephone wire it would give us six lines to the sun,

and about 380 besides to the moon. The exports of linen in 1894 measured about 156,000,000 yards, which would make a girdle for the earth at the Equator three yards wide, or cover an area of 32,000 acres, or it would reach from end to end of the County of Down, one mile wide.

Recovering from the loss of its 13 American colonies in 1783, the British Empire had become the most extensive the world had ever seen. By the middle of the nineteenth century, the United Kingdom was unquestionably by far the greatest trading state on earth and its foremost industrial power. Glasgow and Belfast played a crucial role in generating that strength.

Intimately connected, Belfast and Glasgow together formed a thriving commercial and industrial hub, making the North Channel one of the busiest waterways in the world. The growth of these two imperial cities had been uneven. In 1801 Belfast had been only a minor provincial port, with a population of less than 20,000. Glasgow at the same time had some 70,000 citizens. Its prosperity had been based on importing and re-exporting tobacco from America. Now Glasgow drew on the rich resources of its hinterland.

Unlike Ulster, Scotland had extensive deposits of coal, particularly in Lanarkshire. In the Monkland area of Scotland's central belt, rich veins of blackband stone – a variety of coal containing up to 35 per cent iron ore – were mined to smelt immense quantities of iron. James Neilson invented the hot blast method of smelting iron in 1828, which required a quarter of the coal previously needed. By the middle of the century Scotland was producing a quarter of Britain's iron output.

Along the Clyde skilled engineers converted this iron and steel into ships to defend the Empire and to keep its trade expanding across the globe. The world's first transatlantic steamship, the *Sirius*, was launched at Leith in 1838. The elegant tea clipper *Cutty Sark* was completed at Dumbarton in 1869. John Brown's yard built ocean vessels for the Cunard line. Around half the Royal Navy's ships were built on the Clyde; and by the end of the century the Clyde employed 50,000 in shipbuilding. Glasgow's cotton industry never quite recovered from the American Civil War, but when J. & P. Coats merged with Clarks in 1896 it was the largest manufacturing firm in Britain and the fifth-largest in the world.

What is remarkable about Belfast is that it became a great industrial city without local natural resources – coal, iron and steel had all to be imported across the Narrow Sea, principally from the Clyde. Nevertheless, this cross-channel trade made it possible for Belfast to become not only Ireland's largest city but also by 1900 the port of third importance in the United Kingdom after

London and Liverpool. By the end of the nineteenth century Harland and Wolff, and on more than one occasion the smaller Workman Clark shipyard, were launching the largest vessels ever constructed. For some years to come it would continue to build the world's largest ships. Though smaller than Glasgow, Belfast had become Ireland's industrial powerhouse. A veritable forest of tall gantries, towering flax mills, tapered factory chimneys and masted vessels moored below the Queen's Bridge marked this city out as one of the United Kingdom's most vibrant centres of production.

Considerable numbers of Scots crossed the North Channel to take up the comparatively well-paid skilled jobs available in Belfast's shipyards and engineering works. But their numbers were dwarfed by the numbers of people from Ulster seeking work in the Clyde and beyond.

EPISODE 92

A NEW LIFE IN SCOTLAND: NAVVIES AND MINERS

The 1870 census report for Scotland declared that around 1820:

> an invasion or immigration of the Irish race began, which slowly increased till it attained enormous dimensions after 1840 ... This invasion of Irish is likely to produce far more serious effects on the population of Scotland than even the invasions of warlike hordes of Saxons, Danes or Norsemen.

It observed that between 10 and 30 per cent of the population in many Scottish towns 'consist of the Irish Celtic race' and concluded that the 'immigration of such a body of labourers of the lowest class, with scarcely any education, cannot but have most prejudicial effects on the population'. The census revealed that natives of Ireland amounted to 207,770 persons or 6.184 per cent of the total population and that, if Scots-born children of Irish parents were included, the number would be raised to around 400,000. The report continued:

This very high proportion of the Irish race in Scotland has undoubtedly produced deleterious results, lowered greatly the moral tone of the lower classes, and greatly increased the necessity for the enforcement of sanitary and police precautions wherever they are settled in numbers.

The percentage of Irish immigrants began to drop somewhat thereafter but remained high: the census returns for 1881 gave the figure of 218,745 Irish-born in a total population of 3,735,573, the percentage being 5.856.

The great majority of Irish immigrants came from Ulster: 8,191 came from Ulster in 1876, with only 364 from the other three provinces. This human flow across the Narrow Sea provided more than half of the vast industrial army that built the railways of Scotland. The 60 miles (90 km) that formed the Edinburgh to Hawick line of 1846 had increased in the North British system to over 1,200 miles (1,931 km) by 1880. The second half of the century saw the completion of the 400 miles (644 km) of the Highland railway and the 300 miles (483 km) of the Great North of Scotland railway. The majority of these navvies were natives of Donegal. This was low-paid, difficult and often dangerous work. Navvies travelled the country, sleeping in verminous bunkhouses and forced to buy their food and moleskins at prices above the current ones in 'tommy shops' run by the contractors. Payment days were too widely separated and were celebrated by bouts of drinking and subsequent quarrelling referred to as 'Donnybrooks'. On more than one occasion, on the Kelso branch of the Edinburgh to Hawick line, local people attacked the navvies' huts, threw out the bedding and bits of furniture and set fire to them. Several navvies lost their lives in such incidents.

Navvies were also engaged in the building of docks and harbours for steamers run by the railway companies, especially at Greenock, Granton, Leith, Dundee, Stranraer and Grangemouth. In the 1850s they were employed in the making of the great aqueduct between Loch Katrine and Glasgow. These men and their wives were lodged in caves, 6 to 10 feet (1.8 by 3 metres) wide, in a peat bog in the glen above Loch Chon. Later in the century navvies were involved in the making of suburban underground railways, tramways, Glasgow's subway system, and sewage works.

The principal agent of the Duke of Hamilton's estates described the 'male collier population' to the duchess in 1851 as 'rude, vulgar, ignorant and savage in the extreme'. This condition had sunk even lower 'owing to the vast influx of Irish of the lowest grade'. He continued:

The great increase of the iron trade in this part of Scotland, i.e. Lanarkshire, where the number of iron blast furnaces has been augmented, since the year

1806 to this date, from fourteen to ninety, and the coal mining from a few pits, comparatively speaking, to no less than nearly 200, has occasioned this immigration into it.

In 1868 Alexander McDonald, president of the Miners' National Association, was asked: 'Taking the thirty years since you have had experience of the mines of Scotland, what do you suppose was the proportion of Irish at the beginning of that time to what it is now?' He replied: 'It is a hundred per cent more I should think now'. In 1854 368 Scottish collieries produced 7,500,000 tons; by 1874 there were 470 collieries with an output of over 20,000,000 tons. Lanarkshire and Ayrshire were responsible for 70 per cent of the coal mined. Over the same period the number of coal miners had risen from 33,000 to 53,000. In 1880 the iron industry of Scotland's central belt employed 50,000. The production of pig iron grew from half a million tons in 1850 to 1,126,000 tons in 1882. The *Ordnance Gazetter of Scotland* in 1885 provided the following statistics:

In 1882 there were in Scotland 182 blast furnaces in 23 works, 22 iron mills and forges with 380 puddling-furnaces, and 74 rolling-mills. Steel was manufactured by the open-hearth method in 57 furnaces (Glasgow, Motherwell, Holytown and Wishaw), and by Siemen's gas furnaces in Glasgow and Coatbridge.

The great majority of immigrants of 'the Irish Celtic race' came from Ulster. A total of 8,9191 came from Ulster in 1876, with only 219 from Connacht, 111 from Munster and a mere 34 from Leinster. This pattern remained consistent: in 1905, for example, 1,378 arrived from Ulster, 86 from Connacht, 76 from Leinster and 36 from Munster. Co. Donegal may have provided most of the migrant seasonal workers but Co. Antrim supplied more permanent immigrants than any other county. In 1877 the statistics were: Antrim 2,342; Armagh 609; Cavan 240; Londonderry 1,403; Donegal 739; Down 957; Fermanagh 249; Monaghan 242; and Tyrone 702.

EPISODE 93

'THE DEATH RATE FROM CHEST AFFECTIONS IS VERY HIGH': HARSH WORKING CONDITIONS

The development of mass production drew families in from the countryside to rapidly growing industrial towns and cities to seek work in spinning mills, weaving sheds, factories, foundries and engineering works. Such concentration was strikingly evident on both sides of the Narrow Sea: in Ulster along the Lagan valley, in Derry and numerous mill villages; and in the Scottish Lowland belt, particularly along the Clyde, the Tay and the Firth of Forth. For much of the Victorian era this employment, especially for those classed as unskilled, was dangerous, low-paid and injurious to health.

Writing an account of the influence of flax-spinning on the health of mill workers in Belfast in 1867, Dr John Moore concluded that 'the employment will be found, if not the most lucrative, at least one of the most healthy in the whole range of our manufactures'. Ten years later damning reports by Dr C D Purdon, certifying surgeon of the Belfast factory district, exposed the complacency of Moore's conclusion.

Examining boys engaged in hackling flax (drawing handfuls of fibre through boards fitted with iron pins), Purdon concluded that their 'mortality from Phthisis, etc., is very high' and that army surgeons 'have forbidden recruiting sergeants to enlist any from this department'. Next the flax was sent for combing to separate the 'tow', or short fibre, from the 'line', the best long fibre. The 'pouce' (flax dust) quickly entered the lungs of the machine boys leading to a 'paroxysm of cough and dyspnoea' that 'does not pass off until the contents of the stomach are ejected, and often blood is spat up'. The next process was 'preparing' and 'carding'; girls working there, Dr Purdon continued, 'suffer in the same manner as the males, but in a far more aggravated degree ... in this department the death rate from chest affections is very high.'

'Doffers', girls who replaced bobbins in the spinning rooms, suffered from 'the moisture and heat of the rooms, which often causes them to faint, and accidents have occurred by their falling on machinery'. New recruits often suffered from 'mill fever' brought on by the odour of oil and flax, the symptoms being 'rigors, nausea, vomiting, quickly followed by pain in the head, thirst, heat of skin, etc.'

Dr Moore did refer to 'the deformity of the foot – a species of talapsis' and 'onychia' caused by contaminated water washing round barefoot doffers, which 'requires for its remedy a most painful operation, either the dissecting out or wrenching out the entire roots of the great toe-nail'. In weaving sheds the temperature and humidity were kept very high by steam and hundreds of gas jets. Here, Dr Purdon noted, weavers 'suffer greatly from chest affections ... The constant stooping' over heavy looms, he continued, 'renders the death rate very high'. Linen workers also ran the risk of being maimed or killed by exposed machinery. On 1 May 1854 a girl engaged in carding at Rowans of York Street had her hair 'entangled in the machinery in which the greater part of the scalp was removed from the head'.

On the eastern side of the Narrow Sea official enquiries and reports provide ample evidence of harsh working conditions. A parliamentary commissioner visited 38 bleach and dye works in the west of Scotland in 1855. Labour for these was recruited almost exclusively from Irish and Highland girls because only women of robust constitution found in farming stock could stand up to the exacting conditions of work. He found that women spent their entire working hours in drying rooms heated to a temperature of between 90 and 130 degrees Fahrenheit (32 to 54 degrees Celsius). Most were aged between 15 and 25, but he found many girls and some boys aged between 11 and 15. 'The recognised hours of work at the largest proportion of these bleach-works', he reported, 'were from 67 to upwards of 70 hours per week; in addition to which ... overtime was not uncommon'. Some girls were too exhausted after 19 hours of work to go home and lay down in a store room 'coming out of those hot places dripping with perspiration, and their clothes wet through with it'.

Two years later a Paisley surgeon reported that employees in bleaching mills suffered from varicose veins. 'I have known the workers bleed almost to death in a very short time', he said. 'Rupture is another thing that is very common in consequence of the constant standing ... most of these females are young girls from the Highlands and from Ireland; they frequently come with a plump and healthy appearance but that very soon disappears ...' Children of immigrants were also employed in the pottery, tobacco and clay-pipe factories of Scottish industrial towns. One 13-year-old said that after running moulds and wedging clay in a pottery between 6 a.m. and 6.30 p.m. 'I have to work for my father when I go home. I teaze ropes. We get sixpence a stone for the tow – 20lb to the stone'.

ORANGE AND GREEN IN SCOTLAND

Those moving out of the Ulster countryside to Belfast and other industrial towns brought with them their folk memories, fears and entrenched beliefs. Just as intercommunal distrust periodically erupted in street violence in urban Ulster, so those who had crossed the Narrow Sea transferred over the water age-old tensions as they settled in Scotland's thriving industrial centres.

In Belfast in the late nineteenth century the number of low-paid unskilled Protestants and Catholics was around the same. However, the better-paid skilled trades were then almost entirely dominated by Protestants. This was not the case amongst Irish immigrants in Scotland. Because skilled workers were rather better paid in Ulster than in Scotland, they tended to stay at home. But as the unskilled were considerably better paid in Scotland (where wages were a third higher than in Belfast) there were sound reasons why they would cross the North Channel to get a better living there. Protestants and Catholics settling in Scottish ports and industrial centres, therefore, were at the same economic level. Their living and working conditions were almost the same – but their allegiances and cultural traditions, of course, were diametrically opposed.

A detailed analysis based on the 1891 census for six Clydeside shipbuilding communities (Greenock, Dumbarton, Clydebank, Linthouse, Govan and Partick) showed that Catholic and Protestant immigrants there had identical occupational and demographic profiles. 'This was so in terms of age, family size, skill level, size of house occupied and types of occupation entered', the researchers concluded.

In Govan's shipbuilding yards, the skilled men, predominantly boilermakers and platers, were Lowland Scots. But large numbers of unskilled labourers, such as caulkers and stokers, were needed and almost all of these workers were recruited from immigrants living in the immediate area. Protestants were no better able to afford better-quality housing than Catholics. They did, however, do their best to select their homes (one-room tenements for the most part) in separate streets. In Govan, for example, Protestants lived in Harmony Row, a street which ran parallel, north to south, around 50 yards from the Catholic-inhabited Hamilton Street. Both streets ended opposite the Elder family's huge Fairfield yard. In Kinning Park, St James Street was overwhelmingly Catholic while Plantation Street, 300 yards away, was correspondingly Protestant. However, from the beginning of the twentieth century this segregation in Clydeside – unlike that in Belfast – eased considerably. To a very notable extent this was due to the success of trade unions in Glasgow in building up a sense of workers' solidarity.

In Greenock and the adjacent town of Port Glasgow, Protestant and Catholic Irish worked alongside each other in the sugar refineries and the quays. Here vicious faction fights, often involving as many as 400, were frequent on Saturday and Sunday evenings. In October 1855, ferocious fighting broke out between shipyard workers in Dumbarton. According to the *Free Press* this trouble arose 'from a preconcerted plan of the Orange scoundrels of the place to give the Papists a milling, or in other words to drive the Catholic population out of the town and destroy their chapel'. Messrs Denny and Rankine in consequence dismissed all their Irish employees regardless of religious affiliation.

For year after year intercommunal battles broke out during and immediately after the 'Twelfth'. In the wake of violence at Airdrie and Coatbridge, the sheriffs of Lanarkshire, Renfrewshire, Stirlingshire and Dumbartonshire 'proclaimed', that is, banned all Twelfth processions in their counties in 1858. The following year, however, the ban was lifted in Renfrewshire. As the parade came to an end in Paisley, Orangemen fell into conflict with Catholic miners. Firearms, knives, bludgeons and paling stobs were used: a Catholic was stabbed to death and many were injured. 'One very extraordinary feature of the day's proceedings', the *Glasgow Herald* observed, 'was the encouragement given to the Orangemen by the police'.

The places most persistently convulsed by this sectarian battling were Partick, Govan, Coatbridge, Motherwell and surrounding districts. Here parades by Orangemen on the Twelfth were followed by equally large Catholic nationalist demonstrations every 15 August to celebrate the Feast of the Assumption. The violence accompanying the Coatbridge parade on 12 July 1883 was eclipsed in scale by the vicious warfare which erupted a few weeks later in mid-August. When the Home Rule march reached Sunnyside, the Protestants attacked with stones. A charge by mounted police drove the attackers back but only for a time. Fighting also broke out at Bellshill. At Motherwell, the local priest issued posters declaring that parishioners joining a nationalist demonstration were 'acting in direct opposition to ecclesiastical authority'. His appeal was fruitless. This street warfare continued through Sunday into Monday when both sides got fresh recruits from workers coming off the day shift. Revolvers were used and order was only gradually restored by mounted police charges.

Lives were lost in these encounters but the sectarian battles between Protestant and Catholic immigrants were nowhere as lethal as those in Ulster during the same period. The Belfast riots of 1886, when the first Home Rule Bill was being debated and defeated, extended from early June, all through the summer and into September and cost around 50 lives. There were no riots at all, for example, in Govan in 1886.

EPISODE 95

'THIS HIBERNIAN INVASION HAS ... STAMPED ITS IMPRESS ON THE COUNTRY'

The *Scotsman* reported on 11 August 1846 that in the preceding week from Belfast via Ardrossan and from Belfast and Derry direct to the Broomielaw upwards of 14,000 Irish reapers equipped with sickles had arrived in Glasgow. During the next few years they continued to travel in great numbers. The vessels transporting them were often alarmingly overcrowded. the *Scottish Guardian* observed in August 1849:

> The *Londonderry* brought over from Ireland the extraordinary number of 1,700 human beings at one trip, but a still more incredible fact was noticed on Friday when the *Thistle* steamer arrived at Greenock from Londonderry with upwards of 1,900 deck passengers ... The poor creatures filled every corner from stem to stem, clustering round the bulwarks as thick as bees.

These two ships had each a tonnage of less than 300 tons. In 1850 the *Herald* remarked that 'it is pleasing to notice [passengers] are this year better attired, and altogether in a better condition of body. Formerly rags and squalor were the rule; now they are the exception'. In 1851 a veritable army of 12,000 Irish reapers was employed, 'accompanied by women and children at least to another 1,000'.

It required six shearers, at 2s 4d each, to cut in a day a Scotch acre (equal to one and a quarter English acres). Scythes were only rarely preferred to sickles for cutting corn as opposed to hay, but the introduction of the mechanical reaper in the 1850s saw a steady drop in demand for Irish shearers. Despite teething difficulties, especially on undulating land, mechanical reapers were preferred by farmers to having to create large encampments for unruly Irish workers, especially unruly when idle in wet weather. Local people often resented the migrant hordes, as the journal *Witness* observed in October 1857:

> We deeply lament and condemn the introduction into counties like East Lothian of a set of low Popish Irish that bring with them their debasing habits, their turbulence, their blind superstition, and deteriorate our native population wherever they settle.

The introduction of reaping machines did not reduce the demand for immigrant labour. The land was now being cultivated more intensively and migrant labourers were much in demand to effect improvements. 'Nearly the whole of the drainage operations are now executed, not by the native population, but by immigrant Irish – the local labourers being nearly all absorbed by the demand for hired servants as ploughmen, cattle-keepers and barnmen', the *Border Advertiser* reported in 1856. Most of the agricultural labourers who travelled to Scotland came from Ulster, and the vast majority from a small area in Donegal – the area included in the Poor Law Unions of Glenties, Dunfanaghy, Inishowen and Milford strung along the west and north-west of the county. Glenties provided by far the largest number of migrants. The 1858 Report from the select committee on destitution in Gweedore and Cloghaneely concluded that virtually every single able-bodied man from those districts left home every spring to work in Scotland. Outside of Co. Donegal, the largest number of migrants came from south-east Armagh and south-west Down, in and around Newry. In 1862 Robert Skirving, an East Lothian landlord, concluded that:

> this Hibernian invasion has in many respects stamped its impress upon the country ... Good and bad, quiet and disorderly, their labour is absolutely necessary. They have come to fill up a great gap. Without them it is simply impossible that, under present circumstances, the agriculture of some parts of Scotland could be carried on. While this is the state of things as regards the men, the female workers on the farm are still more exclusively immigrants ...

By now the potato was the crop that was replacing corn as the provider of seasonal employment.

EPISODE 96

'RABBLES': THE HIRING FAIRS OF ULSTER

To endure the loneliness and hardships of becoming migrants working in Scotland, thousands of boys and girls in Ulster hired themselves out in preparation as farm servants for six-month terms.

Hiring fairs were to be found across the island but the largest were in the north-west. Here they were known as 'rabbles', the most significant being in Strabane, Derry, Omagh, Letterkenny, Stranorlar, Carndonagh, Raphoe and Milford. These fairs were held in May and November, and the dates were staggered: if work could not be found in one fair there was always an alternative to go to another day.

Róise Rua, who lived on Arranmore Island, recalled:

The hiring fairs in Strabane were held on Old Hallowe'en (12 November) and Old May Day (12 May). Those were two big days in the life of the young ones then; they were every bit as important as Christmas Day and Easter Sunday are for children these days.

Those young people (some as young as nine or ten) generally had to walk many miles, often in bare feet, to the fairs. Hiúdaí Sheáinin, who told his story to Eoghan Ó Domhnaill, was first engaged at the Letterkenny hiring fair in 1867 at the age of 13 or 14. His mother had made him a pair of footless stockings and his small bundle consisted of no more than an old shirt and a pair of working trousers. With his friend Seán Ó Baoighill, who was already crying with loneliness just a few miles from home, he walked 30 miles to Letterkenny where the two boys got lodging for the night. Overnight accommodation could often be got in the Letterkenny workhouse dormitory if empty beds were available.

The extension of light railways in Ireland's 'Congested Districts', encouraged by Conservative governments at the close of the nineteenth century, had the result of increasing the size of hiring fairs. In May 1903 the railway company operating the newly opened line from Burtonport to Letterkenny had no alternative but to pack some passengers onto cattle trucks because the carriages were so overcrowded. Those offering themselves for hire sometimes carried a straw or a peeled willow stick to show that they were seeking work. Farmers, many of them wearing bowler hats, looked over those lining themselves up and bargained with them. Once a wage was agreed, the young people waited until the close of the fair. Then they would be taken by horse and cart to the farms where they would live and work for the ensuing six months.

Hiúdaí was hired by a farmer in Drumquin, Co. Tyrone. He was paid £1 for six months' labour. His evening meal was a bowl of buttermilk and some potatoes and he slept on straw thrown on the ground with an old blanket and a couple of empty bags to cover him. He herded cattle by himself, a job made particularly lonely for a lad speaking only Irish in an area where just one old woman could be found who could speak it to him. Mící Mac Gabhann, aged nine, had been taken by his mother from their home in Cloghaneely to the Letterkenny hiring fair in 1874. His verdict after spending six six-month terms as a servant boy on farms in the Laggan was 'sclábhaíocht, streachailt agus síorobair gan sos gan scíth' (slavery, struggle and working all the time without a rest).

The most likely destination was the Laggan, the fertile area in north-east Donegal where the strong farmers hiring labour were for the most part Presbyterians. Strictly speaking the Laggan is the district between the River Foyle and Lough Swilly, but to the young people hiring themselves out the boundaries could reach deep into the counties of Tyrone, Derry and even Fermanagh. The Taylor family, owners of a large farm at Craigadoos near St Johnston in the Laggan, kept detailed records of those they hired on six-month contracts. These show that their workers were treated exceptionally well. The Taylors were members of the Church of Ireland but paid the local priest half a crown for each worker at Christmas and Easter. Those they employed were given time off to visit local towns and their families. William Gilespy was contracted to be paid £6 for the period 12 November 1872 to 12 May 1873. Unusually, the Taylors gave him advances totalling £1 16s to pay for the repair of boots, a day visit to Derry, a ticket to a concert, 'cash to go to the dance' and 'cash the Sunday you went home'. This meant that on 12 November he had just £4 4s to take home.

After five or six years of selling their labour to 'strong' farmers, learning skills such as milking, herding and thinning turnips, these boys and girls had completed their apprenticeship. Effectively, they had been hardening themselves up to meet the rigorous demands sure to be made on them when joining the squads travelling across the Narrow Sea to labour on Scottish farms.

TATTIE HOKERS: DONEGAL MIGRANT WORKERS IN SCOTLAND

Only the arrival of the railway made the potato an important commercial crop. Before that it had been prohibitively expensive to transport potatoes any great distance except by water. In Ayrshire the potato industry grew rapidly following the extension of the railway to Maybole and Girvan in 1860. It expanded greatly in the 1870s in the Lothians, Fifeshire, Perthshire, Renfrewshire and Dumbartonshire. A striking feature was that Irish migrants (unlike Scots from the Highlands and Islands) brought their womenfolk to join the gangs of 'tattie hokers', the potato harvesters. A report of 1871 stated: 'The extended use of self-binders during the corn harvest has rendered extra labourers at that particular season almost unnecessary, but potatoes can be gathered and separated, the sound from the unsound, only by manual labour'. Fife potato-buyers purchased by the acre, arranging for the tubers to be dressed at the time of gathering before shipping them directly to London.

Patrick MacGill was born into poverty near Glenties in 1890. He was first engaged at the Strabane hiring fair at the age of 12 and later crossed over to work on farms and as a navvy in Scotland. In his semi-autobiographical novel, *Children of the Dead End*, he described the work of harvesting potatoes at the beginning of the twentieth century:

> The job, bad enough for men, was killing for women. All day long, on their hands and knees, they dragged through the slush and rubble of the field. The baskets which they hauled after them were cased in clay to the depth of several inches, and sometimes when emptied of potatoes a basket weighed over two stone. The strain on women's arms must have been terrible. But they never complained. Pools of water gathered in the hollows of the dress that covered the calves of their legs. Sometimes they rose and shook the water from their clothes, then they went down on their knees again … Two little ruts, not at all unlike furrows left by a coulter of a skidding plough, lay behind the women in the black earth. These were made by their knees.

Another task that provided employment, for women in particular, was the thinning, weeding and lifting of turnips. Turnip 'singling and shawing' (thinning, topping and tailing) in the last decades of the nineteenth century were generally paid for by piecework rates of six to eight shillings an acre, with higher rates if pulling turnips was also involved. A job carried out exclusively by women was the gutting of fish. These 'gutters' travelled from Donegal to ports such as Lerwick, Peterhead, Wick and Stornoway.

Some women left for Scotland in March, but most travelled in May or June. They were employed in planting potatoes, thinning turnips, weeding, harvesting and potato lifting, returning home in late autumn. Scottish merchants who bought crops of potatoes while in the ground contacted 'gaffers' in Donegal and elsewhere to collect young women as well as men and accompany them to do the potato lifting, taking them from farm to farm and making all the arrangements for travelling.

A report of 1892 provided much detail on how tattie hokers were housed and nourished:

> In most of the steadings there is a temporary bothy with a fireplace, some chairs or benches, and wooden bedsteads ... They work by the piece at some jobs, rising very early and often toiling till sunset ... At turnip singling they sometimes earn as much as 30/- per week, but to do this they work from 4.30 a.m. to 9 p.m. only stopping for a few minutes to take their dinner of bread and cheese, with a cup of cold tea.

It added that a few of the Irish men did not return home, having 'in most cases married Scotch girls, and fallen into Scotch ways'. Migrant workers from Donegal in the counties of Berwickshire and Roxburghshire, engaged in turnip thinning and mowing corn which had lodged too much to be cut by the reaping machine, had to make do with shelter in barns. The food supplied was oatmeal porridge and milk for breakfast and supper, bread and beer for dinner, and potatoes which migrants cooked on a fire outside their sleeping quarters.

A detailed report in 1905 provided information on the places in Ireland where migrant workers came from and how much they earned. There were seventy-one men, most of them from Donegal, who earned between 24s and 19s 10d a week, and seven men from Armagh, engaged in harvesting and potato lifting between 1 August and 1 October earned between 15 and 16 shillings a week. The 'gaffer' in charge of the squad had from 26 to 30 shillings a week. The working day was ten hours with an interval of ten minutes in the morning and afternoon and half an hour for the midday meal.

An outbreak of enteric fever among potato diggers on a farm in Stirlingshire in 1897 was investigated by the county medical officer. He found 17 men and women lodging in a bothy consisting of a single apartment 17 feet square. Their water came from a dip well in an adjacent field. There were no sanitary facilities. Though the 'gaffer' assured him that the accommodation was better than that usually given to potato diggers, the doctor declared that 'I had never myself seen human beings lodged under conditions so utterly indefensible as regards both health and decency'. His report prompted an examination of 15 other farms. At only seven of them was there separation of the sexes. The worst example was a byre provided for the housing of 17 men, 5 women and 6 calves, with a heap of manure at one end and a pile of chaff at the other. A serious defect was the lack of fires to dry clothes worn by workers exposed to rain and standing all day in the turned-up soil of potato fields.

EPISODE 98

PADDY 'THE COPE' GALLAGHER CROSSES OVER TO SCOTLAND

'Paddy the Cope', Patrick Gallagher (Pádraig Ó Gallchóir) from Cleendra in the Rosses, recalled his first journey from Derry in the year 1889:

We walked from Cleendra to Letterkenny, a distance of thirty-six miles and trained from Letterkenny to Derry on the Londonderry and Lough Swilly Railway, built a few years previously. We arrived in Derry in good time for the Glasgow boat. I paid four shillings for my ticket. I suppose we were in the same steerage compartment in which my father often travelled. In any case the cattle and pigs were in the same flat. There was a bench or seat along the side of the ship, not enough sitting room for all the women and men in the compartment. There was no lavatory. (If it came hard on you, you had to go in among the cattle) …

We landed at the Broomielaw at about twelve noon the following day, and broke up into squads. The squad I was with (six of us in all) went to Queen's Street Station, and took our tickets for Jedburgh, Roxburghshire, and as far as I can remember the ticket was six shillings and sixpence. We reached Jedburgh late that night, and got lodgings in Muldoon's Model, fourpence each for a bed. John Biddy and Hughdie Micky collected one shilling from each of us for the supper and breakfast. They went to a small shop and got bread, bacon, tea, sugar and milk, the whole lot coming to four shillings and a halfpenny. I remember the price because we divided the change ...

Next morning we went out amongst the farmers looking for work ... 'I have a field of turnips ready for singling. Can any of you lads single?' We both said we could. We had been practising with small rows of stones before we left home. Hughdie spent a week training us to knock four stones off the top of a drill and leave the next in its bed without touching it. The day before we left for Scotland we were carefully examined by our fathers, Hughdie and the others. We satisfied the examiners, who told us it would be no shame for us to say we could single turnips ... The master told us we could start in the morning. 'I will give each of you seven bob a week until the harvest if you are worth it; if not, off you go,' he said. 'I have no blankets until I get into Kelso next market day, and if you are worth the money, I will get a new blanket for you. You can sleep over the horses, and I will give you plenty of bags to get into ... We were not very long in the barn until we heard the shout: 'Paddies, let one of you come down to the kitchen for your dinners'.

Dinner consisted of a jug of milk and two small loaves of bread. For supper they had porridge and milk.

We had a happy time at the Crow's Farm for the nine weeks we were there. Sam had no corn, and as the farmers who had corn were paying one pound a week and Sam not having sufficient work for us, we had to leave. We were very sorry when it came to the last week. We had to go to the other side of Kelso. We used to meet the other lads every Sunday at Kelso and had always a feed on O'Donovan's Hot Plate.

Patrick Gallagher was to return to the Rosses where he founded 'the Cope', the Templecrone Agricultural Co-operative Society. Opposed by local vested interests ('gombeen men'), he had to buy his own boats to do his own importing. Fishermen, weavers and knitters were able to swap what they had caught and made for items on sale in his local co-operative shops. His biography *Patrick Gallagher: My Story* was published in 1939.

EPISODE 99

INDUSTRIAL MIGHT ... IN ULSTER ...

T hough both Ulster and Scotland had extensive areas of remote, impoverished and sparsely inhabited countryside, they both contained some of the most intensively industrialised regions on the face of the planet. Indeed, on the eve of the Great War they were at the zenith of their global economic power.

In Ulster this manufacturing and commercial might was concentrated in the lower Lagan valley. For a brief moment, during the Boer War, Belfast was the port of third importance in the United Kingdom, after London and Liverpool, before being bypassed by Glasgow soon after peace was signed in 1902. A smaller city than Glasgow, Belfast could boast nevertheless that it had the largest shipyard, ropeworks, linen mill, tobacco factory, tea machinery and fan-making works, aerated waters factory, linen machinery works, dry dock, handkerchief factory and spiral-guided gasometer anywhere on earth.

On 14 January 1899 Harland and Wolff launched the *Oceanic* from Queen's Island. Fitted with four-cylinder, triple-expansion engines, with a gross tonnage of 17,274, it was 13 feet (3.9m) longer than Brunel's *Great Eastern*, the mightiest ship afloat and the largest man-made moving object ever constructed up to that time anywhere in the world. In the years following the company continued to launch the world's biggest ships, including the *Olympic* in 1910 and the *Titanic* in 1911. The tragic sinking of the *Titanic* in April 1912, with the loss of 1,490 passengers and crew, did cast a shadow over the reputation of Belfast and, in particular, over that of the White Star Line, the firm's most valuable customer. There was no fall in orders for the present, however. The output of Workman Clark – inappropriately known as the 'wee yard' – actually exceeded that of Harland and Wolff on several occasions in the years before the outbreak of war in 1914. Entering the Lagan from its slips in 1904, the *Victorian* was to be the first passenger-carrying turbine-driven liner to cross the Atlantic.

Though its profits were dwarfed by those earned by shipbuilding and engineering, the linen industry remained by far the largest employer of labour in the city. Belfast continued to be the most important centre of production but the making of fine linen was by no means confined to it. This was because Ulster was exceptionally well served by its railway network; since goods trains could, speedily and inexpensively, bring flax and coal from the quayside into the heart of the province and take finished cloth back to the ports, many mills sprang up in the countryside. These included the Braidwater, Lisnafallen and Hillmount mills in Ballymena; Dunbar, McMaster & Co. in Gilford; Clark's of Upperlands; Herdman's at Sion Mills; and others at Bessbrook, Drumaness, Shrigley, Killyleagh, Comber and Castlewellan.

Between 1881 and 1911 the population of Derry doubled to over 40,000. This expansion was largely generated by the success there of the shirt-making industry. Cotton shirts, with linen fronts and cuffs, were supplanting those made of flannel. William Scott was the first to exploit the commercial possibilities of these new garments by securing orders in Glasgow for shirts cut out in city workshops and embroidered and sewn up in the countryside. The invention of steam-driven machines for both cutting and sewing brought shirt-making into factories, the most impressive being a five-storey block covering almost an acre in Foyle Road, erected in 1857 by two Scots, William Tillie and John Henderson. By 1891 the firm had added a steam laundry to its premises, exported its products – the 'Celtic' shirt in particular – across the empire and in Latin America. The firm employed 1,500 at its Foyle Road factory and another 3,000 rural workers, more than half of them in Inishowen.

Derry did construct ships for a time. Captain William Coppin had built sailing vessels in the 1830s. He launched the world's largest screw-propulsion vessel, the *Great Northern*, in 1843; but his steamships were not a commercial success. W F Biggar's Foyle shipyard at Pennyburn built 26 sailing vessels and 6 steamers before being forced to close down in 1892. In 1899 the Londonderry Shipbuilding and Engineering Company resumed operations at the Foyle yard and, taken over by Swan and Hunter in 1912, it prospered in a small way with good prospects on the eve of international conflict in 1914.

Derry had become a thriving commercial and industrial centre by the beginning of the twentieth century. Its economy was diversified by busy corn and saw mills, foundries, tanneries, tobacco manufacture, salmon netting, oyster fishing and whiskey distillation – A.A. Watt's Abbey Street distillery was for a time the largest in Ireland.

Though local industries in many towns wilted before the onslaught of more competitive goods brought in by rail, some resisted this trend by specialisation. Kennedy's Coleraine Foundry became one of Ireland's leading makers of agricultural implements and water turbines. Barbour's Hilden Mills near Lisburn had become the largest linen thread manufacturer in the world. The famous works of McBirney & Company drew on the water power of the Erne at Belleek to create a high-lustre, elaborately ornate and extremely delicate china. Likewise, Carrickmacross lace had an international reputation for quality. Founded originally by the Sisters of the Order of St Louis in the 1890s, the success of this industry (worth £100,000 a year by 1907) was largely due to the energetic and sustained patronage of Lady Aberdeen, the viceroy's wife.

EPISODE 100

... AND INDUSTRIAL MIGHT IN SCOTLAND

The industrialised west-central belt of Scotland then made a formidable contribution to Britain's economic predominance. Its core was Glasgow and its satellite towns, a region responsible for producing one third of the United Kingdom's shipping tonnage, one half of its marine engine horsepower, one fifth of its steel, most of its sewing machines and one third of its steam locomotives and rolling stock.

Fuelled by coal mined in Stirlingshire, Ayrshire and Fife, the great steelworks of Motherwell and Coatbridge strove to meet the requirements of a kaleidoscope of industries. The North British Locomotive Company employed 8,300 men in Glasgow. The greatest consumers of steel were the Clyde shipyards, particularly Fairfield's and John Brown's: unlike the Belfast yards, those based on the Clyde depended heavily on orders for the Royal Navy but they also launched large merchant ships and ocean-going passenger vessels, particularly for the Cunard, Clan, Anchor and Donaldson lines. Napier's of Govan made all of Cunard's marine engines. In 1913–14 no fewer than 51,000 men were engaged in shipbuilding on the Clyde, where 18 per cent of the world's vessels were launched. It is thought that some 70 per cent of men employed in Glasgow could be classed as skilled – in Belfast it was no more than 25 per cent.

In 1884 the German-American entrepreneur Isaac Singer built his largest European factory to manufacture sewing machines on a 46-acre site at Kilbowie. By the time Edward VII had succeeded his mother Victoria in 1901, Singer's was employing 10,000 men and women. The Addiewell Works, near West Calder, was the largest producer of paraffin oil in the world; at one time no fewer than 120 firms were engaged in extracting this oil from local shale stone and by 1900 the six biggest were producing around six million tons a year. The chemical complex at St Rollox in Glasgow was the largest in the world. Perhaps half a million workers across the central belt depended on the making of iron and steel goods. That does not include 6,000 men employed clipping tickets and driving trams on the 200 miles of Glasgow's municipal track. Children continued to be employed in their thousands, though now in out-of-school hours. Tom Bell began his milk round when he was eight or nine. He had to carry 20 cans at a time up 4 flights of tenement stairs for 1s 6d a week: 'On winter mornings our hands were cracked and bleeding with frost and cold, and I cried'. Then he got a better job as a van-boy for a mineral water firm, selling lemonade and Irn-Bru round Airdrie and Coatbridge – 'the iron workers in these infernos had a perpetual thirst', he remembered.

A succession of cargo ships steamed up the Tay bringing jute from Calcutta, Bombay and Karachi. Half the population of Dundee was engaged in manufacturing almost all the jute cloth in the United Kingdom, made (after being treated with whale oil) into sacking, backing for carpets and linoleum. Linoleum (known everywhere as 'lino', for much of the twentieth century a ubiquitous floor covering) was made in Kirkaldy from jute canvas and linseed oil. The jute mills of Dundee sought to fend off Indian competition by using low-paid female labour. In that city, there were three women to every two men, aged between 20 and 35, and two-thirds of all heads of households were women. The family culture of Dundee (similar to that in the shirt-making city of Derry) was therefore radically different from the male-dominated one thriving in the densely housed communities abutting the Fife coalfields and Clyde shipyards.

The traditional hosiery industries in the Borders used local fleeces but relied increasingly on wool imported from Australia to make knitwear and tweed. Dunfermline was known for its linen, Paisley for its thread and Aberdeen for its textiles and granite. Edinburgh, reckoned to be Britain's third richest city, prospered as the country's legal heartland and from its financial services, as well as being a producer of a wide range of consumer goods, including its highly regarded India Pale Ale. Scotland established secure niche markets in, for example, printing and publishing; medical and scientific equipment for its world-class teaching hospitals and universities; jams and preserves from farms in the Clyde and Tay valleys; cheese from the Borders and Galloway; kippers from the east coast ports; and confectionary and comic books from Dundee.

This account of economic success needs some qualification. Many firms remained in business only because wages were barely above subsistence level and, in these years, their purchasing power was being eroded by inflation. The largest industries, in particular, were heavily dependent on exports and therefore subject to alarming fluctuations in the trade cycle. The shipyards on the Clyde were over-dependent on Admiralty orders and on Queen's Island the welfare of Harland and Wolff was inextricably bound up with the fate of just one company, the White Star Line of Liverpool and Southampton.

From 9 May 1907 Belfast was brought to a standstill for over nine months as a federation of employers locked out dockers, and eventually most of the unskilled in the city, in an attempt to stop them joining trade unions. Troops, including battalions of Cameron Highlanders, were brought in by 9 warships after 800 members of the constabulary had refused to obey orders. When cavalry charges were repelled by rioters throwing showers of paving stones, soldiers opened fire, killing two people, including Maggie Lennon out looking for her child.

The Belfast Dock Strike had been aggravated by a severe downturn in trade in 1907–8. Glasgow was one of the worst affected places in the United Kingdom. By Christmas 1907 7,000 were wholly reliant on what was being offered by a special relief fund. By the autumn of the following year, according to *The Times*, over 16,000 were 'on the verge of starvation'. In the western world the early years of the twentieth century were characterised by violent fluctuations in the economic cycle. Manufacturing tended to be most acutely affected. In 1908 unemployment in Clydeside shipbuilding soared to 28 per cent, provoking a new militancy amongst skilled men, especially those who had joined the Marxist Social Democratic Federation. Boom conditions returned in 1909 and on the eve of the Great War the unemployment rate in Glasgow had fallen to 1.8 per cent.

During the Dock Strike, Catholics and Protestants in Belfast had campaigned shoulder to shoulder. But it would take more than faith in workers' solidarity to detach them from their traditional political allegiances. By 1912 clashing aspirations in Ulster were plunging the whole of the United Kingdom into a constitutional crisis.

'YOU AND I ARE JUST ABOUT FIT TO MEND HIS PENS': WILLIAM THOMSON, LORD KELVIN, SCIENTIFIC GENIUS

On 12 June 1798 the weather was perfect as armed United Irishmen assembled on rising ground overlooking Ballynahinch. James Thomson, a boy of 12, helped women to carry food to the rebel encampment. He later wrote a vivid account of what he had seen that day. As these insurgents awaited the approach of the forces of the Crown, he described how many sheltered 'themselves from the scorching rays of a burning sun under the shelter of trees' and that they 'wore no uniforms; yet they presented a tolerably decent appearance being dressed, no doubt, in their Sunday clothes'. The ladies swiftly took young James from the field as the government's cannon opened up.

Twenty years later this farmer's son from County Down was a teacher of mathematics and engineering in the Royal Belfast Academical Institution, a degree-awarding college modelled on Scottish academies founded in 1810. He had married Margaret Gardner in 1817 and six of the children she bore survived infancy. James insisted on tutoring his two older boys, James and William, at home. William was only six when his mother died in 1830.

In 1833 James Thomson was appointed Professor of Mathematics at Glasgow University. Extraordinary though it seems today, William became a student of that university at the age of 11, then a not unusual starting age for talented pupils. Certainly, William showed every sign of being astonishingly precocious. He was 12 when he won a prize for his translation from Latin of Lucian's *Dialogues of the Gods* and at 16 he wrote a paper entitled 'On the uniform motion of heat in homogeneous solid bodies'. On summer vacations his father took him to Paris, Prussia and the Netherlands on the assumption that learning languages was his career ambition. But on his return, William had decided that, like his father, he wanted to be a mathematician and a scientist.

Almost from the moment he became a student of Peterhouse at Cambridge in 1841, William Thomson attracted attention by his brilliance. He was the first Smith's prizeman of 1845, receiving an award which was a test of original research: one of his examiners turned to another and said: 'You and I are just about fit to mend his pens'.

In 1842 he put together the mathematical technique that solved important problems in electrostatics. Three years later he gave the first mathematical development of Michael Faraday's concept of an electromagnetic field.

In 1846 Thomson was appointed Professor of Natural Philosophy in Glasgow University. He was only 22 years old. In this post for the rest of his career, he was to publish no fewer than 650 scientific papers, establishing himself as a pioneer in electromagnetism and thermodynamics. In 1848 he proposed an absolute temperature scale: he put forward the view that a point would be reached at which no further heat could be transferred, the point of absolute zero.

Thomson was asked to advise on the laying of a submarine telegraph cable across the Atlantic. He was delighted to accept this challenge: his goal had always been the practical application of science and, in any case, he loved being at sea. He was on board to witness hugely expensive mistakes when the cable being laid from HMS *Agamemnon* broke in 1857 and, again in 1865, when a fresh cable put out from the *Great Eastern* parted 1,200 miles out to sea. Had not Thomson the following year worked out what the correct current should be and how the cable capable of carrying it should be constructed, it might have been decades later before Britain and America had a working telegraphic connection. Thomson's reward was fame, a knighthood and riches.

A raft of patented inventions generated most of Thomson's riches. Using piano wire, he devised a method of deep-sea sounding that could be operated from a ship sailing at full speed. Now that iron vessels were replacing wooden ones, compasses were giving too many false readings; Thomson made an adjustable compass to correct errors arising from such magnetic deviation. He constructed absolute, portable and quadrant electrometers, and ampère-meters, volt-meters and watt-meters, suitable alike for the electrical workshop and laboratory. However, it was in pure science that Thomson did his incomparable work. This included thermodynamic researches especially on how energy is dissipated; a significant contribution to the theory of elasticity; and his research in hydrodynamics, notably in wave-motion and vortex motion.

In 1892 he was created a peer with the title of Lord Kelvin of Largs (Kelvin is a stream that flowed past his laboratory in Glasgow). All his life he was a devout Presbyterian, and attendance at the university chapel was part of his daily routine. He was not unduly disturbed by what he read in Charles Darwin's *Origin of Species*: the theory of evolution did not overturn his belief that God created the universe, even if the earth (as he wrote) 'certainly a moderate number of million of years ago, was a red-hot globe'.

He died in 1907, and was buried in Westminster Abbey, appropriately close to the tomb of Sir Isaac Newton.

Some memorable observations made by Lord Kelvin:

'Mathematics is the only true metaphysics'

'I have no satisfaction in formulas unless I feel their arithmetical magnitude'

'Do not imagine that mathematics is harsh and crabbed, and repulsive to common sense. It is merely the etherealization of common sense'

'When you can measure what you are speaking about, and express it in numbers, you know something about it'

'I am never content until I have constructed a mechanical model of the subject I am studying. If I succeed in making one, I understand. Otherwise, I do not'.

EPISODE 102

A QUESTION OF IDENTITY: THE ULSTER CRISIS AND AFTER

When the Act of Union came into force in January 1801, most ordinary Irish people did not have strong feelings one way or another about being governed directly from Westminster. By the middle of the century, however, attitudes on Ireland's political future had become passionate and polarised. Catholics now sought an end to the Union and a parliament in Dublin. The great majority of Protestants sank their former differences in a drive to prevent this. They viewed the growth of the Home Rule movement from 1870 onwards with alarm.

A crisis point was reached when, in 1912, a majority at Westminster supported a Home Rule Bill for Ireland. Though this provided for a parliament in Dublin with devolved powers no greater than possessed today by the Welsh Assembly in Cardiff, Ulster Unionists prepared themselves to resist its introduction. Ulster Unionists elected Sir Edward Carson, a distinguished Dublin lawyer, to lead them.

The high point in Carson's campaign was 'Ulster Day', 28 September 1912. That Saturday all those who could prove Ulster birth were invited to sign Ulster's Solemn League and Covenant. This was a pact with God modelled on two Scottish documents, the National Covenant of 1638 and the Solemn League and Covenant of 1642, pledged to uphold Presbyterian rule and to resist Charles I's attempt to impose the Book of Common Prayer. Now, those signing this Ulster Covenant pledged themselves:

> to stand by one another in defending for ourselves and our children our cherished position of equal citizenship in the United Kingdom and in using all means which may be found to defeat the present conspiracy to set up a Home Rule Parliament in Ireland.

That day 471,414 men and women signed the Covenant. 'All means' included the threat of force. As early as March 1911 the Ulster Unionist Council had voted its first cash allocation for the buying of rifles. Carson declared: 'I am convinced that unless a steady supply is started, we will be caught like rats in a trap'.

In January 1913 the Ulster Volunteer Force (UVF) was established – a paramilitary army of 100,000 men who had signed the Covenant. Before the end of the year the Irish Volunteers were formed in Dublin to defend Home Rule. Half of the Irish Volunteers were in Ulster. In Belfast only narrow streets separated Ulster Volunteers marching with rifles down the Shankill Road and armed Irish Volunteers parading down the Falls Road. In April 1914 the UVF successfully landed 24,000 modern rifles and 5,000,000 rounds of ammunition, brought ashore at Larne, Bangor and Donaghadee.

Then in July, in a blaze of publicity, Irish Volunteers landed 1,500 rifles at Howth near Dublin. Carson thought that civil war was unavoidable: 'I see no hopes of peace. I see nothing at present but darkness and shadows ... We shall have once more to assert the manhood of our race'.

But it was in France, not Ireland, that so many Ulster Volunteers and Irish Volunteers – fighting on the same side – were to assert the manhood of their race. As the Great War got under way, Home Rule was suspended until the end of the conflict. On 1 July 1916, the bloodiest day in the history of the British Army, 5,700 men of the Ulster Division (for the most part members of the UVF) fell as the Battle of the Somme got under way. Irish Volunteers had already sustained fearful casualties at Gallipoli and, in September 1916, they fought side-by-side with the Ulster Division at Guillemont and Ginchy.

On Easter Monday 1916 militant nationalists of the Irish Republican Brotherhood (IRB) and the Irish Citizen Army (ICA) as well as smaller organisations, including the women's paramilitary organisation Cumann na mBan, had risen in rebellion in Dublin.

Though they were crushed in less than a week and their leaders executed, the republican cause – championed by Sinn Féin – gained in strength. The Representation of the People Act, passed in the spring of 1918 more than doubled the Irish electorate from 701,475 in 1910 to 1,936,673. For the first time tens of thousands of agricultural labourers and urban workers could vote, together with women over the age of thirty who were ratepayers or married to ratepayers. Then in December 1918, a month after the war had ended, Sinn Féin scored an electoral triumph by sweeping aside the more moderate Home Rulers of the Irish Party. Ulster Unionists also increased their strength, raising their representation from 18 to 26 MPs at Westminster.

Ireland was more politically polarised than ever before. What would the British government do? The political scene at Westminster had also been transformed. Though the Prime Minister continued to be a Liberal, David Lloyd George, he led an overwhelmingly Conservative coalition. The Conservatives, who had backed the Ulster Covenant, were now in a position to look after the interests of Ulster Unionists. The Government of Ireland Act of December 1920 created the United Kingdom's first devolved region by giving Home Rule to Northern Ireland, six counties which remained in the United Kingdom but with its own parliament in Belfast.

The remaining 26 counties were also given Home Rule with a devolved parliament in Dublin. The Act satisfied neither the nationalists of Ulster nor the Sinn Féin MPs. The civil war, postponed in 1914, now got under way.

EPISODE 103

A SCOTTISH RADICAL'S ROAD TO AN IRISH REVOLUTION: JAMES CONNOLLY

On 20 October 1856 John Connolly, a manure carter, married Mary McGinn in Edinburgh. Both had come to this city from rural Ulster in search of work. The couple moved from lodging to lodging with their two young children. On 5 June 1868, their third child, James, was born at 107 Cowgate. This was in a densely packed warren, inhabited mainly by Irish immigrants, where work was low paid and precarious. James seems to have got a good education at the nearby elementary school of St Patrick's. Later he was to recall reading at home by the light of embers, and using charred sticks as pencils to write. His legs became slightly bow-legged as a result of rickets brought on by malnutrition.

James was variously employed from the age of 11 as a printer's devil, in a bakery and in Messrs Hawley's in Frederick Street, a depot for supplying marbles and chimney pieces. Then, falsifying his age (he was only 14) and his name, he joined the Royal Scots. As an army recruit, Connolly was brought to Ireland for the first time. Stationed at Cork at first, his regiment was transferred to Dublin. Here, while waiting for a tram, he met Lillie Reynolds, a housemaid. Soon they were engaged. When his regiment was ordered to Aldershot, prior to being sent overseas, Connolly – unable to endure the thought of leaving his fiancée – deserted and made his way back to Scotland. While Lillie followed him by a tortuous route, James was obtaining a dispensation from the Bishop of Dunkeld to marry her, since she was a Protestant. They were married at St John's Church, Perth, on 20 April 1890. The young couple set up home at 22 West Port, on the corner of Grassmarket in Edinburgh.

Connolly – to his surprise – was never apprehended for army desertion. He got casual work as a carter with Edinburgh Corporation. He quickly immersed himself in left-wing politics, and joined the Socialist League. Connolly attended three meetings a week, the most important of which was a public meeting each Sunday, in East Meadows in summer and in various trades halls in winter. In this way Connolly was participating in the emergence of the Independent Labour Party. He became Secretary of the Scottish Socialist Federation and soon became well known as an engaging public speaker. He extended the organisation to Leith and became closely acquainted with Keir Hardie. But times were hard; he lost his job as a carter and made an ill-advised attempt to set up as a cobbler. In his desperation, Connolly was considering emigration to Chile. Instead, he accepted the offer of a job as the organiser of the Dublin Socialist Club.

In Dublin he found a one-room tenement for his family at 76 Charlemont Street. The club's first meeting was in the snug of a public house in Thomas Street, where Connolly, with five other total abstainers out of an attendance of eight, sipped lemonade. There they set up the Irish Socialist Republican Party. Connolly found it difficult to get anyone to join. He tried to promote the cause by public meetings in the Phoenix Park and at St James's Street Fountain. These were broken up with onlookers throwing cabbage stalks and shouting 'You're not an Irishman!' Connolly rarely received the £1 a week promised.

At Christmas 1900 Connolly brought home just two shillings and the family had no Christmas dinner and no presents. He decided to emigrate to the United States. When he embarked on 18 September 1903, not one of his Irish comrades came to see him off.

In America he moved from one precarious job to another. Though usually working 14 hours a day, in 1906 Connolly found time to become involved in the affairs of the Socialist Labor Party and the Industrial Workers of the World. The family lived in one of the notorious 'fire-trap' tenements in the Bronx. It was here that Connolly was able to finish his *Labour in Irish History*, his most enduring work, still in print today.

Connolly's reputation as a compelling speaker and a writer grew. This was noticed back in Ireland. Here James Larkin had been busy organising the unskilled and drawing them into the Irish Transport and General Workers' Union (ITGWU). Connolly accepted an invitation to return as a paid union official. He landed in Derry on Tuesday 26 July 1910 and travelled on to Belfast where he lodged with a colleague at 5 Rosemary Street. He often spoke at the Custom House steps and became involved in organising industrial action by dockers in dispute with the Head Line.

In October 1911 mill girls approached Connolly for advice. They were going on strike because of the introduction of a fresh system of fines for singing, laughing, talking or 'adjusting the hair during working hours'. Connolly advised them to return to work but to disregard the rules. For example, if one girl was checked for singing, then all would sing. The rules became a dead letter. Encouraged by this, Connolly set about organising the textile workers' section of the ITGWU.

Then on 29 August 1913 Connolly received a telegram summoning him to Dublin. Larkin had been arrested as the titanic struggle with the employers, the Great Lock-Out, got under way. Connolly himself was arrested there and went on hunger strike. He was released on the order of the viceroy and recuperated in Belfast. He was to travel to Scotland to speak at Edinburgh, Leith, Dundee, Glasgow and Kilmarnock, seeking help for the strikers.

When Connolly returned to Dublin he was set on a fresh course: he now prepared to establish an Irish socialist republic by force of arms. Connolly was on the road which would lead him to the GPO on Easter Monday 1916 and execution by firing squad, wounded and seated on a chair, on 12 May in Kilmainham Gaol.

WAR, INDUSTRIAL UNREST AND INTERCOMMUNAL CONFLICT: SCOTLAND AND ULSTER 1914–21

S cotland in wartime was almost entirely free of upsets equivalent to the bouts of turbulence and violence which then convulsed much of Ireland. In many other respects, however, the inhabitants of both sides of the Narrow Sea experienced much in common in those years.

Scots and Ulstermen had rushed to volunteer for the armed forces with equal enthusiasm. Thanks largely to the recruiting enthusiasm of the Irish Party MP for West Belfast, Joseph Devlin, a slightly higher proportion of Catholics than Protestants in Belfast joined up: many nationalists served with the Connaught Rangers and the Dublin Fusiliers. More than one Scottish miner in four joined up in the first year of war; the workers in the Glasgow slums thronged to enlist in the Highland Light Infantry; and Dundee had a higher proportion of serving soldiers than any other British city – here, because of the predominantly female labour force in the jute industry, the armed forces at least provided secure employment. Ulster would never forget the grim toll of the Somme; the equivalent for Scots was the bloodletting during the Battle of Loos. Scotland's wartime dead numbered close to 110,000. Glasgow lost 10 per cent of all adult males but the proportion killed from country districts was twice as great – Lewis and Harris suffered some of the highest casualties, in proportion to its population, of any British region.

The industries on both sides of the North Channel did much to fulfil the insatiable demands of total war. Harland and Wolff built monitors for shelling coastal defences; two cruisers, one adapted as a seaplane carrier; and from 1917 'standard' ships, simplified cargo vessels urgently needed to replace losses on the high seas. During 1918 alone, the company launched 201,070 tons of merchant shipping, 120,000 tons more than its nearest United Kingdom rival. Workman Clark constructed boom defence vessels, patrol boats, sloops and cargo ships totalling 260,000 tons during the war. The first year of war brought at least 20,000 munitions workers into the Glasgow area, concentrated in Govan, Clydebank and Parkhead. Textile mills and factories in Belfast, Dundee, Derry, Glasgow and elsewhere in Scotland and Ulster worked at full stretch to meet the demand for uniforms, tents, knapsacks, stretchers and aeroplane fabric. The Belfast Ropeworks produced 50 per cent of the Royal Navy's cordage requirements.

For more than a year after the Armistice of November 1918 the industries of the United Kingdom experienced a hectic boom. During this time skilled workers in both Belfast and Glasgow used this as an opportunity to strike for shorter hours and higher pay. 'The War is over in the Fields but not in the Shipyard,' Lord Pirrie, the managing director of Harland and Wolff, declared in a manifesto to his employees, '… there must be no slackening of effort'. The skilled marine engineers responded early in the new year by downing tools and demanding a 44-hour week. Soon they were joined by all the shipyard men, the gas workers and the electricity station workers. The trams could not run, picture houses closed, thousands of linen employees were laid off and, after the first week bread was running short. Only when the army occupied the gasworks and electricity station at 6 a.m. on 14 February did the strike collapse.

Engineers in Glasgow – particularly in factories such as Beardmores, Weirs, Albion Motors, and Barr and Stroud – had been taking unofficial action even while the war was still on. In defiance of their own unions, shop stewards formed the militant Clyde Workers' Committee. They campaigned against 'dilution', that is the employment of women in munitions jobs. Then, in January 1919, they went on a 'forty-hour strike' but, despite a huge demonstration baton-charged by the police, their attempt to make this a general strike in Glasgow failed. Nevertheless, the army was called in. For a time there were tanks, machine-gun nests and even a howitzer in the centre of the city. Just a little over a year after the Russian Revolution, a frightened government feared a Bolshevik-style uprising. But 'Red Clydeside' proved to be a figment of some cabinet ministers' imagination.

As the Anglo-Irish War edged into Ulster any feelings of workers' solidarity surviving there quickly evaporated: this 'War of Independence' triggered off a sectarian conflict there more vicious and lethal than all the northern riots of the previous century put together. It began in April 1920 when republican prisoners were brought to Bishop Street gaol, straddling the Catholic Bogside and Protestant Fountain Street area in Derry. Fierce battles at the corner of Long Tower Street developed into gun battles. The death toll for the city eventually reached 40.

On 21 July hundreds of apprentices and rivet boys from Workman Clark marched into Harland and Wolff and ordered out 'disloyal' workers, Catholics and socialists. During the ensuing weeks around 10,000 men and 1,000 women were expelled from Belfast's shipyards and engineering works. After being driven out of local mills and factories, virtually the entire Catholic populations of Lisburn, Banbridge and Dromore were forced to flee.

While the violence continued to rage the six north-eastern counties were formed into the first devolved region of the United Kingdom, Northern Ireland. On 22 June 1921 George V was in Belfast City Hall for the state opening of the Northern Ireland parliament. 'I can't tell you how glad I am I came', he said to the Prime Minister, Sir James Craig, 'but you know my entourage were very much against it'.

The King's entourage had good reason to be anxious: the worst blood-letting was yet to come.

EPISODE 105

TROUBLES: POLITICAL, SECTARIAN AND INDUSTRIAL

In a metaphorical sense the Narrow Sea grew wider from 1921 onwards. There would be no more dramatic migrations, whether westwards from Scotland by those seeking land, as in the seventeenth century, or eastwards from Ulster by those escaping poverty and famine, as in the nineteenth century.

Intercommunal violence had been convulsing Ulster since the spring of 1920. The Government of Ireland Act of December 1920 had partitioned the island and created Northern Ireland, formally established in May 1921. The Irish Republican Army (IRA) called a truce in July 1921 but, while the fighting halted in the south, it actually intensified in the north. IRA volunteers crossed the Border to carry out raids and set up ambushes on lonely country roads. In Belfast isolated Catholic and Protestant families were particularly vulnerable. House-burning, rioting and assassination drew the lines between the two communities more tautly than ever. Atrocity followed atrocity, counter-assassination followed almost every death, and large areas of Belfast were virtually at war.

In April 1922 the Northern Ireland parliament voted to set up an armed police force, to augment the Special Constabulary created 18 months earlier by Westminster, and to give the government special powers to detain suspects. Meanwhile representatives of Dáil Éireann had signed the Anglo-Irish Treaty in Downing Street on 6 December 1921: the other 26 counties (including the Ulster counties of Donegal, Cavan and Monaghan) became the Irish Free State, a self-governing Dominion of the British Empire. This was not the independent 32 county republic the IRA had fought for. Attempts to prevent civil war broke down at the end of June 1922 when the Free State army shelled the Four Courts in Dublin occupied by republicans opposed to the Treaty.

Armed volunteers moved south to take part in the civil war and this, together with draconian measures taken by the devolved government, brought peace for the first time to Northern Ireland. The price in blood had been heavy: between July 1920 and July 1922 the death toll in the 6 counties was 557 – 303 Catholics, 172 Protestants and 82 members of the security forces. Remarkably, there was not a single sectarian killing in the region between 1923 and 1933.

The Ulster 'Troubles' did not spill over into Scotland. Perhaps awareness of the violence did encourage the Liberal and Labour parties in Scotland to drop from their programmes the aspiration to seek home rule there and to persuade the Scottish Unionists to sever their connection with the Orange Order. However, in one important respect the experience of Northern Ireland and Scotland during the interwar years was very similar: both had to endure mass unemployment. The post-war boom had juddered to a halt in 1921. Then the slump developed into a protracted depression affecting whole communities for years on end.

The origins of the malaise were the same on both sides of the Narrow Sea. There was an over-dependence on staple, traditional industries producing, mainly for export, a narrow range of goods to a limited range of customers. Some 30 per cent of the world's merchant fleet had been lost during the war. After the Armistice, on the assumption that demand would now be unprecedented, the shipbuilding concerns on both Queen's Island and Clydeside increased capacity and output. But this overlooked the sudden freeze on the Admiralty's orders for warships and the great increase of berthage in other parts of the world such as the United States, Sweden and Japan. Throughout the 1920s and 1930s the capacity of world shipping was greater than was needed. Freight rates all but collapsed and demand fell for coal, steel plates and sections, ventilation equipment and pumps, marine engines and the like. As workers lost their jobs and much of their purchasing power, all other sectors of the economy were adversely affected.

In 1913 Scotland's coalfields had produced 42 million tons; within 20 years output was to fall by a quarter. In any case, the richer seams were becoming exhausted. Between 1920 and 1931 Scottish pig-iron output contracted by more than three-quarters. The traumatic changes in world trading conditions hit Northern Ireland at least six months earlier than Clydeside. Economic distress in this new devolved region had little to do with political troubles, sectarian violence, the creation of a new land border, or government inaction. Here, in the most economically disadvantaged part of the United Kingdom, the Depression began early. Nearly 23 per cent were unemployed in 1922 and for the rest of the decade on average around one fifth of all insured workers had no jobs.

Both Clydeside and Queen's Island enjoyed a modest recovery in the late 1920s. Then, on 23 October 1929, security prices on the Wall Street stock market crumbled in a wave of frenzied selling and in less than a month the securities lost more than 40 per cent of their face value. The speculative orgy of 1928–9 was followed by an unrelieved world depression lasting ten years. In just four years the volume of international trade was barely one third of what it had been on the eve of the crash.

Not a single ship was launched at Queen's Island between 10 December 1931 and 1 May 1934, and the number of yardmen in Belfast was reduced from 10,428 in 1930 to 1,554 in 1932. The world crisis was too much for Workman Clark: after the delivery of the tanker *Acavus*, ship number 536, in January 1935, the 'wee yard' had no more orders and was forced to close down. Throughout the 1930s a quarter of insured workers were out of work. In Scotland the unemployment rate in 1932 reached 27.7 per cent and in some staple industries unemployment levels of 70 per cent were being registered. The great steel-making firm of Stewarts and Lloyds moved its entire operations to Northamptonshire.

The self-confidence of the Victorian and Edwardian era had become but a memory.

EPISODE 106

'WHAT ABOUT THE 78,000 UNEMPLOYED WHO ARE STARVING?': THE BELFAST OUTDOOR RELIEF RIOTS OF 1932

On Friday 30 September 1932 Prime Minister Lord Craigavon rose to speak to a motion thanking Belfast Corporation for the use of the City Hall for meetings of the Northern Ireland Parliament, shortly to move to new premises at Stormont. This was too much for the east Belfast Labour MP, Jack Beattie: he seized the mace and shouted out that his motion had been unaccountably refused, a motion to bring 'to your notice the serious position of the unemployment in Northern Ireland'. Uproar followed as Beattie refused to withdraw and Tommy Henderson, Independent Unionist MP for the Shankill, joined in, declaring: 'I condemn the way the Government have treated the unemployed; it is a disgrace to civilisation'. Ignoring the Speaker's pleas for order, Beattie again shouted out: 'I am going to put this out of action ... The House indulges in hypocrisy while there are starving thousands outside'. He then wrested the mace from the sergeant-at-arms, threw it upon the floor, and walked out. Henderson roared out above the tumult, 'What about the 78,000 unemployed who are starving?'; to a cry from the Government benches of 'God Save the King', he responded 'God Save the People'; and then he withdrew leaving only one MP remaining on the opposition benches.

Relief for those out of work was more niggardly than in any other region of the United Kingdom. The dole, known as the 'b'roo', ran out after six months and those unemployed for extended periods were forced to turn to the Poor Law as the only official alternative to starvation. The Belfast Board of Guardians applied the old workhouse test with rigour: nothing would be given until savings had been exhausted; relief (which had to be earned by unpaid labour) was in the form of groceries obtained by 'chits' from named shops; and the names of successful applicants were posted on gable walls.

Now in 1932 the prevailing distress in the city brought working-class people of both religions together in common protest. The lead was taken by men resurfacing the streets in task work, without which the unemployed could not qualify for relief payments. Outdoor-relief workers agreed to strike to force their demands for an increase in levels of assistance and for an end to task work and payments in kind. The strike began on Monday 3 October and that evening 60,000 from all over Belfast – led by bands playing 'Yes, We Have No Bananas' – marched from Frederick Street Labour Exchange to a torch-lit rally at the Custom House. Next day 7,000 people accompanied a deputation to the Union Workhouse, where the Guardians were meeting, and men lay down on the tramlines to stop traffic on the Lisburn Road.

The Northern Ireland government banned all marches when the Unemployed Workers' Committee planned a great protest demonstration for Tuesday 11 October. That day the police converged on five assembly points, starting in east Belfast. The *Belfast Telegraph* described what happened in Templemore Avenue: 'As the crowd continued to advance an order was given: "Draw-Ready-Charge!" Men went down like nine-pins, and the rest fled helter skelter'.

The worst violence was in the lower Falls, where the people put up barricades in an attempt to impede the police who used their firearms freely. According to the *Belfast Telegraph*:

> The screams of the women who were trapped in the streets and could not reach home were heard above the din. Police reinforcements were summoned. Constables wearing bandoliers filled with bullets and with rifles at the ready were speedily jumping out of caged cars. Other constables with revolvers in hand peered cautiously round the street corner as the hail of stones came out of Albert Street. Batons were useless and the police were compelled to fire.

It was here that Samuel Baxter, a Protestant flower-seller, was shot dead; John Geegan, a Catholic from Smithfield, was mortally wounded in the stomach; and 14 others suffered gunshot wounds. James Kelly, reporting for the *Irish Press* on the Shankill Road, heard a woman shouting out: 'They're kicking the shite out of peelers up the Falls. Are you going to let them down?' 'I took refuge in a shirt factory in Agnes Street', Kelly continued, 'and we saw some of the Protestant workers actually shooting at the police'.

Order was restored by nightfall when a curfew came into force. The last major eruption was in the York Street area the following evening when police armed with rifles opened fire on crowds of looters. John Kennan, of Leeson Street, was shot dead and the list of wounded filled newspaper columns.

By now a thoroughly alarmed government was forcing the Guardians to relent and on 14 October substantial increases in relief were announced. Next day the British trade-union leader Tom Mann led the funeral procession of Samuel Baxter in the most impressive demonstration of working-class solidarity Belfast has ever seen.

EPISODE 107

TWO DISASTERS: ARRANMORE AND KIRKINTILLOCK

ARRANMORE 9 OCTOBER 1935

During the interwar years people from the coastlands and islands of the north-west and west of Ireland – boys and girls as well as men and women – continued to take part in the annual migration to lift potatoes on Scottish farms. This 'tattie hoking' became a particularly vital source of income in the 1930s when the world depression was being aggravated by the 'Economic War' being waged between de Valera's government in Dublin and the coalition governments at Westminster.

These migrant workers were absent from home for months at a time, their labour being in demand throughout the summer and reaching a peak in September. On 9 October 1935, having travelled from Glasgow by boat and train, 13 arrived in Burtonport in the Rosses for the last stage of their journey over the sea to Árainn Mhór, Arranmore island. The group were met by seven islanders who had crossed over to greet them and travel back with them. It was very dark but not stormy when the *Yawl*, an open sailing boat, left Burtonport harbour. On the way across, the *Yawl* struck one of the many rocks encountered on the passage. The craft overturned and, since no distress signals were heard or seen, it was a fearfully long time before anyone either on the mainland or on the island was aware that a disaster had occurred.

Tragically nineteen people were drowned that night. There was only one survivor, Paddy Gallagher: he lost his father, four brothers and two sisters in the tragedy.

Peadar O'Donnell, who taught in a National School on Arranmore, a republican socialist who was becoming one of Ireland's best-known writers, wrote about the disaster in the *Irish Press*:

> Morning. And the world hears. And the world says it was a rock. And the world says: Put up a beacon. And the world says it was a fog … but it was not a rock. It was Society. The world has spelled out one of its crimes in the corpses. The order of life that impounds the Gael, that drags him to sleep on the steps of Glasgow Central, to slave in the tattie fields of Scotland may decree beacons along Arranmore coast. And the quicker the better. But if the agony of that moment of breathed prayer, that comes as close to us as our own breathing, does not flash into a decision to end the impounding of the Gael, and the trek to the Scottish tattie fields, the beacons around Arranmore are not a remedy for a wrong, but a hush-hush to ease settled consciences …

KIRKINTILLOCK 16 SEPTEMBER 1937

On the evening of 15 September 1937 potato merchants, Messrs W & A Graham of Hunter Street, Glasgow, took 26 migrant workers in 2 lorries from a farm near Edinburgh where they had been working for the previous three weeks. These were 'tattie hokers' preparing to begin their last job before returning to Achill. Their destination was a 'bothy', a shed, at Kirkintillock – this was where 12 men and boys would sleep. The females, 14 in total, most of them just girls, were to be put up in a 4-room cottage adjacent.

Since work was to begin early next morning, they were all eager to get some rest. The bothy simply had inverted potato boxes covered with straw and old blankets to serve as beds. The bothy's entrance was a sliding door fastened by a basic slip bolt. The windows, which opened inwards, were covered with wire netting.

Tom Duggan, the son of the foreman, got up because he could not sleep and found the bothy ablaze at around 1:00 am. He raised the alarm but no one could open the bothy door or discover how to open and get out of the windows. Only when one of the potato merchants, John Mackey, arrived was a way found to open the bothy. Tragically 10 young men and boys, aged between 13 and 23, had already died. Men from the fire brigade were hampered in their efforts to identify the bodies because the survivors were only able to speak Irish.

The inquest found that the victims had died from carbon monoxide poisoning caused by the overloading of a coal stove.

Back in September 1924 nine tattie hokers had died in very similar circumstances in a bothy at Dundonald in Ayrshire.

The bothy in Kirkintillock where the 10 Achill migrant workers died in 1937 was the *very same one* in which the 13 Arranmore migrant workers had lodged in 1935 before their return to the Rosses.

EPISODE 108

FROM PEACE TO WAR

In the autumn of 1932 Catholics and Protestants had marched and campaigned side by side to force the Belfast Board of Guardians to improve outdoor relief for the unemployed. That solidarity did not last: 13 were killed in vicious sectarian fighting in the city's York Street area during the summer of 1935. Later that year 2,000 Catholics had been driven from their homes. At an inquest on riot victims, the city coroner blamed political leaders: 'The poor people who commit these riots are easily led and influenced', he said. Indeed, poverty was the prevailing feature of these years in Northern Ireland. This was the United Kingdom's most depressed region: in 1938 the unemployment rate reached 28 per cent at a time when it had fallen to 16.3 per cent in Scotland.

On 1 December 1930 John Brown and Company signed a contract to build the two biggest ships in the world. By the next spring the skeleton of the *Queen Mary* had risen up from the gantries overlooking the Clyde but – six months later – the company was bankrupt. On 11 December 1931 the entire workforce was laid off and, since this collapse led to the cancellation of dozens of other orders, 10,000 men and women were left jobless. Eventually Westminster, in an uncharacteristic act of intervention, bailed out Cunard. Work resumed on 3 April 1934, the first task being to remove 130 tons of rust from the frame. Then, on 26 September 1934, watched by a quarter of a million people, the great liner was launched. Work had already begun on the sister ship, *Queen Elizabeth*. Mass unemployment continued to blight the country, but Scots now felt that better times were in prospect.

Living standards in Scotland were only marginally better than in Northern Ireland, however. In 1937 1 in 20 in Scotland (1 in 12 in Glasgow) were in receipt of poor relief – the figure for England and Wales was 1 in 40. But the conviction that another world war was inevitable led the government to place urgent orders in Scotland for warships and munitions. Unemployment had all but disappeared when Britain went to war on 3 September 1939.

In March 1938 Annie Chamberlain, the Prime Minister's wife, performed the opening ceremony for Sydenham aerodrome alongside the Musgrave Yard in Belfast. By then work was well advanced on the adjacent aircraft factory. Shorts Brothers of Rochester had extended its operations here, primarily to be well away from the threat of German assault. Nearby, HMS *Belfast* was launched in the same month and completed its sea trials in August 1939. Work was well under way on the 28,000-ton aircraft carrier HMS *Formidable*. By the beginning of September Shorts had built 11 Bristol Bombays and 4 Hereford bombers and design work had begun on the first of the heavy bombers, the four-engined Stirling. Northern Ireland's recovery came very late but since the beginning of 1939 the region's unemployment register had fallen by over 30,000.

'An attack on Northern Ireland would involve a flight of over 1,000 miles'. Edmond Warnock, parliamentary secretary at the Ministry of Home Affairs, was addressing the Northern Ireland cabinet on 19 June 1939. He continued: 'For aeroplanes of the bombing type, loaded, this is a very big undertaking ... it is possible that we might escape attack.' For the next year and more Lord Craigavon's government felt so reassured by these remarks that almost nothing was done to protect citizens from air attack. Ministers remained complacent even when Warnock resigned in disgust in May 1940 because his government 'has been slack, dilatory and apathetic'.

Meanwhile, the Irish premier, Éamon de Valera, had torn up most of the Anglo-Irish Treaty of 1921 and given the 26 counties of the Irish Free State a new name, Éire. He made it clear that Éire would be neutral if Britain went to war. The implications of that decision were made very clear on the very first night of the war when the liner *Athenia* was torpedoed by U-30 off the north-west coast of Donegal and sank with the loss of 112 lives.

In the spring of 1940 the vortex of total war suddenly swung westwards: the Germans overran Norway and Denmark at the beginning of April; a month later they swept over the Netherlands and Belgium; and then the Wehrmacht forged through the Ardennes, reaching Paris in June. As the shattered remains of the British army gathered on the Dunkirk beaches Winston Churchill, who had just replaced Neville Chamberlain as Prime Minister, is said to have remarked gloomily in his map room that the only properly armed and disciplined force left in the United Kingdom was the Ulster Special Constabulary.

Then, as the Battle of Britain got under way, the Battle of the Atlantic intensified. The fall of France enabled U-boats to operate from Brest and Lorient, and long-range Focke-Wulf Condor bombers flew out from French air bases in search of British ships off the west coast of Ireland to land eventually at Stavanger in Norway. Britain was forced to divert its convoys around the headlands of Co. Donegal and into the North Channel – a decision strengthened by Churchill's failure to get Éire to abandon its neutrality. Northern Ireland now had a crucial role to play as U-boats continued to wreak havoc on merchant shipping in the Western Approaches. 'All had to come in around Northern Ireland', Churchill said later. 'Here by the grace of God, Ulster stood a faithful sentinel'.

Éire's neutrality notwithstanding, approximately 70,000 southern Irish men and women joined the British armed forces and no attempt was made to stop them. Travel permits were freely issued, and some 200,000 of Éire's citizens worked in British factories or as nurses during the war. And Irish food exports to the UK proved vital.

EPISODE 109

THE BLITZ

The Third Reich's western advance brought Birmingham, Coventry, Manchester and Liverpool within range of German bombers. Both Glasgow and Belfast were crucial destinations for the North Atlantic convoys coming in to the North Channel; and both were playing a vital role in wartime production. In short, if these two cities could be reached, they were tempting targets for the Luftwaffe.

On the night of 13-14 March and again on the night of 14-15 March 1941 a total of 460 German bombers attacked Clydeside. Targets on the first raid were the shipyards and industrial installations, and the second was designed primarily to strike terror into the civilian population. The town of Clydebank in west Dunbartonshire was almost totally razed: 4,000 houses were completely destroyed, 4,500 were severely damaged and – out of a total of 12,000 – only 7 houses were left undamaged. In what was to be the worst civilian loss of life in Scotland during the war, 528 people were killed and 617 severely injured. In just 1 house, 78 Jellicoe Street, 31 people died, including 15 members of the Rocks family. The Beardmore engine works, the Singer factory and Aitchison Blair engineering firm were left devastated. The Admiralty oil storage facility at Dalnottar became an inferno and burned for four weeks. RAF fighters had brought two bombers down but a sustained barrage from the Polish destroyer, *Piorun*, moored in John Brown's shipyard, failed to find a target.

Over 35,000 had been left homeless by these two raids. The authorities acted quickly to evacuate the majority of them in buses; the remarkable achievement was that by 17 March 11,350 had been given accommodation and soon after the remainder found shelter in rest centres or with family or friends in Glasgow.

'All sorts of rot going on here', Lady Londonderry wrote to her husband soon after the outbreak of war; 'Air raid warnings and blackouts! As if anyone cared or wished to bomb Belfast'. But on 24 March 1941 John MacDermott, Minister of Public Security, sent a memorandum to John Andrews, Prime Minister since the death of Craigavon the previous November. Aircraft cover was less than half the approved strength in Belfast; the city did not possess a single searchlight; and no other town in Northern Ireland had any defence at all. He concluded:

Up to now we have escaped attack. So had Clydeside until recently. Clydeside got its blitz during the period of the last moon ... The period of the next moon from, say, the 7th to the 16th of April, may well bring our turn.

On the night of 7-8 April a small German squadron raided Belfast and delivered damaging blows to the docks. Luftwaffe crews reported that the city's defences were 'inferior in quality, scanty and insufficient'. Then, on the evening of Easter Tuesday, 15 April 1941, 180 German bombers flew in formation over the Irish Sea and, as they approached the Ards, they dropped to 7,000 feet. At 10.40 p.m. sirens wailed in Belfast. Casting intense light, hundreds of flares drifted down, then incendiaries, high-explosive bombs and parachute mines rained on the city. It was not the industrial heartland but the congested housing north of the city centre that received the full force of the attack. The result was fearful carnage in the New Lodge, the lower Shankill and the Antrim Road. At 1.45 a.m. a bomb fell at the corner of Oxford Street and East Bridge Street, wrecking the city's central telephone exchange. All contact with Britain and the anti-aircraft operations room was cut off. At 4.35 a.m. an appeal for help to Dublin was sent by railway telegraph. De Valera was awakened and agreed without hesitation to send help. Altogether 70 men and 30 fire engines sped northwards. But there was little the firemen could do to fight the flames – the water pressure had fallen too far.

The official figures were 745 people dead and 430 seriously injured. The actual total was at least 900 dead. Some 6,000 people arrived in Dublin from Belfast, including an air-raid warden still wearing his helmet. Tens of thousands left the city for the countryside.

On Sunday 4 May 1941, before Northern Ireland had the opportunity to improve its defences, the Luftwaffe returned. Until 1.55 a.m. the pathfinders of Kampfgruppe 100 over Belfast dropped 6,000 incendiaries almost exclusively on the harbour, the aircraft factory and the shipyards; then the rest of the bombers were led in by the rapidly spreading conflagration.

Three corvettes nearing completion were totally destroyed; the transport ship *Fair Head* sank at her moorings; three ships received direct hits in the Abercorn yard; and altogether Harland and Wolff suffered the devastation of two thirds of its premises. By now 53.5 per cent of Belfast's housing stock had been destroyed or badly damaged. The death toll for this May raid was 191 – a surprisingly low figure largely explained by two facts: that in this Sabbatarian city the centre was largely deserted when the attack began; and a very large number of people had already fled to the countryside. By the end of May some 220,000 had left the city. Radio Paris, under German direction, informed its listeners in the middle of May: 'Fearing air raids, 20,000 women and children escape every evening from Belfast to the outskirts of the city'. This was a considerable underestimate.

Over two nights on 6-7 May 1941 around 350 German aircraft bombed Greenock. The targets were ships and shipyards but the brunt of the attack was taken by civilians. The toll was 271 dead and over 10,000 injured. About 5,000 homes were destroyed. This was the last of the major air raids. The reason soon became evident. Hitler was turning his attention eastwards and on 26 June 1941 the Wehrmacht crossed the borders of the Soviet Union. The isolation of the United Kingdom had come to an end.

EPISODE 110

ARSENALS OF VICTORY

On the night of 15-16 April 1941 nearly a thousand men, women and children had been killed in Belfast, in part a consequence of it being the most unprotected city in the United Kingdom. No other city, except London, had lost so many lives in one air raid. But the Blitz inflicted heavier losses on Scotland: a toll of around 6,000 civilian deaths. More than 500 air attacks on Scotland were recorded.

The Battle of the Atlantic continued to rage but, when Hitler concentrated his military resources to invade the Soviet Union, the civilian population of the United Kingdom no longer had the same constant fear of terror from the skies. For some time to come that did not include Scotland's north-east, vulnerable to attack from German bases in Norway. The ports of Peterhead, Fraserburgh and Montrose were frequently targeted, and Aberdeen suffered 33 raids, the biggest in April 1943: 25 bombers attacked the city and the last wave of aircraft swept low to machine-gun the streets.

By December 1941 German troops could see the minarets of Moscow glimmering in the sun; but this was the moment the tide of the conflict began to change. That month Hitler sealed his fate, shortly after the Japanese assault on Pearl Harbour, by casually declaring war on the richest nation on earth – the United States.

Since the summer of 1941 Americans, describing themselves as 'civilian technicians', had been building bases in Derry and on Lough Erne as unobtrusively as possible. Then on 26 January 1942, now that the USA was officially at war, the first American troops stepped ashore at Belfast's Dufferin Quay. The United States took over responsibility for the defence of Northern Ireland. Derry became the most important escort base for convoys; at one stage 149 vessels, together with 20,000 sailors, used this port to patrol the Western Approaches. Americans built a new town at Langford Lodge on the eastern shores of Lough Neagh to assemble, repair and maintain aircraft. From Lower Lough Erne at Castle Archdale Catalina and Short Sunderland flying boats flew out in pursuit of U-boats. The Taoiseach, Éamon de Valera, created the 'Donegal Corridor' to allow Allied aircraft to fly unhindered between the Erne estuary and Mullaghmore in Co. Sligo – though he took good care to have 'ÉIRE' written in large white letters, most prominently on Slieve League and close to Malin Head, to indicate his state's neutrality.

During the autumn of 1942, after training in the Ulster countryside, the first contingents of American troops had moved on to North Africa in preparation for the invasion of Italy. A year later greater numbers arrived in readiness for the Normandy landings. The total exceeded 120,000. Indeed, over 4 years there was an influx of some 300,000 and this at a time when the population of Northern Ireland was less than one and a half million. Meanwhile the industrial zones on both sides of the Narrow Sea were becoming arsenals of victory.

The Singer Sewing Machine Company, turned over to the making of munitions in 1939, lost over a quarter of a million square feet of floor space and its timber yard in the blitz of March 1941. Within just six weeks it had returned to normal production. By the end of the war the firm had manufactured

60,000 rifle components, 1,125,000 bayonets, 250 Sten guns,15,000 tank tracks and 125 million bullets. The rerouting of convoys around Donegal and Ulster's north coast into the North Channel turned the Clyde into Britain's principal wartime port. Around 52 million tons of cargo were landed on its quays. Here the number of shipyard workers reached 100,000. Amongst the hundreds of vessels constructed were the aircraft carrier *Indefatigable* and the capital ships *Vanguard, Duke of York* and *Howe.*

As many as a hundred businesses were engaged in making floating pierheads, known as Mulberry Harbours, ready for the Normandy landings of June 1944. A great factory at Bishopton produced prodigious quantities of explosives, and Rolls-Royce employed 25,000 manufacturing Merlin engines. A quarter of Scotland's workers were engaged in the making of munitions, engines and ships. Dundee's jute industry sprang back to life, to meet the need for sand bags in particular, and the woollen factories in the Borders worked to full capacity.

On the other side of the North Channel a return to full production after the air raids took much longer than in Clydeside. After a year, however, Northern Ireland finally was making a valuable contribution to wartime output. At Harland and Wolff the workforce in Belfast rose steadily to reach a peak of 30,800 in December 1944. Altogether Queen's Island launched almost 170 Admiralty and merchant ships between 1939 and 1945. These included 40 corvettes; 27 minesweepers; 11 frigates; 3 aircraft carriers; 8 tank-landing craft; 3 tank-carrying ships; and submarine and aircraft support vessels. In addition, the firm launched from its Clydeside yards at Govan and Pointhouse another 84 ships. It repaired or converted 30,000 vessels, manufactured 13 million aircraft parts, over 500 tanks, thousands of field and anti-aircraft guns and hundreds of searchlights.

Short's dispersed as many as its processes as possible in case of further attacks from the air. By the end of the war it had completed almost 1,200 Stirling bombers and 125 Sunderland flying boats. Mackies undertook substantial fuselage assembly for Short's and made 75 million shells and 65 million parts for bombs. The Sirocco Works produced grenades, radar equipment and gun-mountings, and the Belfast Ropeworks made one third of the cordage and ropes required by the War Office. The linen industry was severely dislocated when the Germans overran its principal sources of flax in Russia and Belgium. The growing of flax at home revived and mills then produced great quantities of parachutes, machine-gun belts, canvas covers, uniforms and 'blitz cloth' for reroofing damaged buildings. Ulster's farms played a crucial role in helping to keep Britain fed: for example, every day in wintertime up to 17,000 gallons of milk were shipped across the Narrow Sea.

EPISODE 111

BETTER TIMES IN SCOTLAND ...

T he new Labour government, with Clement Attlee as Prime Minister, elected after peace returned to Europe in 1945, was determined that alarming fluctuations in the economic cycle that had followed the 1918 Armistice must not recur. The United Kingdom did experience a postwar boom but it was controlled – in any case the international conflict had been so destructive that shortages remained to be filled in the rest of Europe and beyond for years to come.

In retrospect it is not wrong to conclude that, in the years following the war, the citizens of the United Kingdom, especially in Northern Ireland and Scotland, enjoyed a more sustained improvement in living standards, and in their quality of life overall, than anyone could remember. That improvement began even while the conflict was still raging.

Those engaged in war work may often have felt exhausted by excessive hours of overtime but they enjoyed regular wages and – even if the fare was dull and limited – they were probably better fed than ever before. On the Clyde, for example, the management of John Brown and Company shipbuilders resisted setting up canteens until Churchill gave the management his personal assurance that the associated costs would be tax-deductible.

In his wartime coalition Churchill had been content to appoint Labour politicians to posts concerned with domestic matters, which no doubt he regarded as devoid of glamour. His choice of a stalwart of the Scottish Labour Party, Tom Johnston, as Secretary of State for Scotland proved to be inspired. Johnston got approval to create the state-run Scottish Hydro-Electric Board in 1943, which he was sure would help regenerate the Highlands. One of his finest achievements was to give Scotland effective health care well before the National Health Service was set up in 1947. For the first time ordinary Scots had access to readily available free medical attention. Johnston made sure that the poorest districts got fair access to available food supplies, and that free milk and vitamins were given out to under-fives. The outcome was that infant mortality fell by 27 per cent during the war years, the biggest fall anywhere in Europe.

Heavy industry continued to play a central role in the economy for a decade and more after 1945. As in Northern Ireland, the expected postwar slump in shipbuilding did not materialise, averted in part by the devastation of German and Japanese yards, the maintenance of state controls, and the unprecedented aid given by the United States to western Europe under the Marshall Plan. No fewer than 26 shipyards along the Clyde prospered as they strove to meet demand. To feed the near-insatiable appetite of the steel mills, around 80,000 miners were employed in Scotland (almost as many as in 1914) even though the great Lanarkshire coalfield was close to exhaustion. Attlee's government nationalised coal, steel, transport and power but this did not bring with it much of a zeal for modernisation. When new processes were brought in they were often resisted by conservative-minded unions and they triggered damaging demarcation disputes. But for the time being traditional practices were serving Scotland well.

This was the era of ambitious planning and in Scotland this prompted the construction of the New Towns, most notably East Kilbride begun in 1947, Glenrothes in 1949 and Cumbernauld in 1957. New industrial estates were established such as Newhouse near Glasgow and Kingsway near Dundee. Attempts to bring new industries to Scotland met with only limited success; and strong persuasion was needed to persuade Rolls-Royce to remain at Hillingdon making aircraft engines after the war. But between 1946 and 1951 Scotland succeeded in attracting over 70 per cent of United States investment into Britain. By the mid-1950s the volume of this American investment was greater than in all the rest of Europe put together.

The decade following the Second World War was a time of negligible unemployment. There was no urgent need to move to get a job. The conviction that everything was getting better was justified. Certainly, Scots were becoming much healthier. One by one killer diseases for both children and adults were successfully combated. The medical profession had mobilised to resist plans for a national health service. Four hundred of them met in St Andrew's Hall in Glasgow to pour scorn on the Labour government's proposals, contemptuously rejecting the threat of becoming 'servants of the state'. Fortunately for the great majority of Scots, they failed.

A huge amount of effort had been required for reconstruction after the Blitz. However, the sterling crisis of 1947 caused the most ambitious plans for house building to be shelved. In 1951 a third of all Scottish households still had to share a toilet. It was actually after the Conservatives returned to power in that year that most was achieved – by 1954 40,000 council houses were being built every year. New estates sprang up with homes equipped with modern amenities and gardens, for example Pollok and Knightshood in Glasgow, Sighthill in Edinburgh, the Inch at Liberton, and Whitfield and Menzieshill in

Dundee. Unfortunately, funding did not extend to making proper provision for shopping centres, local schools and community halls. Rab Butler's 1944 Education Act, for all its imperfections, together with the provision of grants to university students who needed them, brought about greatly enhanced social mobility.

EPISODE 112

... AND BETTER TIMES IN NORTHERN IRELAND

In 1943 Sir Basil Brooke had replaced John Andrews as the Prime Minister of Northern Ireland. His Unionist government was more secure than any before and, indeed, any subsequent one. Éamon de Valera's neutral Éire was economically stagnant, inward-looking and diplomatically isolated. Not only had Northern Ireland been promised parity with Britain in its social services (with the support of the central exchequer) but also successive Westminster governments expressed in practical ways their gratitude to Stormont for standing by the Allies in their hour of need. This also was the view of President Harry Truman's American administration. On 24 August 1945 General Dwight Eisenhower returned to Northern Ireland, inspected troops in front of Belfast's City Hall, and received the Freedom of the City. In his acceptance speech he said:

> I have received honours in a number of cities but never have been more impressed with the sincerity and friendliness exhibited towards me than in Belfast ... without Northern Ireland, I do not see how the American forces could have been concentrated to begin the invasion of Europe.

Brooke, along with most of his colleagues, loathed socialism and was deeply suspicious of the Attlee government's welfare legislation – but since the Treasury in London would be underwriting most of the additional costs, he did not oppose it. It was fortunate that he chose a shipyard worker, William Grant, as his Minister of Health and Local Government. His private secretary, John Oliver, wrote later: 'Billy Grant was unique. He was a huge rugged man ... an

Orangeman; a Labour Unionist; a man of immense courage ... He was one of those ministers who attract business'.

In 1945 Grant set up the Northern Ireland Housing Trust, modelled on the Scottish Special Housing Association, with power to borrow from the Government to build houses and pay back the capital with interest over 60 years. With difficulty he persuaded his party that subsidy was essential, for 'without a very substantial measure of Government aid, not a brick can be laid of houses which ordinary people can afford to rent'. The Trust was run by men who set a new standard of probity and dedication in public life, making certain that houses were allocated with strict fairness. Grant's targets proved to be over-ambitious but the achievement was vastly more impressive than that of the interwar years.

At Westminster the Butler Act of 1944 was revolutionising the education system in Britain and in December 1944 the education minister, Lieutenant-Colonel Samuel Hall-Thompson, published his proposals to extend its provisions to Northern Ireland. But three long and rancorous years were to pass before he could get his education act approved. Catholic bishops condemned them as putting their schools under severe pressure to join the state system. Protestants objected to the increase in funding for 'voluntary' (mainly Catholic) schools and were outraged by the plan to scrap compulsory Bible instruction in state schools. At one rowdy meeting Reverend Professor Robert Corkey (Hall-Thompson's predecessor as minister, dismissed for inattention to his duties in 1944) asserted that state schools would be thrown open to 'Jews, Agnostics, Roman Catholics and Atheists'.

Despite all the opposition, Hall-Thompson had his way and his bill became law in 1947. But he was forced to resign two years later when the Prime Minister, soon after being promoted to the peerage as Lord Brookeborough, agreed to a demand by the Orange Order to cut superannuation and national insurance payments to Catholic teachers. During the bitter debates and unedifying wrangling, very little had been said about the major features of the legislation. As in Britain, pupils would leave primary school at 11 years old; selected by a qualifying examination, the most able 20 per cent would proceed to grammar school and the remaining 80 per cent were to go on to 'intermediate' or 'technical' secondary school. Despite the controversial 'eleven plus' test, unprecedented opportunities were created by this great reform making secondary education available to all, and for many the opportunity to go to university with local authority financial assistance.

The Belfast Blitz of 1941 had revealed to public gaze, in a way cold statistics could not, the appalling low standards of health of the working class. Those in the countryside who had thrown open their homes to evacuees were horrified to find so many children from Belfast infested with lice and wasting away from tuberculosis. School children were the first to benefit from the region's vastly improved health services. The Belfast Education Committee provided milk to needy children from October 1942 and a general schools meals service from January 1943.

Tuberculosis was responsible for almost half the deaths in the 15-25 age group, and in this field Stormont did not wait to take a lead from Westminster. The Tuberculosis Authority was set up with a mission to find and treat victims and eventually to extirpate the disease altogether. The campaign was so determined and effective that by 1954 the death rate was reduced to the same level as that in England and Wales. So well had the Authority done its work that it was dissolved in 1959.

In July 1948, the National Health Service, open to all, totally free and almost completely comprehensive, came into operation in Britain. In the same year an almost identical act passed through Stormont but, because of past neglect, the impact of this new service was more profoundly felt than in any other region of the United Kingdom.

On 8 October 1951 the *Belfast Telegraph* gave readers a general account of Harland and Wolff's work in progress:

> Already the yards have launched eight ships of more than 100,000 tons, and at least two more are likely to reach the water before the end of the year. Sixteen slipways are now occupied and preparations are being made for the laying of keels in the remaining two.

Later that month the company delivered the aircraft carrier HMS *Eagle*, the largest vessel in the Royal Navy, and *Juan Perón*, the world's biggest whale factory ship. Throughout the 1950s Harland and Wolff outperformed other yards in the United Kingdom. The workforce at Queen's Island rarely fell below 20,000. On 16 March 1960 Dame Pattie Menzies, wife of the Australian prime minister, broke a bottle of Australian red wine on the bows of *Canberra* and the 45,270-ton P&O liner entered Belfast Lough. The ship was the largest liner built in the United Kingdom since the *Queen Elizabeth*.

For most of the 1940s the only brake on Northern Ireland's linen industry seemed to be shortage of raw material. Then as flax supplies increased the industry flourished as it had not done for a quarter of a century. By 1951 around 76,000 workers in Northern Ireland were employed in textiles, the great majority in linen. Then in July 1953 the Korean War ended and prices dropped alarmingly. But the industry remained a major employer of labour, albeit by paying very low wages.

Short's aircraft factory had employed 10,500 at Sydenham during the last year of the war and then the workforce fell to a plateau of around 6,000. For a time the firm developed a market for passenger flying boats. The company developed the first tailless aircraft, the Sherpa, in 1951, and pioneered the vertical take-off SC1 in 1955.

In both Northern Ireland and Scotland the glory days of the traditional staple export industries were coming to an end. From 1953 prices collapsed in the linen industry. The conclusion of the Korean War ended shortages; new processes were making cotton much cheaper than linen; working women were unwilling to spend time ironing a material that creased so easily; and new synthetic fibres were competitively making their appearance. At Upperlands a three-day week had to be imposed and the firm that had orders for 33,000 webs in January had only 3,000 on order by December. This was no temporary downturn and from now on the industry was in a state of near-terminal decline. Across the Narrow Sea an absence of orders from 1957 onwards signalled the slow and painful contraction of shipbuilding on the Clyde. The workforce fell from 60,000 to 20,000 over the ensuing 10 years. No one could have predicted that when the *Canberra* slid down the ways into the Lagan in March 1960 it would be the last great launching of its kind in Belfast.

Across the Scottish Lowlands coal pits closed one by one. The great steel mills were increasingly exposed as being outdated and uncompetitive. Textile mills and factories struggled to survive. In Northern Ireland over a 7-year period 25,000 jobs were lost in the linen industry, leaving only 51,000 employed by 1958. Attempts to bring in new light industries were poorly rewarded. Those that came to Scotland steered clear of established industrial areas where unions were ensconced; they preferred greenfield sites, industrial estates and the New Towns. British firms, persuaded to establish branches here, regretted doing so: parts for motor vehicles, for example, were usually brought north from England and, to compensate for additional transport costs, companies generally paid wages lower than in the south. These branches proved particularly vulnerable in times of recession.

But the horrors many still remembered from the 1930s did not return. In the 1960s Northern Ireland and Scotland found new ways of earning a living. During a time of unparalleled and sustained growth multinational concerns were attracted in. Living standards continued to rise. The benefits of postwar welfare legislation were being reaped.

To a remarkable degree the experience of Northern Ireland and Scotland had been very similar from the middle 1920s, the Great Crash at Wall Street in 1929, though the Depression and war years all the way to the 1960s. But there was one striking difference: society in Northern Ireland was dangerously fractured in a way it never was in Scotland. The ancient divisions of the region had survived the war intact and were older and more profound than the political frontier weaving its erratic way through the historic province of Ulster.

For all their undeniable benefits, welfare legislation and increased public expenditure failed to ease tensions. Sometimes they magnified them. For example, educational reform had a modernising effect in Northern Ireland only within the limits of a strictly segregated system. Children now were longer at school and therefore officially separated on religious lines longer than before. The awarding of jobs in local authorities was not done in a fair and open manner. The Housing Trust allocated houses for rent with admirable impartiality but in the end most public housing was built by councils that blatantly failed to apply the same even-handed standards. Insufficient advantage was taken of the long period of comparative peace to remedy obvious wrongs and soothe intercommunal resentment still stubbornly alive, especially where pockets of disadvantage were dangerously concentrated.

EPISODE 113

THE *PRINCESS VICTORIA* DISASTER

Towards the end of January 1953 Europe was assailed by fierce storms. In the Netherlands over a million – one-tenth of the entire population – had been made homeless by flood waters. The death toll there had risen to 340. It was Holland's worst natural disaster since the year 1421.

Britain suffered the most devastating attack of sea and wind since 1703. The gravitational pull of the full moon on the ocean was at its peak six minutes before midnight on Friday 30 January and this created great tides. High tide coincided with a cyclone that moved across Scotland from the Irish Sea to the North Sea whipping up gales of 113 miles per hour. Bodies of over a hundred people had been found on Canvey Island in Essex and 400 were still unaccounted for. Lifeless bodies were found on rooftops with water lapping at their feet and entangled among branches of trees.

The new Larne–Stranraer steamer *Princess Victoria* nosed out of Loch Ryan at 7.45 am on Saturday 31 January. The ship struggled to make headway in a violent gale, now gusting up to 120 miles per hour. As Fusilier Walter Baker said afterwards:

> The *Princess Victoria* took a terrific beating from the mountainous seas as soon as she left Loch Ryan. Finally, one very high wave burst one of the ramp doors at the stern used for loading vehicles, and the water poured in. The ship took a list and then we realised we were in a very serious position.

Captain James Ferguson sent out a distress signal:

> Four miles north-west of Corsewall, car deck flooded, 35 degree list to starboard, require immediate assistance. Ship not under command.

In response the destroyer HMS *Contest* set out from Rothesay. Co. Down lifeboats from Cloughey and Donaghadee, the tugs *Warrior* and *Brigadier* and the salvage ship *Salveda* also raced to the aid of the stricken vessel. Distress rockets were fired but the visibility was so poor they were seen only by the keeper of the Copeland Lighthouse. The *Princess Victoria* drifted helplessly south and west in the raging storm. A plane searching overhead could not find the ferry ship to pinpoint its exact position.

Then at 2:00 pm the Captain sent out his last message:

> Starboard engine room flooded. Ship on her beam ends. Preparing to abandon.

Seas were breaking over the vessel, one side of which was under water. When one lifeboat arrived the line between it and the ship snapped. John Ross of Carrickfergus said afterwards:

> The men formed a human chain to get the women and children out of the lounge, but some of them were not able to get out. Once we reached the deck we clung to the rail as long as we could and were then forced to clamber over the side as the list got worse. Eventually I had to jump into the sea and was picked up in a lifeboat.

Kenneth Harrison of Skipton tried to get two women out:

> The sea came over and smashed the windows of the dining-room and the
> ship started to go over. Somebody shouted: 'she's going,' and one of the crew
> helped me up onto the hull on the port side, where we tried to get the two
> women over, but there was no chance, as they were completely exhausted.
> They were swept away.

Then at 2.30 pm, five miles off the Copeland Islands, the *Princess Victoria* sank.
One lifeboat got away full of passengers. James Kerr, from the Serpentine road
in Belfast, told a reporter afterwards:

> The other lifeboat was swept across her keel and overturned, and that was
> the last we saw of any of the passengers ... On a raft which passed us were a
> woman and a child, and later we sighted a baby in the water in a life jacket.

An oil tanker, *Pass of Dromochty*, dropped oil to calm the waters. Several
in the water owed their lives to the courage and strength of a passenger from
Alliance Avenue in Belfast, Billy Copley, who swam to their rescue.

It seemed clear that most of those who had taken to rafts had perished.
Among the 45 bodies landed at Belfast was that of Major J Maynard Sinclair,
Unionist MP for the constituency of Cromac in Belfast and Minister of Finance
in the Northern Ireland government. He had been seen by many as the natural
successor to the Prime Minister, Lord Brookeborough. His Parliamentary
Secretary, Sir William Scott, was fortunate to have been too late to board the
Princess Victoria on his return from London. Another victim was Sir Walter
Smiles, Unionist MP for North Down and son of William Smiles, founder and
managing director of the Belfast Ropeworks, which became the biggest of its
kind in the world. Altogether 128 people lost their lives in the disaster.

'I HOIST MY SWAG ON MY BACK': AUSTRALIA

Between 1788 and the ending of enforced transportation in 1853, around 48,000 Irish men, women and children were shipped to the penal colonies in Botany Bay and Van Diemen's Land. Sentences were harsh even for trivial crimes. William McKeown from County Antrim was given seven years for stealing two-and-a-half yards of cloth. Tom McKibbon, from the same county, got 14 years for attempting to pass a forged banknote. Chained up, poorly fed and often flogged for insubordination, many died on board before reaching Australia. Those who survived and served their sentences stayed on to make Australia their home.

Since the fare from Ireland to Australia was three or four times more expensive than the passage across the Atlantic, most Irish emigrants preferred North America and Canada. Then in 1851 gold was discovered at Buninyong in Victoria and soon after this strike richer finds followed at Ballarat and Bendigo. Suddenly Australia had become very attractive.

Ulster Presbyterians were amongst the keenest 'diggers' in this gold-rush. One of them was Noah Dalway from Bellahill near Carrickfergus, a descendant of John Dalway, a Scots planter who had built Dalway's Bawn in 1609. He abandoned his job as a bank clerk to find gold in Australia. He invested all his savings in a mine at Simson's Diggings 110 miles (183 km) from Melbourne. But in three weeks he managed to dig up only £2 worth of gold. Soon he was living on bread and water and sleeping rough. Eventually, a Carrickfergus man, William Reid, helped him find a job as a groom at a wage of £6 10s a month.

William Carlisle emigrated from Ulster to try his hand at the diggings in 1854. He went up to Bendigo with some of his shipmates but was forced to give up for lack of capital:

> I hoist my swag on my back which consisted of a blanket, a little tea and sugar, a few matches and a pint tin to make it ready; in such a way came into Melbourne after travelling nearly 200 miles with blistered feet and

wet clothes; the following day overhauled myself with a little decency and joined the Police.

Two brothers from Coleraine, Charles and Sampson Lawrence, also lost their savings in the quest for gold. George McLean, writing home to Richhill in County Armagh, observed that 'Gold digging is both dangerous and uncertain ... Store keeping is a much shurer game'. But nearly all of those who went over to Australia stayed there.

By now colonial governments in Australia were subsidising passages to encourage people to come over. By 1872 140,000 Irish migrants had been assisted to make the passage. A quarter of the white population in Australia were by then of Irish origin – a much higher proportion than in the United States. Some preferred to become outlaws, like the notorious Ned Kelly, born in 1854 in Victoria, the son of Irish parents from Tipperary. Andrew George Scott, son of a Rathfriland clergyman, became a particularly notorious bushranger before his life finished at the end of a noose.

The majority of Irish emigrants to Australia were Catholics from the Midlands, but Protestants from Fermanagh, Tyrone and Cavan also formed a significant group. Slightly more of them were Church of Ireland members rather than Presbyterians. Then for ten years before the outbreak of the First World War in 1914, Ulster provided the majority of Irish emigrants.

Most coming from Ireland became farmers. Those with even small amounts of capital could acquire large tracts of land for raising cattle and sheep. Ulster provided some of the greatest landowners. They included 'Bullocky' Sam Wilson from Ballycloughan in mid-Antrim who made a vast arid estate productive by careful irrigation. His nephew, Sam McCaughey, ended up owing three million acres. He lived to make a large donation to the Ulster Volunteers to buy guns.

Having spent years building up his fortune, Joseph McGaw from Mallusk finally considered marriage. He wrote home to his sister: 'Bespeak me a sweetheart to be ready in two or three years time but not too young as I am now getting grey-haired'.

That the lands they were now farming had been the hunting grounds of the aboriginal people for tens of thousands of years hardly cost these European settlers a thought. Incomers shot or poisoned Australian natives with impunity. Alexander Crawford from Belfast, who had created a sheep station in Western Australia, declared that he enjoyed a 'niggerhunt'. Writing to his fiancée in May 1882, he described how he tracked down some natives who had been killing sheep. He shot one, clubbed another with his revolver butt and tied three by the neck to a tree before having one of them flogged. Back in Ulster, his fiancée,

Elizabeth Matthews, did not approve of her Alexander's manhunts: 'It is a dreadful thing to be continually hunting down one's fellow creatures ... when really in your heart you cannot blame them for taking the sheep ... the whites will have a deal to be answerable for some day'.

EPISODE 115

NEW ZEALAND: AN ULSTER PLANTATION AT KATIKATI

In 1845 the *Dublin University Magazine* noted that New Zealand was 'the most recent, remotest, and least civilized of our colonies'. Then in 1858 it observed: 'Favoured with a climate that shames that of Australia, and with a soil exuberant in the highest degree ... those islands are every year more largely engaging the attention of emigrants.'

However, it was not until Maori resistance had been ruthlessly crushed in the 1860s that New Zealand become an attractive destination for Irish emigrants. For long the government there attempted to keep Irish Catholics out, but New Zealand needed settlers. And the colony was desperately short of women. Single Irish women were much more willing to emigrate from their homeland than were English, Scots or Welsh women. By 1901 Irish Catholics formed just over 14 per cent of New Zealand's white population and Irish Protestants 4.5 per cent. Most of these Irish, Catholic as well as Protestant, had come from Ulster.

Despite their comparatively small number, Ulster Protestants were to make a remarkable contribution to the development of New Zealand. One of these was George Vesey Stewart. Son of Captain Mervyn Stewart of Martray near Ballygawley, he was directly descended from a seventeenth-century Scottish undertaker in the Plantation of Ulster. Indeed, the way his project in New Zealand was planned and organised had much in common with British colonisation of Ulster in the early 1600s.

Sailing out in 1873, he obtained a grant of 10,000 acres at Katikati by the Bay of Plenty on the east side of North Island. Back in Ulster he launched an energetic campaign to find suitable colonists. He circulated all the Orange lodges in the province, gave public lectures and wrote promotional literature, describing the climate at Katikati as 'the finest and most healthy in the world'. The land, after being surveyed, would be divided into portions of 40 acres and an additional 20 for every child. All had to bring suitable farming equipment, seed and ready money. The subsidised fare was fixed at £5 for each person, except that females aged between 15 and 35 travelled free. Almost all those who crowded aboard two sailing vessels in Belfast Lough in June 1875 were tenant farmers.

The ships reached Auckland Harbour in September and as the settlers came ashore the Artillery Band played 'See the Conquering Hero Comes'. That evening the Mayor entertained them at a banquet. Then they transferred to two government steamers and, as they left for the Bay of Plenty the guns at the Armed Constabulary Station thundered out a salute.

At Katikati, the lots for the land portions were drawn by two small boys. There was much to be done. Household goods had to be dragged in across tidal estuaries. The bush was anything up to 12 feet high and there was no road. But, taking the advice of some local Maoris, the newcomers simply set fire to the bush to prepare the land for planting. Enriched by the potash left by the burned ferns, the yields were spectacular in the first season. One settler, Sandy Turner, wrote back to his relations in Ulster:

> I have, without manure, potatoes nine inches long and 3½ inches broad, and half a pound in weight, and oats 7½ feet high … Peas, beans and cabbages will grow all the year round, and melons of all kinds will grow in the fields, which require hot houses at home, and grow to perfection, too, some to the weight of 50 pounds.

'Better than that', he added, the settlers would never be brought to a land court for falling behind in rent, 'for the land will be theirs and their heirs for ever'. Only around a hundred Maoris remained in the area and, Vesey Stewart remarked, 'they vanish like moths before the blaze of civilisation'. A couple of years later, however, the fertility that had been provided by burning ferns was almost gone. Henceforth, as in Ulster, they would have to apply fertilisers and plant more suitable grasses.

Soon the restless Vesey Stewart was busy negotiating with the New Zealand government for another block of land. He returned to Ulster in 1877, published a promotional pamphlet in Omagh, and was overwhelmed with applications. On 20 May 1878, the *Lady Jocelyn* sailed out of Belfast Lough with 378 passengers. This time Stewart attracted many from the upper ranks of society, including some sons of the gentry and two generals.

The colony struggled during the 1880s when prices for agricultural produce were falling fast. However, after the discovery of gold at nearby Waihi in 1886 the farmers did good business supplying the miners' townships with provisions. Stewart built himself a splendid mansion, which he named Mount Stewart, and there he set up a farming school for army officers. When a dairy factory was built in 1902 the future prosperity of this Ulster plantation was assured.

EPISODE 116

'O YES, HIBERNIANS, I BEHELD THE BARD'

On 6 July 1794 Henry Joy, proprietor of the *Belfast News-Letter*, on returning from a tour of the Lake District with Rev. Dr William Bruce, stopped at Dumfries 'desirous to devote the rest of the day to Robert Burns, the Ayrshire poet'. Both men had championed the cause of political reform (though neither would have countenanced the Antrim insurrection led by Joy's nephew, Henry Joy McCracken, just four years later). They were keenly interested in the radical opinions Burns had expressed in his verse. They found that Burns 'preferred a republic' since it would give 'dignity and importance to every individual in society and tends to the cultivation often lost in an inequality of ranks'. Joy asked him about his method of composition:

His muse was most propitious, he said, at night, when his family were at rest. At that time he usually sat down with his box of Lundy Foot's 'Irish Blackguard' and a tumbler of spirits and water; and as often as he found himself 'gumm'd' in a passage, he started to his feet, and was sure to find relief in a hearty pinch of 'Lundy'.

'Irish Blackguard' was a brand of snuff manufactured in Dublin.

Joy and Bruce were not the first from Ulster to call on Burns. Just a few weeks earlier the schoolmaster and poet Samuel Thomson, known as the 'Bard of Carncranny', celebrated this visit subsequently in verse:

O yes, Hibernians, I beheld the Bard,
Old Scotia's jewel, and the muses' darling,

Joy had obtained an edition of Burns published in September 1787 by James
Magee in Belfast. Pirated reprint though it was, it was the first volume of his
poems to appear outside Scotland. Joy, indeed, was responsible for being the
first to print Burns in Ulster; 'Fragments of Scotch poetry', at the poet's request,
appeared in his newspaper in October 1786. More Burns poems appeared
regularly throughout every year thereafter – indeed, Joy had to apologise to
his readers on 11 December 1792 for failing to print any new material from 'the
Ayrshire Bard' who had 'not, as it was feared, taken leave of his muses': simply,
his latest volume of verse was still being printed.

Burns was making a strong appeal to people in Ulster very conscious of their
Scottish roots, people who shared his language, culture and religion and very
often sympathised strongly with his democratic political ideology. After Burns
died prematurely in 1796, at the age of 37, the popularity of his poetry and songs
became stronger in Ulster than perhaps in any territory outside Scotland. There
were 16 locally published editions of Burns' work by 1817. This intense interest
in Burns was noted by John McCloskey in his statistical reports on south Co.
Londonderry in 1821. He observed that:

> the dialect abounds in Scotticisms ... the Presbyterians retain the broad
> Scotch of their ancestors; they require no glossary to understand the
> language of Ramsay or Burns ... Burns is universally a favourite of these
> parishes ... Burns' poems occur more frequently than any other work and
> his beautiful songs often cheer the country-girl at the interesting labour of
> her spinning wheel.

Robert Burns, the poet's eldest son, came over to Belfast in August 1844 to visit
his widowed daughter, Elizabeth, who had settled in the town. Hearing of this,
citizens quickly organised an evening's entertainment in the Burns Tavern in
Long Lane. Then, on 4 September, Burns's son was the guest of honour at a
public breakfast chaired by the Mayor of Belfast in the Donegall Arms Hotel in
High Street. The *Belfast News-Letter* reported 'that the company included men
of all religious and political classes – Protestants, R. Catholics, Presbyterians,
Unitarians, and Quakers, while, as politicians, there were Repealers, Anti-
repealers, Whigs, Tories and radicals, all associated together in the utmost
cordiality for the purpose of doing united homage to the genius of Robert
Burns'. The man leading the campaign against repeal of the Act of Union, Revd

Dr Henry Cooke, said grace. The Mayor, John Clarke, told the company that in 'the North of Ireland … you can scarcely enter the house of any farmer there, who has the least pretensions to a library, but you are sure to find in it the poems of Burns, and, I am happy to say the Bible also'.

In 1859, the centenary of the poet's birth, the *Northern Whig* was overwhelmed when it organised a competition for the occasion – only two winners were to be published but, having received 110 poems, the newspaper had to keep publishing many more over the ensuing months. A grand banquet followed in Belfast Music Hall – one of the largest events outside Scotland – and the same night a centenary dinner in the Corn Exchange ('got up principally by the working classes', according to the *Northern Whig*) and another organised by the Eglington Bowling Club in the Albion Hotel in York Street.

The numerous events organised around the centenary of Burns's death in 1896 seem to have had a healing effect at a time when opinion was bitterly divided on the issue of Home Rule. Burns was one of the few writers who could cross cultural and political boundaries in Ulster. This is how a Catholic ploughman in south Armagh responded when Lynn C. Doyle, still in his teens, tried to interest him in the poetry of another Scot: 'No, Master Lynn, Rabbie'll do for me. Rich or poor, drunk or sober, there's always somethin' in him to suit a body. He'll last me my time'.

A shipping agent in Belfast, Andrew Gibson, had created a great collection of Burns texts – including no fewer than 728 distinct editions of the works of Robert Burns, numbering more than 1,000 volumes. Described as 'the most unique collection of Burns and Burnsiana in the world' this was bought by public subscription in 1900 and deposited in the Linen Hall Library.

Thereafter, though civic events marked the bicentenaries of 1959 and 1996, enthusiasm for Burns became more muted. Then, as the new millennium opened, a strong revival of interest began in Ulster and it did not seem to falter. Burns Night, commemorating the bard's birth every 25 January, is probably celebrated now with more élan and in a greater number of venues across Ulster than ever before.

Seamus Heaney warmly acknowledged his debt to Burns, in his poem 'A Birl for Burns'. In it he recalls that the poet's speech was reflected in that of his neighbours about Bellaghy where he grew up:

> From the start, Burns' birl and rhythm,
> That tongue the Ulster Scots brough wi' them
> And stick to still in County Antrim
> Was in my ear.

From east of Bann it westered in
On the Derry air

He acknowledged that this speech was being lost and concluded:

And even words like stroan and thrawn
Have to be glossed
In Burns' rhymes they travel on
And won't be lost.

EPISODE 117

BLUEGRASS: 'PLAYED FROM MY HEART TO YOUR HEART'

Every September more than 5,000 people gather for the annual Bluegrass Festival at the Ulster American Folk Park in Omagh. This is the most respected and usually the largest festival of its kind in Europe which showcases such world-famous bands as Michael Cleveland & Flamethrower and Dan Paisley and The Southern Grass. The venue is highly appropriate: Bluegrass has its roots in Kentucky, Tennessee and the Carolinas, states that were densely settled from the early 1700s by Ulster Scots.

North America was, and continues to be, a melting pot. Ulster Scots, known in America as the Scotch-Irish, intermarried with other neighbouring immigrants from the rest of the British Isles, with Germans and, indeed, with the Native American Cherokee. Scotch-Irish speech, customs, traditions and music, enriched and altered by this blending, remained strong and distinctive. The Appalachian mountain range was the heartland of this unique culture. The people who farmed and hunted in this high country became known as 'hillbillies', because, it is thought, they were eager to celebrate the deliverance of their forbears in Ulster by William of Orange.

On Saturday evenings neighbours would come together, often at some distance from isolated farms, to exchange news, find partners and drink moonshine. They danced to the fiddle and listened to ballads freshly composed to ancient melodies brought across the Atlantic. In the eighteenth century the

Presbyterian Church and some other strict sects disapproved of too much emotion and forbade the playing of musical instruments in the House of the Lord. Music in church was restricted to the plain singing of versified psalms. Most Ulster Scots arrived as Presbyterians but in time the majority chose to join the Baptists. Enthusiasm characterised the worship of Baptists, Methodists and other evangelical sects, and this included rousing singing in harmony.

To this blend of gospel music and traditional melodies brought over from the Old World was added the music of the African slaves on the tobacco plantations of Kentucky and the cotton fields of the Carolina lowlands. The banjo evolved on the plantations as a stringed instrument brought over in its original form from West Africa. African American music here and in the Deep South became known as jazz and the blues which, together with black gospel music, made their impression on the 'mountain music' or 'country music' of the Appalachians.

The invention of the phonograph and the spread of radio broadcasting in the early 1900s brought this old-time music to people all over the United States and beyond. Few people in the mountains had access to electricity and so music here continued to depend on traditional acoustic instruments. From this country music emerged Bluegrass during the Second World War.

Bill Monroe was the founding father of Bluegrass. The Bluegrass style was named for his band formed in 1939, the Blue Grass Boys. Kentucky is often referred to as the Blue Grass state. As in some forms of jazz, in Bluegrass each instrument takes its turn in playing the melody and improvising around it, while the others perform accompaniment – a style most typically heard in tunes called 'breakdowns'. This is in contrast with old-time music, in which all the instruments play the melody together or one instrument carries the lead throughout while the others provide accompaniment. Bluegrass, unlike mainstream country music, relies on acoustic stringed instruments: the fiddle, five-string banjo, mandolin, upright bass and acoustic guitar played with either a flatpick or a thumb-and-finger pick. Soon after, a new instrument was added to the ensemble, the Dobro, the brand name of a resophonic or resonator guitar invented by a Slovak immigrant family.

Another distinguishing characteristic of bluegrass is vocal harmony composed of two, three, or four parts, often with a dissonant sound delivered in a high-pitch vocal style. The layering of this harmony is called the 'stack'.

Bill Monroe, the solo lead singer and mandolin player, described his Bluegrass as:

Scottish bagpipes and ole-time fiddlin'. It's Methodist and Holiness and Baptist. It's blues and jazz, and it has a high lonesome sound. It's plain music that tells a good story. It's played from my heart to your heart, and it will touch you. Bluegrass is music that matters.

In 1945 the banjo player Earl Scruggs joined the Blue Grass Boys. He added a three-finger roll, universally known as 'Scruggs style', which immediately became a feature of Bluegrass. At first bluegrass was used for dancing in the rural areas, a dancing style known as 'buckdancing', 'flatfooting', or 'clogging'. Soon broadcasting spread its popularity and new bands emerged, including: the Foggy Mountain Boys, Hilo Brown and the Timberliners, and Carl Story and his Rambling Mountaineers.

Lester Flatt and Earl Scruggs, former members of Bill Monroe's band, gave Bluegrass music an enormous boost when they played the soundtrack for the 1967 film *Bonnie and Clyde* and for the television show *The Beverley Hillbillies*.

EPISODE 118

THE OLD FIRM

From late medieval times the main flow of migration across the Narrow Sea had been from east to west. Then, in the nineteenth century, the direction of that flow reversed as tens of thousands escaped from hunger and destitution in the congested Ulster countryside to seek a better life in Scotland's thriving industrial heartland. It is true that by the start of the twentieth century migration had been reduced to a trickle. This ensured that by then the great majority in Scotland with Irish roots were native-born. However, the immigrant community had neither jettisoned atavistic hatreds nor erased memory of ancient wrongs and these continued to fester dangerously in the new homeland.

Actually, periodic eruptions of sectarian conflict in Scotland – however alarming to the authorities at the time – were far less destructive than those on the other side of the North Channel. Annual 'Walks' during the summer parading season did regularly produce violent confrontations, most notably in 1923, 1925, 1927 and 1930, reported in newspapers with headlines such as,

'Garnad Midnight Melee', 'Police in action with the "Billy Boys"', and 'Pitched Street Battles'. These episodes were altogether benign by comparison with the fearsome intercommunal bloodletting in Ulster that had accompanied the birth of Northern Ireland in 1920-22. In Scotland the festering bitterness fuelling fierce loyalties on each side of the religious and cultural divide was in an extraordinary way funnelled into the football stadium.

In Britain association football, described more than once as the country's most durable export, had without question become the most popular spectator sport. Soccer had come of age during the industrial revolution. The game was a great release for young men working long hours, for example, treading perilously narrow beams underneath gantries, tossing red-hot rivets to be hammered into giant steel plates, or carrying out repetitive and often dangerous tasks in enclosed workshops, in engineering shops and in deafening steam-filled mills. All that was required for players was a ball, a hard, flat surface and a relatively small number of players where agility, strategic collaboration and a keen eye counted for more than size or strength. By comparison with most other sports, a football match was easier to stage for very large numbers. And spectators, who so often had played amongst themselves in the narrow streets, could be counted on to have an intimate knowledge of the rules of the game.

The population of greater Glasgow exceeded that of Northern Ireland as a whole and it is no surprise that such a great city became home to Scotland's two mightiest teams. Glasgow Rangers Club was formed in 1872 on the initiative of Peter Campbell, William McBeath and the brothers Moses and Peter MacNeill. Brother Walfrid, originally from Sligo, formed Glasgow Celtic and Athletic Club in 1888 to provide the St Vincent de Paul Society 'with funds for the maintenance of the "Dinner Tables" of our needy children' in the Catholic parishes in the city's east end and 'to have a large recreation ground where our Catholic young men will be able to enjoy the sports which will build them up physically'. It was not long before its Edinburgh counterpart, the Hibernian Football Club, lost its pre-eminence, vanquished repeatedly by Celtic.

Rangers proved to be the only club in Scotland with the necessary drive capable of fielding players of sufficient calibre, and backed by a following formidable and faithful enough to take on Celtic as an equal. The two clubs played each other for the first time in May 1888. From the outset support for each club was so passionate that Celtic Park and the Rangers ground, Ibrox – for long the two biggest soccer stadiums in the world – were almost always filled to capacity. In consequence, handsome receipts were virtually guaranteed; this prompted one journalist to name matches between these two powerful teams (on average more than four a year) as 'The Old Firm'.

Few arenas in the world attracted followers in such imposing numbers as Old Firm games. Undoubtedly Glasgow's highly efficient transport system, composed first of horse-drawn brakes and then of electric trams, buses and a sophisticated underground subway, opened in 1896, helped to bring supporters easily and inexpensively to fixtures. But it was the intensity of the passion in support of (or in hated opposition to) the teams that counted for most. George Macdonald Fraser observed that others 'played football on Saturday afternoons and talked about it on Saturday evenings, but the Glaswegians, men apart in this as in most things, played, slept, ate, drank and lived it seven days a week'.

Acrid emotions, which two centuries earlier had fuelled battles between Peep o' Day Boys and Defenders in mid-Ulster, now surfaced again in an altered form on the other side of the Narrow Sea to find virulent expression at Old Firm fixtures. Celtic had been an avowedly Catholic club since its foundation. John Lawrence, chairman of Rangers, admitted in 1969 that the policy of not signing Catholics had been with the club since it was formed. Celtic had been the first to sign up players who were not Catholics, without serious reaction. Then, on 10 July 1989, Maurice 'Mo' Johnston, a former Celtic player, signed for Rangers. Some Rangers fans burned their scarves and season tickets. The club's kitsman, Jimmy Bell, refused to wash Johnston's training gear. But the most intense fury came from Celtic supporters. Johnston had to be accompanied by six bodyguards working on a rota.

Year after year, Old Firm fixtures were marred by furious fighting between rival supporters, and by pitch invasions, requiring vigorous intervention by mounted police. A violent confrontation between fans on 10 May 1980 at Hampden Park prompted this editorial in the *Scotsman*:

> The brutal and disgusting scenes which followed as bottles flew and drunken supporters charged and countercharged from one end of the field to the other, brought disgrace upon the two clubs concerned, upon Scottish football generally, and were an affront to Scotland as a nation.

In Northern Ireland the fortunes of Rangers and Celtic were closely scrutinised with a fierce partisan fervour, as in Scotland, along confessional lines. However, the region did not have an exact equivalent to the Old Firm: most soccer clubs were and remain based in Protestant districts. Those most often celebrating triumphs were those with loyalist followers, such as Linfield. Clubs with Catholic followers, including Cliftonville in Belfast, repeatedly found the Irish League, the governing body in Northern Ireland, to be unsympathetic to its concerns about where fixtures should be held. In 1949

Belfast Celtic gave up the struggle and its followers transferred their support to Glasgow Celtic.

Derry City, founded in 1928, remained in the Irish League, winning a title in 1964-65. But its position became impossible with the onset of the Troubles, when the unchained sectarian dragon leaped from its cage as fear, suspicion and recollection of grievance gushed to the surface. Derry City's grounds at the Brandywell was sited in a part of the city most convulsed by the violence. It had to play its home games in Coleraine, 30 miles (48 km) away, where fans were reluctant to travel. When the Army approved a return to the Brandywell, the Irish League continued to insist on Coleraine as a venue for home games. The result was that Derry City left the Irish League in 1971 and became the only Northern Ireland club to join the Republic's League of Ireland. It is remarkable, nevertheless, that well-supported soccer matches continued to be played on schedule throughout more than 30 years of political and intercommunal conflict – a protracted episode which led to a total of 3,651 men, women and children losing their lives as a direct result of the violence by the year 2000.

EPISODE 119

THE HAMELY TONGUE

In 1860 David Patterson, teacher at the Industrial Institution for the Deaf and Dumb and the Blind, published a book with the title *The Provincialisms of Belfast and the Surrounding Districts Pointed Out and Corrected*. His purpose was to persuade his pupils to drop local speech and pronunciation and use Standard English. He wrote:

It must be evident to any intelligent and unprejudiced observer, that the pronunciation given to the English words used in ordinary conversation by the people of Belfast and the surrounding districts, is, in general, very different from that recommended by English orthoepists, and taught in our common school dictionaries ... mistakes are made in the use of almost every elementary sound in the language. In Belfast and the surrounding districts, the uneducated, and sometimes even the educated, err in the pronunciation of the following sounds and letters ...

Patterson then made long lists showing how words were pronounced locally, including Besom, Bizzim; Gold, Goold; Idiot, Eedyet; Whip, Whup; America, Americay; Soft, Saft; Turpentine, Torpentine; and Canal, Canaul. He also included a list with translations entitled 'Words not to be met with in our Ordinary English Dictionaries'. They included: Wheen, a quantity; Sleekit, sly; Skelly, to squint; Skelf, a small splinter; Farl, a cake of bread; Curnaptious, crabbed; Boke, to make an offer to vomit; Thole, to endure or suffer pain or annoyance; Hoke, to make holes; Scundther, to disgust; Sheugh, a ditch; Stoor, dust; and Cowp, to upset.

With the exception of sheugh, which comes from the Gaelic, all of these words are of Lowland Scots origin.

Lowland Scots or Lallands is derived from Old Northumbrian or northern forms of Anglo-Saxon. Originally it was spoken only in the south-east of Scotland from the Tweed River to the Firth of Forth. Scots Gaelic was the language over most of the rest of Scotland. Then, from the time that King David I was crowned at Scone in 1124, Lowland Scots became the language at court and rapidly spread up the east coast as far as Caithness (where it became known as Doric) and throughout the Lowlands.

The great majority of Scots who colonised Ulster from the early 1600s onwards came from the Lowlands and they brought their Lallands with them. At this time Lowland Scots was the language of commerce, taught as a written language and used in legal and other official documents printed in Edinburgh. The official standing of Lallands, however, was slowly undermined after the Union of Crowns in 1603 and the publication of the King James Authorised Version of the Bible in 1611. But, apart from the Highlands and Islands, it remained the everyday speech of Scots from the humblest labourer to the highest ranks of the nobility.

This speech was planted most securely in Ulster where Scots settled in the greatest numbers. Its strongholds were, and remain, north, mid and south-east Antrim; north-east Londonderry, north-east Down; north-west Tyrone; and north-east Donegal. Elsewhere in Ulster the vernacular tongue is also strongly influenced by Scots, but it is arguably closer to the dialects of English colonists, and is known to scholars as 'Hiberno-English'. For example, 'crack', meaning fun and often attributed to Irish and spelt 'craic' (often used with the definite article 'the craic'), was brought over from England. Gaelic, the language of the native Irish, was still spoken in every Ulster county, but by the beginning of the twentieth century it was the language of only six per cent of the province's population.

In Ulster this speech imported from Scotland developed its own characteristics. Speakers referred to it as 'Scotch' or 'Braid Scotch'. In 1777 the *Hibernian Magazine* said of Newtownards: 'The language spoken here is a broad Scotch hardly to be understood by strangers'. Elsewhere it appeared in verse written by handloom weavers by their looms, and in correspondence, including a bill in Ulster Scots attached to two parcels sent by Friend Thomas Stott of Dromore to his fellow-Quaker Friend James Gilmour of Garvagh. It concludes:

> On baith to this bit paper joined
> The bill o' parcels ye will find.
> An' we hae placed the fair amount
> Right cannily to your account,
> Which, if we cast the figures straight,
> Is just of pounds four score and eight,
> Five Irish siller shillins smug
> And six bawbees – to buy a mug.

Just like Gaelic, Ulster Scots retreated under pressure from formal education and modern communications. It survived, however, cherished in newspaper articles and novels in the 1800s, by the poet and broadcaster W F Marshall in the 1900s, and its most admired exponent today is James Fenton, who celebrates the vernacular speech of his native County Antrim as 'The Hamely Tongue'.

The influence of Ulster Scots on the speech of people in America's Appalachian Mountains is strong. This has been a lifetime study of Professor Michael Montgomery of South Carolina whose dictionary includes words such as hap, nebby, scunner, bannock, blatherskite, clart, coggly, drewth, foutery, forenenst, hove up, hunker, jeuk, kist, piggin, red up, skitter and unbeknownst.

EPISODE 120

EPILOGUE

Modern nationalism, which could be said to have originated in revolutionary France, sped along rapidly extending railway lines to engulf every part of Europe by the end of the 1800s. As modern communications steadily eroded parochial sentiment, peoples discovered their national identity. Every nationality emphasised its individuality and distinctiveness. In Ireland, as the debate on the island's political future intensified from the 1830s onwards, citizens seemed divided sharply into two ethnic groups with profoundly divergent aspirations. Ulster joined in the developing European debates on racial typifications and national traits. Many of those northern unionists who were opposed to a Home Rule parliament in Dublin took pride in their Scottish ancestry, looking upon themselves as a distinct people, Ulster Scots, quite different from nationalist Catholics now seeking a form of independence for Ireland.

The *Ulster Journal of Archaeology*, founded in 1852, in its first issues ran a series of articles entitled 'The origin and characteristics of the population in the counties of Down and Antrim'. These informed readers that Protestants in eastern Ulster were Anglo-Saxon in race, possessing the inherited virtues of thrift, capacity for hard work and respect for law and order. Using such words as 'staunch' and 'stalwart' to describe themselves, northern Protestants had no difficulty in accepting this theory. Nationalists largely accepted Protestants' assumption of their racial separateness, for they at the same time were emphasising their Celtic origins and laying claim to inherent characteristics such as hospitality, passion and love of poetry.

A similar movement developed in the United States. Some descendants of Ulster Presbyterians who had settled in America were becoming alarmed not only by the influx of Catholic Irish but also by the arrival of great numbers from eastern and southern Europe. On 8 May 1889 the Scotch-Irish Society of America was inaugurated at Columbia, Tennessee, and over the next 12 years held 10 congresses largely to define and celebrate 'Scotch-Irish American' identity. Robert Bonner, the permanent president of the society, declared that the proceedings reflected

the cordial good will, the patriotic fervour, the indomitable spirit, the tenacity of purpose, and the stern integrity, which have always characterised the Scotch-Irish.

Certainly Governor William McKinley of Ohio, elected 28th President in 1897, regarded the Scotch-Irish as a distinct race. He remarked:

The Americanised Scotch-Irishman is the perfection of a type which is the commingling and assimilation process of centuries ... Before he loses his racial distinctiveness and individuality he should be photographed by history's camera.

The Scotch-Irish, he believed, should distance themselves from the Celtic-Irish as

the most undesirable, the most mischievous, the most damnable element of population that could have been scraped out of the corners of the earth.

Clashing political aspirations in Ireland resulted in fearful bloodletting while the island was being partitioned between 1919 and 1923. Such convulsions ensured that descendants of natives and newcomers alike continued to emphasise their separate origins. In doing so, they had academic approval at a time when eugenics remained a respectable and approved area of study.

The government of the Irish Free State gave enthusiastic backing to Harvard University's five-year archaeological research programme in Ireland in the 1930s. This was to determine the racial and cultural heritage of the Irish people. The Harvard mission included the examination of prehistoric skulls, complemented by the physical examination of thousands of volunteers who came forward to have their skulls and nose shapes measured and their hair colour graded. The chief adviser to the Harvard mission was the Director of the National Museum of Ireland, Adolf Mahr, an Austrian archaeologist who had joined the Nazi Party in 1932, a year before Hitler came to power in Germany. Mahr declared that Ireland 'is not the cradle of the Celtic stock, but she was its foremost stronghold at the time of the decline of the Celts elsewhere'. 'Ireland is now the only self-governing State with an uninterrupted Celtic tradition', he continued, the 'last refuge' of the Celtic spirit, 'pre-eminently *the* Celtic country'. Those on both sides of the Atlantic who funded this mission considered it politically and economically important to confirm the identity of the Irish as white, Celtic and northern European. There appeared to be no recognition that Vikings, Normans, Flemings and English had made significant contributions to the Irish gene pool from early medieval times onward. The Harvard mission returned largely satisfied that it had established that the Irish were the truest descendants of the Celtic race. As the magazine *Life* put it in its issue of 7 August 1939: 'No long upper-lipped, baboon-faced Irishmen common in political cartoons were found'.

Meanwhile, there were many in Northern Ireland continuing to give assurance to Protestants there that they were ethnically different from the rest of the inhabitants of Ireland. In 1922, Cyril Falls, an officer of the Royal

Inniskilling Fusiliers who had led his men over the top on 1 July 1916 at the Somme, published his history of the 36th (Ulster Division). Those who came forward to enlist in the division he classed as a distinct people with special qualities. 'There is a slow-burning flame in the Ulster blood', he wrote, 'that keeps her sons, once raised to the passion of great endeavour, at a high and steady pitch of resolution'. He singled out 'that great accretion of moral force' to be found in descendants of Borderers, including Armstrongs, Wilsons, Elliots, Irvines, Johnstons and Hannas. Few nationalists joined the Ulster Division, it is true, but it is worth pointing out that during 1914–18 in Belfast a slightly higher proportion of Catholics voluntarily enlisted, joining the 10th and 16th divisions for the most part, than Protestants.

In 1942, the United States of America took over responsibility for the defence of Northern Ireland and established bases on Lough Erne and Lough Foyle to combat the U-boat campaign. At the same time Northern Ireland became the training ground for American troops preparing to invade North Africa and then the Normandy beaches. Altogether some 300,000 Americans were stationed at one time or another in the region. In 1943 the Presbyterian minister of Castlerock, Co. Londonderry, W. F. Marshall – well known as a poet and broadcaster – published *Ulster Sails West*. This book was designed to provide incoming Americans 'with an outline of the part played by Ulstermen in building the United States'. This lucid and carefully researched account gives the reader a comprehensive catalogue of Ulster Scots and their descendants who became presidents, distinguished statesmen, outstanding generals, leading churchmen, great inventors and successful businessmen.

At the same time *Ulster Sails West* was a broadside, a vehement counterblast against those who classed the achievements of the Scots-Irish in America as 'Irish'. He argued that it was 'most dishonest and unfair' to claim 'this contribution as Irish, and then use it as the basis of propaganda against the Ulster that made it'. He concluded:

> We are not willing to lose the credit for these achievements of our people.
> We are not willing that this credit should be stolen from those to whom it
> belongs, and made part and parcel of a tireless propaganda for our political
> extinction.

Here Marshall is referring to the publicity campaign by Éire's Taoiseach, Éamon de Valera, to end partition, a campaign intensified in the immediate post-war years. For all the strength of his arguments, Marshall makes one point clear: he regards northern Protestants, 'our people', as a completely separate group. Most nationalists, still considering themselves heirs of the Celtic race, agreed entirely with this viewpoint.

The robust celebration of the achievements of both the 'Celtic' Irish and the Scots-Irish, viewed as two disparate entities, continues most prominently in the United States. Perhaps the best-known publication on this subject in recent years is *Born Fighting: How the Scots-Irish Shaped America* by James Webb, a former Secretary of the Navy in the Reagan administration. Webb's publishers described the Scots-Irish as 'this remarkable ethnic group' and, in a warm review of *Born Fighting*, the novelist Tom Wolfe labels them as 'the all-but-invisible ethnic group'.

Such assumptions made about ethnic groups in and from Ireland can be shown to be seriously flawed. In the wake of two world wars, Hitler's programme of genocide and the ethnic slaughter which accompanied the break-up of Yugoslavia in the 1990s, the hollowness of extreme claims of racial distinctiveness have been exposed. Like all the inhabitants of Ireland, Ulster Scots are a blend. This was ensured from the earliest times by constant coming and going across the Narrow Sea.

Lowland Scots and their descendants who arrived in Ulster as colonists in the 1600s did not separate themselves from the native Irish population quite as much as was formerly believed. In western Ulster, Scots settlers, particularly those of low status, sometimes married local women and within a generation their descendants could well be speaking Irish. On the other side of the province the incoming flood of British colonists encouraged many native Irish to embrace Protestantism, speak English and drop the 'O' or 'Mac' from their surnames. Some O'Flynns changed their surname to Lynn and many O'Neills and MacNeills adopted the surname Neill. A cursory glance at registers in segregated schools past and present will show many Lowland Scots surnames – such as Hume, Adams and Sands – in Catholic roll books. Native Irish surnames – such as McCusker, O'Neill and Magennis – frequently appear in Protestant school registers.

The 1800s saw a dramatic fall in the number of people who could speak Irish and, as surnames were anglicised, translated or given pseudo-translations, the memory of ancestral connections was often lost. Hebridean warriors settling in Ulster were known as *gallóglaigh*, 'young foreign warriors'. Some adopted this as a surname which, in some cases, became anglicised as Gallogley. Others, not knowing of family origins in the Western Isles, assumed that the *gall*, 'foreigners', were English and so adopted it as an anglicised surname – at the time of writing English is a far more common surname in Ulster than Gallogley. During the nineteenth century the many Catholics who joined Protestant churches during the evangelical revivals often changed their surnames. Laverys on the eastern shore of Lough Neagh became Armstrongs; the surname Johnston was borrowed by McKeowns and MacShanes; and the O'Carrolls of Dromore almost all changed their surname to Cardwell. Following a quarter of a century of research, the historian Douglas Carson found that all in Ulster bearing his surname are related to each other, however distantly, and that there are almost as many Catholics as Protestants in Northern Ireland possessing the Lowland Scots surname of Carson – a name of Norman origin.

However blended, a great many people in Ulster take pride in their Scots ancestry and culture ... and with good reason: the influence of Ulster Scots across the globe has been out of all proportion to their numbers.

REFERENCES

Where the title of a book, article or pamphlet is not given, the complete reference will be found in the bibliography.

EPISODES

Preface: Mallory, 2017, pp 30–36, pp 42–47

1. Cary and Warmington, 1929, p. 43; Mallory, 2017, pp 29–30 and pp 71–90; Oliver, 2009, pp 11–13

2. Fraser, 2009, pp 17–23 and 44–50; Oliver, 2009, pp 28–31; Clarkson, 2013, pp 17–26

3. Fraser, 2009, pp 22–29; Clarkson, 2009, pp 64–5

4. Fraser, 2009, pp 96, 121, 144–149, 159–160; Dáibhí Ó Cróinín in Ó Cróinín (ed.), 2005, pp 210–219; Hamlin and Lynn, 1988, p. 21; Clarkson, 2013, pp 59–64; Campbell, 1999, 17–30; Cormac McSparran in Roulston (ed.), 2018, pp 66–71

5. Fraser, 2009, pp 97–105; Clarkson, 2009, pp 138–145; Campbell, 1999, pp 31–41

6. Fraser, 2009, pp 109–113 and 155–174; Campbell, 1999, pp 34–41; Clarkson, 2009, pp 112–117, 124–128 and 159–161; Driscoll, 2002, pp 14–24; McNally, 1965, p. 125; Ó Croinin, 2005, p. 217; Adamson, 1979, p. 19 and 74–5

7. Fraser, 2009, p. 346; Driscoll, 2002, pp 24–32; F.J. Byrne in Ó Cróinín (ed.), 2005, pp 609–631; de Paor, 1964, p. 132; *Annals of Ulster* AD 811

8. Clarkson, 2009, pp 170–180 and 188–9

9. Oram, 2011, pp 16–24 and 269–277; Oliver, 2009, pp 61–82; Lynch, 1991, pp 53–63 and 74–90; Houston and Knox (eds), 2001, pp 84–90 and 155–170; Lynch (ed.), 2001, pp 360–1

10. Scott and Martin (eds), 1978, p. 175, 177 and 181; Flanagan, 1998, pp 79–167; *Annals of Inisfallen* AD 1177

11. Brown, 2016, pp 50–165; Hamlin and Lynn, 1988, p. 38; McNeill, 1980, pp 7–9

12. Brown, 2016, pp 165–211; McNeill, 1980, pp 40–1, 45, 53, 79–81 and 92–3; Bardon, 1992, pp 45–7

13. Oram, 2011, p. 229; Taylor, 2016, pp 81–83; Lynch, 1991, pp 58–60, 88 and 91; Oliver, 2009, pp 63–4 and 73–6; James Lydon in Cosgrove (ed.), 1987, pp 156–175

14. J.A. Watt in Cosgrove (ed.), 1987, pp 353–4; James Lydon in Cosgrove (ed.), 1987, pp 187–8 and 197–200; Oliver, 2009, pp 88–99

15. Clark, 1996, pp 70–74; Oliver, 2009, p. 114; Ulster-Scots Agency, 2007, *Robert the Bruce 700: 1307–2007*

16. James Lydon in Cosgrove (ed.), 1987, pp 275–284; Lynch, 1991, pp 116–124; Oliver, 2009, pp 96–99 and 110–121; Lynch (ed.), 2001, pp 524–525; Steel, 1984, pp 39–44; Ulster-Scots Agency, 2007, *Robert the Bruce 700: 1307–2007*

17. McNamee, 1997, pp 166–180; James Lydon in Cosgrove (ed.), 1987, pp. 284–294; *Annals of Connacht* AD 1315 and AD 1318; Orpen, 1913–5, part 4, p. 167; Gilbert, 1884–6, p. 297 and 345; Ó Baoill, 2008, p. 12 and 18–24

18. McNamee, 1997, pp 180–199; Ó Baoill, 2008, p. 12; James Lydon in Cosgrove (ed.), 1987, p. 275 and 282–294; Bardon, 1992, pp 49–54

19. Seán Duffy in Duffy (ed.), 2017, pp 1–2 and 17–24; Kenneth Nicholls in Duffy (ed.), 2017, pp 86–105; David H. Caldwell in Duffy (ed.), 2017, pp 144–168; *Calendar of State Papers*, Henry VIII, Correspondence, vol. 3, p. 44

20. Kingston, 2004, pp 49–52; Hill, 1873, pp 21–23, 26–29, and 35; Williams, 1997, p. 149 and 169–179; Lynch, 1991, p. 67; Oliver, 2009, pp 157–158; Lynch (ed.), 2001, pp 294–295 and 341

21. Clarkson, 2009, pp 61–64; Campbell, 1999, pp 17–27; Lynch (ed.), 2001, pp 257–258 and 505, Bardon, 1992, p. 42; Kenneth Nicholls in Duffy (ed.), 2017, p. 88; Hill, 1873, p. 23; Kingston, 2004, p. 50

22. Kingston, 2004, pp 66–70; Oliver, 2009, pp 138–140; Lynch (ed.), 2001, p. 635; Williams, 1997, pp 186–187; Lynch, 1991, pp 142–143 and 167–168

23. Hill, 1873, p. 18 and 27–31; Lynch, 1991, pp 144–145; Williams, 1997, pp 199–200; Lynch (ed.), 2001, p. 295

24. 'Pibroch of Donald Dhu': Gaelic verse and Scott's poem in www.online-literature.com/walter_scott/2567

25. Williams, 1997, pp 223–240; Lynch, 1991, pp 146–151; Lynch (ed.), 1991, p. 295

26. Lynch, 1991, pp 155–158; Art Cosgrove in Cosgrove (ed.), 1987, pp 531–532; Hill, 1873, p. 37; Bardon, 1992, pp 66–68; Ó Baoill, 2008, p. 29

27. Darren McGettigan in Mac Laughlin and Beattie (eds), 2013, pp 135–147; Darren Mac Eiteagáin in Nolan, Ronanyne and Dunlevy (eds), 1995, pp 203–224

28. Darren Mac Eiteagáin in Nolan, Ronanyne and Dunlevy (eds), 1995, pp 211–212; Goodwin, 2014, p. 155; Darren McGettigan in Mac Laughlin and Beattie (eds), 2013, p. 146

29. Goodwin, 2014, p. 118, 155 and 157–161; Lynch, 1991, pp 158–161; Oliver, 2009, pp 168–169

30. Goodwin, 2014, pp 191–213

31. Lynch, 1991, pp 187–190; Smout, 1969, pp 49–57; Mac Culloch, 2003, pp 378–379; Steel, 1984, pp 64–66; Houston and Knox (eds), 2001, pp 184–186

32.   Oliver, 2009, p. 178; Smout, 1969, pp. 49–57; Steel, 1984, pp 64–70

33.   *Calendar of State Papers*, Henry VIII, Correspondence, vol. 3, p. 15; Bardon, 1992, pp 72–73; Darren Mac Eiteagáin in Nolan, Ronayne and Dunlevy (eds); Elliott, 2000, pp 61–64

34.   Maxwell, 1923, p. 145; Mac Culloch, 2003, pp 202–203, 395–396 and 398

35.   Steel, 1984, pp 77–88; Oliver, 2009, pp 179–196; Lynch, 1991, pp 517–519

36.   Mac Culloch, 2003, pp 380–381; Smout, 1969, pp 101–106; Lynch (ed.), 1991, p. 512 and 517–519.

37.   *Annals of the Four Masters* AD 1567; *Calendar of State Papers, Ireland*, vol. 21, p. 8; Bardon, 1992, pp 76–79

38.   Hill, 1873, pp 155–156; Clark, 1996, pp 94–97; *Annals of the Four Masters* AD 1574

39.   Lennon, 1994, pp 274–283; Hill, 1873, pp 159–180; Bardon, 1992, pp 85–87; Clark, 1996, pp 103–110

40.   Lennon, 1994, pp 292–296; Bardon, 1992, pp 89–92

41.   Hill, 1873, p. 188; Bardon, 1992, pp 100–104 and 108–114; Fynes Moryson, *An History of Ireland, From the Year 1599 to 1603*, London, 1617, Book 3, p. 177, 197, 99, 283, and 285

42.   Hiram Morgan in Morgan (ed.), 2004, pp 128–132; Hill, 1873, pp 194–196

43.   Perceval-Maxwell, 1973, p. 53; Hill, 1869, pp 16–26 and 32–33; Bardon 2011, pp 70–75

44.   Fynes Moryson, *An History*, 1617, p. 283; Hill, 1869, p. 66; Perceval-Maxwell, 1973, pp 52–57 and 66; Bardon, 2011, pp 77–80

45.   Hill, 1869, pp 37–39 and 44–47; Perceval-Maxwell, 1973, pp 52–54, 56–57, 66 and 85–86; Bardon, 2011, pp 78–79

46.   Alison Cathcart, 'Scots and Ulster: the late medieval context' in Kelly and Young (eds), 2009, pp 74–83

47.   Hill, 1873, p. 194; Hector McDonnell in Morgan (ed.), 2004, pp 272–273 and 275; Perceval-Maxwell, 1973, pp 47–49 and 62–64; Turner, 1974, pp 64–158; Bardon, 2011, pp 80–85

48.   McCavitt, 2002, pp 88–92 and 124; Bardon, 2011, pp 91–94; *Calendar of State Papers, Ireland*, 1606–8, p. 270 and 273; Hill, 1877, p. 70

49.   *Annals of the Four Masters* AD 1608; *Calendar of State Papers, Ireland*, 1606–8, pp 504–506; Bardon, 2011, pp 102–108; Hill, 1877, p. 70

50.   Robinson, 1984, p. 63; Moody, 1939, p. 31; Bardon, 2011, pp 142–146

51.   Smyth, 2006, p. 21, 25–28, 31, 35 and 49–53; Hill, 1877, p. 70; Canny, 2001, p. 195 and 197; Bardon, 2011, pp 112–129

52.   Hill, 1877, pp 133–134; Moody, 1939, pp 31–32; Bardon, 2011, pp 135–138

53.   Gilbert, 1879, vol. 1, pp 318–326; Perceval-Maxwell, 1973, pp 323–358; Robinson, 1984, pp 205–208; Hill, 1877, pp 283–309; Bardon, 2011, pp 153–159

54.   Perceval-Maxwell, 1973, pp 323–338; Robinson, 1984, pp 205–208; Hill, 1877, pp 283–309; Bardon, 2011, p. 163

55.   Fraser, 1971, pp 361–362 and 366–373; Perceval-Maxwell, 1973, p. 84; Robinson, 1984, p. 77 and 79; Fraser, frontispiece map, and Bell, 1988, for distribution of Borderer surnames

56.   Roulston, 20101, pp 21–29; William Roulston, 'The Ulster Plantation in the manor of Dunnalong, 1610–70' in Jefferies and Dillon (eds), 2011, pp 82–85; Robinson, 1984, p. 200 and 204

57.   Perceval-Maxwell, 1973, pp 26–27; Gillespie, 1985, p. 31; Bardon, 2011, p. 243 and 262–3

58.   Aidan Clarke in Moody, Martin and Byrne (eds), 1978, pp 292–293; Bardon, 2008, pp 184–185; Bardon, 2011, pp 259–260

59.   Curl, 1986, p. 91; Stevenson, 1981, pp 54–55, McGettigan, 2010, p. 38; Elliott, 2010, pp 101–104; Bardon, 2011, pp 272–281

60.   Reid, 1867, vol. 2, pp 260–269; Bardon, 2011, pp 291–293

61.   Steel, 1984, pp 125–126, McBride, 2009, p. 126; Bardon, 2011, pp 298–303

62.   Gillespie, 'Scotland and Ulster: A Presbyterian perspective 1603–1700' in Kelly and Young (eds), 2009, pp 84–85; Bardon, 2011, pp 305–307

63.   Delbourgo, 2017

64.   McBride, 2009, pp 70–79; Smith, 1995, p. 142 and 144; Ruth Smith, *Handel's Oratorios and Eighteenth-Century Thought*, Cambridge, 1995, pp 48–50

65.   Reid, 1867, vol. 3, p. 30; Public Record Office of Northern Ireland, T 781/1 p. 50; Bardon, 1992, pp 168–175

66.   McMaster, 2009, pp 40–57 and 73; Smyth, 2006, pp 427–429

67.   Dickson, 1966, p. 22, 28–29, 33 and 41; Public Record Office of Northern Ireland T.S.P.I. T 659/1352; Boulter, 1770, vol.1, pp 209–210, 224

68.   McMaster, 2009, p. 73; Smyth, 2006, p. 439

69.   Herman, 2001, p. 25, 31–38, and 58; Oliver, 2009, pp 286–294

70.   Stewart, 1993, pp 71–73 and 95–101; Herman, 2001, pp 68–81

71.   Herman, 2001, pp 2–8, 21–23, 60–73, 82–101 and 181–201; Lynch (ed.), 2001, pp 137–143; Smout, 1969, pp 451–483

72.   Dickson, 1966, pp 26–28, 64, 86 and 209–212; voyage of the *Sally* in *Belfast News-Letter*, 13 May 1763, reprinted in Dickson, 1966, pp 288–290

73.   Fitzpatrick, 1989, pp 74–87

74.   Fitzpatrick, 1989, pp 88–98

75.   Fitzpatrick, 1989, pp 98–106

76. Bruce Clark, 'The Man Who Told The Truth', BBC Northern Ireland, 11 February 2018; Fitzpatrick, 1989, pp 95–97; Claire Simpson, 'The United States founding father from the Derry Countryside', *Irish News*, 10 February 2018

77. Joy, 1817, p. 138; O'Connell, 1965, p. 28 and 63; Bardon, 1992, pp 218–224; Public Record Office of Northern Ireland, Education Facsimile, 'Volunteers', pp 141–143, 148 and 152

78. Joy, 1817, p. 165, 183, 348–353 and 358; O'Connell, 1965, p. 325 and 354; Stewart, 1995, pp 102–121 and 205–234; Bardon, 1992, pp 218–224

79. Dickson, 1960, p. 106, 109, 111–112, 119, 138 and 142–7; McNeill, 1960, pp 165–192; Bardon, 1992, pp 225–237

80. Dickson, 1960, pp 227–231

81. Geoghegan, 1999, pp 41–96; Bardon, 2008, pp 327–332

82. McNeill, 1960, pp 43–77, 217–226, 257–287 and 295; Courtney, 2013, pp 130–131

83. Crawford, 1972, p. 46, 51, 63 and 87; Ferguson (ed.), 2008, pp 1–10 and 135–143; see also John Hewitt, *Rhyming Weavers and Other Country Poets of Antrim and Down*, Belfast, 1974

84. Ferguson (ed.), 2008, pp 207–208

85. Holmes, 1981, pp 8, 12, 31 and 66; Kirkpatrick, 2006, pp 55–61; Courtney, 2013, pp 148–150; Bardon, 1992, pp 249–253; Holmes, 2000, pp 84–105

86. 'The Repealer Repulsed', 1841, p. 110 in the Linen Hall Library, Belfast; see also Patrick Maume (ed.), *The Repealer Repulsed* by William McComb, Belfast, 2003; Bardon, 1992, pp 255–257; Ulster-Scots Community Network, *Henry Cooke: An introduction*, Belfast, n.d.

87. Handley, 1947, pp 25–38 and 43–46

88. Fitzpatrick, 1989, pp 124–130; Meacham, 2008, pp; Kennedy, 1996, pp 61–69; Ulster-Scots Community Network, *Ulster & Tennessee*, Belfast, n.d.

89. Fitzpatrick, 1989, pp 133–139; Marshall, 1950, pp 41–44; Ulster-Scots Community Network, *Confederate Generals: Lee's Ulster-Scots commanders*, Belfast, n.d., and *Union Generals: President Lincoln's Ulster-Scots commanders*, Belfast, n.d.

90. Fitzpatrick, 1989, pp 73, 208–221 and 261

91. Lynch (ed.), 2001, pp 39, 103–4, 189, 199–200 and 269–272; *Belfast Directory* 1896; Smout, 1987, pp 85–105; Bardon, 1992, pp 390–392; Steel, 1984, pp 234–246; Handley, 1947, pp 126–127

92. Handley, 1947, pp 123–127, 240 and 244–245

93. Purdon, 1877, p. 8, 9, 37 and 47–48; Handley, 1947, pp 130–133; Brooke, 1973, p. 157 and 176–177; Bardon, 1992, pp 329–334

94. Foster, Houston and Madigan in Mitchell (ed.), 2008, pp 69–87; Handley, 1947, pp 111–120

95. Handley, 1947, pp 164–165 and 173

96. Seán Beattie, 'The Hiring-fair System in Donegal' in McLaughlin and Beattie (eds), 2013, pp 253–262; Anne O'Dowd, 'Seasonal Migration to the Lagan and Scotland' in Nolan, Ronayne and Dunlevy (eds), 1995, pp 625–628 and 631–647

97. Brian Lambkin, 'The Migration Story of Mící Mac Gabhann, 1865–1948' in McLaughlin and Beattie (eds), 2013, pp 287–292; Patrick MacGill quoted in Bardon, 1992, p. 319; Handley, 1947, pp 173–187

98. 'Service in Scotland', Chapter 2 of *My Story* by Pat the Cope Gallagher quoted in Handley, 1947, pp 183–184

99. Stephen A. Royle, 'Workshop of the Empire' in Connolly (ed.), pp 199–236; *Belfast Directory*, 1887 and 1896; Maguire, 1993, pp 59–88; Bardon, 1992, pp 336–340 and 386–399

100. Cameron, 2010, pp 37–45; Peter L. Payne, 'The Economy' in Devine and Finlay (eds), 1996, pp 13–16; Devine, 1999, Chapter 12, 'The World's Workshop'; Graeme Morton and R.J. Morris, 'Civil Society: Governance and Nation, 1852–1914', pp 369–373, and John Foster, 'The Twentieth Century, 1914–1979', pp 417–423, in Houston and Knox (eds), 2001; Lynch, 1991, pp 404–414; Smout, 1987, pp 32–57; Lynch (ed.), 2001, pp 212–213

101. Sharlin, 1979, pp 1–12, 84–105 and 137–147; Lindley, 2004, pp 114–163 and 309–315

102. Alvin Jackson, 'The Origins, Politics and Culture of Irish Unionism, c. 1880–1916', pp 86–116, David Fitzpatrick, 'Ireland and the Great War', pp 223–257, and Fearghal McGarry, 'Revolution, 1916–1923', pp 258–295, in Bartlett (ed.), 2018; Brian Barton, 'Northern Ireland, 1920–25', in Hill (ed.), 2003, pp 161–196; Bardon, 1992, pp 437–479

103. Greaves, 1961, pp 9–282

104. Devine, 1999, pp 266–272; Steel, 1984, pp 292–305; Lynch (ed.), 2001, pp 199–201; Mackie, 1978, pp 357–360; Lynch, 1991, pp 422–428; John Foster, 'The Twentieth Century, 1914–1979', pp 448–465, in Houston and Knox (eds), 2001; Bardon, 1992, pp 448–465; Peter L. Payne in Devine and Finlay (eds), 1996, pp 16–21; Cameron, 2010, pp 102–124

105. Brian Barton, 'Northern Ireland, 1925–39', in Hill (ed.), 2003, pp 199–234; Susannah Riordan, 'Politics, Economy, Society: Northern Ireland, 1920- 1939', in Bartlett (ed.), 2018, pp 296–322; Bardon, 1992, pp 466–525

106. Devlin, 1981, pp 110–145; Susannah Riordan in Bartlett, 2018, p. 320; Bardon, 1992, pp 527–529 and 539–542; Brian Barton in Hill (ed.), 2003, pp 210–233

107. Peadar O'Donnell, 'The Arranmore Disaster' in McLaughlin and Beattie (eds), 2013, pp 358–360; Handley, 1947, pp 187–188

108. Cameron, 2010, pp 127–135; Devine, 1999, pp 266–272; Steel, 1984, pp 292–319; Brian Barton, 'Northern Ireland, 1925–39' in Hill (ed.), 2003, pp 214–234; Bardon, 1992, pp 539–40 and 552–561

109. Cameron, 2010, pp 175–179; Devine, 1999, pp 545–549; Steel, 1984, pp 320–324; Lynch, 1991, pp 436–437; Barton, 1989, pp 80–208; Brian Barton, 'Northern Ireland, 1939–45' in Hill (ed.), 2003, pp 235–245; Bardon, 1992, pp 564–574

110. Cameron, 2010, pp 182–193; Steel, 1991, pp 320–324; Barton, 1989, pp 246–260; Patterson, 2002, pp 36–44; Bardon, 1992, pp 579–581

111. Devine, 1999, pp 549–565; Cameron, 2010, pp 236–250; Steel, 1984, pp 324–329; Wood, 2002, pp 53–66 and 81–109; Oliver, 2009, pp 354–359; Lynch (ed.), 2001, pp 213–214, 357 and 279–280; John Foster, 'the Twentieth Century, 1920–1979' in Houston and Knox (eds), 2001, pp 459–472

112. J.H. Whyte in Hill (ed.), 2003, pp 270–276, 286–287 and 305–307; D.S. Johnson and Liam Kennedy, in Hill (ed.), 2003, pp 470–477; Patterson, 2002, pp 116–147; Bardon, 1992, pp 587–599

113. *Belfast Telegraph*, 2 and 3 February 1953; *Northern Whig*, 2 February 1953; *Irish News*, 2 February 1953

114. Fitzpatrick, 1989, pp 222–243; David Fitzpatrick, *Oceans of Consolation: Personal Accounts of Irish Migration* to Australia, Ithaca, 1994, pp 6–19; Inglis, 1974, pp 168–211

115. Gray, 1950, pp 1–11, 17–42, 53, 71–72 and 135–142; Fitzpatrick, 1989, pp 240–243 and 261

116. John Erskine, 'Scotia's jewel: Robert Burns and Ulster, 1786–c. 1830', pp 15–36, and Frank Ferguson, John Erskine and Roger Dixon, 'Commemorating and collecting Burns in the north of Ireland, 1844–1902', pp 127–147, in Ferguson and Holmes (eds), 2009; 'A Birl for Burns' © Seamus Heaney in Douglas Gifford (ed.), *Addressing the Bard: Twelve contemporary poets respond to Robbie Burns*, Edinburgh, 2009

117. Ritchie and Orr, 2014, pp 200, 237, 260–270 and 276; interviews with Richard Hawkins and Alister McReynolds

118. Wilson, 2012, pp 24–39 and 225–243; Murray, 1984, pp 9–32, 154–158 and 246; Alan Bairner and Paul Darby, 'Divided Sport in a Divided Society: Northern Ireland' in Sugden and Bairner (eds), pp 51–72

119. Ferguson, 2008, pp 505–516; Robinson, 1997, pp 1–11, 44–48 and 215–229; Fenton, 1995, Forward, pp v–xiii and Part 1 (pp 1–182)

120. Marshall, 1950, p. 8 and 51; Falls, 1922, pp. 12–13; Webb, 2009, pp xiv-xix; Carew, 2018, pp vii–viii, 1–4, 32–33, 60, 64 and facing 215; Bell, 1988, pp. 25–6, 31–2, 55, 92, 103–5, 114, 122, 1634, 174 and 202–3; information about the surname English from the late Aodán Mac Póilin

BIBLIOGRAPHY

Adamson, Ian, *Bangor, Light of the World*, Belfast, 1979

Adamson, Ian, *The Cruthin*, Bangor, 1974

Akenson, Donald Harman, and Crawford W. H., *James Orr: Bard of Ballycarry*, Belfast, 1977

Bardon, Jonathan, *A History of Ireland in 250 Episodes*, Dublin, 2008

Bardon, Jonathan, *A History of Ulster*, Belfast, 1992

Bardon, Jonathan, *The Plantation of Ulster: The British colonisation of the north of Ireland in the seventeenth century*, Dublin, 2011

Barton, Brian, *The Belfast Blitz: The City in the War Years*, Belfast, 2015

Bartlett, Thomas (ed.), *The Cambridge History of Ireland*, vol. IV, Cambridge, 2018

Beattie, Seán, 'The Hiring-fair System in Donegal', in Jim McLaughlin and Seán Beattie (eds), *An Historical, Environmental and Cultural Atlas of County Donegal*, Cork, 2013

Bell, Robert, *The Book of Ulster Surnames*, Belfast, 1988

Boulter, Hugh, *Letters*, 2 vols., Dublin, 1770

Brooke, Peter (ed.), *Problems of a Growing City: Belfast 1780–1870*, Belfast, 1973

Brown, Daniel, *Hugh de Lacy, First Earl of Ulster: Rising and Falling in Angevin Ireland*, Woodbridge, 2016

Buchanan, George, and Aikman, James, *The History of Scotland, translated from the Latin of George Buchanan; with notes and a continuation to the Union in the reign of Queen Anne*, Vol. III, Glasgow and Edinburgh, 1827

Cameron, Ewen A., *Impaled upon a Thistle: Scotland since 1880*, Edinburgh, 2010

Campbell, Ewan, *Saints and Sea-kings: The First Kingdom of the Scots*, Edinburgh, 1999

Canny, Nicholas, *Making Ireland British, 1580–1650*, Oxford, 2001

Carew, Mairéad, *The Quest for the Irish Celt*, Newbridge, Co. Kildare, 2018

Cary, M., and Warmington, E.H., *The Ancient Explorers*, London, 1929

Clark, Wallace, *The Lords of the Isles Voyage*, Naas, 1993

Clark, Wallace, *Rathlin, Its Island Story*, Coleraine, 1996

Clarkson, Tim, *The Makers of Scotland: Picts, Romans, Gaels and Vikings*, Edinburgh, 2013

Connolly, S. J., *Contested Island: Ireland 1460–1630*, Oxford, 2007

Connolly, S.J. *Divided Kingdom: Ireland, 1630–1800*, Oxford, 2008

Connolly, S.J. (ed.), *Belfast 400: People, Place and History*, Liverpool, 2012

Cosgrove, Art (ed.), *A New History of Ireland, II: Medieval Ireland, 1169–1534*, Oxford, 1987

Courtney, Roger, *Dissenting Voices: Rediscovering the Irish Progressive Presbyterian Tradition*, Belfast, 2013

Cowan, E.J., and R. Andrew McDonald, *Alba: Celtic Scotland in the Medieval Era*, East Linton, East Lothian, 2000

Crawford, W.H., *Domestic Industry in Ireland: The Experience of the Linen Industry*, Dublin, 1972

Curl, James S., *The Honourable the Irish Society and the Plantation of Ulster, 1608–2000*, Chichester, 2000

Delbourgo, James, *Collecting the World: The Life and Curiosity of Hans Sloane*, London, 2017

Devine, T.M., *The Scottish Nation: 1700–2000*, London, 1999

Devine, T.M., and David Dickson (eds), *Ireland and Scotland 1600–1850: Parallels and Contrasts in Economic and Social Development*, Edinburgh, 1983

Devine, T.M., and R.J. Finlay (eds), *Scotland in the 20th Century*, Edinburgh, 1974

Devlin, Paddy, *Yes We Have No Bananas: Outdoor Relief in Belfast, 1920–1939*, Belfast 1981

Dickson, Charles, *Revolt in the North: Antrim and Down in 1798*, Dublin and London, 1960

Dickson, R. J., *Ulster Emigration to Colonial America, 1718–1775*, London, 1966

Driscoll, Stephen, *Alba: The Gaelic Kingdom of Scotland AD 800–1124*, Edinburgh, 2002

Duffy, Seán (ed.), *The World of the Galloglass: Kings, warlords and warriors in Ireland and Scotland, 1200–1600*, Dublin, 2016

Dunlop, John, *A Precarious Belonging: Presbyterians and the Conflict in Ireland*, Belfast, 1995

Elliott, Marianne, *The Catholics of Ulster: A History*, London, 2000

Falls, Cyril, *History of the Ulster Division*, Belfast, 1922

Fenton, James, *The Hamely Tongue: a personal record of Ulster-Scots in County Antrim*, Belfast, 1995

Ferguson, Frank (ed.), *Ulster-Scots Writing: An Anthology*, Dublin, 2008

Ferguson, Frank and Andrew R. Holmes (eds), *Revising Robert Burns and Ulster: Literature, religion and politics, c. 1770–1920*, Dublin, 2009

Ferguson, Frank, and James McConnel (eds), *Ireland and Scotland in the Nineteenth Century*, Dublin, 2009

Fitzgerald, Patrick, and Ickringill, Steve (eds), *Atlantic Crossroads: Historical Connections between Scotland, Ulster and North America*, Newtownards, 2001

Fitzpatrick, Rory, *God's Frontiersmen: The Scots-Irish Epic*, London, 1989

Flanagan, Marie Therese, *Irish Society, Anglo-Norman settlers, Angevin Kingship: Interaction in Ireland in the Late 12th Century*, Oxford, 1998

Foster, John, Muir Houston and Chris Madigan, 'Sectarianism, Segregation and Politics in Clydeside in the Later Nineteenth Century' in Martin J. Mitchell (ed.), *New Perspectives on the Irish in Scotland*, Glasgow, 2008

Ford, Alan, *The Protestant Reformation in Ireland, 1590–1641*, Dublin, 1997

Fraser, George MacDonald, *The Steel Bonnets: The Story of the Anglo-Scottish Border Reivers*, London, 1971

Fraser, James E., *From Caledonia to Pictland: Scotland to 795*, Edinburgh, 2009

Garvin, Wilbert, and Des O'Rawe, *Northern Ireland Scientists and Inventors*, Belfast, 1993

Gilbert, J.T. (ed.), *Chartularies of St Mary's Abbey*, 2 vols., Dublin, 1884–6

Gillespie, Raymond G., *Colonial, Ulster: The Settlement of Eastern Ulster, 1601–1641*, Cork, 1985

Gillespie, Raymond G., *Seventeenth-Century Ireland*, Dublin, 2006

Geoghegan, Patrick M., *The Irish Act of Union: A Study in High Politics 1798–1801*, Dublin, 1999

Goodwin, George, *Fatal Rivalry: Flodden 1513*, London, 2014

Gray, Arthur J., *An Ulster Plantation at Katikati*, Wellington, 1950

Greaves, C. Desmond, *The Life and Times of James Connolly*, London, 1961

Hamlin, Ann, and Chris Lynn, *Pieces of the Past*, Belfast, 1988

Handley, James E., *The Irish in Modern Scotland*, Cork, 1947

Herman, Arthur, *The Scottish Enlightenment: The Scots' Invention of the Modern World*, London, 2001

Hewitt, John, 'The Rhyming Weavers', in *Fibres, Fabric and Cordage*, Belfast, 1950

Hill, G., *An Historical Account of the Macdonnells of Antrim, Including Notices of Some Other Septs, Irish and Scottish*, Belfast, 1873

Hill G., *An Historical Account of the Plantation of Ulster at the Commencement of the Seventeenth Century, 1608–1620*, Belfast, 1877

Hill, G., *The Montgomery manuscripts, 1603–1706, Compiled from Family Papers*, Belfast,1869

Hill, J.R. (ed.), *A New History of Ireland VII: Ireland 1921–1984*, Oxford, 2003

Holmes, R.F., *Henry Cooke*, Belfast, 1981

Holmes, R.F., *The Presbyterian Church in Ireland: A Popular History*, Dublin, 2000

Houston, R.A. and W.W.J. Knox (eds), *The New Penguin History of Scotland From the Earliest Times to the Present Day*, London, 2001

Hunter, Robert J. (ed.), *Strabane Barony during the Ulster Plantation, 1607–1641*, Belfast, 2011

Inglis, K.S., *The Australian Colonists: An exploration of social history 1788–1870*, Melbourne, 1974

Kearney Walsh, Micheline, *An Exile of Ireland: Hugh O'Neill, Prince of Ulster*, Dublin, 1996

Kelly, William, and Young, John R. (eds), *Ulster and Scotland 1600–2000: History, Language and Identity*, Dublin, 2004

Kelly, William P., and Young, John R. (eds), *Scotland and the Ulster Plantations: Explorations in the British Settlements of Stuart Ireland*, Dublin, 2009

Kennedy, Billy, *The Scots-Irish in the Hills of Tennessee*, Londonderry, Belfast and Greenville, South Carolina, 1996

Kingston, Simon, *Ulster and the Isles in the Fifteenth Century: The Lordship of the Clann Domhnaill of Antrim*, Dublin, 2004

Kirkpatrick, Laurence, *Presbyterians in Ireland: An Illustrated History*, Belfast, 2006

Lambkin, Brian, 'The Migration Story of Mící Mac Gabhann, 1865–1948' in Jim McLaughlin and Seán Beattie (eds), *An Historical, Environmental and Cultural Atlas of County Donegal*, Cork, 2013

Lennon, Colm, *Sixteenth-Century Ireland: The Incomplete Conquest*, Dublin, 1994

Lindley, David, *Degrees Kelvin: The Genius and Tragedy of William Thomson*, London, 2004

Lindsay, Robert, *The History of Scotland from 1453 to 1565 by Robert Lindsay of Pitscottie, to which is added, A Continuation, by another Hand, till August 1604*, Glasgow, 1749

Lynch, Michael, *Scotland: A New History*, London, 1991

Lynch, Michael (ed.), *The Oxford Companion to Scottish History*, Oxford, 2001

Lysaght, Liam and Marnell, Ferdia (eds), *Atlas of Mammals in Ireland, 2010–2015*, Waterford, 2016

McBride, Ian, *Eighteenth-Century Ireland*, Dublin, 2009

McBride, I. R., *Scripture Politics: Ulster Presbyterians and Irish Radicalism in the Late Eighteenth Century*, Oxford, 1998

McCavitt, John, *The Flight of the Earls*, Dublin, 2002

Mac Cuarta, Brian, *Catholic Revival in the North of Ireland 1603–41*, Dublin, 2007

Mac Cuarta, Brian (ed.), *Reshaping Ireland, 1550–1700: Colonisation and its Consequences*, Dublin, 2011

MacCulloch, Diarmaid, *Reformation: Europe's House Divided, 1490–1700*, London, 2003

McDonald, R. Andrew, *The Kingdom of the Isles: Scotland's Western Seaboard c. 1100–c.1336*, East Linton, East Lothian, 1998

McGettigan, Darren, *The Donegal Plantation and the Tír Chonaill Irish, 1610–1710*, Dublin, 2010

Mac Laughlin, Jim, and Beattie, Seán (eds), *An Historical, Environmental and Cultural Atlas of County Donegal*, Cork, 2013

MacMaster, Richard K., *Scotch-Irish Merchants in Colonial America*, Belfast, 2009

McNally, Robert (ed.), *Old Ireland*, Dublin, 1965

McNamee, Colm, *The Wars of the Bruces: Scotland, England and Ireland, 1306–1328*, East Linton, East Lothian, 1997

McNeill, Mary, *The Life and Times of Mary Ann McCracken 1770–1866: A Belfast Panorama*, Belfast, 1960

McNeill, T.E., *Anglo-Norman Ulster: The History and Archaeology of an Irish Barony 1177-1400*, Edinburgh, 1980

McReynolds, Alister, *Kith & Kin: The Continuing Legacy of the Scotch-Irish in America*, Newtownards, 2013

McReynolds, Alister, *The Ulster Scots and New England*, Belfast,

Mackie, J.D., *A History of Scotland*, 2nd Edition, Harmondsworth, 1978

Maguire, W.A., *Belfast*, Keele, 1993

Mallory, J.P., *The Origins of the Irish*, London, 2017

Mallory, J.P. and McNeill, T.E. *The Archaeology of Ulster: From Colonisation to Plantation*, Belfast, 1991

Marshall, William F., *Ulster Sails West: The Story of the Great Emigration from Ulster to North America in the 18th Century. Together with an Outline of the Part Played by Ulstermen in Building the United States*, Belfast, 1950, and Baltimore, 1979

Mason, Roger, and Norman MacDougall (eds), *People and Power in Scotland: Essays in Honour of T.C. Smout*, Edinburgh, 1992

Maxwell, Constantia, *Irish History from Contemporary Sources (1509–1610)*, London, 1923

Meacham, Jon, *American Lion: Andrew Jackson in the White House*, New York, 2008

Mitchell, Martin J. (ed.), *New Perspectives on the Irish in Scotland*, Edinburgh, 2008

Montgomery, Michael, *From Ulster to America: The Scotch-Irish Heritage of American English*, Belfast, 2006

Moody, T.W., Martin, F.X., and Byrne, F.J. (eds), *A New History of Ireland, IX: Early Modern Ireland, 1534–1691*, Oxford, 1978

Morgan, Hiram (ed.), *The Battle of Kinsale*, Bray, 2004

Murphy, Eileen M., and Roulston, William J. (eds), *Fermanagh: History & Society*, Dublin, 2004

Murray, Bill, *The Old Firm: Sectarianism, Sport and Society*, Edinburgh, 1984

Nicholson, Ranald, *Scotland: The Later Middle Ages*, Edinburgh, 1974

Nolan, William, Ronayne, Liam and Dunlevy, Mairéad (eds), *Donegal History & Society*, Dublin, 1995

Ó Baoill, Ruairí, *Carrickfergus: The Story of the Castle & Walled Town*, Belfast, 2008

O'Connell, Maurice R., *Irish Politics and Social Conflict in the Age of the American Revolution*, Philadelphia, 1965

Ó Cróinín, Dáibhí, *A New History of Ireland: Prehistoric and Early Ireland*, vol. 1, Oxford, 2005

O'Dowd, Anne, 'Seasonal Migration to the Lagan and Scotland' in William Nolan, Liam Ronayne and Mairéad Dunlevy (eds), *Donegal History & Society*, Dublin, 1995

Ohlmeyer, Jane, *Civil War and Restoration in the Three Stuart Kingdoms: The Career of Randal MacDonnell, Marquis of Antrim, 1609–83*, Cambridge, 1993

Oliver, Neil, *A History of Scotland*, London, 2009

Oram, Richard, *Domination and Lordship: Scotland 1070–1230*, Edinburgh, 2011

Orpen, Goddard H., 'The Earldom of Ulster' in *Journal of the Proceedings of the Royal Society of Antiquaries of Ireland*, 1913–15

Patterson, Henry, *Ireland since 1939*, Oxford, 2002

Perceval-Maxwell, M., *The Scottish Migration to Ulster in the Reign of James I*, Belfast, 1973

Purdon, C.D., *The Sanitary State of the Belfast Factory District (1863 to 1873 Inclusive)*, Belfast, 1877

Ritchie, Fiona, and Orr, Doug, *Wayfaring Strangers: The Musical Voyage from Scotland and Ulster to Appalachia*, University of North Carolina Press, Chapel Hill, 2014

Robinson, Philip, *The Plantation of Ulster: British Settlement in an Irish Landscape, 1600–1670*, Dublin and New York, 1984

Robinson, Philip, *Ulster-Scots: A Grammar of the Traditional Written and Spoken Language*, Belfast, 1997

Roulston, William J. (ed.) *Antrim and Argyll: Some Aspects of the Connections*, Belfast, 2018

Roulston, William J., *The Story of the Presbyterians in Ulster: Pocket History and Heritage Trail*, Belfast, 2015

Roulston, William J., *Three Centuries of Life in a Tyrone Parish: A History of Donagheady from 1600 to 1900*, Strabane, 2010

Roulston, William J., 'Seventeenth-century manors in the barony of Strabane', in J. Lyttleton and T. O'Keefe (eds), *The Manor in Medieval and Early Modern Ireland*, Dublin, 2005

Roulston, William J., 'The Ulster Plantation in the manor of Dunnalong, 1610–70,' in H.A. Jefferies and C. Dillon (eds), *Tyrone: History & Society*, Dublin, 2000

Scott, A. B., and Martin, F. X. (eds), *Expugnatio Hibernica: The Conquest of Ireland, by Giraldus Cambrensis*, Dublin, 1978

Sharlin, Harold Issadore, *Lord Kelvin: The Dynamic Victorian*, Pennsylvania State
    University Press, 1979

Smout, T.C., *A Century of the Scottish People 1830–1950*, London, 1987

Smout, T.C., *A History of the Scottish People, 1560–1830*, Glasgow, 1969

Smyth, William J., *Map-making, Landscapes, and Memory: A Geography of Colonial
    and Early Modern Ireland, c. 1530–1750*, Cork, 2006

Steel, Tom, *Scotland's Story: A New Perspective*, London, 1984

Stevenson, David, *Scottish Covenanters and Irish Confederates: Scottish-Irish
    Relations in the Mid-Seventeenth Century*, Belfast, 1981

Stewart, A.T.Q., *A Deeper Silence: The Hidden Origins of the United Irishmen*,
    London, 1993

Stewart, A.T.Q., *The Summer Soldiers: The 1798 Rebellion in Antrim and Down*,
    Belfast, 1995

Sugden, John, and Bairner, Alan (eds), *Sport in Divided Societies*, Aachen, 1999

Taylor, Alice, *The Shape of the State in Medieval Scotland, 1124–1290*, Oxford, 2016

Turner, Brian S., 'Distributional Aspects of Family Name Study Illustrated in the
    Glens of Antrim', PhD thesis, Queen's University, Belfast, 1974

Ulster-Scots Agency and Ulster-Scots Community Network publications:
  Confederate Generals: Lee's Ulster-Scots commanders
  Cultural encounters between Ulster & China
  Hamilton & Montgomery 400 Years 1606–2006 … from Ayrshire to Ulster
  Henry Cooke: an introduction
  Herstory: profiles of eight Ulster-Scots women
  Herstory II profiles of eight more Ulster-Scots Women
  Robert the Bruce 700 1307–2007
  The Covenanters in Ulster
  The Covenanters in Ulster, 2009
  The Covenanters in Ulster: Heritage Trail
  The Desert Generals
  The Ulster-Scots & New England
  Union Generals: President Lincoln's Ulster-Scots commanders
  Ulster & Canada: Ulster-Scots and the making of modern Canada
  Ulster & New Zealand
  Ulster & Pennsylvania: Ulster-Scots and 'the Keystone State'
  *Ulster & Tennessee: The Ulster-Scots contribution to the making of 'the Volunteer
    State'*

Webb, James, *Born Fighting: How the Scots-Irish Shaped America*, Edinburgh, 2009

Williams, Ronald, *The Lords of the Isles: The Clan Donald and the early Kingdom of
    the Scots*, Colonsay, 1997

Wilson, Richard, *Inside the Divide: One City, Two Teams, The Old Firm*, Edinburgh, 2012

Wood, Emma, *The Hydro Boys: Pioneers of Renewable Energy*, Edinburgh, 2002

INDEX

Donegal 57, 58, 70, 204
Donegal Abbey 72
Donegal Castle 60, 85
Donuil Dhu (piper) 52
Douglas, James (The Black Douglas) 32
Douglas, Margaret 75
Douglas, William Douglas, 8th Earl of 53
Down County 9, 20
Downham, George, Church of Ireland
    Bishop of Derry 119, 120
Downpatrick 15, 23, 26, 69–70
Doyle, Lynn C. 254
Drake (Royal Navy sloop) 164
Drake, Sir Francis 80–1
Drogheda 126
Drowes Abbey 72
Dublin 16, 39, 40, 45, 147–8, 165
Dublin Castle 39, 46, 73, 84, 85
Dublin Socialist Club 221
Dublin University Magazine 250
Dumbarton Rock 18
Dumfries 45, 117
Dunadd, Argyll 10, 11, 14
Dunaverty 31, 32, 45
Dunbar, Gavin, Archbishop of Glasgow
    116–17
Dundas, James, Bishop 121
Dundee 214, 223
Dundonald 9, 26, 232
Dundrum Castle 23, 24, 25
Dunfermline 20, 214
Dunfermline, Alexander Seton, Earl of 75
Dungannon 85, 88, 108, 125, 144, 164
Dungannon Castle 86
Dunkeld 12
Dunlap, John 158, 162
Dunluce 78, 84
Dunluce Castle 83, 86–7
Dunnalong 119, 120
Dunseverick, Antrim 10, 78
Duntreath 94, 101
dwellings 9

Easter Rising (1916) 219–20
Economic War 230
Edinburgh 20, 214, 258
Edinburgh Castle 54, 55, 60–1
Edmonston, William, 7th Laird of
    Duntreath 94, 101
Education Act (1944) 241, 242
Edward I, King (Hammer of the Scots) 25,
    29, 30–1, 33
Edward II, King 34–5, 36, 39
Edward IV, King 54
Edward VI, King 68
Egil's Saga 18
Éire 233, 234, 237, 241
Eisenhower, General Dwight 241
Elizabeth I, Queen 73, 75, 77, 78, 83, 84
    conquest of Ireland, cost of 104
    death of 90, 91, 102
    Shane O'Neill and 78, 79
    Spanish Armada and 85
    Ulster and 80, 81, 85, 86–8, 93, 98
Elizabeth, Queen of Scots 34, 35, 39
Elliots 117, 118
emigration
    coffin ships and 193
    from Ulster 141–2, 143, 144–5, 151–2, 155,
        156
    Great Famine and 185–6, 189, 192–3
    indentured servants 144
    redemptioners 144
    to America 141–2, 143, 144–5, 151–3
    to Australia 248–9
    to Canada 192
    to New Zealand 250–2
    to Scotland 185–7, 196–7, 201, 257
    Ulster Presbyterians 152, 153, 155
Emmet, Robert 175
English Civil War 126
Enlightenment, the 133, 145, 156, 158, 162,
    163
    in Belfast 165, 174
Enniscorthy, County Wexford 168